Maharashtra Human Development Report 2012

Thank you for choosing a SAGE product! If you have any comment, observation or feedback, I would like to personally hear from you. Please write to me at contactceo@sagepub.in

—Vivek Mehra, Managing Director and CEO,
SAGE Publications India Pvt Ltd, New Delhi

Bulk Sales

SAGE India offers special discounts for purchase of books in bulk. We also make available special imprints and excerpts from our books on demand.

For orders and enquiries, write to us at

Marketing Department
SAGE Publications India Pvt Ltd
B1/I-1, Mohan Cooperative Industrial Area
Mathura Road, Post Bag 7
New Delhi 110044, India
E-mail us at marketing@sagepub.in

Get to know more about SAGE, be invited to SAGE events, get on our mailing list. Write today to marketing@sagepub.in

This book is also available as an e-book.

Contributors

Leading Team
K. P. Bakshi, Additional Chief Secretary, Planning Department, Government of Maharashtra
Sanjay Chahande: Director General, Yashwantrao Chavan Academy of Development Administration (YASHADA)
Minal Naravane: Director, Center for Human Development, YASHADA

State Steering Committee
Principal Secretary, Planning Department, Chairperson
Additional Chief Secretary, Education, Member
Principal Secretary, Health, Member
Secretary, Women and Child Development, Member
Secretary, Rural Development, Member
Executive Chairman, Human Development Commissionerate, Member
Joint/Deputy Secretary, Planning Department Member, Secretary

Coordinators, Planning Department, Government of Maharashtra
A. K. Jagtap, Joint Secretary; S. N. Shinde, Under Secretary; A. A. Khandare, Officer on Special Duty

Lead Author and Editor
Usha Jayachandran

Background Paper Writers
Suryanarayana M. H., Indira Gandhi Institute of Development Research, Mumbai
D. P. Singh, Tata Institute of Social Sciences (TISS), Mumbai
Rohit Mutatkar, TISS, Mumbai
R. K. Mutatkar, Maharashtra Association of Anthropological Sciences (MAAS), Pune
Anuja Jayaraman, Consultant, Mumbai
Rukmini Banerji, Pratham, Mumbai
Usha Rane, Pratham, Mumbai
Oommen Kurian, Centre for Enquiry Into Health and Allied Themes (CEHAT), Mumbai
Suchitra Wagle, CEHAT, Mumbai

Support Group in YASHADA
Shashikant Lokhande, Officer on Special Duty; Vinay Kulkarni, Research Assistant; Atul Naubde, Research Assistant; Nilesh Ingale, Project Assistant

Maharashtra Human Development Report 2012

Towards Inclusive Human Development

Yashwantrao Chavan Academy of Development Administration
Rajbhavan Complex, Baner Road, Pune 411 007

ISO 9001:2008

Copyright © YASHADA, 2014

All rights reserved. No part of this book may be reproduced or utilized in any form or by any means, electronic or mechanical, including photocopying, recording or by any information storage or retrieval system, without permission in writing from the publisher.

First published in 2014 by

SAGE Publications India Pvt Ltd
B1/I-1 Mohan Cooperative Industrial Area
Mathura Road, New Delhi 110 044, India
www.sagepub.in

Yashwantrao Chavan Academy of Development Administration
Rajbhavan Complex, Baner Road, Pune 411 007

SAGE Publications Inc
2455 Teller Road
Thousand Oaks, California 91320, USA

SAGE Publications Ltd
1 Oliver's Yard, 55 City Road
London EC1Y 1SP, United Kingdom

SAGE Publications Asia-Pacific Pte Ltd
3 Church Street
#10-04 Samsung Hub
Singapore 049483

Published by Vivek Mehra for SAGE Publications India Pvt Ltd, typeset in 10.5/12.5 Adobe Jenson Pro by RECTO Graphics, Delhi, and printed at Saurabh Printers Pvt Ltd, New Delhi.

Second Printing 2014

Library of Congress Cataloging-in-Publication Data Available

ISBN: 978-81-321-1136-8 (PB)

The SAGE Team: Rudra Narayan, Shreya Chakraborti, Rajib Chatterjee and Dally Verghese

मुख्य मंत्री
महाराष्ट्र

Chief Minister
Maharashtra

MESSAGE

Maharashtra Human Development Report, 2012 is an effort to evaluate the development process in the State in terms of equitable access of people across regions and socio economic segments, to education, health and economic opportunities. The first State Human Development Report was published in 2002. During the intervening period, the HDI for Maharashtra has shown significant improvement on all the parameters. Improvement in the HDI has been greater in districts, positioned at the lower end of the HDI ranking scale. Thematic approach of this report is focused on inclusive growth, which is the core objective of XII Plan adopted by the National Development Council. I am sure that Human Development Report 2012 will result in informed policy interventions, required to achieve sustainable growth with equity and dignity.

(Prithviraj Chavan)

DEPUTY CHIEF MINISTER
MAHARASHTRA STATE

Message

Maharashtra is a well-diversified State with a fast-growing economy. As a State, we have always strived for the well-being of our people, training our focus on sustained increases in their quality of life.

Over the last two decades, the concept of Human Development has acquired greater significance across the world with Maharashtra preparing its first State Human Development Report (SHDR) in 2002. Several changes have taken place in the last ten years in Maharashtra's socio-economic profile and performance and the current State Human Development Report 2012 attempts to capture the trends and transitions witnessed in all the key human development parameters at the state, district/regional levels. In keeping with the XII Five Year Plan ideology of inclusive growth, this report keeps its theme central to inclusion in growth, income and human development across various economic and social indicators.

We are sure that this Report will provide the State Government with appropriate inputs for decision-making at various administrative levels. Our financial allocations and development policy need to increasingly incorporate the human development factor in order to ensure rapid growth and widespread sharing of the gains from growth. The SHDR could thus serve as an authentic basis for designing state plans, programs and policies.

(Ajit Pawar)

**MINISTER OF STATE FOR
FINANCE & PLANNING,
ENERGY, WATER RESOURCES,
PARLIAMENTARY AFFAIR AND EXCISE,**

GOVERNMENT OF MAHARASHTRA,
Mantralaya, Mumbai 400 032.

MESSAGE

Planning for human development has been an intrinsic part of policy formulations in Maharashtra. The main objective of development planning is keeping the most deprived, marginalised and unrechable as the focus with the aim of reaching equitably all development opportunities to them and consequently leading to capability enhancements. With inclusive growth and development as the aim, it is now imperative for development policy and planning to bridge the social, economic, gender, sectoral and regional gaps. This State Human Development Report for Maharashtra takes step in the right direction by identifying and highlighting the progress that has been made as well as the gaps that need to be addressed for the state to move effectively towards faster and more inclusive growth and human development.

(Rajendra Mulak)

J. S. Saharia
Chief Secretary

Chief Secretary's Office
6th Floor, Mantralaya,
Mumbai 400 032
Tel.: 22025042/22028594(F)

MESSAGE

I congratulate YASHADA for preparing the Second Human Development Report for the State of Maharashtra.

The First Human Development Report of the State was prepared in 2002. The present report has taken the overview of the progress in the human development aspects, such as economic growth, education, health, housing, water and sanitation since 2002. The report, with the central premise of inclusive human development, focuses on five cross cutting themes of regional, rural-urban, social groups, gender and income groups. It has led to the greater understanding of human development issues for the disadvantaged sections of the society. Hence, the report is of interest to a wide range of planners, policy makers, administrators and opinion leaders.

It will be joint responsibility of stakeholders to ensure that the State continues to build up on the progress it has made in the last decade. I welcome the practical suggestions contained in this Report to address the lacunae in human development. The Government of Maharashtra will leave no stone unturned to achieve inclusive growth, based on the findings of the report.

(J. S. Sahariya)

Tel. (0) 022-2202 50 42/2202 87 62, Fax : 2202 85 94, E-mail : chiefsecretary@maharashtra.gov.in

United Nations Development Programme

Empowered lives.
Resilient nations.

MESSAGE

Maharashtra's 2012 Human Development Report confirms the impressive progress being made in the state. With per capita income well above the national average, Maharashtra has improved overall literacy and, at the same time, reduced the literacy gender gap. The Report shows that the state has made excellent progress in reducing Infant mortality by 20 points during the past decade, one of the most dramatic improvements recorded across the country.

The Government of Maharashtra's commitment to human development is long-standing and carries through to regular monitoring of indicators at district and blocks level. This kind of tracking is a pioneering model which alerts stakeholders to trends and changes in social conditions and is the kind of approach that other states may wish to replicate.

Data from the State's first Human Development Report has been used by the Government of Maharashtra to establish policy and budgetary priorities for marginalized communities and regions that need particular attention. This is exactly the kind of impact that human development reports are intended to generate. We hope that the important evidence and recommendations in this Report help to frame the Government's future plans and budgets.

The United Nations Development Programme is proud to have supported this important report and salutes the Government of Maharashtra for its steadfast commitment to human development.

Lise Grande
United Nations Resident Coordinator
Resident Representative United Nations Development Programme

UNDP in India • 55, Lodi Estate, Post Box No. 3059, New Delhi 110 003, India
Tel: 91-11-2462 8877 • Fax : 91-11-2462 7612 • E-mail: info.in@undp.org • www.in.undp.org

Contents

List of Tables	xix
List of Figures	xxiii
List of Boxes	xxvii
List of Abbreviations	xxix
Executive Summary	xxxiii
Foreword by K. P. Bakshi	xliii
Preface by Dr Sanjay Chahande	xlv

1.	**Setting the Framework**	1
	Human Development: A Global Overview	1
	Towards Social Inclusion: The India Human Development Report (IHDR) 2011	3
	The MHDR 2002	5
	Human Development in Maharashtra: From Analysis to Action	7
	Inclusive Growth and Human Development	7
	The MHDR 2012: Content Highlights	8
2.	**Human Development: Progress Made, Milestones to Be Reached**	11
	Human Development in Maharashtra: A District Profile	11
	District HDIs	13
	The Components of HDI	17
	Human Development across Districts: A Radar Profile	21
	The IHDI	21
	Summing Up	24
	Annexure 2.1: Technical Note: The HDI	25
3.	**Growth, Equity and Inclusion**	27
	Introduction	27
	Economic Growth	28
	Economic Growth: Distributional Performance	33
	Calorie, Protein and Fat Intake: The Nutrition Intake Dimension	41
	Summing Up	43
4.	**Education: A Means for Enhancing Capabilities**	45
	Motivation	45
	Demographic Profile of Maharashtra	46
	Education and Its Interlinkages	47
	Literacy Achievements	48
	Increasing Access and Rising Enrolment	51
	Female Enrolment in Education	52
	Attendance Matters More	54

Out-Of-School Children and Dropouts	56
Schooling Incentives	60
The Quality of Education	61
School Resources	63
Education for the Katkari Tribe	64
Education Budget: Allocations and Achievements	66
Summing Up	67
5. Health and Nutrition: Imperative for Capability Enhancement	**71**
Motivation	71
Health: Outcome Indicators	72
Health: Input Indicators	77
Health: Process Indicators	90
Cost of Health Care	90
Availability and Pricing of Essential Drugs	91
New Government Initiatives	91
Nutrition: Essential for Health and Education	94
Under-Nutrition in Maharashtra	94
Overweight and Obesity in Maharashtra	97
Anaemia	97
Vitamin A Coverage	98
Childhood Diarrhoea	99
Childcare and Feeding Practices	99
Summing Up	100
6. Housing, Water and Sanitation: Interlinked with Capability Enhancement	**105**
Motivation	105
Interlinkages with Health and Well-Being	105
Urbanization and the Proliferation of Slums	106
Migration: Implications for Support Infrastructure and Amenities	107
Housing Amenities in Maharashtra: Trends and Patterns	110
Condition of Dwellings	111
Housing Programmes	113
Water: An Important Resource for Human Development	113
Sanitation Conditions	117
Summing Up	121
Annexure 6.1: Definition of Slums in Maharashtra	124
7. Inclusive Human Development: Looking Ahead	**125**
Human Development Policy Imperatives	126
Recommendations for Data Collection and Management	131
Appendix A: Maharashtra Human Development Report, 2012: Preparation Process	132
Appendix B: District Indicators	135
Appendix C: Further Data	137
Bibliography	200
Index	208

List of Tables

1.1	Ranking of Indian States According to HDI Value	4
2.1	District-Wise Human Development Indicators: 2001 and 2011	12
2.2	Relative Human Development Status of Districts: 2001 and 2011	14
2.3	Rank Correlation between HDI and Its Component Scores: 2001 and 2011	16
2.4	IMR (Rural Maharashtra), 2003–10	19
2.5	Per Capita NDDP (at Current Prices), Maharashtra, 2001–02 and 2011–12	21
2.6	Key Human Development Indicators: States and India	22
2.7	Estimates of HDI and IHDI across States and India: 2010–11	23
3.1	Growth Performance of Maharashtra: 1999–2000 to 2008–09: A Summary Report	29
3.2	NDDP: A Profile (2008–09)	32
3.3	Median MPCE by Sector in Major States: 2009–10	34
3.4	WPR: India and Maharashtra	35
3.5	Incidence of Poverty: Maharashtra and India	36
3.6	Incidence of Poverty across Social Groups, by Region, in Maharashtra: 2004–05	39
3.7	Incidence of Child Poverty across Social Groups, by Region, in Maharashtra: 2004–05	40
4.1	Total Population (1951–2011)	46
4.2	Girls' Enrollment in Elementary Schools across Regions and Social Groups	54
4.3	NAR at the Primary and Upper Primary Levels (1995–96 and 2007–08)	55
4.4	Reasons for Never Enrolling or Discontinuing or Dropping Out (2007–08)	59
4.5	Proportion of Children (6–13 years) Attending School and Receiving Free Education, by Type of Institution Attended (2007–08)	61
4.6	Percentage of Students Who Passed in Board Examinations: 2010–11	63
5.1	Life Expectancy at Birth: Maharashtra	74
5.2	Public Health Expenditure: Maharashtra	78
5.3	Average Population per Sub-Centre: Maharashtra (2011)	81
5.4	Average Population per PHC: Maharashtra (2011)	81
5.5	Maternal Health Indicators as per Targets: Maharashtra	89
5.6	Percentage of HIV/AIDS Prevalence: Maharashtra (2007)	91
5.7	Prevalence of Under-Nutrition, by Place of Residence, Sex, Social Group and Wealth Index: Maharashtra	95

5.8	Prevalence of Malnutrition among Children (0–23 Months), by Administrative Divisions: Maharashtra	97
6.1	Early Childhood Mortality Rates, by Wealth Quintiles: Maharashtra	106
6.2	Inter-District and Interstate In- and Out-Migrants: Maharashtra (1991–2001)	108
6.3	Distribution of Households, by Type of Dwelling Structure: India	110
6.4	Percentage of Households, by Condition of Structure Occupied: Maharashtra (2001–11)	111
6.5	Classification of Districts Based on Proportion of Households Living in Dwellings in Good Condition: Maharashtra (2011)	112
6.6	Classification of Districts Based on Proportion of Urban Residing in Owner-Occupied Houses: Maharashtra (2011)	112
6.7	Distribution of Households, by Access to Drinking Water: Maharashtra and India (2008–09)	116
6.8	Statistics on Rural Drinking Water Supply: Maharashtra (2012–13)	118
6.9	Percentage of Households and Bathroom Facility: Maharashtra and India (2011)	119
6.10	Report Card Status of TSC as on 14 March 2012: Maharashtra	121
2A.1	Classification of Districts by HDI: 2001	136
2A.2	Classification of Districts by HDI: 2011	137
2A.3	Status of Districts (Dimension-Wise): 2001 and 2011	138
2A.4	Radar Scores for Human Development Indicators: 2011	139
2A.5	District-Wise Radar Graphs for Human Development Indicators in Maharashtra: 2011	140
2A.6	Estimates of Sub-Indices by Dimension, with and without Adjustment for Inequality: 2010–11	146
3A.1	Sector-Wise Growth Performance across Districts: Maharashtra (1999–2000 to 2008–09)	147
3A.2	Sector-Wise Annual Growth Performance in Maharashtra	148
3A.3	District-Wise Shares in Growth Performance	149
3A.4	Ordinal Distribution of Districts in Terms of Per Capita NSDP (At 1999–2000 Prices)	150
3A.5	Sectoral Share in Employment: Maharashtra	151
3A.6	Unemployment Rate (Percentage) (Daily Status): Maharashtra and India	152
3A.7	Distribution of Workers (PS and SS) by Category of Employment: Maharashtra and India	152
3A.8	Decile Group-Wise Estimates of Per Capita Consumption Distribution: Rural Maharashtra	152
3A.9	Decile Group-Wise Estimates of Per Capita Consumption Distribution: Urban Maharashtra	153
3A.10	Estimates of Average (Mean and Median) Consumption across Social Groups, by Region: Maharashtra (2004–05)	153
3A.11	Average Consumption, Inequality and Poverty across Districts: Rural Maharashtra	154
3A.12	Average Consumption, Inequality and Poverty across Districts: Urban Maharashtra	155

3A.13	Estimates of Per Capita Cereal Consumption: Rural and Urban India	156
3A.14	Monthly Per Capita Cereal Consumption by Select Decile Groups: Maharashtra	156
3A.15	Per Capita Intake of Calories, Protein and Fat Per Diem by Decile Groups: Rural Maharashtra	157
3A.16	Estimates of Energy Intake: Rural and Urban India	158
3A.17	Average Per Capita Intake of Calorie Per Diem over NSS Rounds, by Major States: Rural Sector	158
3A.18	Per Capita Intake of Calories, Protein and Fat Per Diem by Decile Groups: Urban Maharashtra	159
3A.19	Food and Non-Food Expenditure and Share: Rural Maharashtra (2004–05)	160
3A.20	Food and Non-Food Expenditure and Share: Urban Maharashtra (2004–05)	161
4A.1	Literacy Rates, by Sex, for State and Districts: 2001 and 2011	162
4A.2	Literacy Rate (7+), by Social Groups, Sex and Sector: 2007–08	163
4A.3	Adult Literacy Rate (15+): 2007–08	165
4A.4	Adult Literacy Rate (15+), by Social Groups, Sex and Sector: 2007–08	165
4A.5	Growth of Schools, Teachers and Students: Ratios (1970 to 2010–11)	166
4A.6	Upper Primary versus Secondary School Ratios	167
4A.7	Secondary Schools by School Type	168
4A.8	Female Participation in Education	169
4A.9	Blocks/Municipal Corporations (MNC) with Percentage of Girls Lower than the State Average at Elementary Level	169
4A.10	Region-Wise NAR, Primary and Upper Primary Level: 2007–08	172
4A.11	NAR by MPCE Quintiles: Primary and Upper Primary Level: 2007–08	173
4A.12	NAR, by Social Groups, Primary and Upper Primary Level: 2007–08	173
4A.13	NAR, Secondary Levels: Maharashtra: 2007–08	174
4A.14	Percentage of Out-Of-School Children: 2007–08	174
4A.15	Percentage of Out-Of-School Children, by Sector: 2007–08	175
4A.16	Percentage of Out-Of-School Children, by Social Groups: 2007–08	175
4A.17	Dropout Rates: 2007–08	176
4A.18	Dropout Rates, by Social Groups and Sectors: 2007–08	176
4A.19	Survival of Cohorts by District	177
4A.20	PS of 6–13-Year-Olds Never Enrolled in School: 2007–08	178
4A.21	Proportion of Children (6–13 years) Attending School and Receiving Free Education: 2007–08	178
4A.22	Results of ASER Tests	179
4A.23	Percentage of Primary and Upper Primary Schools Who Reported Receiving Grants in Two Recent FYs: Maharashtra and India (2009–10 and 2010–11)	179
5A.1	Child Sex Ratio	180
5A.2	Per Capita Health Expenditure: Rural	181
5A.3	Per Capita Health Expenditure: Urban	182
5A.4	Population Per Public Health Facility in 1991, 2001 and 2011	183
5A.5	Population Per Government Bed	184
5A.6	HR for Health in Maharashtra	185
5A.7	Select Background Characteristics and Place of Antenatal Care: Maharashtra (2007–08)	185

5A.8	Percentage of Women Who Received any ANC and Full Antenatal Care, by Districts: Maharashtra (2007–08)	186
5A.9	Institutional Deliveries	187
5A.10	Vaccination of Children (12–23 Months), by Background Characteristics: Maharashtra (2007–08)	188
5A.11	Nutritional Status of Women (15–49 Years) in Maharashtra	189
5A.12	Percentage of Children below Five Years Classified as Undernourished and Anaemic in Select States of India: 2005–06	190
5A.13	Prevalence of Anaemia among Children below Five Years in Maharashtra	190
5A.14	Vitamin A Coverage in Maharashtra	191
5A.15	Knowledge and Practices Related to Diarrhoea Management	192
5A.16	Coverage of Nutrition-Related ICDS for Children in Maharashtra	193
5A.17	Breastfeeding Practices in Maharashtra	194
6A.1	IMR and U5MR in Slums and Non-Slums	195
6A.2	Nutritional Status of Children (Percentage of Children Stunted, Wasted and Underweight)	195
6A.3	Distribution of Households, by Material of Roof: Maharashtra and India (2001–11)	196
6A.4	Percentage of Households Having Tap Water as a Source of Drinking Water, by Districts: Maharashtra (2011 and 2001)	197
6A.5	Percentage of Households Having Latrines within Their Premises	198

List of Figures

2.1	HDI across Districts: 2001 and 2011	13
2.2	HDI: 2001 and 2011	15
2.3	Improvements in HDI: 2001–11	15
2.4	HDI: Relative Categories of Districts: 2001 and 2011	16
2.5	Literacy Rate: 2001 and 2011	17
2.6	GER: 2001 and 2011–12	18
2.7	IMR: 2003 and 2010	19
2.8	IMR: Indian States 2012	20
2.9	NDDP: 2001–02 and 2011–12	20
2.10	HDI, IHDI and Loss Due to Inequality across States and India: 2010–13	
3.1	Per Capita NSDP and Its Annual Growth Rate	28
3.2	Decade-Wise Growth Performance	28
3.3	Sectoral Annual Growth Performance: 1999–2000 to 2008–09	30
3.4	Sectoral Distribution of NSDP at 1999–2000 Prices	30
3.5	Per Capita NDDP at 1999–2000 Prices and Its Average Annual Rate of Growth across Districts: 1999–2000 to 2008–09	31
3.6	District-Wise Distribution of NDP at 1999–2000 Prices	33
3.7	Incidence of Rural Poverty: Maharashtra versus India	37
3.8	Incidence of Urban Poverty: Maharashtra versus India	37
3.9	Incidence of Rural and Urban Poverty: Maharashtra versus India	38
3.10	District-Wise Food Security Profile: Rural Maharashtra	42
3.11	District-Wise Food Security Profile: Urban Maharashtra	43
4.1	Decadal Population Growth Rate: India and Maharashtra (1951–61 to 2001–11)	46
4.2	Trends in Urbanization: Maharashtra and India (1901–2011)	47
4.3	Percentage of Women and Men Aged 20–49 Who Have Completed At Least 10 Years of Education, by Wealth Quintile, NFHS-3: India	47
4.4	Trends in Male and Female Literacy: Maharashtra (1951–2011)	49
4.5	Block-Wise Literacy Rate	50
4.6	Primary and Upper Primary School Enrolment: Maharashtra (2005–11)	52
4.7	Ratio of Primary to Upper Primary Schools: Maharashtra (2010–11)	53
4.8	Types of Schools	53
4.9	Gender Gap in Enrolment, by Social Groups	54
4.10	Primary-Level NAR: India and Maharashtra (2007–08)	55
4.11	Upper Primary NAR: India and Maharashtra (2007–08)	56

4.12	Primary-Level NAR, by Social Groups: Maharashtra (2007–08)	57
4.13	Upper Primary NAR, by Social Groups: Maharashtra (2007–08)	57
4.14	Reading and Arithmetic Ability of Children in Std I and Std II: Maharashtra (2006–11)	62
4.15	Reading and Arithmetic Ability of Children in Std III and Std IV: Maharashtra (2006–11)	62
4.16	PTR	64
4.17	Infrastructure Facilities in Elementary Schools	65
4.18	Infrastructure Facilities in Secondary Schools	65
4.19	Percentage Increase in SSA Annual Work Plan and Budget: 2006–07 and 2009–10	67
4.20	Per-Child Expenditures versus State Budgets	68
5.1	Trends in TFR: Maharashtra	73
5.2	District-Wise Child Sex Ratio: Maharashtra (2001 and 2011)	73
5.3	Life Expectancy at Birth: Maharashtra	74
5.4	IMR and PCDDP: Maharashtra	75
5.5	District-Level IMRs (Rural Areas Only): Maharashtra (2010)	76
5.6	U5MR: India and Maharashtra (2009)	76
5.7	NMR, IMR and U5MR, by Social Groups: Maharashtra	77
5.8	MMR: India and Maharashtra (1997–98 to 2007–09)	77
5.9	Percentage of Health Budget to State's Total Budget: Maharashtra (2000–01 to 2008–09)	78
5.10	Percentage of Utilization of Budgeted Outlay (State-Level Plan Scheme): Maharashtra (2006–07 to 2011–12)	79
5.11	Public Health Care Infrastructure: Maharashtra (2012)	80
5.12	District-Wise Trends in Population per RH: Maharashtra	82
5.13	Availability of Hospitals (per 100,000 Population): Maharashtra	82
5.14	Availability of Beds (per 100,000 Population): Maharashtra	83
5.15	Availability of Allopathic Doctors (per 100,000 Population): Maharashtra	83
5.16	Availability of Nurses (per 100,000 Population): Maharashtra	84
5.17	Utilization of Private Facilities for OP and IP Care: Maharashtra	85
5.18	Use of Public Facilities, by Social Groups: Maharashtra	86
5.19	Hospitalization Rates and Financial Reasons for Not Seeking Treatment, by Social Groups: Maharashtra	86
5.20	Access to Maternity Services across MPCE Classes: Maharashtra	89
5.21	Access to Maternity Services, by Social Groups: Maharashtra	90
5.22	Borrowings and Sale of Assets for Accessing Health Care: Maharashtra	91
5.23	Prevalence of Under-Nutrition among Children: Maharashtra	94
5.24	Trends in Nutritional Status of Children below Two Years: Maharashtra (2012)	96
5.25	Prevalence of Under-Nutrition in Children (0–23 Months): Rural and Urban Maharashtra	96
5.26	Prevalence of Malnutrition among Children below Two Years, by Social Groups: Maharashtra	97
5.27	Adult Males and Females with Low BMI: Maharashtra (2005–06)	97
5.28	Percentage of Women (15–49 Years) Having BMI Less than 18.5: Maharashtra (2005–06)	98
5.29	Prevalence of Overweight and Obesity: Maharashtra	98

5.30	Comparison between Prevalence of Anaemia Reported in NFHS-2 and NFHS-3: Maharashtra	98
6.1	Projected Slum Population: Maharashtra and India (2011–17)	107
6.2	Percentage of Migrants into Million-Plus Cities, Other Towns and Rural Areas of Maharashtra (2007–08)	109
6.3	Proportion of Households with Drinking Water within Their Premises, Electricity for Domestic Use and Toilets: Maharashtra and India (2008–09)	110
6.4	Classification of Households by Ownership Status: Maharashtra (2001–11)	112
6.5	Distance of Tap Water Source from Households: Maharashtra and India (2001–11)	114
6.6	Percentage of Households Having Drinking Water Facility within Their Premises, by Districts: Maharashtra (2001–11)	115
6.7	Access to Drinking Water, by Wealth Quintiles: Maharashtra (2007–08)	117
6.8	Percentage of Households Having Latrine Facility within Their Premises: India and Maharashtra (2001–11)	120
6.9	Percentage of Households Having Different Types of Drainage Facility: India and Maharashtra (2001–11)	121

List of Boxes

1.1	Inclusive Growth	7
2.1	Maharashtra: Significant Improvement in IMR (as per SRS)	20
3.1	Children in Poverty: Rural–Urban Profile	40
4.1	Human Development: Speaking to the People: School Enrolment	52
4.2	Increasing Enrolment in Maharashtra: ASER Survey	53
4.3	Out-Of-School Children in Maharashtra	58
4.4	Human Development: Speaking to the People: School Attendance and Dropout	60
4.5	Primary Schooling for Tribals in Nandurbar District	66
4.6	Planning for Improvements in Education in Rural Maharashtra	66
4.7	The PAISA Survey (2011)	68
5.1	Human Development: Speaking to the People: Some Sociocultural Factors Affecting IMR and CMR	77
5.2	Availability of Health Personnel	84
5.3	Human Development: Speaking to the People: Perceptions on Health Issues: Sarpanch's Speak	87
5.4	Human Development: Speaking to the People: Institutional Deliveries	90
5.5	HIV Prevalence in the State	91
5.6	CBM of Health Services	93
5.7	RJMCHNM	95
5.8	ICDS Scheme	99
5.9	Malnutrition and Child Health amongst Tribals in Maharashtra: A Case Study	100
6.1	Admissible Components: BSUP under JNNURM	113
6.2	Government Initiatives for Improving Access to Water	118
6.3	Nirmal Gram Puraskar (NGP)	122
6.4	A Success Story: Borban, A *Hagandari Mukt Gaon*	122

List of Abbreviations

AG	Accountant General
AHP	Affordable Housing in Partnership
AIDS	Acquired Immune Deficiency Syndrome
AIICOFF	Inclusive Coefficient All-India
AIMPCE	Median Per Capita Expenditure All-India
ANC	Antenatal Check-Up
ANM	Auxiliary Nurse Midwife
APL	Above Poverty Line
ASER	Annual Status of Education Report
ASHA	Accredited Social Health Activist
AWC	*Anganwadi* Centre
AWW	*Anganwadi* Worker
AYUSH	Ayurveda, Yoga, Unani, Siddha and Homoeopathy
BMI	Body Mass Index
BPL	Below Poverty Line
BSUP	Basic Services to Urban Poor
CAGR	Compound Annual Average Growth Rate
CBM	Community-Based Monitoring
CBR	Crude Birth Rate
CDR	Crude Death Rate
CEB	Children Ever Born
CEHAT	Centre for Enquiry into Health and Allied Themes
CHD	Center for Human Development
CHC	Community Health Centre
CMR	Child Mortality Rate
CNSM	Comprehensive Nutrition Survey in Maharashtra
CRM	Common Review Mission
CS	Children Surviving (Out of Those Ever Born)
CSO	Central Statistical Office
CSR	Child Survival Rate
DDP	District Domestic Product
DES	Directorate of Economics and Statistics
DH	District Hospital
DISE	District Information System for Education
DLHS	District-Level Household and Facility Survey
DPT	Diphtheria Pertussis and Tetanus Vaccine
EWS	Economically Weaker Sections
FRU	First Stage Referral Unit
FY	Financial Year
GER	Gross Enrolment Ratio

GI	Galvanized Iron
GoI	Government of India
GoM	Government of Maharashtra
GPI	Gender Parity Index
GSDP	Gross State Domestic Product
HDI	Human Development Index
HDIs	Human Development Indices
HDR	Human Development Report
HIV	Human Immunodeficiency Virus
HMIS	Health Management Information System
HR	Human Resources
IAY	Indira Awas Yojana
IC	Inclusion Coefficient
ICDS	Integrated Child Development Services
ICP	Inclusion Coefficient in a Plural Society
IEC	Information Education and Communication
IGIDR	Indira Gandhi Institute of Developmental Research
IHDI	Inequality-Adjusted Human Development Index
IHDR	India Human Development Report
IHSDP	Integrated Housing and Slum Development Programme
IIPS	International Institute for Population Sciences
IMR	Infant Mortality Rate
IP	Inpatient
IPD	Inpatient Department
IPHS	Indian Public Health Standards
ISR	Infant Survival Rate
ITDP	Integrated Tribal Development Project
JNNURM	Jawaharlal Nehru National Urban Renewal Mission
JSY	Janani Surksha Yojana
kcal	Kilocalorie
kg	Kilogram
Kg/m^2	Kilogram/Square Metre
km	Kilometre
LEB	Life Expectancy at Birth
LHV	Lady Health Visitor
LIG	Lower Income Group
lpcd	Litres Per Capita Per Day
LPG	Liquefied Petroleum Gas
m	Metre
MCL	Municipal Councils
MDG	Millennium Development Goals
MDM	Midday Meal
MHDR	Maharashtra Human Development Report
MICOFF	Inclusive Coefficient Maharashtra
MIG	Middle Income Group
MMPCE	Median Per Capita Consumer Expenditure Maharashtra
MMR	Maternal Mortality Ratio
MO	Medical Officer
MPCB	Maharashtra Pollution Control Board
MPCE	Monthly Per Capita Consumer Expenditure
MPSP	Maharashtra Prathamik Shikshan Parishad
NACO	National AIDS Control Organisation
NAR	Net Attendance Rate

NDDP	Net District Domestic Product
NDP	Net Domestic Product
NEERI	National Environmental Engineering Research Institute
NFHS	National Family Health Survey
NGO	Non-Governmental Organization
NGP	Nirmal Gram Puraskar
NIPFP	National Institute of Public Finance and Policy
NMR	Neonatal Mortality Rate
NRHM	National Rural Health Mission
NRLM	National Rural Livelihood Mission
NSDP	Net State Domestic Product
NSS	National Sample Survey
NSSO	National Sample Survey Office
NT	Nomadic Tribe
NUEPA	National University of Educational Planning and Administration
NVBDCP	National Vector Borne Disease Control Programme
OBC	Other Backward Classes
OP	Outpatient
OPD	Outpatient Department
ORS	Oral Rehydration Salts
ORT	Oral Rehydration Therapy
PCDDP	Per Capita District Domestic Product
PCN	Per Capita Net
PCNDDP	Per Capita Net District Domestic Product
PCPNDT Act	Pre-Conception and Pre-Natal Diagnostic Techniques (Prohibition of Sex Selection) Act, 1994
PDS	Public Distribution System
PHC	Primary Health Centre
PIB	Press Information Bureau
PIP	Programme Implementation Plan
PNC	Postnatal Check-Up
PPP	Purchasing Power Parity
PRI	Panchayati Raj Institution
PS	Usual Principal Activity Status
PTR	Pupil-Teacher Ratio
RAY	Rajiv Awas Yojana
RCH	Reproductive and Child Health
RGGNY I	Rajiv Gandhi Gramin Niwara Yojana I
RGGNY II	Rajiv Gandhi Gramin Niwara Yojana II
RGI	Registrar General & Census Commissioner of India
RGJAY	Rajiv Gandhi Jeevandayee Arogya Yojana
RH	Rural Hospital
RHS	Rural Health Statistics
RJMCHNM	Rajmata Jijau Mother–Child Health and Nutrition Mission
RNTCP	Revised National Tuberculosis Control Programme
RRGGNY II	Revised Rajiv Gandhi Gramin Niwara Yojana II
RSBY	Rashtriya Swasthya Bima Yojna
RTE	Right to Education
RTE Act	The Right of Children to Free and Compulsory Education Act, 2009
SAM	Severe Acute Malnutrition
SBR	Still Birth Rate
SC	Scheduled Caste/s
SCD	Survey of Causes of Deaths

SCR	Student-Classroom Ratio	
SD	Standard Deviation	
SDH	Sub-District Hospital	
SDP	State Domestic Product	
SEMIS	Secondary Education Management Information System	
SHDR	State Human Development Report	
SHSRC	State Health Systems Resource Centre	
SNDT	Shreemati Nathibai Damodar Thackersey	
SNP	Supplementary Nutrition Programme	
SRS	Sample Registration System	
SS	Usual Subsidiary Activity Status	
SSA	Sarva Shiksha Abhiyan	
ST	Scheduled Tribe/s	
TB	Tuberculosis	
TBA	Traditional Birth Attendant	
TFR	Total Fertility Rate	
TLM	Teaching Learning Material	
TRTI	Tribal Research & Training Institute	
TSC	Total Sanitation Campaign	
TSP	Tribal Sub-Plan	
TT	Tetanus Toxoid	
U5MR	Under-Five Mortality Rate	
UA	Urban Agglomeration	
UEE	Universalization of Elementary Education	
ULB	Urban Local Body	
UN	United Nations	
UNDP	United Nations Development Programme	
UNFPA	United Nations Population Fund	
UNICEF	United Nations Children's Fund	
US	United States	
VHSC	Village Health and Sanitation Committee	
VJ	Vimukt Jati	
WH	Women's Hospital	
WHO	World Health Organization	
WPR	Workforce Participation Rate	
YASHADA	Yashwantrao Chavan Academy of Development Administration	

Executive Summary

The Maharashtra Human Development Report (MHDR) 2012 keeps its central ideology as 'inclusive growth'. Progress in human development needs to be assessed not just by improvements in the human development index (HDI), but also by how well the poor, underprivileged and marginalized groups are included into the mainstream development processes. Hence, an attempt is made to study whether advancements in income as well as various social development indicators have been 'inclusive', what the achievements as well as shortfalls have been, and what could be the possible broad policy interventions or actions that could be taken to address the same. Although inclusiveness is a multidimensional concept, we train our focus on inclusive human development with respect to five cross-cutting themes, namely, gender, social groups, rural–urban sectors, regions and income. Such a study is also in keeping with the emphasis laid on inclusive growth by the Eleventh and Twelfth Five Year Plans.

The Context

The roots of our study of the human development scenario in the state of Maharashtra lie in the global human development report (HDR) 2010, which describes human development to be a dynamic and evolving concept. Human development is sustainable, equitable and empowering and facilitates the participation of individuals in household, community and country-level activities. By providing a broader human development perspective, the global HDR points to the fact that human development is different form economic growth and that progress in health and education can also drive improvements in human development. A similar conclusion is found in the first Maharashtra HDR published in 2002. The state did not report a very high HDI then, with high levels of per capita income not seeming to be getting translated into high human development outcomes. While the Report highlighted the rural–urban and regional disparities in health and education-related indicators, it made the point that it is the pattern of growth and not just growth in itself or by itself that is important for human development. The present MHDR 2012 takes its cue from the MHDR 2002 on the importance of the patterns of growth and the contributions it makes to capability advancements. For this purpose it keeps *inclusive human development* central to the presentation.

Human Development Scenario

The HDI is a summary measure of development, capturing three dimensions of education, health and income. Over the period 2001–11, the HDI for Maharashtra has shown an improvement from 0.666 to 0.752. The HDI for all districts has shown progress, reflecting advancements in the literacy rate, school enrolments, infant mortality and income. The highlight is that over 2001–11, improvements in the HDI have been greater in districts positioned at the lower end of the HDI ranking scale (Nandurbar, Gadchiroli, Jalna, Hingoli and Washim report greater improvements in their human development indices (HDIs), compared to progressive districts such as Mumbai, Pune, Thane and Kolhapur). While all districts have shown improvements in their HDI over the two time points under consideration, some have done relatively better and moved up in ranking. Some others have shown a positive change but have moved down in relative ranking. The positive and significant rank correlation between district per capita income scores and the HDI reported in the MHDR 2002 continues to persist in 2011 as well. The inequality-adjusted human development index (IHDI) calculated for the state as per the revised United Nations Development Programme (UNDP) methodology reveals that in 2010–11 Maharashtra ranks higher than the all-India estimate and finds a place in the very high human development quartile amongst the Indian states. The district radar profiles for four indicators (literacy rate, enrolment rate, infant survival and income) also prominently indicate persistent inter-district inequality in the performance of these indicators amongst the districts.

The logical next step after studying the HDI for Maharashtra and its districts is to explore issues pertaining to economic growth and income distribution, whether there has been any reduction in inter-district disparities with respect to them and whether the growth process has been inclusive.

Economic Growth, Equity and Inclusion

Income measures place Maharashtra in second position amongst the major states as far as per capita income is considered. The net state domestic product (NSDP) (at current prices) in 2008–09 being 46 per cent more than the all-India average. Sectoral profiles reveal the continued dominance of the non-agricultural sector in total NSDP with respect to growth rate and size, a majority of the segments in the tertiary sector growing at double-digit rates and the agricultural sector reporting a decline in its share. Inter-district disparities in per capita income measured by the net district domestic product (NDDP) (at constant prices) show a negligibly small change since publication of the MHDR 2002. This could be ascribed to better economic performance by some of the poorer districts, including Dhule, Jalna, Jalgaon and Nandurbar, which have shown faster growth rates than the state as a whole. Despite this improved performance, these districts do not show a higher performance at the aggregate macro level because of their very small share in the state total. Richer districts such as Mumbai continue to lead the growth scenario, with Mumbai alone contributing to 23 per cent of the state's growth since 1999–2000. The state has enjoyed a high level of per capita income made possible by rapid progress in the non-agricultural sectors. This feature, along with the restricted geographical spread of economic development, has implied that both the average level of income and the degree of inequality in its distribution across persons in the state has remained high.

The distribution of the workforce across sectors in 2009–10 remains similar to that reported in the MHDR 2002, with the primary sector showing a sustained decline and the secondary and tertiary sectors showing near stagnation. While the primary sector absorbed more than half the workforce in the state but contributed to less than 12 per cent of the income generated, the non-agricultural sector, which contributed to 88 per cent of the income generated, employed less than 50 per cent of the workforce. Unemployment rates are higher in rural Maharashtra, where virtually half the workforce is employed as casual labour, pointing towards the existence of high rural–urban disparities in income, levels of living and poverty. Combined workforce participation rates (WPRs)—male and female—registered a decline in rural areas and an increase in urban areas over the period from 1993–94 to 2009–10 in Maharashtra as well as India. The decline in rural employment is lesser in Maharashtra vis-à-vis India, while the increase in urban employment is higher in Maharashtra in comparison to all-India figures.

Estimates of consumption distribution (2004–05 to 2009–10) report a decline in the incidence of rural as well as urban poverty in Maharashtra, as per Tendulkar Committee report. Furthermore, in rural and urban areas of the state, the consumption distribution (2004–05), within and across social groups, shows inter-regional variations when measured by consumption levels. The Inland Northern region (revenue division: Nashik) is the poorest in rural Maharashtra and the Inland Western region (revenue division: Pune) is found to be the richest. In urban areas, the Coastal region (revenue divisions: Konkan and Mumbai) is found to be richest and the Inland Central region (districts in the revenue division of Aurangabad, except Washim) the poorest. Amongst the social groups, the incidence of poverty in rural areas is found to be lowest for the Others category, followed by the Other Backward Classes (OBC), Scheduled Castes (SC) and Scheduled Tribes (ST), in that order. In the urban areas there is a slight change in the social group ranking, with the SC moving to the bottom of the ladder preceded by the ST, OBC and Others. District-level profiling shows that across districts, the extent of inequality in consumption distribution is more in urban areas vis-à-vis rural areas of the state.

While there has been a clear improvement in the measures of economic access across decile groups in both rural and urban parts of the state, they still do not translate into improvements in cereal consumption and calorie intake. In rural parts of the state, cereal consumption has seen a continuous decline from the mid-1970s until 2004–05. Average calorie intake by the rural populace saw a decline across all decile groups between 1983 and 1993–94 and across a majority of decile groups until 2004–05. This is in consonance with the all-India trend and may be due to technological advancements and a consequent change in lifestyle of the rural populace. Urban Maharashtra reports a somewhat uneven pattern for cereal consumption with the average calorie intake also experiencing a decline for all the decile groups between 1983 and 2004–05.

Subsequent to the macroeconomic performance of the state, the performance of each of the sectors, including education, health, housing and sanitation is analysed through a five-way lens.

Education

Maharashtra is the second most populous state in the country, accounting for approximately 9.3 per cent of India's population. A larger proportion of the population resides in rural areas (54.7 per cent). Over 1951–2011, the rate of urbanization has been high with a population growth rate of 23.7 per cent, with Maharashtra accounting for 13.5 per cent of India's urban population in 2011.

The state shows improved performance for all education-related indicators at the aggregate level; however inter-sectoral (rural–urban) and social-group disparities persist. Maharashtra reports a literacy rate of 82.9 per cent in 2011, well above the national average. While the male literacy rate has reached a plateau, there has been an overall narrowing in the gender gap, although the gender gap in literacy is higher in rural areas vis-à-vis urban areas (19 and 8.4 percentage points respectively). Inter-district variations in the literacy rate persist, with Nandurbar reporting the lowest literacy rate at the aggregate level as well as for females (63.0 per cent and 53.9 per cent respectively). The literacy rate disaggregated by social groups (based on data from the 64th round of the National Sample Survey [NSS] 2007–08) shows two useful features: *first*, across all the social groups, male and female literacy was higher in urban areas compared to rural areas; *second*, the ST had the lowest literacy rate (61.9 per cent) and a gender gap of 24 percentage points, highlighting a cause for concern. Finally, in 2011, 13 blocks reported literacy rates lesser than some of the low-literacy-rate states in the country, highlighting another cause for concern.

In Maharashtra, there has been a clear increase in primary and upper primary school infrastructure, including human resources (HR), which has contributed to rising enrolments over the period from 1970 to 2010–11. While elementary education is provided mainly through government schools in the state, secondary education is catered mainly by privately aided institutions. Secondary schools have also grown in number with enrolments in secondary schools increasing by approximately 46 per cent per decade during 2000 to 2011–12.

Going beyond provisioning, actual participation in schooling is essential for capability enhancements and this can be captured by the net attendance rate (NAR). In 2007–08, the NARs for the primary and upper primary levels (90.8 per cent and 67.1 per cent, respectively) were lower than the corresponding gross enrolment ratios (GERs) (101.8 and 86.8 for the primary and upper primary levels), reflecting that attendance had not kept pace with enrolments, more so at the upper primary level. This is not to undermine the progress made in the elementary-level NARs, which reported an increase over the period from 1995–96 to 2007–08 across rural and urban areas and for female children, with a narrowing in the gender gap. Social-group stratification of the NARs finds ST children lagging behind in both the primary and upper primary levels. An interesting finding though is the female advantage in primary and upper primary NARs for the ST and SC at the state level as well as in a few regions, which could be a reflection of the effectiveness of interventions aimed at promoting school participation for these social groups that are already in place. School attendance at the elementary level is also found to increase as households move up the monthly per capita consumer expenditure (MPCE) ladder. NARs for the secondary level show a sharp decline in comparison to those at the elementary level, with rural areas and ST children facing a clear disadvantage. Schooling incentives are known to have an important role to play in encouraging school participation as well as retention. In 2007–08, an advantage was seen for female children (in rural and urban areas), children attending school in rural areas, those attending government schools and ST children in terms of proportions receiving free education.

In 2007–08, 6.8 per cent of children in the age group of 6–14 years in the state were out of school, showing a bias against rural areas but no gender disadvantage. The ST reported the highest proportions of out-of-school children. What is of consequence is that never-enrolled children constituted a higher proportion of the out-of-school children. At the secondary schooling level, a quarter of children in the age group of 14–16 years were out of school, with a clear gender gap as well as disadvantage faced by ST children. Here the proportion of children enrolled but not attending school was higher, implying retention to be more of a problem.

Whether school provisioning and rising enrolments have converted into acceptable learning outcomes is an area for which not much data is available. The survey data from the Annual Status of Education Report (ASER) shows that for Maharashtra over the period 2006–11, while children in Std I and Std II have shown improvements in their reading and arithmetic abilities, children in Std III and Std IV have shown deterioration. For higher class levels, one out of every four children in Std V is unable to read textbooks from Std II, implying that approximately 25 per cent of children graduate from primary school without being able to read properly. A similar scenario is found for mathematics where more than half the children in Std V report being unable to carry out simple three-digit-by-one-digit division problems. Despite being above the India average on the ASER performance tests, Maharashtra still has a long way to go in reaching high school achievement levels.

Education expenditures via the Sarva Shiksha Abhiyan (SSA) in the state over 2006–07 have seen a 12 per cent increase. Also, in 2009–10, approximately 92 per cent of the state-allocated SSA funds were utilized. On a per-child basis, Maharashtra spends approximately ₹9,635 per child per year, which is much higher than states such as West Bengal, Madhya Pradesh and Rajasthan. The ASER–PAISA survey of 2010 reports that in Maharashtra, the proportion of schools receiving maintenance, development and teaching learning material (TLM) funds was 92.6 per cent, with 87.6 per cent schools reporting timely receipt of maintenance funds by mid-year.

To summarize, Maharashtra reports considerable progress in access to education, especially in terms of schooling infrastructure with enrolments in the primary and upper primary levels almost universalized. There have also been improvements in the inclusion of the marginalized groups, including female children and children from backward social groups, in school participation. Yet the quality of schooling is an issue that needs to be addressed urgently.

Health

Maharashtra has reported progress in all the outcome indicators of health from 2001–11. The highlights in terms of achievements include a sharp drop in the crude birth rate (CBR), a decline in the fertility rate to below replacement levels, a marginal improvement in the adult sex ratio with the sex ratio for the ST well above the state average and improved life expectancy, with a female advantage reported in the same. A significant decrease in the infant mortality rate (IMR) (a drop of 20 points over 2001–11) is reported with a narrowing of the male–female, rural–urban gap in this indicator. A steady drop in the under-five mortality rate (U5MR), a maternal mortality ratio (MMR) that was half the national average in 2007–09 are clear indicators of progress, although there is still a long way to go to achieve the Millennium Development Goals (MDG) for the MMR.

On the flip side is the low child sex ratio (for children aged 0–6 years) of 883 in 2011, which could reflect not just male child preference but also neglect of the female child in terms of the quality of care given. There continue to also exist inter-district, spatial as well as gender and social-group disparities in all these indicators, pointing towards specific interventions that need to be put into place to tackle the same.

To make the prevailing health scenario in Maharashtra easier to study and understand, it can be arranged under two broad heads, namely, input and outcome indicators. Public spending on health is an important input indicator as it has implications for the availability, provisioning and effectiveness of services provided in this social sector. With less than 2.5 per cent of the state budget allocated to health in 2008–09, Maharashtra reports low public spending on health. On a per capita basis, at the district level, it is found to be higher for the urban population vis-à-vis the rural population. The spread of public health infrastructure and manpower in the state is vast, following a three-tier system and can be considered well above the national average. What needs to be recognized is the presence of a sizeable tribal population spread across 15 districts and the challenges it poses to the outreach of health facilities in the state. Rural hospitals (RHs) have seen a small improvement in population ratios and a lessening in inter-district inequities, which could be a result of the upgrading they have undergone in recent years. Although there has been an upward trend in the availability of hospitals and beds per lakh population, the latter shows an urban bias. At the district level, many districts report an increase in population per hospital bed over the last decade, pointing towards the need for improvements on this front.

Adequate and trained health personnel are essential for the functioning of health infrastructure, and in Maharashtra the numbers of doctors and nurses has been on the rise. Nevertheless, inter-regional variations exist, with urban areas having an advantage in terms of staffing. There is a shortage of auxiliary nurse midwives (ANMs) at the sub-centre level, nurses at the primary health centre (PHC) level and specialists in the Indian Public Health Standards (IPHS) hospitals, with serious consequences for the poor who either have to forgo specialized health care or bear the expenses for availing it. Gadchiroli reports the best doctor-population ratio, but it also has poor utilization of health facilities, which is captured by the very low proportion of institutional deliveries and child immunization rates, demonstrating that mere availability of health facilities and good doctor-population ratios may not necessarily convert to improved utilization rates although they are essential for improving the same.

Population proportions for inpatient (IP) and outpatient (OP) care are a good reflection of the efficiency of any health care system. In Maharashtra, while there has been an increase in IP and OP cases by around 15 percentage points over the period from 1986–87 to 2004, the private sector is found to cater to OP care and hospitalization in larger proportions. Despite such a trend, a large proportion of the poor populace, especially women, access health care from the public sector. There also exists a clear caste disparity with ST households showing very low utilization rates of public health facilities, which could be because of the scattered nature of their habitation and the weak presence of the private sector in tribal-dominated areas. There is thus a pivotal role that the public health sector can play in facilitating inclusion of such excluded social groups into the health-care system in the state.

While there has been an improvement in the coverage of antenatal care in the state, especially for ST mothers, the third district-level household and facility survey (DLHS-3) reports that only a third of women in the state received full antenatal care during pregnancy. The percentage has improved to 70 per cent in rural area and 61 per cent in urban area in 2011–12. (Government of Maharashtra 2012). Inter-district disparities are present in the outreach of antenatal care. Women with more years of education, those living in urban areas and those belonging to higher wealth classes were found to access antenatal care in greater proportions. SC and ST women accessed such care from government facilities in larger proportions. One of the highlights of the achievements of the state has been a clear and unambiguous improvement in the proportion of institutional births, an important element for maternal and neonatal survival, seen over the period between the DLHS-1 and DLHS-3 surveys. Combined with it is an increase in the proportion of safe deliveries. Overall, while institutional births show an urban bias, the increase in their rates has been higher for rural areas of the state (between DLHS-2 and DLHS-3). What is a matter of concern is the wide inter-district variations in this indicator, with institutional births varying from 93.5 per cent in Mumbai suburban to as low as 24 per cent and 25 per cent in Gadchiroli and Nandurbar respectively, which also report the lowest proportions of safe deliveries. The interventions under the National Rural Health Mission (NRHM) in Maharashtra have had some notable beneficial outcomes, including a marked increase in institutional deliveries to 96 per cent, increase in the per cent of safe deliveries to 98 per cent in 2011–12 (Government of Maharashtra 2012), and OP care, enhanced coverage of the beneficiaries under the Janani Suraksha Yojana (JSY), community mobilization by accredited social health activists (ASHAs), community-based monitoring (CBM) instituted in its first phase and increases in health-care manpower in the state.

Maharashtra has made progress in tackling under-nutrition for all three measures, indicating improvements in curbing the incidence of child malnutrition, with a considerable reduction in the proportion of underweight children, stunted and wasting children between the second national family health survey (NFHS) and CNSM. The proportion of children suffering from stunting though has not shown a significant decrease and flags a priority area for interventions. Malnutrition is seen to have a larger rural presence, higher prevalence in urban slums and a gender bias. Disaggregated by social groups, the occurrence of malnutrition is found to be higher amongst children belonging to the SC and the ST. NFHS-3 data shows around a third of women have low body mass index or BMI and a little less than half to be anaemic (based on low haemoglobin levels). Women belonging to the lower wealth classes, rural areas and SC and ST groups report low BMI and haemoglobin levels. Maharashtra also reports of high obese or overweight women (higher in urban areas) and a higher proportion of obese men in rural areas.

Two vital elements for addressing under-nutrition are oral rehydration therapy (ORT) and child-feeding practices. In 2007–08 (DLHS-3), close to a fifth of children in Maharashtra suffered from childhood diarrhoea. Awareness about diarrhoea management practices is found to be influenced by a mother's age and education, place of residence, social group and wealth quintile. Maternal illiteracy and belonging to SC households contribute to low proportions of children being breastfed.

Maharashtra launched the flagship Rajmata Jijau Mother–Child Health and Nutrition Mission (RJMCHNM) in March 2005 with the primary aim of reducing grade III and IV malnutrition in children in the age group of 0–6 years. The RJMCHNM stresses the notion of 'the 1,000-day window of opportunity' (−9 to 24 months), during which a significant lifelong difference can be made to the lives of children. With this underlying ideology the second phase of the RJMCHNM was initiated in 2011 with the focus on reductions in under-nutrition amongst children of less than two years of age through a continuum of care. Inclusion of the most vulnerable, youngest, poorest, socially excluded, severely undernourished and difficult-to-reach children is the main aim of the interventions under the RJMCHNM.

Maharashtra is now positioned such that, although it has a vast health infrastructure, it needs to be operationalized better so as to be more equitable and inclusive. A multi-pronged strategy is needed: to tackle regional disparities in the access to and utilization of health care, for effective functioning of referral mechanisms, more efficient utilization of resources, medicine availability and pricing, public–private partnerships and spread of CBM to all districts, deal with the health-care implications of rapid urbanization and last, but not the least, to improve data availability, which could immensely contribute to the formulation of evidence-based interventions for health care. Also, to be more socially equitable, the spread of tribal population across the 15 districts needs to be understood better to facilitate improved provisioning of health-care facilities and personnel in these areas. Improvements in the nutrition status of women and children needs increased awareness generation on various fronts, including the benefits of breastfeeding practices, usefulness of colostrum, initiation of complementary foods at the age of six months for infants and usefulness and effectiveness of home-based protocols to tackle under-nutrition.

Housing and Sanitation

In 2008–09, Maharashtra accounted for approximately 35 per cent of the notified and non-notified slums in the country. In a rapidly urbanizing state such as Maharashtra which also experiences a fair amount of in-migration as well as has a high proportion of slum-dwelling population, the availability housing as a bundle of basic amenities becomes all the more relevant. One of the immediate consequences of rising urbanization is increasing rents, which has two fallouts, *first*, a shortage of affordable housing giving rise to squatter settlements and slums and *second*, an expansion in urban boundaries with areas in the urban peripheries characterized by lower rents and poor housing and sanitation conditions. Data studied on housing amenities (in terms of households with drinking water within their premises, electricity for domestic use and the availability of toilets) reveal that in Maharashtra, between 2002 and 2008–09 (NSS, 58th round and 65th round), there was a marked improvement in these facilities in rural areas while urban areas showed only a small change in the same. Despite such a trend though, in 2008–09, households in urban areas had an advantage in the availability of all these three facilities.

The household census of 2011 reports a 37.7 per cent increase in households in urban areas of the state and a 25.6 per cent in rural areas. The data shows a clear improvement in the proportion of households having dwellings in good condition over the period 2001–11, with a clear urban bias (17 percentage points in 2011). Disaggregated by social groups, SC and ST households also report a similar improvement over the same decade, which is a sign of better inclusion. NSS data (2008–09) brings forth quite clearly the relationship between household consumption expenditure (MPCE) and condition of dwellings, the latter showing improvements with rising MPCE in both rural and urban areas of the state. Various housing programmes are currently underway in the state under the aegis of the Jawaharlal Nehru National Urban Renewal Mission (JNNURM), Affordable Housing in Partnership (AHP) and Rajiv Awas Yojana (RAY) programmes. Under the JNNURM, the Basic Services to Urban Poor (BSUP) is operational in Mumbai, Pune, Nashik, Nanded and Nagpur while the Integrated Housing and Slum Development Programme (IHSDP) covers all the other cities not under the BSUP.

The availability of and access to clean and safe drinking water is a human development imperative as well as an essential input for achieving the MDG on health. In Maharashtra, around two-thirds of households access drinking water from taps (Census 2011), the proportion being higher for urban areas (89.1 per cent) vis-à-vis rural areas (50 per cent). Wide inter-district variations exist in this indicator, with households in Mumbai and Mumbai (Suburban) districts at the higher extreme (97.8 per cent and 96.5 per cent respectively) and those in Gondia, Gadchiroli and Sindhudurg at the lower extreme (less than a third households accessing tap water). Census 2011 data indicates that in Maharashtra 59.4 per cent households had their source of drinking water within the premises which has shown a marginal increase from 53.4 per cent in 2001. What must be mentioned are a few trends observed over the decade 2001–11 and they are: *first*, an increase in the proportion of households having tap water within their premises (nearly six percentage points); *second*, a small but notable increase in the proportion of SC and ST households having access to tap water; *third*, a substantial increase (10 percentage points) in the proportion of SC households having tap water within their premises and an increase of two percentage points for ST households. The rural–urban disparity in all the water-related indicators is yet to be bridged. In 2008–09 a higher proportion of rural households reported community use for the same (56.9 per cent) when compared to 15.6 per cent of urban households. In rural and urban parts of the state, households with higher MPCE and the OBC reported exclusive use of water in higher proportions while ST households relied more heavily on community use drinking water facilities pointing towards the need for more equitable distribution of drinking water sources for better social inclusion. Various central- and state-sponsored programmes have been put into place in Maharashtra for improving access to drinking water and some of these include the National Rural Drinking Water Programme, The Rural Water Supply Project 'Aaple Pani', the Jalswarajya Programme and the Maharashtra Sujal and Nirmal Abhiyan, to name a few.

The availability of water and sanitation facilities are two essential development imperatives that go hand-in-hand and are essential for good health and hygiene. In Maharashtra, there has been an improvement in the proportion of households having a bathing facility within their premises (by 24.3 percentage points over the decade 2001–11). In urban areas a very small proportion of households report not having any type of bathroom (4.6 per cent) while in rural areas approximately a fifth of households report the same. Inter-district variations are seen in the availability of this facility, with Gadchiroli reporting about 43 per cent of households not having this facility. Although there has been an improvement in the proportion of households having a latrine facility within their premises (18 percentage points over the decade 2001–11), the problem of open defecation still persists in the state. In 2011, 38 per cent of households in rural areas reported having a latrine facility within their premises, which is much lower than in urban areas (close to 75 per cent), bringing to fore the rural–urban disparity that also exists. There has been progress made in terms of the inclusion of backward social groups, shown by an increase in the proportion of SC and ST households having this facility over the decade 2001–11 (approximately 16 and 10 percentage points respectively). A finding to be highlighted is that in some districts where the proportion of households not having a latrine facility within their premises is high, the usage of public facilities is also high (Dhule and Jalgaon), giving a useful policy direction which could also facilitate inclusion. Under the aegis of the Total Sanitation Campaign (TSC), in rural Maharashtra, over the period 2005–12, a substantial number of individual household toilets, sanitary complexes, school toilets, *anganwadi* toilets and rural sanitary marts have been constructed. To summarize, while there has been a move towards improving the condition of dwellings, availability and access to drinking water and sanitation conditions, with the provisioning for the same remaining above the all-India averages, Maharashtra still needs to achieve better inclusion in terms of sectoral, social and income groups in the provisioning and utilization of these facilities.

Looking Ahead

This HDR for Maharashtra encapsulates and presents the progress that the state has made and the gaps it still needs to breach in terms of inclusive human development. Using a five-way lens to study the same, inclusiveness in terms of rural–urban sectors, regions, gender, social and income groups has been analysed, with the achievements as well as gaps identified and suggestions for policy interventions elucidated. While all the major findings, lessons learnt and the policy interventions that emerge are discussed in detail in the concluding chapter of the report, a few of the main evidence-based policy prescriptions are elaborated here. It is suggested that the district-specific policies need to be evolved in order to explore each district's potential in enhancing its income. Further, strategies need to be evolved for better targeting of the poor by interventions such as insurance, direct cash transfers for essential health and education expenditure, etc. One important policy direction that emerges is that the distribution of resources needs to be based on existing gaps in outcome indicators rather than supply/demand based norms. For the effective provisioning of health-care and education services in the state, performance assessments of districts, which reflect the proportions of the poorest and socioeconomically disadvantaged population covered, emerges as a policy imperative.

Education and health are two important pillars of human development and some of the main policy implications for these, with a focus on inclusion, which emerge from this MHDR need highlighting.

Qualitative improvements in educational attainments and learning achievements still remain a challenge for the state and can be facilitated and enhanced by providing improved teacher training and support. District-level action plans through consultations with various stakeholders in education as well as achievement-based rankings of schools could contribute towards improved academic performance and learning attainments. A multi-pronged strategy for health interventions could include: facilitating access for the poor to private health care through interventions such as cash transfers and coupons; strengthening of health facilities through improved infrastructure, skilled HR and use of standard protocols for patient management; health-care planning focused on tribal areas; expansions in the network of special care newborn units at facilities with high institutional deliveries with standard treatment protocols and scaling up accredited health facilities as 24×7 PHCs and sub-centres based on IPHS.

Certain critical policy attention areas in the health and education sectors have been identified and need to be addressed through special interventions to facilitate better outreach and inclusion. The mission mode could be adopted in the identified 13 blocks, which have literacy rates below some of the low-literacy states in the country as well as in districts where the gender gap in literacy is high and/or the literacy rate for ST females is low. Focus needs to be trained on improvements in the female enrolment rates in the 125 blocks and eight municipal corporations where it is lower than the state average. Improvements are needed in the NARs at the upper primary level in general, for ST male and female children at the primary, upper primary and secondary levels and in rural areas at the secondary level.

For interventions in the health sector, the areas of vital importance include reductions in the IMR for socioeconomically disadvantaged groups; reductions in the U5MR in rural areas and for female children; reductions in the neonatal mortality rate (NMR) in rural areas; improving outreach of antenatal care in districts of the Marathawada region, as well as in the districts of Dhule, Nashik and Jalgaon with special focus on ST women; improvements in access to health care in tribal and poor districts and improved immunization of ST children. In addition, water and sanitation programmes in the state need to work in tandem given the close association found between households having water and latrine facilities within their premises.

Finally, for future studies as well as analyses of how the state has been working and making progress towards the goal of inclusive human development, data availability at various levels of disaggregation is vital. To satisfy this need, there is a need for setting up institutional capacity at the state as well as more decentralized levels to collect and compile data at various levels of disaggregation (including gender, rural–urban sector, districts and regions, social groups, income groups, etc). This exercise would definitely enhance as well as enrich human development studies and debates as well as provide concrete evidence-based policy guidelines for the state.

K. P. Bakshi
Additional Chief Secretary

Planning Department
Government of Maharashtra
Mantralaya, Mumbai 400 032.

FOREWORD

We are delighted to present the MHDR 2012 *Towards Inclusive Human Development*. This is a unique Report, documenting the progress made by the state over the last decade on key human development indicators with inclusive growth as the main underlying ideology.

Along with presenting the progress that has been made and the milestones that need to be reached, the report discusses and analyses the prevailing human development scenario in the state across regions and districts, sectors, gender, social groups and income groups. It indicates the challenges that lie ahead and outlines the policy measures required to meet various human development challenges to ensure 'shared prosperity' for all the people of our state in the near future. We are sure that for Maharashtra's future socioeconomic policy and planning with inclusive growth and human development as the central paradigm, the present state HDR will make a very useful and constructive guiding tool.

I compliment Dr Sanjay Chahande, Director General, YASHADA, for bringing out this analytical and exhaustive Report. Dr Minal Naravane and her team at the Center for Human Development (CHD), YASHADA, deserve a special mention for their untiring efforts. Ashok Jagtap, Joint Secretary, and Amol Khandare, Officer on Special Duty of Planning Department also need a special appreciation for their continuous interest and support in the preparation of SHDR. Dr Usha Jayachandran has been instrumental in conceptualizing, compiling and editing all the background material, contributing various invaluable inputs and enriching the analytical content of the final Report. We gratefully acknowledge all the authors for their background papers, which form the backbone of the Report. Our sincere thanks to Dr Seeta Prabhu, Former Senior Advisor, UNDP and Planning Commission, Government of India, for the technical inputs and oral guidance. We place on record our deep appreciation of all the experts and panellists who participated in various workshops, meetings and brainstorming sessions organized by YASHADA. The data support rendered by Directorate of Economics and Statistics (DES) is appreciated.

I believe that the present report will surely find a place in the state's effort on evidence-based policy making aimed at moving towards more inclusive human development.

(K. P. Bakshi)

यशवंतराव चव्हाण विकास प्रशासन प्रबोधिनी, पुणे
(महाराष्ट्र शासनाची अंगीकृत संस्था)

YASHWANTRAO CHAVAN ACADEMY OF DEVELOPMENT ADMINISTRATION, PUNE
(A Government of Maharashtra Organisation)

Dr. Sanjay Chahande, IAS
Director General

PREFACE

Human development is a fundamental part of growth and equity aspirations of every nation today. In the Indian context, Maharashtra prepared first State Human Development Report (SHDR) in the year 2002. The state has come a long way in the ensuing decade with human development becoming one of the guiding principles for overall development strategy of the State.

In keeping with Twelfth Five Year Plans' focused agenda of 'inclusive growth' it is the endeavour of the present Maharashtra SHDR to capture the extent of equity and inclusion the state has managed to achieve in all the key human development parameters in recent years. This has been attempted by studying not only district-wise trends and transitions in all the key HDI parameters but also an analysis of the extent of inclusion achieved across social groups, gender, income groups, sectors and regions, data permitting.

The preparation of this Report has been an enriching experience for all those involved. The various stages of its preparation included several workshops, where experts were consulted and debated with for deciding various human development indicators and methodologies; people's consultations at block and district levels, that helped capture grass-roots-level perceptions about human development; and sharing the draft Report with national and international experts and incorporating their recommendations. The content presented in various chapters of the Report has been contributed by eminent academicians who have attempted to quantify and analyse human development in its various dimensions with 'inclusion' as the underlying theme.

Though the Report is a culmination of academic analyses, its endeavour is to bring forth evidence-based policy prescriptions which the state could use to suitably formulate its interventions for inclusive and effective human development. Given the pressing need for development policies and budgetary allocations to take cognizance of various human development imperatives, we hope the present SHDR for Maharashtra will contribute towards helping the state government in designing its plans, programmes and policies towards more inclusive human development.

It has been a privilege for YASHADA to be associated with the preparation of this prestigious Report and I would like to thank the State Government for giving us this opportunity. My sincere thanks to Shri Sitaram Kunte, ex-Principal Secretary, Planning Department, Government of Maharashtra, for his support and guidance during early stages of the preparation of this Report. This Report could not have been possible but for continuous support and guidance of Shri

K. P. Bakshi, Additional Chief Secretary, Planning, Government of Maharashtra, throughout the preparation phase. My special thanks to all Steering Committee members, for their valuable inputs in the preparation of the SHDR. I also take the opportunity to extend my gratitude to Dr Seeta Prabhu, Senior Advisor, UNDP, for all technical and other inputs. My appreciation to all the background paper writers whose contributions have enriched this Report qualitatively. I would also like to applaud Dr Usha Jayachandran, the lead author and editor of this Report, who had worked and contributed immensely in enhancing the analytical and editorial quality of this Report. Finally, this exhaustive publication was possible only because of the tireless efforts, hard work and complete commitment of Dr Minal Naravane, Director, CHD, YASHADA, and the efforts of her team. My congratulations to her and her team!

(Dr. Sanjay Chahande)

1
Setting the Framework

Human Development is defined as expanding the range of people's choices. The poor are poor because their set of capabilities is small—not because of what they don't have, but because of what they can't do. Well-being is possible by things people can do rather than things people have. If their set of *capabilities* grows larger, people can do more of the things they would like to do. Economic development expands the choices people have over their capabilities. It has meaning only when the resources and access to the gains crafted from them are evenly spread across the population.

It is the pattern of growth, not just growth in itself or by itself that is important for human development; it has to enable improvements in the productive capabilities of the people and their participation in value added activities thereby increasing their purchasing power.
(Government of Maharashtra 2002)

Human Development: A Global Overview

The idea central to the first HDR published in 1990 was that 'people are the real wealth of a nation'. Development was seen as more than just economic growth and was taken to encompass the development of the people of a country. A new vision of development was envisaged by Mahbub-ul-Haq and Amartya Sen who emphasized the need to 'put people at the centre' of all development efforts and the necessity to enlarge people's choices by providing them with the means to lead an educated, healthy life with a decent standard of living. "Plural principles such as equity, sustainability and respect for human rights are thus key" (UNDP 2010).

Celebrating 20 years of human development, the global HDR 2010 published by the UNDP documents the various "pathways to human development" that have been addressed and studied ever since the inception of human development as a concept. We present here a brief overview of the same to set the underlying context for our study of the human development scenario in the state of Maharashtra.

The global HDR 2010 stresses the need for human development to be, *first*, sustainable; *second*, equitable and *third*, empowering, such that it enables individuals to exercise their choices and helps them to participate in processes at the household, community and national levels. It also emphasizes the need to look at human development as an evolving concept and not as a fixed or static dictum. "Inherent in the human development tradition is that the approach be dynamic, not calcified" (UNDP 2010). An interesting observation the global HDR 2010 makes is that countries performing well on the HDI front not only include those who have done well on income indicators but also include those who have shown remarkable progress in the non-income dimensions of human development (for example, Nepal, Oman and Tunisia).

> "Human development is different from economic growth and substantial achievements are possible even without fast growth"

By providing a broader human development perspective, the global HDR 2010 points to the fact that progress in health and education alone can also drive improvements in human development. "Human development is different from economic growth and substantial achievements are possible even without fast growth" (UNDP 2010). The HDR 2010 clearly states that these achievements were possible because growth had decoupled from the processes determining progress in the non-income dimensions of human development. Such a finding is very relevant to the Indian context as it points towards the possibility that states not doing too well on the economic growth front should be able to increase their progress in human development by focusing on achievements in social sectors such as education and health. This does not, however, undermine in any way the importance of income for economic growth and the role that higher incomes play in increasing the access to goods and services, especially of the poor and the underprivileged.

Another significant aspect that the global HDR 2010 highlights is the differences in HDI achievements among countries that initially had similar starting points. The reasons for this include country-specific factors such as policies, institutions and geography which become significant in determining the extent of achievements in human development indicators. Such a finding can also be applicable to the existence of variations in human development outcomes at the state and district levels in a country such as India and, within it, a state such as Maharashtra where policies, institutions and geography do play important roles.

The relevance and importance of institutions and the need to ground human development policies in existing institutions to bring forth change comes out quite strongly in the same Report.

> The policies and reforms compatible with progress vary widely across institutional settings and depend on structural and political constraints. Attempts to transplant institutional and policy solutions across countries with different conditions often fail. And policies must be typically informed by the prevailing institutional setting to bring about change.
>
> (UNDP 2010)

Such an inference can also be applied to country-specific contexts like that within a country. For example, in India, there are large interstate disparities in the availability and functioning of institutions that have a direct bearing on human development outcomes and replicating institutions and policies across the board may not facilitate progress in human capabilities. Often, state- and district-specific interventions (and at even lower levels of administration such as blocks or tehsils) are needed to impact the delivery of the institutional mechanisms already in place.

Looking at the way forward, the global HDR 2010 rationalizes that although the global experience for human development has been encouraging, one needs to move ahead with caution. It states:

> Progress is possible even without massive resources; the lives of people can be improved through means already at the disposal of most countries. But success is not guaranteed, and the pathways to human development are varied and specific to a country's historical, political and institutional conditions.
>
> (UNDP 2010)

What is of essence to the global scenario on human development today is the need to put people at the centre of development by making 'progress equitable and broad-based'. There is also a pressing need for people to participate actively in the change processes as well as to take steps that in no way jeopardize the development needs of the generations to come.

The basis of highlighting some of the main conclusions from the global HDR 2010 here is the very appropriate and applicable nature of these recommendations to the Indian context in general and for Maharashtra in particular. These findings at the global level are relevant to efforts aimed at enhancing human capabilities in developing countries such as India and there is a lot to learn from the experiences and wisdom shared therein. The Report very aptly reaffirms:

> Human development is not only about health, education and income—it is also about people's active engagement in shaping development, equity and sustainability, intrinsic aspects of the freedom the people have to lead lives they have reason to value. There are fewer consensuses about what progress on these fronts entails and measures are also lacking. But lack of quantification is no reason to neglect or ignore them.
> (UNDP 2010)

The HDRs brought out at the state and district levels in India also endeavour to keep the ideologies on human development, as reflected in the global HDR, central to their presentation and analysis on the subject.

Towards Social Inclusion: The India Human Development Report (IHDR) 2011

The IHDR 2011 points towards an improvement in the HDI for the country by 21 per cent over the period from 1999–2000 to 2007–08 and attributes this progress to mainly improvements in the education index (28 per cent) over the same period. It also cites a convergence in HDIs across Indian states, with the poorer states showing higher increases in their HDIs. Keeping social inclusion as the main focus, the report highlights the various input- and output-related synergies that operate in the form of 'feedback loops' during the development process. It states that the expansion of human functioning in terms of health and educational attainments, reduction of income poverty, and economic growth are linked in a synergistic manner through these feedback loops.

Citing various examples to explain the concept of feedback loops, the IHDR 2011 elaborates how education, when taken as an input, can facilitate improvements in health and nutritional outcomes which then feedback into improved school attendance rates and consequently lead to better learning outcomes. Similarly there are feedback loops seen from small family size to better nutrition as well as from better health status of mothers to enhancements in child nutrition. The IHDR 2011 thus focuses on whether large sections of the underprivileged and excluded groups in the country have been able to reap the benefits from these feedback loops and whether the social indicators for these groups have seen improvements or have deteriorated vis-à-vis the rest of the country's population.

In the state-wise analysis of human development scenarios in the IHDR 2011, Maharashtra is reported as having a higher HDI (0.572) than that of the country (0.467) (see Table 1.1).[1] Ranking Maharashtra seventh in terms of its HDI for 2007–08, it cautions the reader to interpret such a ranking with care given the presence of wide regional disparities in the state.

The IHDR 2011 also draws attention to three important facts in this context. *First*, Maharashtra is one of the four states where there has been an increase in the population of the poor between 1993–94 and 2004–05,

Human development is not only about health, education and income—it is also about people's active engagement in shaping development, equity and sustainability, intrinsic aspects of the freedom the people have to lead lives they have reason to value.

---

[1] The set of indicators used in the IHDR 2011 to construct the HDI for India and the states are: adjusted mean years of schooling and literacy rate of the population aged seven years and over (the education index), life expectancy at birth (the health index) and the mean per capita expenditure (at 1999–2000 prices) weighed by the Gini coefficient of inequality of consumption expenditure (the income index).

TABLE 1.1
Ranking of Indian States According to HDI Value

State	HDI Value	Rank (2007–08)
Kerala	0.790	1
Delhi	0.750	2
Himachal Pradesh	0.652	3
Goa	0.617	4
Punjab	0.605	5
North-Eastern States (Excluding Assam)	0.573	6
Maharashtra	0.572	7
Tamil Nadu	0.570	8
Haryana	0.552	9
Jammu and Kashmir	0.529	10
Gujarat	0.527	11
Karnataka	0.519	12
West Bengal	0.492	13
Uttarakhand	0.490	14
Andhra Pradesh	0.473	15
Assam	0.444	16
Rajasthan	0.434	17
Uttar Pradesh	0.380	18
Jharkhand	0.376	19
Madhya Pradesh	0.375	20
Bihar	0.367	21
Odisha	0.362	22
Chhattisgarh	0.358	23
India	**0.467**	

Source: Institute of Applied Manpower Research (2011).

Going beyond growth and poverty, the human development dimensions for the state are reported to be a mixed bag. On the one hand, health indicators such as the U5MR and the proportion of underweight children amongst the SC and ST are seen to be better than the India averages. On the other, one in two ST women is reported to have a BMI of less than 18.5 kilogram/square metre (kg/m^2), with the ST not doing too well on other health indicators too. At the aggregate level, the Report highlights that health-related indicators, such as BMI of women, U5MR and underweight children, point towards less-than-functional health services in the state, in spite of the state having the third highest NSDP per capita in the country. On the education front, with near-universal enrolments at the primary level and a high literacy rate, the Report shows the existence of stark disparities in these indicators when disaggregated by social groups, especially for the ST. In terms of public expenditure on health and education as a proportion of total expenditure, Maharashtra is reported to spend much less on social or human development sectors than the poorer northern Indian states.

The vital observation that the Report makes in the context of Maharashtra is that location matters. It is administratively difficult to service rural and remote areas and logically it becomes best to leave them out. "Seen logistically as well, setting up hospitals or schools for small scattered rural communities is arduous if not unfeasible" (Institute of Applied Manpower Research 2011). The Report suggests a possible solution to this problem, namely, relocation of the poor and unreachable to places such as block or district headquarters, where they can better avail of health and education facilities by offering them attractive income-earning opportunities. Given the more current and concise observations and analysis of the human development scenario in Maharashtra in the IHDR, the MHDR for 2012 was conceptualized and put into action with inclusive human development as its central ideology.

making it important to understand how on the one hand Maharashtra ranks high in terms of per capita income amongst the major states and on the other it also houses large proportions of the poor (10 per cent of the country's poor population in 2004–05). *Second*, the proportion of population below the poverty line is higher in the urban areas of the state, which also conflicts with the pattern seen in the country (where generally the proportion of population below the poverty line is higher in rural areas). Such a pattern, says the Report, could be a reflection of migration of the poor into urban areas in search of productive employment. *Third*, close to 50 per cent of the ST households in the state are below the poverty line.

The MHDR 2002

Maharashtra published its first HDR in 2002, which profiled the human development scenario in the state and set the context for discussions and debate on the subject. It highlighted the prevailing levels of socio-economic achievements and deprivation at the state and district levels along with the need for accurate policy directives on issues related to population, poverty, education, health, nutrition and gender. The Report also highlighted the problems of data availability for human development indicators. Here, we touch upon the main findings cited in the first MHDR on the various dimensions of human development, to benchmark the scenario prevailing in 2002. This will also facilitate a better understanding of whether the state has made any progress in promoting human development related issues which are studied and reported in detail in the various chapters of this report.

Maharashtra has been a state that has consistently done well in terms of economic growth. The state has the second largest per capita net (PCN) state domestic product (SDP) in the country, and the growth in the state has been urban-centric and non-agricultural, having visible consequences of pockets of urban affluence with shades of poverty and a continuing draw of migrants (Government of Maharashtra 2002). The primary sector has continued to be the major source of livelihood in terms of employment despite its falling share in output, while the secondary and tertiary sectors have shown uneven growth performances. The weakness of the state has been cited in the uneven distribution of the gains of economic growth coupled with inter-district disparities in growth performance. In 1998–99, Dhule was reported as being the poorest district with a per capita district domestic product (PCDDP) of ₹11,789 while Mumbai was the richest with a PCDDP ₹45,471, almost four times that of Dhule.

Being the second most populated state (98.6 million) in the country in 2001, Maharashtra accounted for 9.4 per cent of India's population. The density of population was reported to have shown an increase of more than two-and-a-half times from 129 persons per square kilometre in 1961 to 314 in 2001. There were also large variations reported in the population size of districts, ranging from the Mumbai suburban district, having a population of 8.6 million (in 2001) to Sindhudurg, with a population of 0.9 million. The sex ratio for the state was 922 in 2001. The child sex ratio (0–6 years) was seen to have declined quite sharply from 946 in 1991 to 917 in 2001 and was highlighted as a cause for concern. The net migration rate into the state was shown to have increased from 10 per cent in 1981–91 to 19 per cent during 1991–2001. Intra-state migration showed the three divisions of Konkan, Pune and Nashik as accounting for 9 out of every 10 migrants (from other districts of the state). Along with rapid urbanization the state was also reported to have the highest slum population (10.6 million) in 2001.

Although ranked high amongst the Indian states in terms of income, Maharashtra did not report a very high HDI, as high levels of per capita income did not seem to have translated into high human development outcomes. The Report stated that there were several anomalies and distortions, chief among them being high levels of poverty, wide inequalities in the distribution of assets and consumer expenditure, high levels of unemployment and regional disparities. The HDI for Maharashtra in the year 2000 was reported as 0.580. District-level HDIs highlighted the backwardness of the Marathwada and Vidarbha regions (with only Nagpur district from this region showing an HDI above that in the state). The Report also found a strong link between the district HDI rankings and the PCDDP. Achievement indices were also calculated for education and health indicators. It was reported that during 1991–2001, there were no major changes in the rankings of districts in literacy achievements (except in Sindhudurg and Akola) with initial conditions in terms of literacy giving certain districts an edge over the

The state has the second largest per capita net (PCN) state domestic product (SDP) in the country, and the growth in the state has been urban-centric and non-agricultural, having visible consequences of pockets of urban affluence with shades of poverty and a continuing draw of migrants.

others. The districts of Marathwada (with the exception of Aurangabad) lagged behind in education achievements as captured by the literacy rate. On the other hand, the districts of the Vidarbha region (with the exception of Nagpur) were reported to lag behind in health achievements as captured by the IMR. Thus, there were wide inter-regional and inter-district as well as rural–urban disparities (along with disparities between Mumbai and the rest of Maharashtra) found in education, health and nutrition achievements.

"Human development depends on expanding opportunities and increasing skills. The underlying assumption is that each stage of education leads to higher capacities because an individual learns more at every step" (Government of Maharashtra 2002). The MHDR 2002 highlighted the improvements in literacy rates in the state, from 35.1 per cent in 1961 to 77.3 per cent in 2001. Improvements in the literacy rate were marked in the decade 1991–2001, showing a progress of 12 percentage points. Female literacy rose to 68 per cent in 2001, although it was reported to be lower than the literacy rate for males in all the districts of the state. Inter-regional disparities in the literacy rate were also reported as reducing, demonstrated by a decline in the value of the coefficient of variation from 32.6 per cent in 1961 to 9.2 per cent in 2001.

It was also reported that Maharashtra showed impressive increase in the access to basic education, with the numbers of primary and secondary schools per capita population having increased substantially. There were hardly any habitations which did not have primary schools. Widespread state provisioning of primary schools was seen to exist along with high levels of private provisioning in the secondary schooling stage. There was also hardly any gender disadvantage faced by girls in primary school participation, although the disadvantage increased at higher levels of education. Enrolments for the SC and ST were also seen to rise, though their performance was seen to lag behind the rest of the state population. Despite high access through widespread provisioning of educational facilities, the state reported high dropout rates and poor success rates in school board exams. Thus, "while the quantitative expansion of schooling opportunities have [sic]been impressive, quality remains a question" (Government of Maharashtra 2002). State budgetary allocations for education were reported as 2.8 per cent of the SDP in 1995–96, with no major restructuring and reallocation of expenditure in favour of the educationally backward districts.

"A true reflection of an individual or a society is to be found in the nutritional and health status attained which can be measured by life expectancy at birth, the infant mortality rate and nutritional attainments" (Government of Maharashtra 2002). The MHDR reported that although Maharashtra had done fairly well in terms of raising life expectancy at birth and reducing the IMR, the nutritional status of households left a lot to be desired. In 2002, more than half the households in the state were found to be below the prescribed standard norm for nutrition, receiving less than 90 per cent of the required level of 2,700 calories per day per person. Nearly half the ever-married women suffered from anaemia, its prevalence being marginally higher in rural areas. Also, 76 per cent of children below the age of three years were suffering from anaemia, the levels being comparatively higher in rural areas. Close to 40 per cent of women reported a BMI of below 18.5 kg/m^2. The state also had a high proportion of undernourished children as observed on the basis of three nutritional status indices, namely, weight for age (50 per cent), height for age (40 per cent) and weight for height (21 per cent). Rural–urban disparities in the provisioning of health services were evident and were compounded by inter-regional disparities with the Vidarbha, Marathwada and northern Maharashtra regions showing a greater disadvantage. For preventive health care, public provisioning continued to play a major role and was responsible for improvements in health outcomes. Finally, reductions

> *It was also reported that Maharashtra showed impressive increase in the access to basic education, with the numbers of primary and secondary schools per capita population having increased substantially.*

in public investment and expenditure in the health sector had contributed to the slowing down in the attainment of health outcomes for the state.

The Report finally charted the way forward on a positive note by emphasizing that "it is the pattern of growth, not just growth in itself or by itself that is important for human development; it has to enable improvements in the productive capability of the people and their participation in value-added activities thereby increasing their purchasing power" (Government of Maharashtra 2002).

Human Development in Maharashtra: From Analysis to Action

One of the main outcomes of the MHDR 2002 was the establishment of the State Human Development Mission in Aurangabad in 2006. The objective of the Human Development Commissionerate, as it is called now, is to work towards improving the HDI of the state. Initially 12 backward districts, which had an HDI of less than 0.430 (as per the MHDR 2002), were selected. Human development committees were formed at village, block and district levels under the chairmanship of the district collector in these 12 districts. These committees selected 2,700 villages in 25 blocks spread over the districts for interventions in health, education and agriculture. Over time, the state government felt the need to identify backward districts and blocks on the basis of levels of human development indicators to facilitate the identification of geographical areas for interventions. This also prepared the ground for the second MHDR.

In this context, the present MHDR has with the following principal objectives:

1. To overview the human development scenario in the state with inclusion as the main ideology.
2. To study inclusive human development through the five-way lens of regions, sectors, gender, social groups and income groups.
3. To facilitate the identification of regions or pockets and sectors that need interventions for improving human development indicators and promoting inclusion.
4. To make suggestions to the state for equity-based policy formulations.

Inclusive Growth and Human Development

'Faster and more inclusive growth' is the main thrust of the Eleventh and Twelfth Five Year Plans. The Eleventh Plan document highlights at the very outset how economic growth had not been 'inclusive' from the mid-1990s and sets out with a vision for a more inclusive and broad-based development experience (see Box 1.1). Keeping with the underlying ideology of inclusion, the goal of the Eleventh and Twelfth Five Year Plans has been to reduce existing disparities between regions, communities, sectors (rural–urban areas) and gender by ensuring access to health and education infrastructure as well as services.

Along with achieving broad-based inclusive growth, the Eleventh Plan also draws attention to the development needs of certain groups that have remained marginalized, that is, children below the age of three years, those belonging to primitive tribal groups, adolescent girls, the elderly and the disabled. Many of these groups lack family support and also do not have an independent voice of their

---

Box 1.1 Inclusive Growth

A key element of the strategy for inclusive growth must be an all-out effort to provide the mass of our people the access to basic facilities such as health, education, clean drinking water etc. While in the short run these essential public services impact directly on welfare, in the long run they determine economic opportunities for the future.

It is important to recognize that access to these basic services is not necessarily assured simply by a rise in per capita income. Governments at different levels have to ensure the provision of these services and this must be an essential part of our strategy for inclusive growth. At the same time it is important to recognize that better health and education are the necessary pre-conditions for sustained long-term growth.

Source: Planning Commission (2006: 2).

own to demand what is rightfully theirs, and the Eleventh Plan stresses the need to address the issues of these marginalized sections. The thrust areas for development efforts in the Eleventh Plan included the provisioning of essential public services to the poor in the areas of education and health, where large gaps exist in minimum access to some of the most basic services such as maternal care (pre- and postnatal), child care and immunizations, access to clean drinking water and sanitation facilities. The Eleventh Plan reiterates that

> a strategy of inclusiveness also calls for new emphasis on education, health and other basic public health facilities. Inadequate access to these essential services directly limits the welfare of large sections of our population, and also denies them the opportunity to share fully in the benefits of growth.
> (Planning Commission 2006: 56)

The Eleventh Plan clearly highlighted the existence of a divide on various development fronts and the imperative need to address and overcome the same through targeted policy interventions. These included *first*, the divide between the rich and the poor, between the haves and have-nots in terms of access to basic services such as education, health, drinking water, sanitation, etc.; *second*, between rural and urban areas; *third*, amongst social groups which include the SC, ST and OBC and the minorities who fall short of the rest of the population in development in terms of access and outcomes; *fourth*, gender differentials in access and attainments and *finally*, regional backwardness reflected in interstate and intra-state (inter-district) disparities such that the benefits of growth and development are found to be inequitable. The Eleventh Plan laid emphasis on the need to "reduce poverty and focus on bridging the various divides that continue to fragment our society" (Planning Commission 2006: 1). Thus the basic ideology of inclusive growth that underlies the Eleventh Plan is also the very essence of the human development philosophy, namely, enhancing capabilities of every individual across social groups, gender, spatial and regional dimensions.

The present MHDR, in keeping with the 'inclusive growth' ideology of the Eleventh and Twelfth Five Year Plans, attempts to report the progress made by the state in terms of economic growth and how it has (or has not) translated into improvements in social infrastructure and human development outcomes. Combined with this is the endeavour to investigate and understand better whether disparities and inequities across social groups, gender, regions, income groups and rural–urban areas have also been addressed by state policy interventions and how effective the outreach of policies aimed at inclusiveness has been.

The MHDR 2012: Content Highlights

Given the above backdrop and the contextual setting from the Eleventh and Twelfth Five Year Plans, the present HDR for Maharashtra endeavours to keep with the main underlying ideology of 'inclusive growth' and reports whether or not the growth processes and policy interventions in the social sectors have been effective in being inclusive. While keeping the MHDR 2002 as its benchmark, an attempt is made to study and analyse the progress made by the state, milestones reached and backlogs that need to be addressed in human development indicators (inputs in terms of infrastructure and manpower as well as outcomes). With the focus trained on whether growth and advancements in human development have led to enhancements in capabilities and improvements in entitlements, five cross-cutting themes of spatial (rural–urban), regional, gender, income and social groups are kept central to the analysis (wherever data is available). The Report is also an attempt to bring to the fore the relevance of human development and the progress made in the social sectors by the state to facilitate public debate, research, data collection as well as the formulation of evidence-based informed policy interventions.

With the focus trained on whether growth and advancements in human development have led to enhancements in capabilities and improvements in entitlements, five cross-cutting themes of spatial (rural–urban), regional, gender, income and social groups are kept central to the analysis.

Going beyond the income dimension of growth and development and in keeping with the contemporary policy emphasis on inclusive growth, Chapter 2 addresses social and human development dimensions which enhance an individual's capabilities and help him/her gain control over his/her life. The three dimensions of the HDI, namely, income, education and health, are first studied individually and then the HDI of the state as well as districts for 2012 are presented.

Taking a cue from the MHDR 2002, the present Report studies whether the state has made any progress in addressing issues concerning economic growth and income distribution in their sectoral and spatial dimensions since 1999–2000. How the incidence of poverty has changed, what the distributional consequences in terms of the extent of inequality across social groups have been and whether there have been any reductions in inter-district disparities in the same are issues that are delved into in detail in Chapter 3. For a better understanding of the distributional consequences of the growth process, data from the NSS is used to arrive at estimates of private household consumer expenditure and employment. In this chapter an attempt has been made to better understand and explain the concept of 'inclusion' in terms of the consumption distribution (for which data was readily available). The aim is to study how inclusive the growth process has been, that is, whether the growth process has been beneficial to those belonging to the bottom rungs of the income distribution. To be sustainable, an inclusive growth process needs to facilitate involvement in participation in the economic activity (employment), receiving rewards for it (income) and enjoying it (consumer expenditure). In other words, conceptually, a sustainable inclusive broad-based growth process could be one which involves an improvement touching upon the three alternative perspectives of the macroeconomy, namely, production, income generation and income distribution (Suryanarayana 2008). To facilitate such an analysis a 'coefficient of inclusion' has been calculated for the population in general, as well as for various social groups in particular, using an order-based perspective of the consumption distribution profile, contributing to a new dimension for studying inclusion. This is presented in Chapter 3.

Access to good and affordable education, health care and nutrition, housing, clean drinking water and sanitation are some of the basic human development imperatives that are closely interlinked with the well-being of individuals and their capabilities. Housing, water and sanitation are critical social infrastructures that support human development and the current Report takes an in-depth look at whether the state has made any progress in the provisioning of these support facilities, their levels of utilization and how inclusive their coverage is across the five cross-cutting themes mentioned earlier in this section. These issues are addressed in Chapters 4, 5 and 6.

Given the importance of social inclusion in human development and the need to pay specific attention to the hurdles faced by backward social groups (SC, ST and OBC) in accessing and utilizing basic social services, it was thought necessary to take a closer look at the socioeconomic profiles of these groups and present a case study on the Katkari tribe that throws light on what prevents these groups from being included into the mainstream development processes. A section each in Chapters 4 and 5 shows how important it is for such excluded groups to be brought into the domain of human development. Finally, in Chapter 7, the main findings pertaining to inclusive human development, data gaps and recommendations for data collection, specific development goals as well as directives for policy formulation for the state are presented.

During the course of preparation of the MHDR 2012, a pressing need was felt to bring to the fore people's own perceptions about human development, the issues that they would like to highlight and their understanding of development and the progress/

> *Access to good and affordable education, health care and nutrition, housing, clean drinking water and sanitation are some of the basic human development imperatives that are closely interlinked with the well-being of individuals and their capabilities.*

deprivation therein. Taking cognizance of the importance of local wisdom and experience and to give a voice to the people, who are the real agents for change and on whom human development processes hinge, block-level consultations of health and education functionaries (ASHAs, *anganwadi* workers [AWWs] and supervisors, beneficiaries, teachers and headmasters of primary schools), people's representatives, non-governmental organizations (NGOs) and block-level government officers were organized in 13 blocks of the state by YASHADA. These were blocks with poor child mortality rates (CMRs), low institutional deliveries, relatively high child malnutrition and low literacy rates. The consultations were carried out in December 2011. The highlights and findings from these consultations could work as very useful guidelines for policy-makers when tackling human development issues in these areas/blocks and become guideline tools for other areas/blocks where similar scenarios prevail. In the various chapters of the MHDR 2012, the wisdom gained from these block-level consultations has been presented and cited as Human Development: Speaking to the People.

2

Human Development: Progress Made, Milestones to Be Reached

Human Development in Maharashtra: A District Profile

In this chapter we study how Maharashtra has fared in terms of HDI as well as its individual dimensions at the state level and disaggregated by districts. The estimation of district-level HDIs for the current study and analysis bristled with problems due to non-availability of data on two indicators for more recent years. For instance, as a measure of income, only estimates of income generated at the district level and not income net of transfers across district or state borders, were available.[1] To facilitate the comparison of HDI at two points of time (2001 and 2011) the PCDDP at constant prices (1999–2000) of 2001 and 2008–09 are taken. Similarly, estimates of life expectancy at the district level for the relevant years were not available and thus estimates of the IMR were utilized to estimate its complement, namely, infant survival rate (ISR). As far as the education component is concerned, data for the total literacy rate was available, while Gross Enrolment Ratios (GERs) for primary, upper primary and secondary levels of schooling were calculated (see Table 2.1). By using data available for the period from 2001 to 2011, the HDIs for the state as well as the districts were computed for two points of time, namely, 2001 and 2011, and have been presented here.[2]

Also, it is worthwhile to note that the state has made substantial progress in IMR and income status after 2008. Hence the data available about rural IMR and the Per Capita Net District Domestic Product (PCNDDP) at current prices is analysed to obtain the proper perspective of growth in these sectors and given after the discussion on HDI.

---

[1] In the IHDR 2011, the indicator used for income is the per capita consumption expenditure, while the indicator used in the MHDR 2012 is NDDP at constant prices. The rationale for doing so is to ensure similarity with the international methodology of constructing HDIs, which would also facilitate comparisons between Maharashtra's HDIs with those of other states and countries at the international level.

[2] The MHDR 2002 used a different set of indicators and methodology to calculate the HDI for the state and the districts. Hence the state and district-level HDIs for 2011 calculated and presented in the MHDR 2012 are not comparable with those presented in the MHDR 2002.

TABLE 2.1
District-Wise Human Development Indicators: 2001 and 2011

District	Total Literacy Rate		GER		IMR		PCDDP Constant (1999–2000) Prices (₹)	
	(1)	(2)	(3)	(4)	(5)	(6)	(7)	(8)
	2001	2011	2001	2011–12	2001	2007–08[3]	2000–01	2008–09
Ahmednagar	75.3	80.2	71.8	87.9	44	41	16,311	27,392
Akola	81.4	87.6	67.0	85.6	44	28	15,822	24,055
Amravati	82.5	88.2	69.7	86.0	61	59	16,211	21,804
Aurangabad	72.9	80.4	80.1	82.2	51	44	19,539	30,690
Beed	68.0	73.5	82.2	90.4	43	33	14,398	21,013
Bhandara	78.5	85.1	71.0	89.3	68	60	16,110	25,735
Buldhana	75.8	82.1	65.4	87.6	49	34	10,729	19,487
Chandrapur	73.2	81.4	73.6	88.9	67	74	19,408	28,730
Dhule	71.7	74.6	64.2	83.7	56	44	13,166	21,442
Gadchiroli	60.1	70.6	69.1	80.7	75	63	11,745	14,913
Gondia	78.5	85.4	73.8	87.2	73	67	15,211	23,091
Hingoli	66.3	76.0	76.4	78.7	54	50	11,203	18,286
Jalgaon	75.4	79.7	69.7	88.2	50	48	16,580	28,939
Jalna	64.4	73.6	71.9	83.7	56	48	11,458	20,565
Kolhapur	76.9	82.9	75.4	88.4	38	13	23,052	36,178
Latur	71.5	79.0	89.4	91.1	50	53	11,811	17,674
Mumbai	77.0	90.3	74.4	85.5	40	18	36,883	58,818
Nagpur	84.0	89.5	76.5	92.6	54	40	23,323	37,995
Nanded	67.8	76.9	73.0	80.3	57	30	11,022	18,155
Nandurbar	55.8	63.0	55.8	67.7	61	75	11,248	19,156
Nashik	74.4	81.0	66.6	82.2	51	46	21,927	35,545
Osmanabad	69.0	76.3	75.7	81.9	47	50	13,011	17,847
Parbhani	66.1	75.2	74.8	86.3	50	51	12,934	23,146
Pune	80.5	87.2	71.3	88.2	32	28	31,624	50,158
Raigarh	77.0	83.9	72.7	88.9	42	35	32,651	34,377
Ratnagiri	75.1	82.4	72.4	89.0	37	25	16,388	27,685
Sangli	76.6	82.6	76.2	87.9	32	33	21,147	30,713
Satara	78.2	84.2	73.5	85.7	32	27	19,610	29,916
Sindhudurg	80.3	86.5	74.6	87.5	35	35	19,794	31,563
Solapur	71.3	77.7	74.1	89.5	43	23	16,891	28,828
Thane	80.7	86.2	73.7	78.5	39	34	31,061	50,408
Wardha	80.1	87.2	67.3	87.9	51	62	16,955	26,130
Washim	73.4	81.7	66.3	88.0	52	46	10,152	14,885
Yavatmal	73.6	80.7	70.3	84.9	61	47	13,562	24,118
Maharashtra	**76.9**	**82.9**	**72.8**	**85.4**	**47**	**44**	**21,892**	**35,033**

[3] Various sources of IMRs for 2011 were explored. IMR was available in the survey of causes of death (SCD) (State Bureau of Health Intelligence and Vital Statistics 2009, 2010), which could not be used for HDI computation as SCD provides only rural IMR figures. The estimations from

Sources:
Column (1): Directorate of Census Operations Maharashtra (2001).
Column (2): Directorate of Census Operations Maharashtra (2011).
Column (3): Calculated from the enrolment data (primary and secondary) in School Education Department (2002) and age population from Directorate of Census Operations Maharashtra (2001).
Column (4): Calculated from the enrolment data (primary, upper primary and secondary) in National University of Educational Planning and Administration (NUEPA) (2011–12) and age population from Directorate of Census Operations Maharashtra (2011).
Column (5): Directorate of Census Operations Maharashtra (2001).
Column (6): Estimated by the International Institute for Population Sciences (IIPS) using data from DLHS-3 upon the author's request.
Columns (7) and (8): Data provided by DES, Government of Maharashtra, upon author's request.
Note: The estimates for IMRs for Census 2001 and DLHS-3 are based on data about children ever born(CEB) and children surviving out of those ever born (CS)using the same methodology (MORTPACK software), although both are based on different sample surveys.

District HDIs

District-wise HDIs were calculated using the dimensions discussed in the previous section[4] (see Table 2.2).

The main findings that emerge from an analysis of the district HDI areas are as follows (see Tables 2.1, 2A.1 and 2A.2):

First, human development in Maharashtra has improved over time. Between 2001 and 2011, the aggregate HDIs show an improvement across districts (see Figures 2.1 and 2.2).

Second, consistent with the profiles presented above, human development is also positively skewed in its distribution across districts in

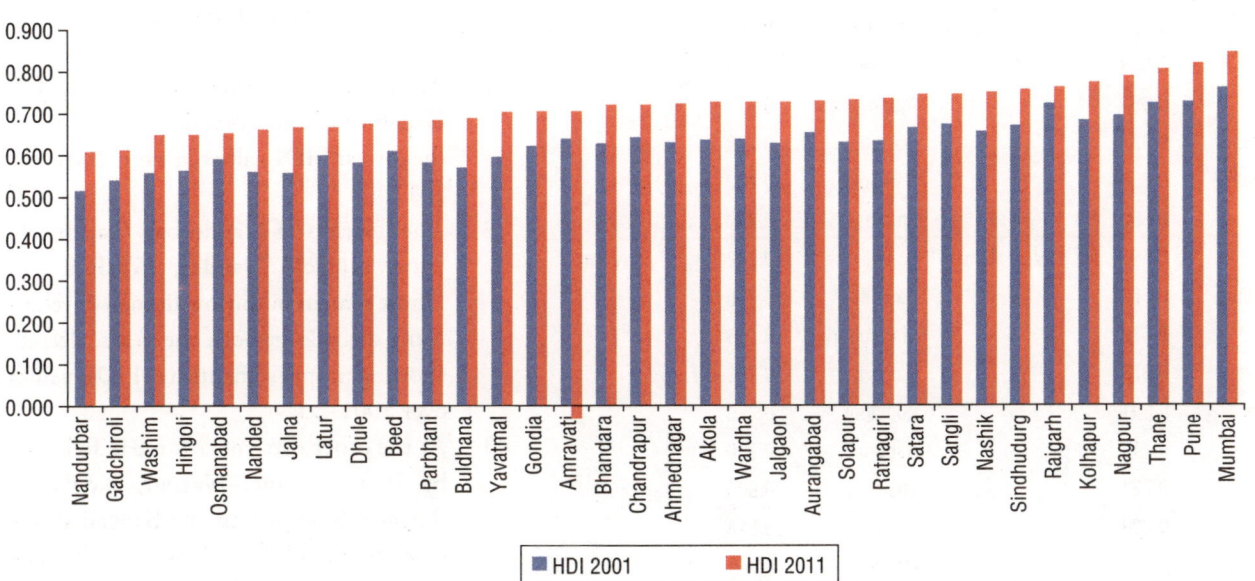

FIGURE 2.1 HDI across Districts: 2001 and 2011

Source: Author's calculations based on data in Table 2.2.

DLHS-3 (IIPS 2010) were the only possible source obtaining estimates of the IMR. To facilitate district-wise comparisons of the HDI for 2001 and 2011, the IMR for 2001 was taken from Census 2001 (Directorate of Census Operations Maharashtra 2001), while in Chapter 5, the IMRs from 2001 to 2011 are sourced from the SRS bulletins, as they provide only state-level data.

[4] Refer also to the technical note in Annexure 2.1.

TABLE 2.2
Relative Human Development Status of Districts: 2001 and 2011[5]

District	HDI 2001	Relative Category	District	HDI 2011	Relative Category
Nandurbar	0.513	Low	Nandurbar	0.604	Low
Gadchiroli	0.538		Gadchiroli	0.608	
Jalna	0.554		Washim	0.646	
Washim	0.554		Hingoli	0.648	
Nanded	0.558		Osmanabad	0.649	
Hingoli	0.561		Nanded	0.657	
Buldana	0.567		Jalna	0.663	
Parbhani	0.578		Latur	0.663	
Dhule	0.579		Dhule	0.671	
Osmanabad	0.588	Medium	Beed	0.678	Medium
Yavatmal	0.592		Parbhani	0.683	
Latur	0.595		Buldana	0.684	
Beed	0.606		Yavatmal	0.700	
Gondiya	0.617		Gondiya	0.701	
Bhandara	0.623		Amravati	0.701	
Jalgaon	0.624		Bhandara	0.718	
Solapur	0.624		Chandrapur	0.718	
Ahmednagar	0.626	High	Ahmednagar	0.720	High
Ratnagiri	0.629		Akola	0.722	
Akola	0.631		Wardha	0.723	
Amravati	0.633		Jalgaon	0.723	
Wardha	0.634		Aurangabad	0.727	
Chandrapur	0.637		Solapur	0.728	
Aurangabad	0.650		Ratnagiri	0.732	
Nashik	0.652		Satara	0.742	
Satara	0.661	Very High	Sangli	0.742	Very High
Sindhudurg	0.667		Nashik	0.746	
Sangli	0.670		Sindhudurg	0.753	
Kolhapur	0.678		Raigarh	0.759	
Nagpur	0.691		Kolhapur	0.770	
Raigarh	0.717		Nagpur	0.786	
Thane	0.721		Thane	0.800	
Pune	0.722		Pune	0.814	
Mumbai	0.756		Mumbai	0.841	
Maharashtra	0.666		Maharashtra	0.752	

Source: Author's calculations based on data in Table 2.1.

both the years of 2001 and 2011. This implies that there are few districts with higher HDI values. The positive skewness is decreased marginally in 2011 (see Figure 2.2).[6]

Third, the range between the extreme HDI values has not changed much. Thus the disparity in HDI among the progressive and backward districts persists.

Fourth, progress in general seems to have been greater at the lower end than at the higher end of districts when ranked by the HDI (see Figure 2.3). Thus the districts of Nandurbar, Gadchiroli, Jalna, Hingoli and Washim show greater improvement in the HDI values than progressive districts such as Pune, Mumbai, Thane and Kolhapur.

Fifth, there is hardly any substantial change in the relative human development status of districts; rather, there are only some marginal changes in ranks over the two time periods considered, which is evident from the following (see Table 2.2 and Table 2A.3):

1. Arranged in terms of the HDI, Gadchiroli and Nandurbar maintain the lowest HDI values in both 2001 and 2011.
2. The districts of Nandurbar, Gadchiroli, Jalna, Hingoli, Nanded, Washim and Dhule remain in the low human development quartile in both the years, despite showing improvements in HDI values over 2001–11.
3. At the other extreme, Mumbai, followed by Pune, Thane, Nagpur, Kolhapur, Raigarh, Sindhudurg and Sangali showcase very high HDI values for both years, staying in the very high human development quartile.

---

[5] The four development-level quartiles have been calculated and presented using standard United Nations (UN) HDR terminologies and formats.
[6] A box plot is a graphic display of distribution in terms of five summary measures: the median, the first (lower) and third (upper) quartiles, and the minimum and maximum sample values. The box represents the central 50 per cent of the data, with its lower hinge corresponding to the first quartile below which 25 per cent of the cases lie and the upper hinge representing the third quartile

Sixth, the movements across HDI quartiles also reflect that despite all districts showing improvements, there are some districts that have performed relatively better, and others that have not managed to perform as well and may have moved down in relative quartile positioning, although they have shown a positive change (see Figure 2.4). Districts that have improved their relative HDI categorization include:

1. Nashik from the high to the very high HDI quartile.
2. Solapur and Jalgaon from the medium to the high human development quartile.
3. Buldhana and Parbhani from the low to the medium human development quartile.

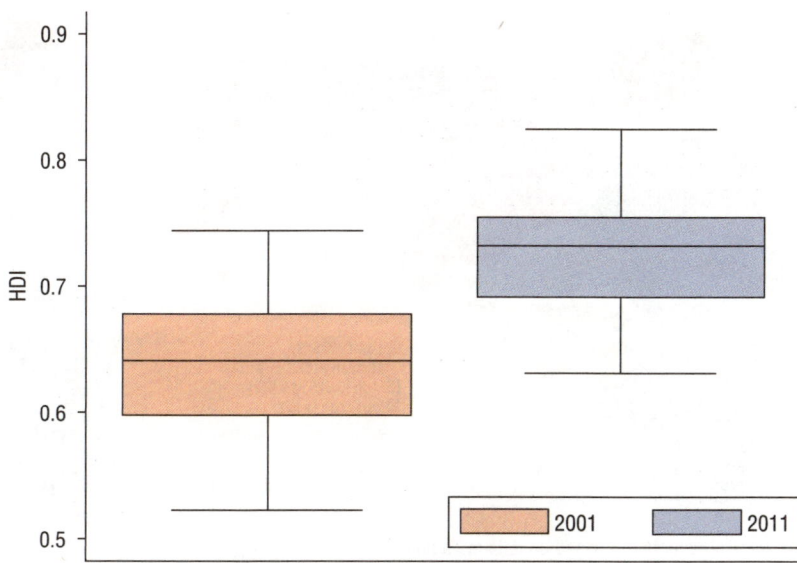

FIGURE 2.2 HDI: 2001 and 2011

Source: Author's calculations based on data in Table 2.2.

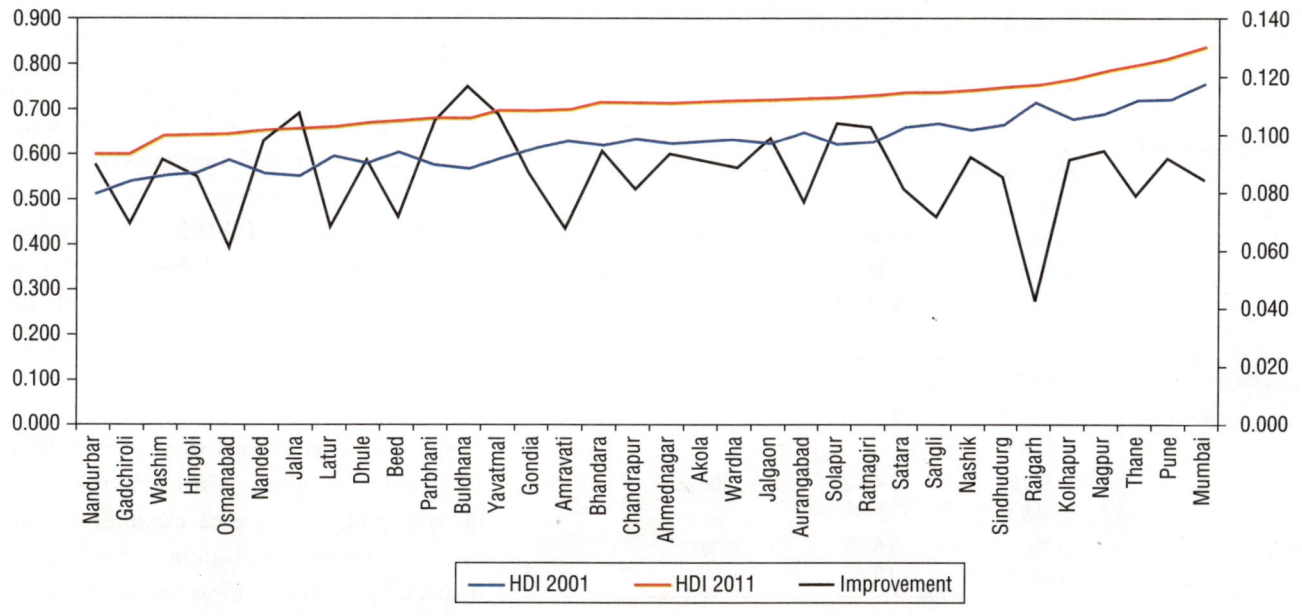

FIGURE 2.3 Improvements in HDI: 2001–11

Source: Author's calculations based on data in Table 2.2.

below which 75 per cent of the cases lie. The line subdividing the box represents the median above which 50 per cent of the cases lie. The difference between the two quartiles is called the inter-quartile range. The larger the box greater the spread of the data. The horizontal lines above and below the box represent the largest and smallest values in the distribution when there are no outliers. Outliers are those values which are less (or more) than the first or third quartile by one-and-a-half times the inter-quartile range. When there are outliers the horizontal lines are the maximum (or minimum) values excluding outliers. The vertical lines drawn from the lower and upper end of the boxes to the largest and smallest value are called whiskers. Such box plots are used to examine location, dispersion, skewness and outliers in distributions. For instance, the box is centrally located between the whiskers when the distribution is normal. In case of achievement indicators if the upper whisker is much longer than the lower whisker it indicates positive skewness and vice versa.

FIGURE 2.4 HDI: Relative Categories of Districts: 2001 and 2011

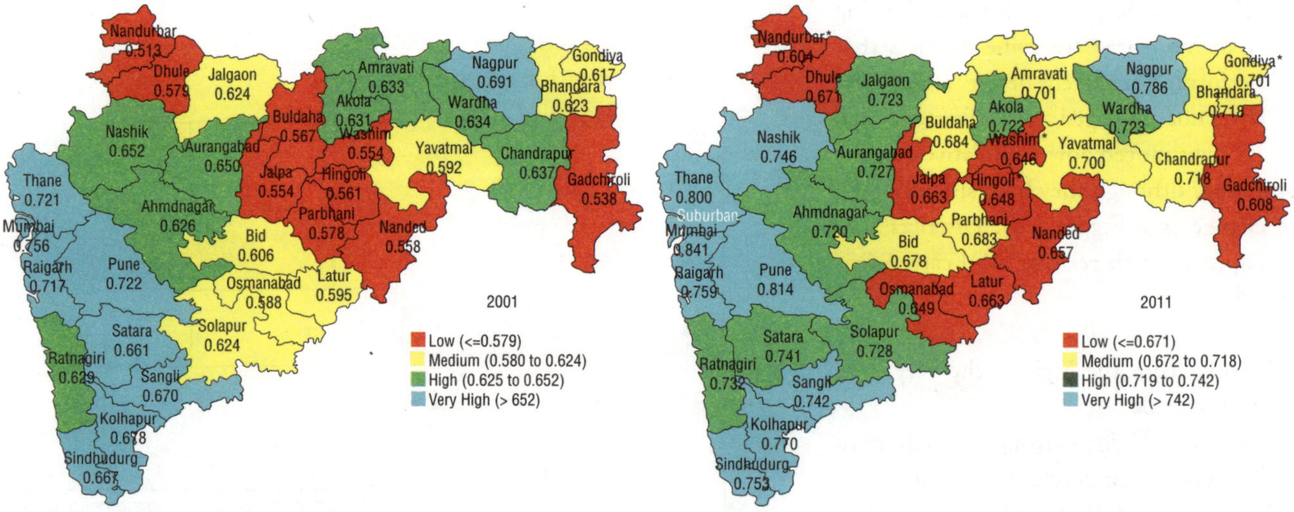

Source: Representation based on data in Table 2.2.

**TABLE 2.3
Rank Correlation between HDI and Its Component Scores: 2001 and 2011**

Index	Literacy	Infant Survival Rate	Income	HDI
		2001		
Literacy	1.0000			
Infant Survival Rate	0.4301 (0.0111)	1.0000		
Income	0.6632 (0.0000)	0.5098 (0.0021)	1.0000	
HDI	0.8181 (0.0000)	0.5719 (0.0004)	0.9708 (0.0000)	1.0000
		2011		
Literacy	1.0000			
Infant Survival Rate	0.3809 (0.0263)	1.0000		
Income	0.5570 (0.0006)	0.4943 (0.0030)	1.0000	
HDI	0.7537 (0.0000)	0.5785 (0.0003)	0.9614 (0.0000)	1.0000

Source: Author's calculations.
Note: Figures in parentheses are p-values.

Districts that have moved down in relative HDI categorization include:

1. Osmanabad and Latur from the medium human development category of districts to the low human development category.
2. Chandrapur and Amravati from the high to the medium HDI category.
3. Satara from the very high human development category to that of high.

Seventh, the MHDR 2002 had reported that generally prosperous districts were also better off in terms of human development. It found positive associations in district ranks in terms of per capita income and HDI. This profile has not changed in 2011. The positive and significant rank correlation between district per capita income scores and HDIs prevails in 2011 as well (see Table 2.3). Positive correlations are also found between district-wise rankings of education and HDI. But this association is not as strong as the one between income and HDI.

Eighth, pair-wise comparisons for HDIs in 2011 show that all the districts in the richest quartile group by income classification also belong to the very high human development quartile by HDI classification. All the poorest districts of Maharashtra also belong to the low human development quartile, barring Dhule, which is in the medium quartile group of income and low human development quartile. Almost a similar profile prevailed in 2001.

Ninth, that development has neither been uniform by dimension, nor across districts. This is borne out by the following (see Table 2A.3):

1. Pune, Mumbai, Nagpur and Sindhudurg are the only districts which have very high human development in terms of

all its three dimensions as well as at the aggregate level in 2001 and 2011.

2. Gadchiroli, Nandurbar, Hingoli, Jalna and Nanded belong to the low HDI quartile for all the three human development dimensions in 2001 and 2011.

3. Although Parbhani belonged to the low HDI quartile in 2001, its health indicator was in the high human development category. By 2011, it had lost its edge in the health indicators, moving to the low human development in terms of health but improved in terms of HDI moving from low to medium. Dhule, a district with low human development in 2001 and 2011, exhibits exactly opposite trend, moving from low quartile group to high quartile group on health indicator from 2001 to 2011.

Lastly, despite the general belief about the existence of a positive association between the three human development dimensions, disaggregated evidence from Maharashtra throws up some surprises:

1. In 2001 and 2011, Gondiya belonged to the medium human development quartile but in terms of education it is in the very high human development quartile and for health it is in the low quartile for both the years.

2. Nanded belonged to the low human development quartiles at aggregate level and for the health as well as education in 2001, but moved up to very high category in 2011 in terms of health but remained in low category in terms of HDI and education.

3. Bhandara belonged to medium human development quartile for both the years. However, it was in the low quartile of health in both the years. It moved up from high to very high in education status from 2001 and 2011.

The Components of HDI

The present section describes the improvements in individual components of HDI. The recent available data for all the four components (literacy rate, GER, IMR and income) is used for analysing the performance of the districts on these components.[7]

Literacy Rate

District-wise performance in the literacy rate (see Table 2.1) is uneven across districts in Maharashtra as shown in their box plot profiles in Figure 2.5.

The salient features are as follows:

1. The distribution of the literacy indicator across districts is negatively skewed as reflected in (*a*) the lengths of the whiskers from the quartiles (the lower whisker is longer than the upper whisker), (*b*) the distance between the median and the lower quartile is higher than that between the median and the upper quartile and (*c*) the distance between

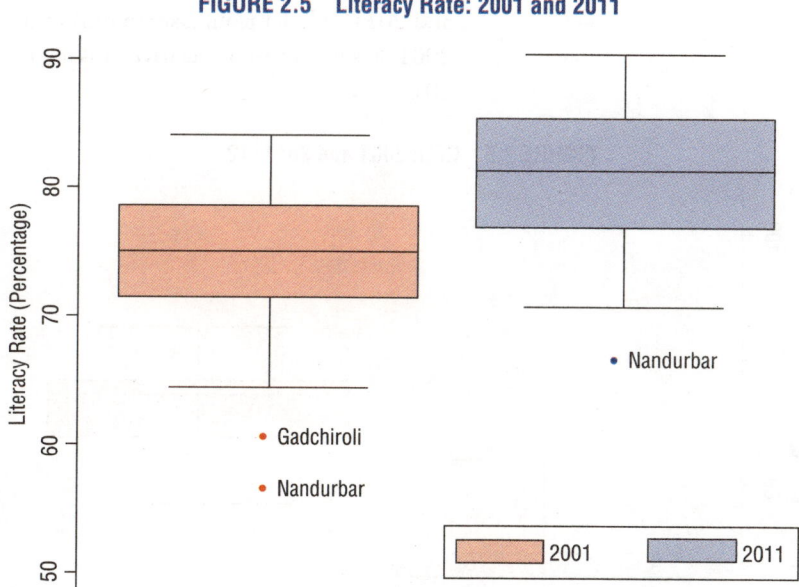

FIGURE 2.5 Literacy Rate: 2001 and 2011

Source: Author's findings based on data in Table 2.1.

---

[7] Same data sets for literacy and GER are used in this section and the previous section on district HDI profile while different data sets for IMR and income are used in this section and the previous section on district HDI profile.

the median and the minimum value is greater than the corresponding distance between the median and the maximum value. This profile holds good for both 2001 and 2011. This means that the districts that performed less are spread over a longer interval due to the slow pace of progress made by the poor performers such as Nandurbar and Gadchiroli in 2001.

2. The profile of total literacy rate for 2011 has registered a general upward shift for all the districts; as a result, the range between the maximum and minimum district literacy rates has shown a decline from 28 to 27 percentage points. But the inter-quartile range has increased from 7 to 8 percentage points; in addition, the negative skewness among them has also increased, implying an uneven progress among the average performing districts.

3. Nandurbar, which was the outlier and had the lowest literacy rate in 2011, has not kept pace with the mainstream; although it has shown an improvement in the literacy rate. But it remains an outlier at the lower end (in both 2001 and 2011). Gadchiroli, also an outlier in 2001, has moved up in relative ranking in 2011.

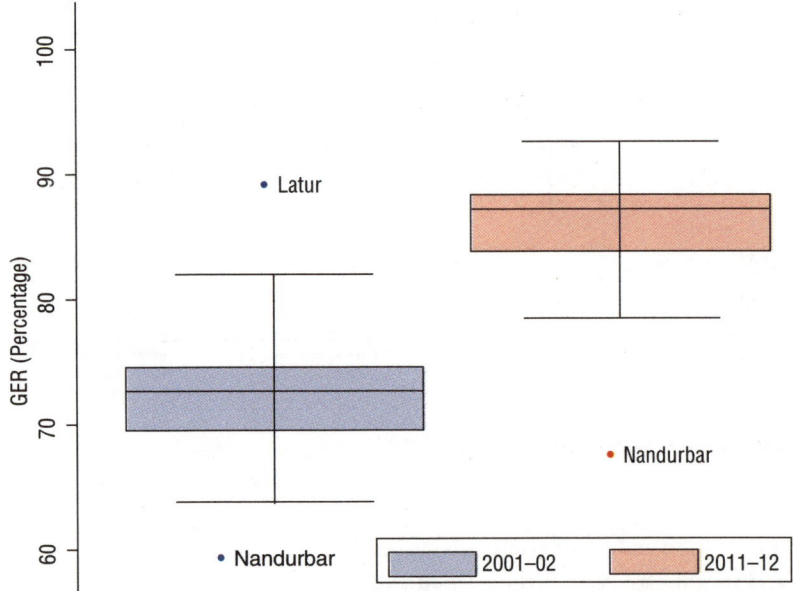

FIGURE 2.6   GER: 2001 and 2011–12

Source: Author's findings based on data in Table 2.1.

GER

Evidence on the GER (see Table 2.1) also shows mixed results (see Figure 2.6).

1. GER of all the districts has improved from 2001 to 2011. Nandurbar (at the lower end) and Latur (at the upper end) were the outliers in 2001 for this indicator, while Nandurbar has remained as outlier in 2011. Its distribution was positively skewed during 2001 while in 2011 it is negatively skewed, indicating that the districts with GER values lower than the average (median) are relatively few as compared to the districts having GER values higher than the median, which is a good sign.

2. The profile of GER 2011 has registered a general upward shift for all the districts; as a result, the range between the maximum and minimum value of GER has shown a decline from 35 to 25 percentage points. The inter-quartile range has decreased as well from 19 to 5 percentage points.

IMR

While computing HDI of 2011 we have taken IMR of 2007–08, which was estimated by IIPS from DLHS-3, due to lack of recent IMR data for the district as a whole. However, the State Bureau of Health Intelligence and Vital Statistics, which publishes vital statistics on health based on the results of Survey of Causes of Death Scheme, has estimated IMR only for the rural part of Maharahstra. Based on that data it is noticed that the state has made substantial progress in reduction of rural IMR after 2007–08. As such, it is imperative to analyse the IMR after 2007–08 so as to obtain the proper perspective of the change in IMR. Hence, even though the classical data for the IMR of the district as a whole is not available after 2007–08, the data obtained from State Bureau of Health Intelligence and Vital Statistics for rural IMR for the districts is used to analyse the progress. The reliable IMR data available with State Bureau of Health Intelligence and Vital Statistics is from 2003 to 2010, which is used for the present analysis. The progress of rural IMR is provided in Table 2.4 below.

TABLE 2.4
IMR (Rural Maharashtra), 2003–10

District	IMR (Rural) 2003	IMR (Rural) 2010
Ahmednagar	37	24
Akola	40	30
Amravati	46	28
Aurangabad	44	32
Beed	46	33
Bhandara	52	30
Buldana	41	33
Chandrapur	56	30
Dhule	41	31
Gadchiroli	64	36
Gondiya	52	34
Hingoli	55	16
Jalgaon	39	28
Jalna	50	23
Kolhapur	37	22
Latur	41	32
Nagpur	41	34
Nanded	42	31
Nandurbar	61	30
Nashik	46	26
Osmanabad	44	32
Parbhani	55	34
Pune	39	19
Raigarh	34	14
Ratnagiri	28	32
Sangli	38	20
Satara	38	26
Sindhudurg	41*	30
Solapur	35	23
Thane	47	25
Wardha	41	39
Washim	40	38
Yavatmal	40	21
Maharashtra	43	28

Source: State Bureau of Health Intelligence and Vital Statistics, 2003 and 2010.
Note: *The figure is of 2001 as figure of 2003 for Sindhudurg is not available.

The following picture emerges as result of the analysis of the IMR data:

1. The rural IMR is seen to have declined over the period from 2003 to 2010 (State Bureau of Health Intelligence and Vital Statistics 2012) which is a good sign. Its distribution in 2003 and 2010 was positively skewed across the districts (see Figure 2.7) indicating that the number of districts with IMR less than the median are more.
2. In 2003, Gadchiroli and Nandurbar were outliers at the negative end implying their IMR was worse than other districts. However, in 2010 there are no outliers indicating that Gadchiroli and Nandurbar have progressed reasonably well and the disparity in IMR among the districts has decreased.

Income

It should be noted here that while computing HDI of 2011 we have taken the PCNDDP at constant prices (1999–2000) for the year 2008-09. The reason was the required consistency of the base year for computing HDI of 2001 and 2011. Since the data about state and district NDDP (for the current prices) is available 2001 onwards till 2011–12, it will

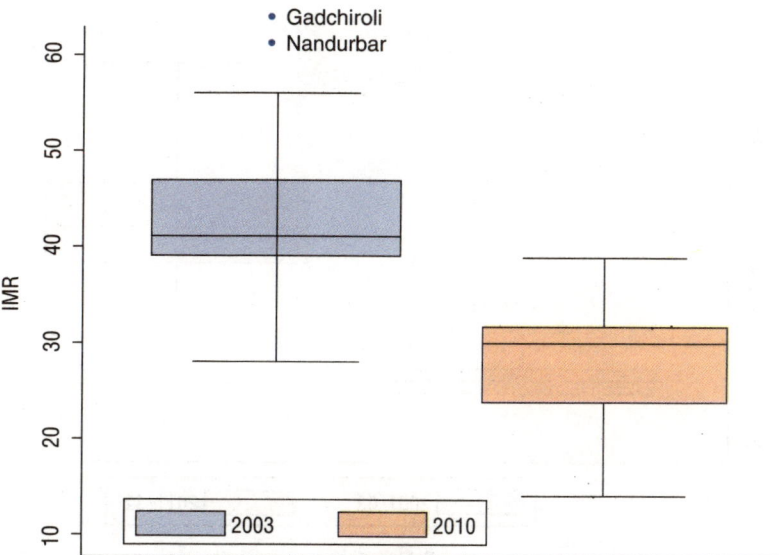

FIGURE 2.7 IMR: 2003 and 2010

Source: Author's findings based on data in Table 2.4.

Box 2.1   Maharashtra: Significant Improvement in IMR (as per SRS)

As far as IMR of the state is considered it is important to note that it has declined by 22 points since 2001 from 47 to 25 in 2011 (Registar General and Census Commissioner of India 2012). In 2011, the IMR of the state was less than the country and other bigger states (except Kerala and Tamil Nadu) (see Figure 2.8).

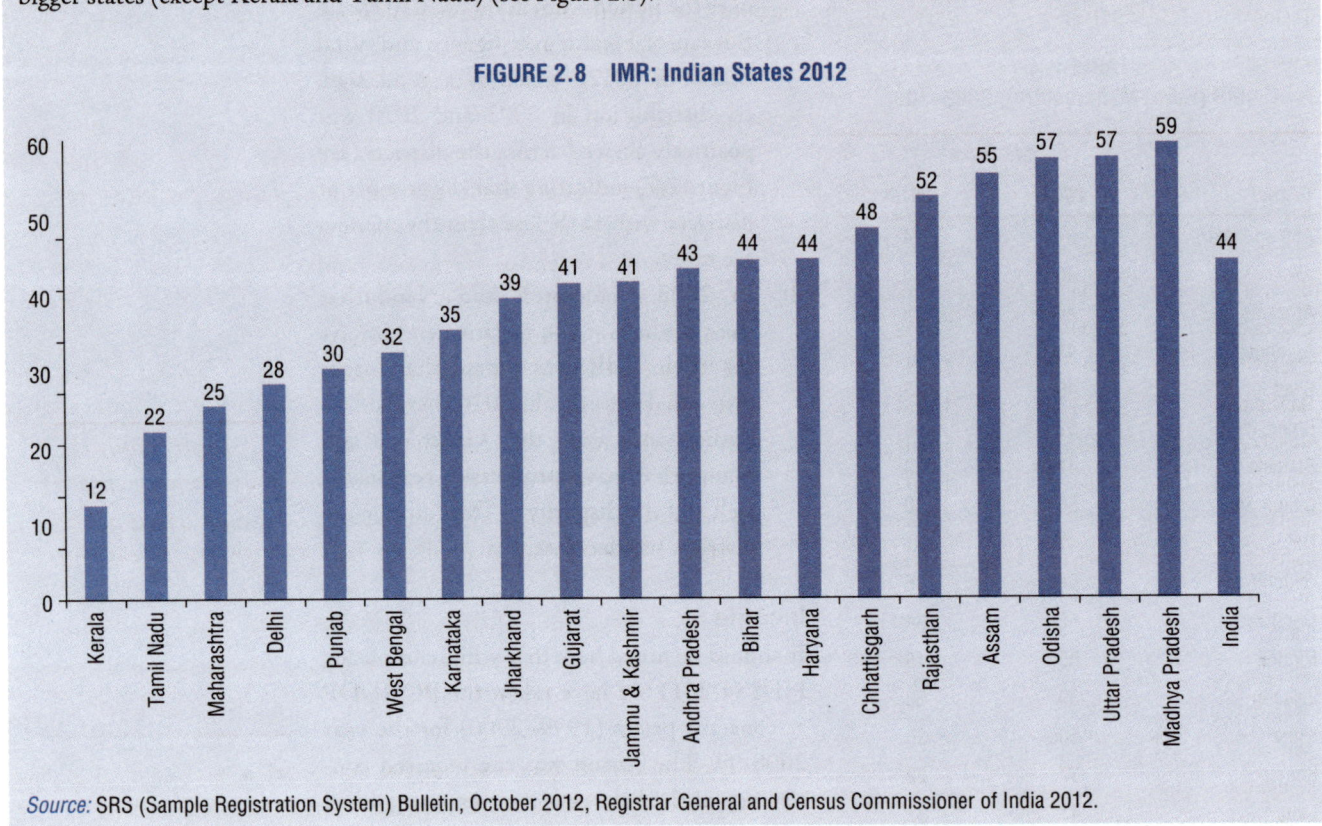

FIGURE 2.8   IMR: Indian States 2012

Source: SRS (Sample Registration System) Bulletin, October 2012, Registrar General and Census Commissioner of India 2012.

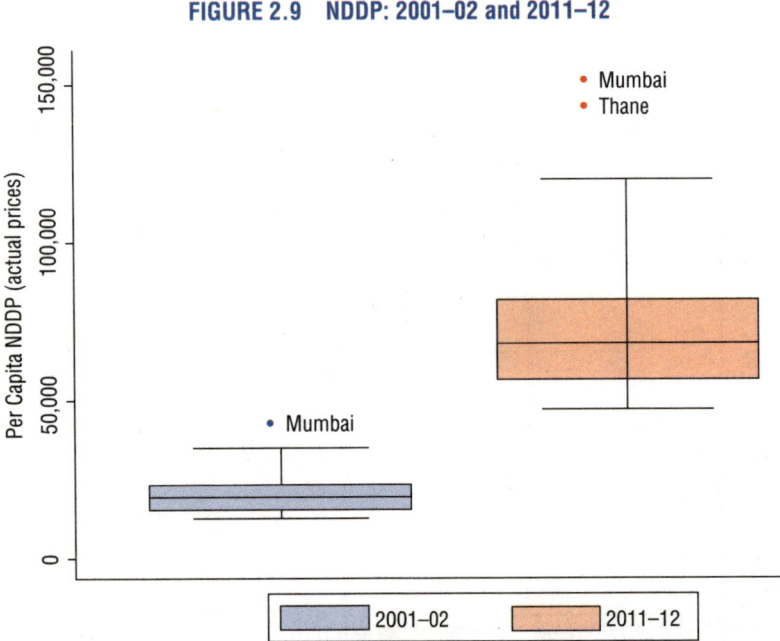

FIGURE 2.9   NDDP: 2001–02 and 2011–12

Source: Author's findings based on data in Table 2.5.
Note: Income (in rupees) per annum at current prices.

be worthwhile to analyse the same separately in this section. The analysis of income data leads to the following picture (see Table 2.5).

Economic growth, when looked at as net income generated across districts, is found to be unequal and positively skewed. Mumbai was an outlier in this category in the year 2000–01. However, with progressive growth across the districts, there has been an improvement in their income-generation status as reflected by the upward movement of the box plot for the year 2011–12. Although marginal, the extent of skewness is seen to have gone down. The profile for the year 2011–12 shows only two outliers (Mumbai and Thane) in terms of income generation per capita (see Figure 2.9).

TABLE 2.5
PCNDDP (at Current Prices), Maharashtra, 2001–02 and 2011–12

District	Per Capita NDDP at Current Prices (₹)	
	2001–02	2011–12
Ahmednagar	18,090	75,233
Akola	17,051	61,423
Amravati	17,795	63,467
Aurangabad	20,174	91,100
Beed	14,094	55,139
Bhandara	17,900	60,764
Buldana	12,755	50,772
Chandrapur	22,290	73,328
Dhule	16,281	66,140
Gadchiroli	13,943	48,311
Gondiya	16,531	53,802
Hingoli	13,184	46,190
Jalgaon	18,601	75,956
Jalna	13,075	55,067
Kolhapur	25,356	101,014
Latur	12,364	59,396
Mumbai	41,032	151,608
Nagpur	25,190	100,663
Nanded	12,742	52,583
Nandurbar	12,116	46,156
Nashik	25,616	91,673
Osmanabad	12,847	54,833
Parbhani	14,523	58,512
Pune	34,358	140,570
Raigarh	31,123	118,885
Ratnagiri	18,753	77,521
Sangli	22,303	80,709
Satara	21,201	80,671
Sindhudurg	18,751	81,201
Solapur	18,699	74,856
Thane	33,171	140,608
Wardha	18,672	68,085
Washim	14,373	55,200
Yavatmal	15,749	54,497
Maharashtra	**24,035**	**95,339**

Source: DES, Government of Mahrashtra.

Human Development across Districts: A Radar Profile[8]

To assess the performance of the districts on each of the human development indicators, radar charts for individual districts were prepared. The following main messages emerge from the district radars:

1. Low human development districts (as reflected by their low HDIs) including Nandurbar, Gadchiroli, Nanded and Osmanabad show poor performance for all the four indicators (total literacy, GER, income and infant survival) on the radar charts.
2. On the other hand, high human development districts such as Raigarh, Thane, Pune and Kolhapur show better performance than the state on all the four indicators.
3. Although the individual radars for districts such as Washim, Gondia, Parbhani, Jalna, Yavatmal and Latur do not reflect much improvement in the income indicator, they show higher convergence with the state average on the GER.
4. Similarly, the radars of Ahmednagar, Hingoli, Jalna and Yavatmal show comparatively lower performances on the income indicator, but better performances on infant survival.
5. Overall, the radars bring forth the inter-district inequalities that persist in all the four human development indicators across the state.

The IHDI

The conventional approach used by the UNDP defines HDI using per capita gross domestic product (GDP) (in terms of purchasing power parity [PPP] in [US$]), the adult literacy rate, GER and life expectancy at

> High human development districts such as Raigarh, Thane, Pune and Kolhapur show better performance than the state on all the four indicators.

---

[8] A radar chart is a graphical method used to display ratings on selected indicators. It is useful to assess performance or achievement in terms of the four human development indicators. Performance or achievement ratings are measured in terms of standardized scores ranging from zero to five, with the former indicating nil achievement. The radar chart depicts areas of relative strength and relative weakness as well, as it provides a snapshot of overall performance. Symmetry

birth, to measure achievements with respect to the three dimensions of income, education and health. The revised methodology focuses on the same three dimensions in terms of the gross national income per capita, mean years of schooling, school life expectancy and life expectancy (see Table 2.6). In addition, it adjusts estimates of these three different indicators for inequalities in their achievements across persons to examine and estimate the potential loss.[10] We have attempted here to calculate the HDI at the state level by using the revised methodology as well as the IHDI. For reasons like lack of comprehensive information on such variables at the more disaggregated district level for Maharashtra, we present only the IHDI estimates as per the revised methodology at the state level and compare achievements in the same relative to the national level as well as other states.

Estimates of the HDI (components as well as aggregate) for Maharashtra and the major states in India show considerable variation in 2011. What we find are as follows:

1. The HDI ranges from 0.442 in Odisha to 0.625 in Kerala covering an interval of 0.183 points (see Figure 2.10 and Table 2.7).
2. The IHDI varies from a minimum of 0.290 in Madhya Pradesh to a maximum of 0.520 in Kerala involving a large difference interval of 0.230 points (see Figure 2.10 and Table 2.7).
3. The extent of human development is higher in Maharashtra than for the country as a whole, both before and after adjusting for inequality (see Table 2.7).
4. When the states are ordered into four quartile groups (low, medium, high and very high human development),

TABLE 2.6
Key Human Development Indicators: States and India

State	PPP Income Per Capita (PPP 2008 in US$)	Life Expectancy at Birth (Years) (2002–06)	Mean Years of Schooling (Years) (2004–05)	School Life Expectancy (Years) (2007–08)
Andhra Pradesh	3,398.8	64.4	3.1	9.7
Assam	2,883.4	58.9	4.0	9.5
Bihar	2,161.8	61.6	3.0	9.6
Chhattisgarh	2,497.0	58.0	3.4	9.3
Gujarat	3,782.9	64.1	4.5	8.8
Haryana	4,574.5	66.2	4.7	9.7
Himachal Pradesh	4,168.4	67.0	4.9	11.0
Jharkhand	2,516.4	58.0	3.3	9.7
Karnataka	3,269.8	65.3	3.9	9.8
Kerala	5,262.9	74.0	6.2	11.3
Madhya Pradesh	2,673.8	58.0	3.4	9.0
Maharashtra	**3,913.1**	**67.2**	**5.1**	**9.9**
Odisha	2,185.8	59.6	3.3	8.7
Punjab	4,885.1	69.4	5.1	9.8
Rajasthan	3,289.3	62.0	3.0	9.2
Tamil Nadu	3,835.0	66.2	4.8	10.6
Uttar Pradesh	2,910.6	60.0	3.6	9.2
Uttarakhand	3,536.1	60.0	5.0	10.2
West Bengal	3,414.1	64.9	4.4	8.9
India[9]	**3,337.3**	**63.5**	**4.1**	**9.6**

Source: Suryanarayana et al. (2011).

in and the extent of the shaded area of the chart would indicate an equally good or bad performance across indicators. Initially the radar scores were calculated by using the same goalposts used for HDI. However, the radars drawn did not depict the differences in the districts clearly. Hence, different goalposts than those used for calculating HDI were used for finding radar scores. The radars drawn then could depict the differences in the performance of various indicators in the districts. The radars for all the districts are presented in Tables 2A.4 and 2A.5.

[9] It needs to be specified here that the set of indicators used to construct the HDI for India and the states in the IHDR 2011 are: adjusted mean years of schooling and the literacy rate of population aged seven and above (education index), life expectancy at birth (health index) and the mean per capita expenditure (at 1999–2000 prices) weighted by the Gini coefficient of inequality of consumption expenditure (income index). Hence HDI of India in the IHDR 2011 (which is presented in Table 1.1 in Chapter 1) and the HDI of India calculated here are not comparable.

[10] For methodological details, see Suryanarayana et al. (2011).

FIGURE 2.10 HDI, IHDI and Loss Due to Inequality across States and India: 2010–11

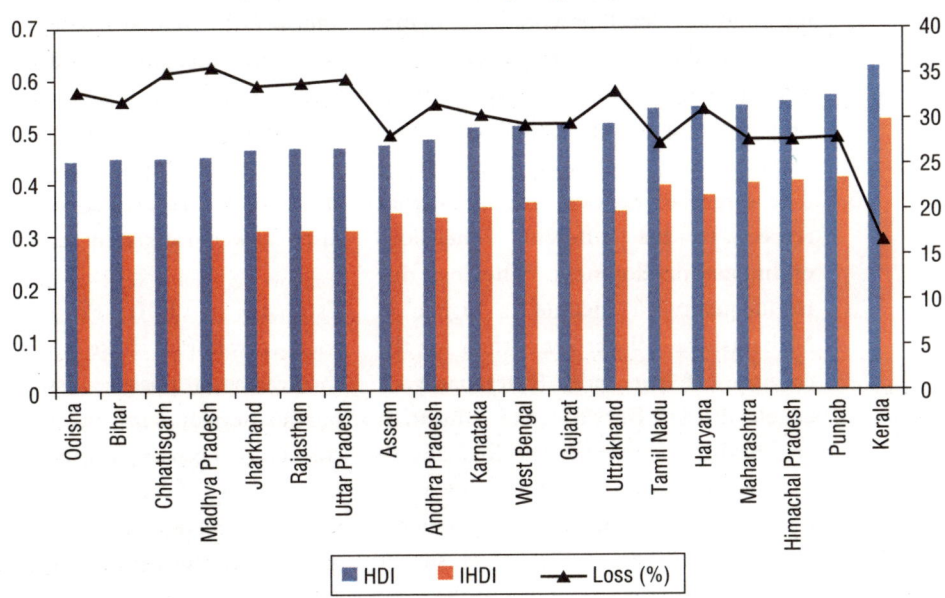

Source: Author's findings based on data in Tables 2.4 and 2.5.
Note: States are arranged in ascending order of HDI.

TABLE 2.7
Estimates of HDI and IHDI across States and India: 2010–11

State	HDI (As per Current International Methodology)	IHDI	Ratio	Loss (Percentage)	Rank HDI	Rank IHDI	Difference*
Andhra Pradesh	0.485	0.332	0.685	31.55	11	12	–1
Assam	0.474	0.341	0.718	28.17	12	11	1
Bihar	0.447	0.303	0.679	32.06	18	16	2
Chhattisgarh	0.449	0.291	0.649	35.14	17	18	–1
Gujarat	0.514	0.363	0.705	29.50	8	7	1
Haryana	0.545	0.375	0.688	31.18	5	6	–1
Himachal Pradesh	0.558	0.403	0.722	27.81	3	3	0
Jharkhand	0.464	0.308	0.663	33.67	15	14	1
Karnataka	0.508	0.353	0.696	30.44	10	9	1
Kerala	0.625	0.520	0.832	16.78	1	1	0
Madhya Pradesh	0.451	0.290	0.643	35.74	16	19	–3
Maharashtra	**0.549**	**0.397**	**0.722**	**27.75**	**4**	**4**	**0**
Odisha	0.442	0.296	0.669	33.11	19	17	2
Punjab	0.569	0.410	0.720	28.04	2	2	0
Rajasthan	0.468	0.308	0.660	34.02	14	13	1
Tamil Nadu	0.544	0.396	0.727	27.28	6	5	1
Uttar Pradesh	0.468	0.307	0.655	34.47	13	15	–2
Uttarakhand	0.515	0.345	0.670	33.03	7	10	–3
West Bengal	0.509	0.360	0.707	29.30	9	8	1
India	**0.504**	**0.343**	**0.680**	**32.00**	–	–	–

Source: Suryanarayana et al. (2011).
Note: * denotes the difference between the 'Rank HDI' and 'Rank IHDI' above, and, therefore, denotes the gain or loss in ranking due to inequality adjustment.

Maharashtra emerges as a state with very high human development, both before and after adjusting for inequality.

5. The percentage loss due to inequality at 28 per cent is less in Maharashtra than for the country as a whole (32 per cent).
6. The extent of relative loss varies with respect to the different dimensions of human development. The loss due to inequality in income is higher in Maharashtra (19 per cent) than for the country (16 per cent) (Suryanarayana et al. 2011). But for the education and health parameters, the loss due to inequality is lesser for Maharashtra (38 per cent and 25 per cent respectively) vis-à-vis India (43 per cent and 34 per cent for education and health respectively, according to Suryanarayana et al. [2011]) (see Tables 2.7 and 2A.6).
7. The loss due to inequality is found to be the least in Kerala. This could be due to two possible reasons: *First*, the high priority assigned to investments in human capital by way of education and health, which have been instrumental in facilitating exports of labour to Arab countries and international remittances accounting for about a quarter of the total income of the state (Centre for Development Studies 2006). *Second*, the relatively limited imbalances in regional development as reflected in limited dispersion in per capita income generated across districts (Centre for Development Studies 2006). Such a finding for Kerala brings forth an important policy message for Maharashtra, which is characterized by regional and sectoral imbalances in growth and development.
8. Finally, Maharashtra, along with Kerala, Punjab, Himachal Pradesh, Haryana, Tamil Nadu, Karnataka, Gujarat, West Bengal and Uttarakhand finds a place in the medium HDI category based on the international classification of countries.

Summing Up

Individual human development indicator scores as well as aggregate HDIs show an improvement across districts between 2001 and 2011 for Maharashtra. There has hardly been any substantial change in the relative human development status of other districts but for some marginal changes in rank permutations. Progress in general was greater at the lower end than at the higher end when districts were ranked by their HDIs.

Estimates of HDIs and income across districts corroborate those in the MHDR 2002, showcasing a positive association between human development and income. The rank correlation between income and HDI is positive and significant. Pair-wise comparisons for HDIs in 2001 and 2011 show that all the districts in the category of richest quartile group by income also belong to the classification of very high human development quartile by HDI. Barring Buldhana, all the poor districts of Maharashtra also belong to the low human development quartile.

It is observed that the districts of Nashik, Solapur, Jalgaon, Buldhana and Parbhani have improved their relative category on the HDI. On the other hand, the districts of Osmanabad, Latur, Chandrapur, Amrawati and Satara, which although have improved their HDI, have moved down relatively in the HDI categorization.

Maharashtra throws up some surprises at the disaggregated level, given the general belief about a positive association among the three human development dimensions.

For example, in 2001 and 2011, Gondiya belonged to the medium human development quartile but in terms of education it is in the very high human development quartile and for health it is in the low quartile for both the years.

When the IHDI is considered, Maharashtra falls in the medium HDI category in terms of the international classification of countries. Amongst the states in India, it emerges as a state with very high human development both before and after adjustments for inequality.

> *It is observed that the districts of Nashik, Solapur, Jalgaon, Buldhana and Parbhani have improved their relative category on the HDI.*

The extent of relative loss is seen to vary with respect to the different dimensions of human development. The loss due to inequality in income is higher in Maharashtra than for the country. But for the education and health parameters, the loss due to inequality is lesser for Maharashtra vis-à-vis India. In other words, there is considerable scope for realizing improvements in human development through a strategy that equalizes achievements across persons with respect to the different human development dimensions.

The radar profiles of the human development indicators across districts point towards the inequalities that prevail in the status of all the four human development indicators (income, literacy ratio, GER and IMR).

Annexure 2.1

Technical Note
The HDI

The HDI is designed to capture average achievements with respect to three critical dimensions, namely, (a) a long and healthy life, (b) knowledge and (c) a decent standard of living. These three critical dimensions are measured in terms of the following indicators: (a) life expectancy at birth; (b) adult literacy rate and combined GER for primary, secondary and tertiary schools and (c) per capita GDP in PPP (US$). However, due to limited information, this Report has made use of the following indicators to measure the three dimensions. They are (a) the literacy rate and the combined GER for primary and secondary school education, (b) ISR and (c) per capita net domestic product (at constant prices) across districts in Maharashtra. To facilitate their aggregation into a single index, corresponding dimension indices are estimated in terms of the following normalized scores.

$$I_X = \text{Dimension index of 'X'} = \frac{(\text{Actual value} - \text{Minimum value})}{(\text{Maximum value} - \text{Minimum value})}$$

The education index has been calculated by allocating two-thirds weight to literacy and one-third weight to GER.

The goalposts used to estimate these scores are as follows:

Maharashtra: Goalposts for District-Wise HDI

Dimension	Maximum	Minimum
ISR	1,000	0
Literacy Rate	100	0
GER	100	0
Per Capita Net Domestic Product (Rupees at current prices)	150,000	10,000

Note: ISR is obtained as (1000−IMR). Normalised scores for the income dimension have been worked out based on log transformation of the estimates of DDP.

Finally, an aggregate HDI for a given district has been calculated as a simple arithmetic mean of the normalized scores for the three dimensions.

Motivation for Choosing the Goalposts

In this second MHDR 2012, the framework for estimating district HDIs should have been ideally the same as the one used in the MHDR 2002. Due to lack of information on the methodology or the goalposts used in the MHDR 2002, one option was to follow the international approach or convention for comparable indices and choose actual limits or extreme values for the sample, as done in some other SHDRs:

1. We have followed the convention for education scores (UNDP 2005).
2. For IMR we have chosen the ideal limits for CSRs.
3. For income, different state governments have followed different norms. While Kerala (Centre for Development Studies 2006) and Uttar Pradesh (Government of Uttar Pradesh 2003) have used the actual goalposts used by the UNDP Odisha (Government of Orissa 2004) and West Bengal (Development and

Planning Department 2004) have used the observed extreme values for per capita incomes across states. In the case of Maharashtra, which is virtually the richest state in the country, the choice of extreme values based on state averages would not have been useful since the richest district (Mumbai) has a value exceeding the richest state's average. Hence, our option was to choose values from the district-wise estimates of per capita income. The sample extreme values on district-wise per capita income for 2008–09 were ₹14,885 (Washim) and ₹58,818 (Mumbai). However, given the need for estimates for at least two points of time to facilitate verification of progress over time, we have taken ₹10,000 (corresponding to the income (₹11,789) for the poorest district, Nandurbar, in 2001) as the lower limit and ₹150,000 as the upper limit. While absolute values of normalized scores would vary depending upon the goalposts used, inferences on progress would not, since the same goalposts have been used for all districts at one point of time and over time.

3

Growth, Equity and Inclusion

Introduction

Income is a significant component of the HDI though the latter has been designed to address the limitations of income as a measure of progress in human development. The relevance of income stems from the fact that it provides an estimate of resources available for realizing a wide range of capabilities, including education and health. Hence, to assess its potential as well as impact on development, there is a need to study (*a*) economic growth and income levels from the resource availability perspective and (*b*) distribution of income, levels of living and food security from the resource distribution and utilization perspectives.

The MHDR 2002 highlighted the positive as well as negative growth features of the state since its very inception. Due credit was given to the state for its material progress in spite of the heavy odds loaded against it by nature, and Maharashtra has continued to be one of the fastest-growing states of the Indian union. However, it was pointed out in the MHDR 2002 that the spatial dimension of the growth process as well as its lopsidedness due to excessive reliance on the manufacturing and services sectors left a lot to be desired. The urban centres of Mumbai, Thane, Pune and Nagpur alone accounted for about half of the total income generated in the state. Levels of income were low and, hence, the incidence of poverty was very high in several districts of Maharashtra. The conscious efforts of the government in alleviating unemployment and poverty seemed to have borne some results. However, the MHDR 2002 pointed out that the state had a long way to go in terms of realizing the goals for food and nutrition security, since the reductions in the statistical estimates of poverty were not corroborated by the estimates of physical cereal consumption and calorie intake.

In this HDR, we seek to examine whether Maharashtra has made any progress in addressing issues concerning economic growth and income distribution by addressing the following questions:

1. What has been the economic growth performance of the state since 1999–2000?
2. What has been the sectoral profile and spatial dimension of this growth process?
3. Has the state been successful in reducing inter-district disparities in the growth process?
4. What are the distributional consequences in terms of the extent of inequality across income groups and districts?
5. What are the changes that have occurred in the intake of calories, proteins and fats?
6. How far has the growth process been inclusive?

Economic Growth

When measured by income, Maharashtra maintains its second position as far as per capita income is considered. In 2008–09, the per capita NSDP at current prices was about 46 per cent more than the all-India average (this difference was 40 per cent in 1998–99). Provisional estimates for 2008–09 show the NSDP at current prices to be ₹5,975,424.2 million and per capita NSDP at ₹54,867 (Government of Maharashtra 2011). The primary sector contributed to 12.3 per cent of total NSDP, the secondary sector 28.6 per cent and the tertiary sector 59.1 per cent, validating the continued dominance of the non-agricultural economy, with the secondary and tertiary sectors accounting for about 88 per cent of the total NSDP (see Table 3.1).

A Macro Profile

Maharashtra has retained its tempo of accelerated growth from its very inception. The NSDP grew[1] at an annual rate of 2.5 per cent in the 1960s, 5.2 per cent in the 1970s, 5.4 per cent in the 1980s, 6.4 per cent in the 1990s (Government of Maharashtra 2002: 182) and 7.5 per cent since the decade 1991–2000 (see Figure 3.1). Maharashtra has sustained its growth in the new millennium too. Growing at an annual rate of 7.5 per cent in 1999–2000, its total NSDP demonstrated an increase of 76 per cent by 2008–09 (see Table 3.1). With the exception of the first year of the new millennium, the growth in per capita NSDP has always been positive (see Figure 3.2). It has shown an increase at an average annual rate of 5.9 per cent, thus showing a 50 per cent increase over the same time period.

The growth profile across sectors reveals that the state continues to retain its past features of the dominance of the non-agricultural sector in terms of growth rate and size with periodic declines in agricultural growth (see Figure 3.3). While the agricultural sector grew at the average annual rate of 5.2 per cent, the industry and service sectors grew at the rates of 7.6 per cent and 8.6 per cent respectively during the period between 1999–2000 and 2008–09. What we therefore see is a decline in the share of the agricultural sector in total NSDP on the one hand and an increase in the shares of the secondary and tertiary sectors shares on the other, with

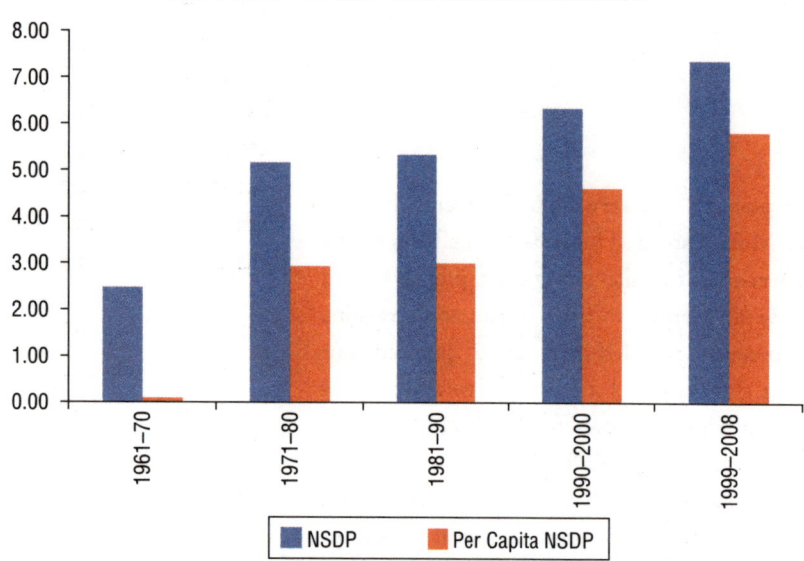

FIGURE 3.1 Decade-Wise Growth Performance

Source: Based on information provided by DES.
Note: Average annual growth rate (percentage) of NSDP and per capita NSDP based on semi-log trend functions.

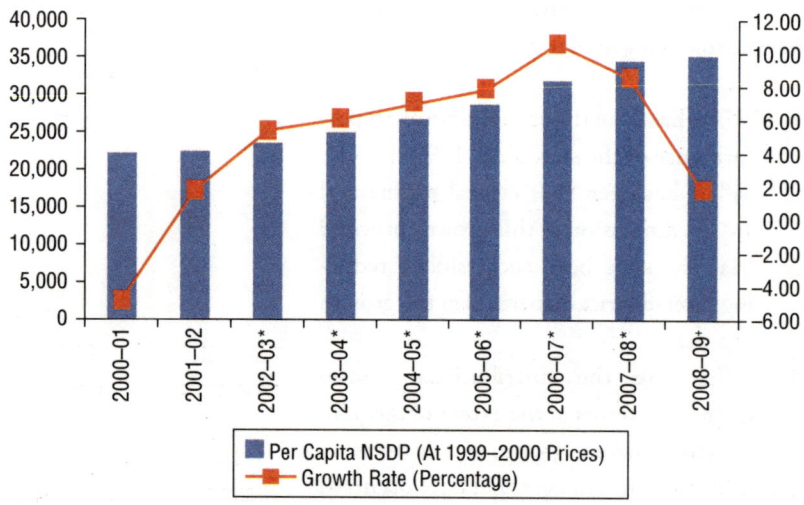

FIGURE 3.2 Per Capita NSDP and Its Annual Growth Rate

Source: Based on information provided by DES.
Notes: (i) * indicates provisional estimates.
(ii) + indicates preliminary estimates.

---

[1] The growth rate is calculated using a semi-log trend function.

TABLE 3.1
Growth Performance of Maharashtra: 1999–2000 to 2008–09: A Summary Report

Sectors	NSDP at Current Prices (2008–09) (₹)	Share (Percentage)	Growth Rate (1999–2000 to 2008–09)@ (Percentage per Annum)	NSDP (₹ Millions) at 1999–2000 Prices 1999–2000 Volume	Share (Percentage)	2008–09 Volume	Share (Percentage)
1.1 Agriculture	655,113.4	11.0	3.5**	345,505.4	15.9	392,966.5	10.3
1.2 Forestry	31,926.6	0.5	(−) 2.4**	17,199.7	0.8	13,643.0	0.4
1.3 Fishing	13,288.1	0.2	(−) 1.0***	8,242.5	0.4	6,908.1	0.2
1. Agriculture and Allied Activities	**700,328.1**	11.7	3.2*	370,947.6	17.1	413,517.6	10.9
2. Mining and Quarrying	35,178.5	0.6	5.2***	15,562.5	0.7	21,996.4	0.6
Primary Sector	**735,506.6**	12.3	3.3**	386,510.1	17.8	435,514.0	11.4
3.1 Registered	747,257.1	12.5	6.5***	312,387.6	14.4	427,680.2	11.2
3.2 Unregistered	235,161.8	3.9	5.9***	101,043.1	4.7	161,173.5	4.2
3. Manufacturing Total	**982,418.8**	16.4	6.3***	413,430.7	19.0	588,853.8	15.4
4. Electricity, Gas and Water Supply	64,893.6	1.1	6.3***	38,285.6	1.8	64,578.5	1.7
5. Construction	662,321.6	11.1	11.1***	129,199.0	6.0	332,804.5	8.7
Secondary Sector	**1,709,634.1**	28.6	7.6***	580,915.2	26.8	986,236.7	25.9
Industry Sector	**1,744,812.6**	29.2	7.5***	596,477.7	27.5	1,008,233.1	26.4
6.1 Railways	33,156.9	0.6	9.2***	14,035.2	0.7	29,393.5	0.8
6.2 Transport by Other Means Storage	164,205.8	2.8	0.66	71,964.0	3.3	68,670.8	1.8
6.3 Communication	174,166.7	2.9	12.0***	49,546.1	2.3	155,144.6	4.1
6.4 Trade, Hotels and Restaurants	1,146,403.1	19.2	10.6***	329,540.8	15.2	719,293.6	18.9
6. Trade, Hotels, Transport, Storage and Communication	**1,517,932.5**	25.4	9.6***	465,086.1	21.4	972,502.6	25.5
7.1 Banking and Insurance	732,689.6	12.3	11.4***	273,943.4	12.6	640,811.4	16.8
7.2 Real Estate, Ownership of Dwellings, business services, public administration and other services.	731,880.8	12.3	9.8***	195,315.2	9.0	457,947.5	12.0
7. Finance, Insurance, Real Estate and Business Services	**1,464,570.5**	24.5	10.7***	469,258.6	21.6	1,098,759.0	28.8
8.1 Public Administration	222,520.7	3.7	2.1**	100,830.2	4.6	124,003.6	3.3
8.2 Other Services	325,259.9	5.4	1.8	169,379.1	7.8	198,390.1	5.2
8. Community and Personal Services	**547,780.6**	9.2	2.0	270,209.3	12.4	322,393.7	8.5
Tertiary/Service Sector	**3,530,283.5**	59.1	8.6***	1,204,554.0	55.5	2,393,655.2	62.7
9. Net State Domestic Product	**5,975,424.2**	100.0	7.5***	217,197.9	100.0	3,815,405.9	100.0
Population (Thousands)	108,908		1.6***	94,388	–	108,908	
Per Capita Income (₹)	**54,867**		5.9***	23,011	–	35,033	

Source: Author's estimates based on information provided by DES.
Notes: (i) @ indicates growth rate computed from an estimated semi-log trend function.
(ii) Annual growth rates and their averages are reported in Table 3A.2.
(iii) *** indicates significance at the 1 per cent level; ** indicates significance at the 5 per cent level; * indicates significance at the 10 per cent level.

Growth, Equity and Inclusion

the increase in tertiary sector share being more pronounced (see Figure 3.4). A more in-depth look at the sectoral composition of growth shows that agricultural performance by itself has been highly unstable, reflected in its wide annual fluctuations (see Table 3A.2). Within the agricultural sector, fishing and forestry have shown a poor growth performance, with a decline in income originating from these two activities. On the other hand, banking and insurance, trade, hotels and restaurants, communication and construction (non-agricultural sectors) have grown at double-digit rates. In sum, the majority of segments of the tertiary sector have grown at double-digit rates.

> *The majority of segments of the tertiary sector have grown at double-digit rates.*

District-Level Profile

Compared to the benchmark scenario set by the MHDR in 2002, there has been a marginal reduction in the profile of inter-district disparities in per capita income (NDDP at constant prices). This marginal reduction can be attributed to the improved economic performance of some of the poorer districts, such as Dhule, Hingoli, Jalna, Jalgaon and Nandurbar across the primary, secondary and tertiary sectors (see Table 3A.1). While these districts have grown faster than the state as a whole, relatively richer districts such as Mumbai have performed less than the state average (see Figure 3.5). In fact, the fastest-growing quartile consists of Nandurbar,

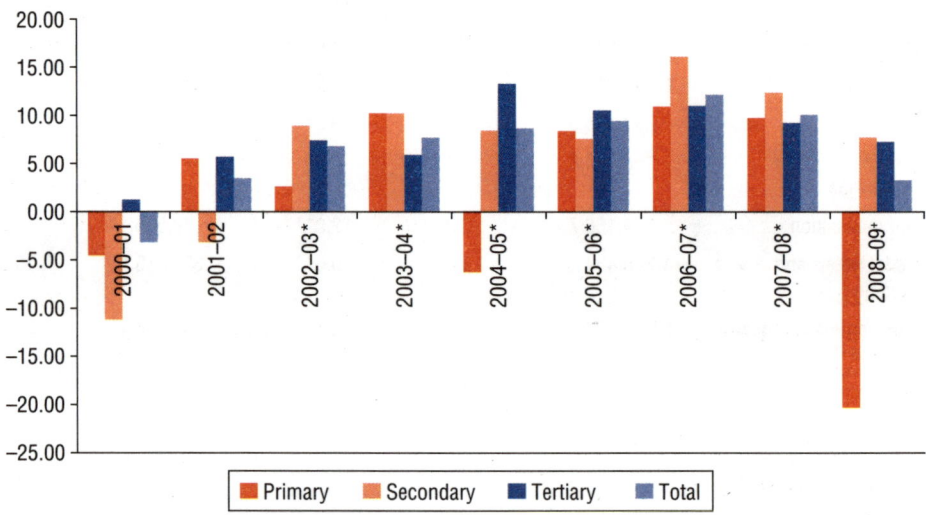

FIGURE 3.3 Sectoral Annual Growth Performance: 1999–2000 to 2008–09

Source: Based on information provided by DES.
Notes: (i) * represents provisional estimates.
(ii) + represents preliminary estimates.

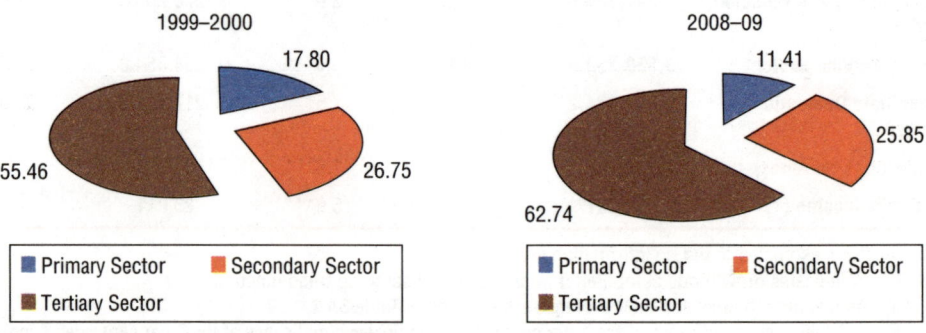

FIGURE 3.4 Sectoral Distribution of NSDP at 1999–2000 Prices

Source: Based on information provided by DES.
Note: Findings are presented in percentage terms.

FIGURE 3.5 Per Capita NDDP at 1999–2000 Prices and Its Average Annual Rate of Growth across Districts: 1999–2000 to 2008–09

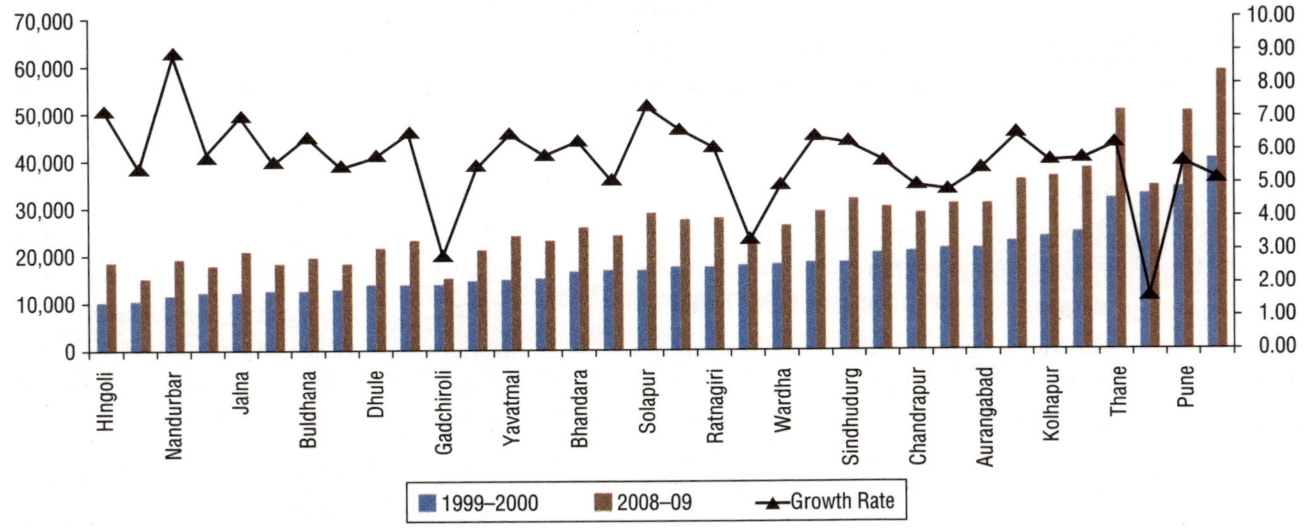

Source: Based on information provided by DES.
Notes: (i) Districts are ordered in terms of PCN domestic product (NDP) in the base year (1999–2000).
(ii) Growth rates are computed from semi-log trend functions.

Solapur, Hingoli, Jalna, Ahmednagar, Parbhani, Yavatmal, Nashik and Jalgaon while Mumbai has fallen into the poorest performing quarter. As a result, the extent of inter-district disparity in per capita income (at constant prices), as measured by the Lorenz ratio, declined from 22.5 per cent in 1999–2000 to 21.2 per cent in 2008–09. The two important findings here are *first*, the poorer districts have improved their income levels over time and *second*, the distribution of per capita income across districts, which was positively skewed in 1999–2000, is seen to have become nearly symmetric by 2008–09 (see Figure 3.5).

Improved performance of the poorer districts, facilitated partly by growth in the primary sector, has however not contributed to similar performance by them at the macro level because of their paltry share in the state total (see Table 3.2). As a result, richer districts such as Mumbai continue to dominate the growth scenario with Mumbai alone contributing 23 per cent of the growth experience since 1999–2000. Also, while the triumvirate of Mumbai, Thane and Pune together contributed to 48 per cent of the growth process, the fastest-growing quartile group managed to contribute just one-fifth to the same

(see Table 3A.3). Going by the estimates of income generated across districts, one would tend to get the impression that Maharashtra owes its prosperity entirely to Mumbai and a couple of urban districts (Thane, Pune and Raigarh). However, the evidence based on estimates of income generation does not corroborate this perception. Even the poorest district of Washim had an income level of ₹23,628 per capita per annum in 2008–09 (see Table 3.2).

The inter-district per capita income profile for the year 2008–09 emerges as follows (see Tables 3.2 and 3A.4):

1. Dhule is no longer the poorest district in Maharashtra. Instead, Washim, with a population share of 1 per cent and income share of less than 0.5 per cent, was the poorest district for most of the years during 1999–2000 to 2008–09.
2. Mumbai continued to retain its position as the most prosperous district, while Mumbai and Pune were also the richest outliers (see Figure 3.6).
3. The districts of Dhule, Jalna, Osmanabad, Nanded, Yavatmal, Latur, Buldhana and Parbhani formed the poorest quarter in 1998–99. In 2008–09,

> *The poorer districts have improved their income levels over time and second, the distribution of per capita income across districts, which was positively skewed in 1999–2000, is seen to have become nearly symmetric by 2008–09.*

TABLE 3.2
NDDP: A Profile (2008–09)

District	Total NDP (₹ Millions at Current Prices)	Share in State Population	Share in State NDP (At Current Prices)	Per Capita NDP (At Current Prices)	Division	
Washim	26,299.0	1.0	0.4	23,628	Amravati	
Gadchiroli	25,464.7	1.0	0.4	24,370	Nagpur	
Latur	65,764.8	2.1	1.1	28,764	Aurangabad	
Nanded	91,251.8	2.9	1.5	28,853	Aurangabad	
Hingoli	31,320.9	1.0	0.5	29,150	Aurangabad	Poorest Quarter
Osmanabad	47,180.6	1.5	0.8	29,155	Aurangabad	
Buldhana	73,801.3	2.3	1.2	30,165	Amravati	
Nandurbar	43,561.3	1.3	0.7	30,516	Nashik	
Jalna	57,540.1	1.6	1.0	32,635	Aurangabad	
Beed	79,434.5	2.2	1.3	33,672	Aurangabad	
Amravati	97,872.8	2.7	1.6	33,710	Amravati	
Dhule	63,773.4	1.7	1.1	33,870	Nashik	
Parbhani	61,318.4	1.6	1.0	36,161	Aurangabad	
Akola	67,036.3	1.7	1.1	36,750	Amravati	Lower Middle Quarter
Yavatmal	99,308.3	2.5	1.7	36,979	Amravati	
Gondia	48,122.0	1.2	0.8	36,986	Nagpur	
Wardha	56,944.6	1.3	1.0	41,757	Nagpur	
Bhandara	51,975.8	1.1	0.9	42,037	Nagpur	
Jalgaon	175,850.6	3.7	2.9	43,184	Nashik	
Chandrapur	99,941.8	2.1	1.7	43,456	Nagpur	
Solapur	192,531.1	3.9	3.2	45,055	Pune	
Ratnagiri	82,785.3	1.7	1.4	45,060	Konkan	Upper Middle Quarter
Sangli	132,750.8	2.6	2.2	46,699	Pune	
Satara	143,478.8	2.8	2.4	47,009	Pune	
Sindhudurg	44,285.6	0.9	0.7	47,183	Konkan	
Ahmednagar	211,577.5	4.0	3.5	47,856	Nashik	
Aurangabad	160,161.1	3.0	2.7	49,465	Aurangabad	
Nashik	312,138.2	5.1	5.2	55,841	Nashik	
Kolhapur	218,215.1	3.6	3.7	55,931	Pune	
Raigarh	138,609.1	2.2	2.3	57,074	Konkan	Richest Quarter
Nagpur	284,235.5	4.3	4.8	60,592	Nagpur	
Thane	743,542.9	8.7	12.4	78,531	Konkan	
Pune	662,246.2	7.6	11.1	79,968	Pune	
Mumbai*	1,285,110.0	13.2	21.5	89,343	Konkan	
Lorenz Ratio (Current Prices) = 21.2 per cent						
Maharashtra	**59,75,430.3**	**100.0**	**100.0**	**54,867**		

Source: Author's calculations based on information provided by DES.
Note: * denotes Mumbai city and Mumbai Suburban district.

this position was held by Washim, Gadchiroli, Latur, Nanded, Hingoli, Osmanabad, Buldhana, Nandurbar and Jalna. In other words, the districts of Washim, Latur, Nanded, Hingoli, Osmanabad, Buldhana, Nandurbar and Jalna have not improved their relative position. Gadchiroli, on the other hand, is a new entrant into the poorest quartile group.

4. The richest quarter consisted of Mumbai, Pune, Thane, Nagpur, Raigarh, Kolhapur, Nashik and Aurangabad, making the Konkan region consistently retain its top position. This quarter together contributed about 64 per cent of the total NSDP in 2008–09, a share which was around 60 per cent in 1998–99.

5. Mumbai's share in the state NDP has reduced (from 25 per cent in 1998–99 to 22 per cent in 2008–09). On the other hand, Thane improved its share from 10 per cent to 12.4 per cent, and Pune from 9 per cent to 11 per cent. These three urban districts continued to retain their cumulative share of 45 per cent of the total NSDP in Maharashtra.

Maharashtra has enjoyed a high level of per capita income made possible by rapid progress in the non-agricultural sectors. This feature, along with the restricted geographical spread of economic development, implied that both the average level of income and the degree of inequality in its distribution across persons in the state has remained high. Thus, the economic growth profile of Maharashtra continues to be lopsided across sectors at the macro level and across districts at the disaggregated level. As a result, though the state ranks high in terms of per capita income or growth rate, in terms of a robust measure of location for a skewed distribution such as

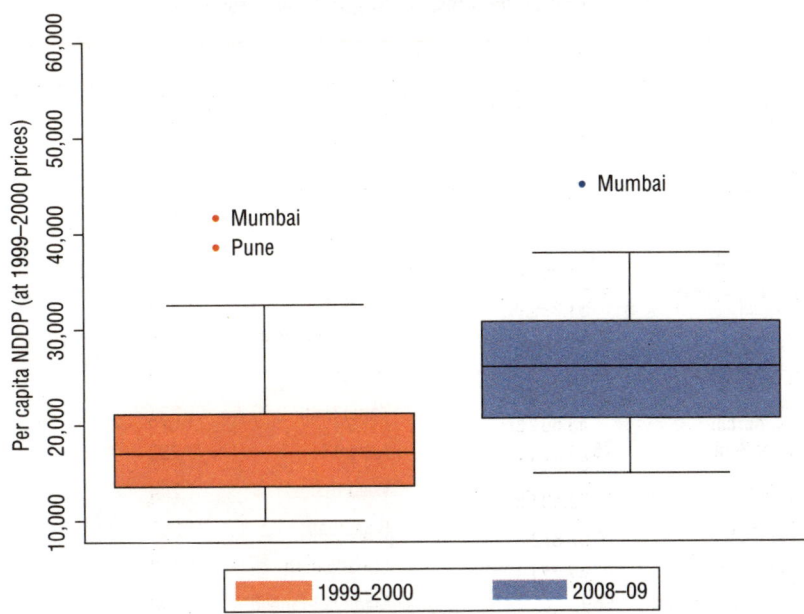

FIGURE 3.6 District-Wise Distribution of NDP at 1999–2000 Prices

Source: Based on information provided by DES.

consumption, namely the median, the performance of rural Maharashtra is a cause of concern.[2] Rural Maharashtra ranks seventh while urban Maharashtra ranks second across the 17 major states of India (see Table 3.3).

Economic Growth: Distributional Performance

This section studies in detail the distributional consequences of the observed growth process in Maharashtra. Data paucity on functional or personal income distribution has restricted the analysis to available NSS estimates of the distribution of employment and private household consumer expenditure.

Distribution of Employment and the Workforce[3]

Given the increasing dominance of the non-agricultural sector in income generation in Maharashtra, it becomes important to examine the profile of workforce distribution across these sectors to determine the

---

[2] As is well known in simple statistics, average per capita income is not an appropriate measure for an unequal distribution. For such a distribution the median is considered a better measure of the average.

[3] Findings presented in this section draw from data analysis of data from of various rounds of the NSS.

TABLE 3.3
Median MPCE by Sector in Major States: 2009–10

Rural		Urban	
State	MPCE (₹)	State	MPCE (₹)
Kerala	1,222	Gujarat	1,536
Punjab	1,206	Maharashtra	1,535
Haryana	1,162	Kerala	1,513
Rajasthan	897	Punjab	1,452
Andhra Pradesh	862	Karnataka	1,413
Gujarat	851	Andhra Pradesh	1,404
Maharashtra	848	Haryana	1,389
Tamil Nadu	817	Tamil Nadu	1,331
West Bengal	751	Assam	1,283
Assam	735	West Bengal	1,244
Karnataka	701	Rajasthan	1,206
Uttar Pradesh	693	Chhattisgarh	1,123
Madhya Pradesh	669	Madhya Pradesh	1,096
Jharkhand	643	Jharkhand	1,072
Bihar	622	Uttar Pradesh	1,019
Odisha	600	Odisha	962
Chhattisgarh	564	Bihar	844
All-India	**765**	**All-India**	**1,307**

Source: National Sample Survey Office (2011).

relative productivity per worker. As regards this parameter, the MHDR 2002 provided evidence of a sustained decline in the primary sector and near stagnation in the secondary and tertiary sectors. This trend is seen to persist. In 2009–10, the share of employment in the tertiary sector in particular did not show an increase commensurate with the increase in its share in income generation (see Table 3A.5). Though the non-agricultural sectors accounted for 88 per cent of the income generated, their share of employment was less than 50 per cent, whereas the primary sector, which provided employment to more than half of the workforce, generated less than 12 per cent of the total income of the state.

When studied at the more disaggregated rural–urban levels, in 2009–10 the primary sector dominated the employment scenario in rural areas, contributing to 80 per cent of the workforce, while it was virtually non-existent in the urban sector with a paltry share of 5 per cent. In addition, at a more macro level, unemployment rates were higher in rural Maharashtra than in the urban areas, and virtually half of the rural employment was casual labour (see Tables 3A.5, 3A.6 and 3A.7). This factor alone can be taken to indicate the prevalence of high rural–urban disparities in income, levels of living and poverty. However, the actual realization of these implications further depends upon the extent of work participation and unemployment rates by gender and sector, which is discussed below.

Although the daily status unemployment rates in Maharashtra have declined in the new millennium, WPRs have been better in the state than in India as a whole. In 2009–10, the rural WPR (principal and subsidiary status) was 48.8 per cent, comparatively higher than the WPR of 40.8 per cent for the country as a whole (see Table 3.4). For the urban sector, the corresponding estimates were 38 per cent and 35 per cent respectively. What is worth noting, however, is the observed difference in the behaviour of the same WPR over time when disaggregated by gender and sectors. During the years 1993–94 and 2009–10, the WPR for rural men, measured by the principal status, showed an increase for the state but declined for all-India, while the WPR by the subsidiary status decreased for both. Female WPR (principal status and subsidiary status) declined at both the state as well as at the all-India level during the same period, although the percentage point decline was more for Maharashtra. Thus, rural areas of the state witnessed a decline in female workforce participation vis-à-vis an increase in the same for males during the years 1993–94 to 2009–10.

In urban Maharashtra and urban India as a whole, the male WPR by principal status saw an increase over the period under study. For women on the other hand, there was an increase only in the WPR by principal status. In sum, it was found that the total WPR (male and female combined) declined in rural areas and increased in urban areas for both

TABLE 3.4
WPR: India and Maharashtra[4]

NSS Round	Rural Sector						Urban Sector					
	Males		Females		Total		Males		Females		Total	
	PS	PS+SS	PS	PS+SS	PS	PS+SS	PS	PS+SS	PS	PS+SS	PS	PS+SS
Maharashtra												
50 (July 1993–June 1994)	53.7	55.1	40.4	47.7	47.1	51.4	52	52.6	13.7	16.9	33.8	35.6
55 (July 1999–June 2000)	52.3	53.1	39.3	43.4	46	48.4	52.8	53.2	12.2	13.7	33.6	34.6
61 (July 2004–June 2005)	55.3	56.6	42.3	47.4	49	52.1	54.8	56	16.2	19.0	36.5	38.4
66 (July 2009–June 2010)	56.6	57.6	35.4	39.6	46.3	48.8	56.9	57.5	14.1	15.9	36.8	38
India												
50 (July 1993–June 1994)	53.8	55.3	23.4	32.8	39	44.4	51.3	52.1	12.1	15.5	32.7	34.7
55 (July 1999–June 2000)	52.2	53.1	23.1	29.9	38	41.7	51.3	51.8	11.7	13.9	32.4	33.7
61 (July 2004–June 2005)	53.5	54.6	24.2	32.7	39.1	43.9	54.1	54.9	13.5	16.6	34.6	36.5
66 (July 2009–June 2010)	53.7	54.7	20.2	26.1	37.4	40.8	53.9	54.3	11.9	13.8	33.9	35

Sources: Government of India (1997a, 2001c, 2006b, 2006c, 2011d).

Maharashtra and all-India during the period under study. Also, the percentage point decline in rural employment was lesser in Maharashtra compared to that in India and the percentage point increase in the urban sector more for Maharashtra than for India. Given the dominance of the non-agricultural sectors in income generation and growth, an improved WPR for the urban sector would imply a better profile of consumption distribution for this sector.

Consumption Distribution

The NSS data for various years reveals that in rural Maharashtra, the estimates of absolute consumption declined between 1999–2000 and 2004–05 and improved proportionately largely by 2009–10 for all the decile groups (see Table 3A.8).[5] This is also confirmed by conventional estimates of poverty, which increased from 23.5 per cent to 29.6 per cent during the period between 1999–2000 and 2004–05 (see Table 3.5). The estimates of

---

[4] Usual principal activity status: The usual activity status relates to the activity status of a person during a reference period of 365 days preceding the date of survey. The activity status on which a person spent a relatively longer time (that is, major time criterion) during the 365 days preceding the date of survey is considered as the usual principal activity status of the person.

Usual subsidiary economic activity status: A person whose usual principal status was determined on the basis of the major time criterion could have pursued some economic activity for a shorter time throughout the reference year period of 365 days preceding the date of survey or for a minor period, which is not less than 30 days, during the reference year. This is the usual subsidiary economic activity.

Usual activity status considering principal and subsidiary status taken together: The usual status, determined on the basis of the usual principal activity and usual subsidiary economic activity of a person taken together, is considered as the usual activity status of the person and is written as usual status (PS+SS). According to the usual status (PS+SS), workers are those who perform some work activity, either in the principal status or in the subsidiary status. Thus, a person who is not a worker in the usual principal status is considered as worker according to the usual status (PS+SS), if the person pursues some subsidiary economic activity for 30 days or more during a period of 365 days preceding the date of survey.

[5] For well-known issues related to the reference period used in data collection during the NSS 55th round (1999–2000) of the NSS, the estimates for this year are not strictly comparable with those for the remaining years.

TABLE 3.5
Incidence of Poverty: Maharashtra and India

Year	Rural Sector		Urban Sector		Combined	
	Percentage of Poor	Number of Poor (Millions)	Percentage of Poor	Number of poor (Millions)	Percentage of Poor	Number of Poor (Millions)
Conventional Approach						
Maharashtra						
1973–74	59.0	21.5	43.8	7.7	54.1	29.2
1977–78	63.3	24.7	38.8	7.8	55.0	32.5
1983	45.3	19.4	37.6	9.1	42.5	28.5
1987–88	42.6	19.5	38.1	10.5	40.9	30.0
1993–94	37.6	19.2	34.9	11.1	36.6	30.3
1999–2000	23.5	12.4	27.5	10.6	25.2	22.9
2004–2005	29.6	17.1	32.8	14.9	31.0	32.0
India						
1973–74	55.9	259.0	47.4	58.1	54.2	317.0
1977–78	50.5	251.5	42.0	60.0	48.6	311.4
1983	43.4	239.5	38.1	66.2	42.1	305.7
1987–88	36.9	219.1	37.6	74.1	37.1	293.1
1993–94	37.2	243.6	32.7	77.2	36.0	320.8
1999–2000	27.4	195.6	24.2	68.2	26.5	263.8
2004–05	28.3	221.2	26.0	81.8	27.7	303.1
Tendulkar Committee Approach						
Maharashtra						
2004–05	47.90	27.8	25.6	11.5	38.1	39.2
2009–10	29.5	18.0	18.3	90.9	24.5	27.0
All India						
2004–05	41.80	325.8	25.5	81.4	37.2	407.2
2009–10	33.80	278.2	20.9	76.5	29.8	354.7

Sources: The estimates per the conventional approach correspond to the poverty lines worked out according to the Lakdawala Committee Report (Government of India 1993); the estimates as per the Tendulkar Committee approach are from the Tendulkar Committee Report (Government of India 2009). Given some reservations about the recommendations of the Tendulkar Committee Report (Suryanarayana 2011), the analysis in this Report is based on estimates of poverty as per the conventional approach.
Note: The analysis in this report is based on estimates of poverty as per the conventional approach. The estimates have been made by the author based on the central sample of the NSS for the corresponding rounds; hence the estimates for Maharashtra are not strictly comparable with those in Tables 3A.11 and 3A.12, which are based on pooled state and central samples.

the extent of inequality as measured by the Lorenz ratio in rural Maharashtra showed an increase between the years 1999–2000 and 2004–05 and a decline thereafter almost to the initial levels by 2009–10. The decile group-wise estimates of shares in consumption also confirm this pattern (see Table 3A.8). Unlike rural Maharashtra, the extent of inequality in urban consumption distribution has increased over the three time periods considered (see Table 3A.9).

The share of the poorer decile groups in consumption in general saw a decline while the incidence of poverty (as per the Lakdawala Committee Report) showed an increase between 1999–2000 and 2004–05. The incidence of rural poverty in Maharashtra relative to its all-India counterpart has tended to decline over time while the corresponding estimate for urban Maharashtra has increased (see Figures 3.7 and 3.8 respectively). Given the large share of the rural poor, the incidence of poverty in Maharashtra as a whole relative to that in India has shown a general tendency to decline (see Figure 3.9). The Tendulkar Committee estimates indicate that the incidence of rural poverty has decreased from 2004–05 to 2009–10 (47.90 per cent to 29.5 per cent). Similarly incidence of urban poverty has also decreased during the same time period (25.60 per cent to 18.3 per cent). The aggregate poverty has reduced as well (38.10 per cent to 24.5 per cent) (see Table 3.5).

Distribution Profile across Social Groups

Levels of Living

This section provides a profile of average levels of consumption, extent of inequality and poverty in Maharashtra at the regional level[6] and across social groups for 2004–05, using unit record data from the NSS central sample (see Table 3A.10). Mean and median are the two alternative measures of averages used in the analysis. While mean is the most commonly used measure of average, it has a limitation in that it is influenced by outliers and hence represents largely changes in the consumption levels of the richer segments. Median, on the other hand, is a relatively more robust measure of average for skewed distributions. Such an analysis is important for a better understanding of the level and extent of social inclusion or exclusion in the growth processes.

In rural Maharashtra, the Inland Western region was found to be the richest by both the mean and median measures of average consumption. In other words, its consumption distribution in general is located above the distributions pertaining to other regions of Maharashtra; that is, its rank is reasonably robust. However, one does not find such

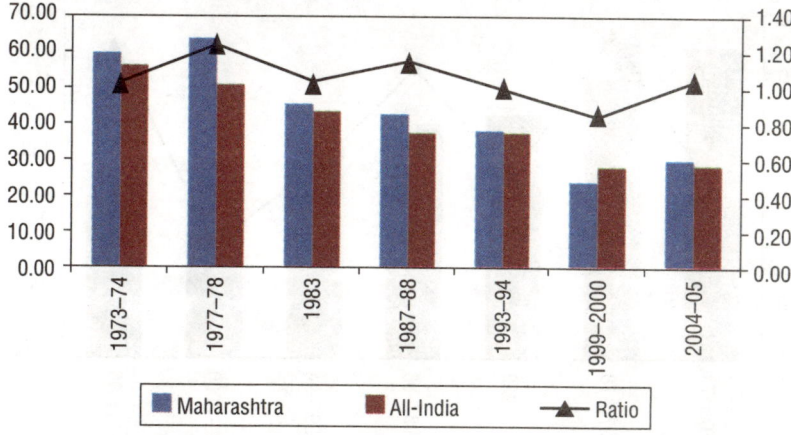

FIGURE 3.7 Incidence of Rural Poverty: Maharashtra versus India

Source: Based on data in Table 3.5.

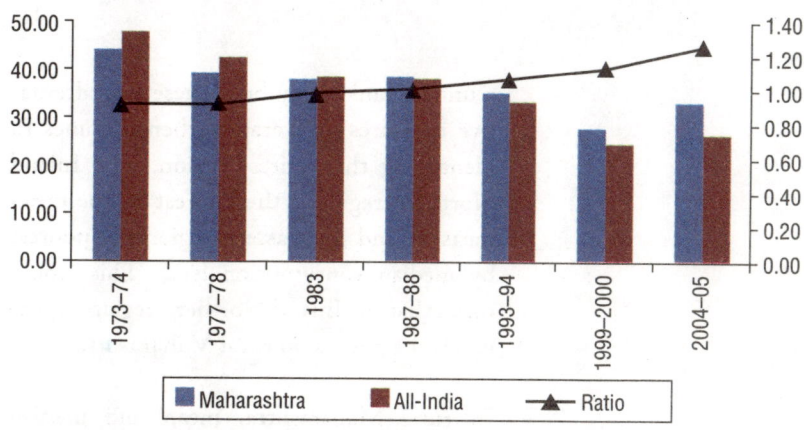

FIGURE 3.8 Incidence of Urban Poverty: Maharashtra versus India

Source: Based on data in Table 3.5.

---

[6] In the NSS data, regions in Maharashtra are classified as follows:

1. Coastal: Greater Mumbai, Suburban Mumbai, Thane, Raigarh, Ratnagiri and Sindhudurg.
2. Inland Western: Ahmednagar, Pune, Satara, Sangli, Solapur and Kolhapur.
3. Inland Northern: Nandurbar, Nashik, Dhule and Jalgaon.
4. Inland Central: Aurangabad, Parbhani, Beed, Latur, Nanded, Osmanabad, Jalna and Hingoli.
5. Inland Eastern: Buldhana, Akola, Washim, Amravati, Yavatmal, Wardha and Nagpur.
6. Eastern: Bhandara, Gadchiroli, Chandrapur and Gondia.

Growth, Equity and Inclusion 37

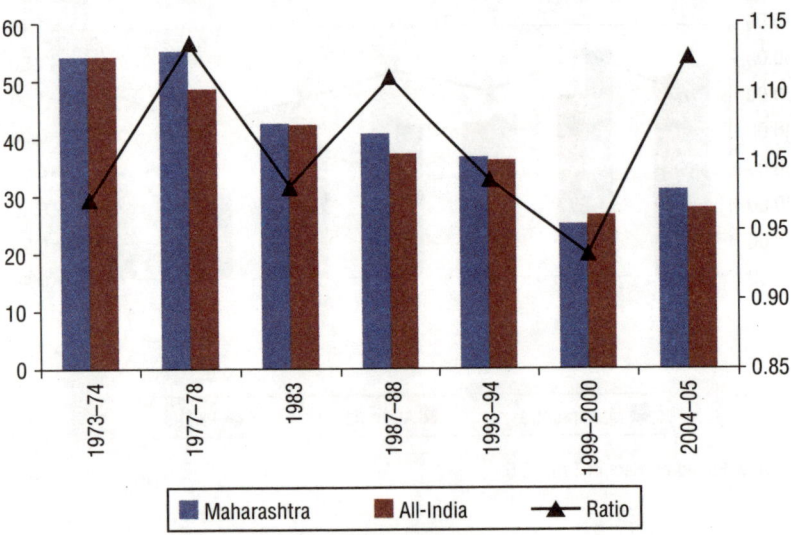

FIGURE 3.9 Incidence of Rural and Urban Poverty: Maharashtra versus India

Source: Based on data in Table 3.5.
Note: Ratio refers to ratio of estimate for Maharashtra to that of India as a whole.

a unique ranking by both these two alternative measures of averages when it comes to identifying the poorest region. The Inland Northern region is the poorest by the mean measure and the Eastern region the poorest by median consumption level. This would mean that the Inland Northern region in general is the poorest in rural Maharashtra.

In rural Maharashtra, mean and median consumption levels disaggregated by social groups find persons belonging to the 'Others' category the most well off, followed by the OBC, SC and ST, in that order. Across the four regions of Coastal, Inland Western, Inland Central and Eastern, persons belonging to the Others category were the most well off. In the remaining two regions, the OBC enjoyed the highest levels of living (mean as well as median) in the Inland Northern region and the highest median consumption levels in the Inland Eastern region, implying that the distribution was much broader based for this social group. Persons belonging to the ST were found to be the worst off in mean and median levels of consumption in four of the six regions, namely, Coastal, Inland Northern, Inland Eastern and Eastern. The SC were the worst off in the Inland Western and the Inland Central region. In sum, the profile of consumption distribution within and across social groups is not the same across regions.

The profile of consumption by social groups in urban areas is very similar to that in rural areas. At the aggregate state level, the Others category was the most well off by mean as well as median consumption levels, followed by the OBC, ST and SC, in that order. Region-wise comparisons showed persons belonging to the 'Others' category to be the most well off in the Coastal, Inland Western and Inland Northern regions. By estimates of median consumption, the OBC were the most well off in the Inland Eastern and the Eastern regions; and the ST in the Inland Central region (by both mean and median estimates). The ST performed the worst, with the lowest mean and median values in the Inland Northern, Inland Eastern and Eastern region. The Coastal region performed the best and the Inland Central region the worst for consumption distribution across regions for all social groups.

Extent of Deprivation (Incidence of Poverty) by Sector

For 2004–05, in the rural areas of Maharashtra, across regions, the profile of poverty by social groups generally tallies with the common perception, namely, it is the lowest for persons belonging to the Others category (in the Coastal, Inland Central and Eastern regions) while the OBC have the least incidence (in the remaining three regions, namely, Inland Eastern, Inland Western and Inland Northern). Deprivation, as measured by incidence of poverty, is found to be the highest amongst the ST in rural parts of all the regions, except the Inland Central region where the SC experience the highest incidence of poverty. At the aggregate state level, the Others category had the lowest and the ST the highest incidence of rural poverty (see Table 3.6). Overall region-wise estimates of rural poverty showed the Inland Western region having the lowest and the Eastern region having the highest incidence of poverty across regions.

In urban areas across regions, poverty estimates reflecting deprivation were the least amongst those belonging to the Others category in all regions, except the Inland Central where the ST had the lowest poverty values and the Inland Eastern region where the OBC had the lowest value for the same. On the other hand, the ST reported the highest incidence of poverty in the Eastern, Inland Eastern and Inland Northern regions, the SC in the Inland Western, and Inland Central and the OBC in the Coastal region. Overall, region-wise estimates of urban poverty revealed that the Coastal region has the lowest and the Inland Central region has the highest incidence of deprivation. As regards social groups, the welfare ranking based on the extent of deprivation in ascending order was Others, followed by the OBC, ST and SC (see Table 3.6).

TABLE 3.6
Incidence of Poverty across Social Groups, by Region, in Maharashtra: 2004–05

Region	ST	SC	OBC	Others	Total
Rural Areas					
Coastal	60.8	26.5	14.3	7.5	26.0
Inland Western	19.9	15.3	7.8	8.3	9.5
Inland Northern	62.8	60.1	18.2	27.9	37.9
Inland Central	44.2	64.9	46.7	30.6	42.6
Inland Eastern	55.5	44.7	2230	42.8	33.5
Eastern	70.8	46.9	40.7	35.8	47.1
Total	56.3	44.8	24.1	18.6	29.6
Urban Areas					
Coastal	18.2	18.5	19.4	12.0	14.5
Inland Western	37.4	55.5	37.0	31.3	36.8
Inland Northern	60.5	55.5	50.2	41.8	48.2
Inland Central	48.1	69.4	65.5	65.2	66.2
Inland Eastern	59.3	49.2	40.7	50.9	46.9
Eastern	64.5	50.6	32.0	25.2	35.8
Total	40.9	42.8	35.6	26.8	32.1

Source: Author's estimates based on the NSS central sample unit record data from the NSS 61st round (2004–05).
Note: Estimates of poverty correspond to the conventional poverty lines of ₹362.3 and ₹665.9 for the rural and urban sectors respectively.

A Disaggregate Profile

District-wise estimates of per capita consumption, inequality in consumption distribution and incidence of poverty (see Tables 3A.11 and 3A.12) were arrived at by pooling the central and state samples of the NSS data for the years 1993–94 and 2004–05. Still, the sample size was inadequate (Government of Maharashtra 2009) for several districts.[7] Given such a scenario, certain computational problems and inconsistencies that needed to be tackled were:

1. Lack of clarity on how far some results were realistic and valid. For instance, the estimates based on the pooled state and central samples showed that about half of the rural population in the Pune division belonged to a single richest expenditure group (greater than → ₹580 per capita per month) while about one-third of the rural population in the Aurangabad division belonged to the single poorest expenditure group (less than ₹365 per capita per month) (Government of Maharashtra 2009: 1). For the urban area it was found that about 52 per cent of the population in the Konkan division belonged to the uppermost group of MPCE (more than ₹1,100) while about 53 per cent of the population in the Aurangabad division belonged to the lowest group of MPCE (less than ₹580) (Government of Maharashtra 2009: 1).

2. Given the observed growth profile across the districts in the preceding sections, one would have expected a uniform pattern of change in the incidence of poverty across districts. However, a comparison

---

[7] Even after pooling the central and state samples, the number of first-stage units were small (16 villages) in the rural sector for Sindhudurg, Hingoli, Parbhani, Akola, Washim, Wardha, Bhandara and Gadchiroli. Similarly the number of urban blocks was less than 20 for Raigarh, Ratnagiri, Sindhudurg, Satara, Nandurbar, Dhule, Hingoli, Parbhani, Jalna, Beed, Latur, Osmanabad, Buldhana, Washim, Yavatmal, Wardha, Bhandara, Gondia and Gadchiroli, which in turn could be expected to adversely affect the reliability and robustness of the estimates.

Box 3.1 Children in Poverty: Rural–Urban Profile

Children in poverty or child deprivation can be defined as the percentage of children living in households below the poverty line. Estimates for the same for 2004–05 reveal the following (see Table 3.7):

In the rural areas of the state:

1. At the aggregate level of the region, the Inland Western region had the lowest incidence of children in poverty and the Eastern region the highest.
2. The incidence of children in poverty was the lowest for children belonging to the Others category amongst the social groups in the Coastal, Inland Western, Eastern and Inland Central regions.
3. It was the least for children belonging to the OBC in the remaining two regions, Inland Eastern and Inland Northern.
4. ST children showed the highest prevalence of poverty in five of the six regions, the exception being the Inland Central region where the SC children experienced the highest extent of deprivation.
5. Ranking of social groups at the aggregate state level for children in poverty in rural areas in ascending order was: Others (lowest), followed by the OBC, SC and ST.

In the urban areas of the state:

1. The incidence of children in poverty was again the lowest for the Others category amongst the social groups in three of the six regions—Coastal, Inland Northern and Inland Eastern. The proportion of children in poverty was the least for the SC in the Inland Central region, for the ST in the Inland Western region and the OBC in the Inland Eastern region.
2. SC children experienced the highest incidence of deprivation in the Eastern, Inland Northern and Inland Western regions; ST children in the Inland Eastern region; OBC children in the Coastal region; and Others in the Inland Central region.
3. At the aggregate level of urban sector, the Coastal region had the lowest incidence of child poverty and the Inland Central region the highest.
4. Ranking of social groups at the aggregate state level for children in poverty in urban areas in ascending order was: Others (lowest), OBC, ST and SC.

TABLE 3.7
Incidence of Child Poverty across Social Groups, by Region, in Maharashtra: 2004–05

Region	ST	SC	OBC	Others	Total
Rural Sector					
Coastal	68.2	33.2	22.2	9.5	35.5
Inland Western	29.1	20.1	11.9	11.1	13.2
Inland Northern	74.1	67.3	25.1	36.2	49.4
Inland Central	48.7	72.3	57.3	39.5	52.5
Inland Eastern	67.5	62.5	28.9	58.1	44.3
Eastern	76.4	55.7	51.5	27.4	55.5
Total	66.0	56.1	32.0	25.0	38.8
Urban Sector					
Coastal	16.4	23.2	25.1	21.6	22.5
Inland Western	38.9	64.9	44.7	40.5	46.1
Inland Northern	54.9	71.6	61.0	47.7	57.8
Inland Central	73.7	72.1	74.2	75.6	74.3
Inland Eastern	72.9	58.5	38.6	62.0	51.9
Eastern	61.1	71.0	34.2	26.6	39.0
Total	43.7	52.7	40.9	38.4	41.9

Source: Author's estimates based on the NSS central sample unit record data from the NSS 61st round (2004–05).
Note: Estimates of poverty correspond to the conventional poverty lines of ₹362.3 and ₹665.9 for the rural and urban sectors respectively.

between the estimates for 1993–94 and 2004–05 did not reveal any such pattern. The direction as well as the extent of change in poverty differed substantially between rural and urban sectors across districts and within administrative divisions. The data did not also reveal any consistent pattern with respect to changes in district domestic product (DDP) or spatial location.

The three broad findings from the district-level analysis (2004–05) of per capita consumption, inequality in consumption distribution and incidence of poverty are:

1. *First*, across the districts, the extent of inequality in consumption distribution was more in urban areas when compared to rural areas. Within the rural sector, the extent of inequality in consumption was relatively higher in the Konkan division while in the urban areas it was the highest in the Pune division.

2. *Second*, in terms of consumption deprivation, the incidence of rural poverty was the highest in the districts belonging to the Aurangabad division (more than 30 per cent) and lowest in the Pune division (less than or around 10 per cent). On the urban front, the incidence of poverty was seen to be the highest again in the Aurangabad division (more than 50 per cent) and lowest in the Konkan division (less than 20 per cent).
3. *Third*, the rural–urban disparity in deprivation was quite pronounced in Amravati division.

Calorie, Protein and Fat Intake: The Nutrition Intake Dimension

Disaggregated Rural–Urban Profile

Measures of economic access point confidently towards improvements across decile groups in rural and urban Maharashtra. It is observed (as already pointed out in the MHDR 2002) that such improvements in economic access have not translated into corresponding increases in cereal consumption (see Table 3A.14) and calorie intake across decile groups in both the rural and urban parts of the state. For rural Maharashtra it is found that:

1. Like the all-India trend, cereal consumption has seen a continuous decline. The total monthly per capita cereal consumption has shown a drop from about 13.5 kg during the mid-1970s to less than 11 kg in 2004–05. The estimates of cereal consumption for the bottom decile groups have also shown a decline (see Tables 3A.13 and 3A.14).
2. As regards the other two nutrients, protein intake has virtually been stable while fat intake has increased for all decile groups (see Tables 3A.15).
3. The average calorie intake in rural Maharashtra has decreased since 1983, similar to the all-India trend. There was a decline in the calorie intake of all the decile groups of rural population between 1983 and 1993–94. Further, for a majority of the rural decile groups as well as the total rural population, the calorie intake further declined by 2004–05 (see Table 3A.15). The decrease in calorie intake might be attributable to technological advancements and hence changing lifestyles.[8] Like in all of India and some other states, Maharashtra is also witnessing calorie intakes less than the normative minimum of 2,400[9] kilocalories (kcal) (see Tables 3A.15, 3A.16 and 3A.17).

For urban Maharashtra on the other hand we find:

1. Cereal consumption shows a somewhat uneven pattern, decreasing until 1986–87, increasing in 1987–88 and then showing a stable decline until 2004–05 (except for a slight increase in 1999–2000) (see Table 3A.14). As regards the other two nutrients, protein intake again shows a decrease for all the decile groups between 1972–73 and 2000–05, while fat intake increased for all decile groups (see Table 3A.18).
2. The average calorie intake declined between 1983 and 1993–94 and further reduced in 2004–05 for all the decile groups (see Table 3A.18).
3. The incidence of calorie deficiency corresponding to the norm of 2,100 calories saw a decline from 70.1 per cent in

---

[8] With economic growth and development involving structural and technological changes, observed consumption patterns have changed. This could be reflecting changes in minimum nutritional requirements. The Government of India (GoI) has also recognized that physical activity level and energy requirement has declined over the decades (Suryanarayana 2009b).

[9] The official definition of 'poor' as stated by the Sixth Planning Commission is: those whose per capita consumption expenditure lies below the midpoint of the MPCE class having a per capita daily calorie intake of 2,400 kcal in rural areas and 2,100 kcal in urban areas.

1972–73 to 67.8 per cent in 1983; it remained about the same level (68.3 per cent) in 1993–94 but increased to 78 per cent in 2004–05. This might be again a consequence of technological advances.

Disaggregated District Profile

For the purposes of a district-level analysis on nutritional intake, data availability was a major constraint. Yet, in order to facilitate analysis at the more disaggregated level of the districts, data for the share of food in total expenditure in rural and urban areas was studied for 2004–05 (see Tables 3A.18 and 3A.19). Some useful and interesting findings emerge and are detailed below.

First, households in rural Maharashtra spend on an average at least half of their total consumption budget on food. Of the 33 rural districts, 16 showed a budget share allocated to food less than the state average (between 43 per cent and 52 per cent). The remaining districts (majority) spent a high proportion of their household budget on food (52 per cent to 58 per cent). The profile of expenditure on food and non-food items under review indicates that the poorest districts, like Gadchiroli, as well as the richest districts, like Sangli, had a larger share of expenditure on food (see Table 3A.19), which would imply that there are factors other than income which necessitate larger budget shares on food.

Second, in rural areas such a finding is also confirmed by the sharp fluctuations across districts in food budget shares (see Figure 3.10). For example, corresponding to a per capita expenditure of about ₹600, household food budget shares vary from as low as 40 per cent to as high as 60 per cent of total expenditure. At the same time, there are households with total expenditure ranging from ₹550 to ₹850, which show the same fraction as their food budget (47 per cent). Thus, what we find is the existence of both multiple food shares for the same total expenditure and multiple total expenditure for the same food share. This is clearly a puzzle because, ceteris paribus,[10] economic theory would predict

FIGURE 3.10 District-Wise Food Security Profile: Rural Maharashtra

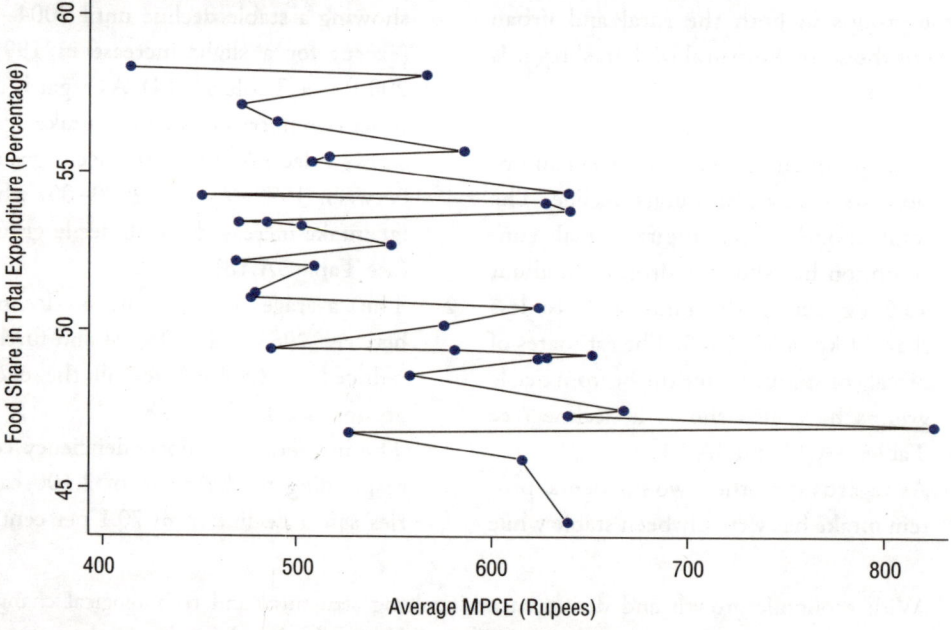

Source: Author's calculations based on Government of Maharashtra (2009).

[10] This is a Latin phrase that translates approximately to 'holding other things constant' and is usually rendered in English as 'all other things being equal'. In economics and finance, the term is used as shorthand to indicate the effect of one economic variable on another, holding constant all other variables that may affect the second variable.

the food budget share to be a smooth single-valued declining function of per capita total real expenditure.

Such sharp fluctuations in the share of food in total household expenditure as exhibited in Figure 3.10 could be due to the following factors: (*a*) per capita total expenditure at current prices per se does not explain food shares, which could be because of inter-district variations in prices and hence, nominal expenditure does not measure real expenditure satisfactorily, (*b*) in addition to income, there are other economic and non-economic factors, which account for sharp variations in food expenditure across districts and (*c*) sample data inadequacies. The non-economic factors could include limited physical access and high costs of procuring food, which further call for food-policy interventions to promote both economic and physical access. Nevertheless, such a finding calls for immediate food-policy interventions on multiple fronts in rural Maharashtra.

The scenario in urban Maharashtra seems to be relatively better from a food share perspective and is reflected in lower estimates for the food budget share. The budget shares across districts are found to be a declining function of per capita total expenditure, which would suggest that inter-district variations in the share of food to total expenditure can be explained in terms of variations in total income or expenditure (see Figure 3.11 and Table 3A.20). Thus, economic access seems to be a major determining factor in the urban scenario, calling for interventions such as income-enhancing programmes by the State.

Summing Up

1. Maharashtra continues to be one of the fastest growing states of the Indian union with the acceleration in it its growth process sustained largely by the tertiary sector.
2. The spatial dimension of the growth process reflects that poorer districts such as Dhule have grown faster than the state as a whole and relatively richer districts like Mumbai have performed less than the average. This has been made possible partly by perceptible growth in the primary sector. Such improvements in the primary sector in the poorer districts, however, are not reflected at the macro level because the share of these districts in the state total is negligible.
3. The fastest growing quarter consists of Nandurbar, Solapur, Hingoli, Jalna, Ahmednagar, Parbhani, Yavatmal, Nashik and Jalgaon, while Mumbai falls into the less performing quarter.

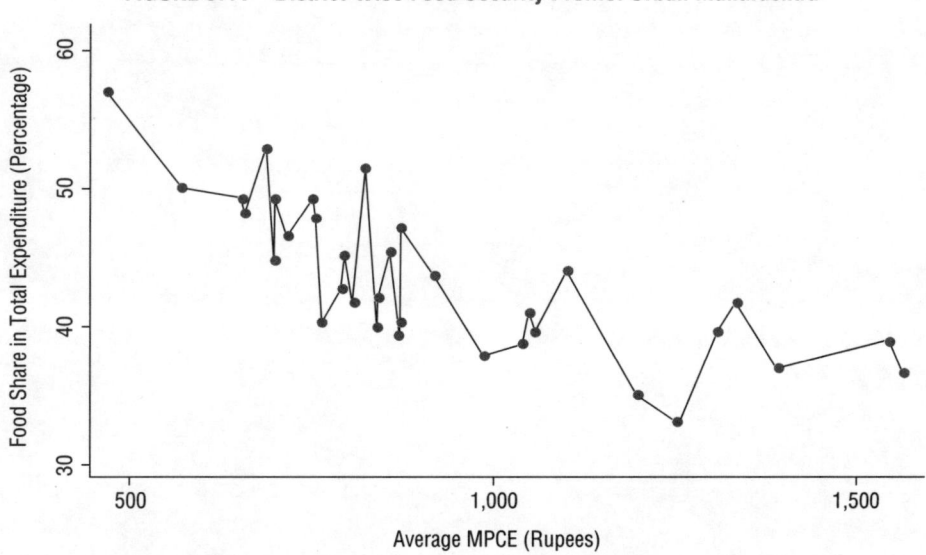

FIGURE 3.11 District-Wise Food Security Profile: Urban Maharashtra

Source: Author's calculations based on Government of Maharashtra (2009).

As a result, there has been a change in the profile of inter-district disparities in per capita income generated.

4. The poorest district of Washim in Maharashtra had an income level of ₹23,628 per capita per annum in 2008–09, which is more than other backward states of India.

5. The incidence of rural poverty in Maharashtra relative to that in rural India as a whole has tended to decline over time while the corresponding estimate for urban Maharashtra has increased. Given the share of the rural poor, incidence of poverty in Maharashtra as a whole relative to that in India as a whole has shown a general tendency to decline.

6. Growth in employment in the non-agricultural sectors has not been commensurate with growth in income generation. Agriculture continues to be the major source of livelihood in the rural sector in particular. Its share in employment is proportionately more than that in income generation. As a result, relative product per worker in agriculture is much less than that in non-agriculture.

7. The dominance of agriculture as a source of employment in the rural sector accounts for much of the rural–urban disparities in income and deprivation.

8. The average calorie intake in rural Maharashtra has decreased since 1983, similar to the trend observed for India as a whole. In the rural and urban populations, the calorie intake declined in 2004–05. The decrease in calorie intake might be due to technological advancements and hence changing lifestyles.

9. Poor districts such as Gadchiroli as well as rich districts such as Sangli have high shares of expenditure on food, which implies that there are factors other than income that necessitate larger budget shares on food.

10. The progress in MPCE has not been inclusive as reflected in the ICs, which are marginally less in Maharashtra vis-à-vis India.

4

Education: A Means for Enhancing Capabilities

Motivation

Enhancing human capabilities is the main motive of efforts aimed at promoting human development outcomes. Amongst the various elements of human development that underlie and facilitate the enhancing of human capabilities, good education can be considered the cornerstone. Education contributes immensely to both social and economic growth by opening doors to human capabilities via empowering individuals with knowledge and skills, which in turn help them access opportunities for productive employment and empowers them with the means to tackle poverty. In the Twelfth Five Year Plan (2007–12) emphasis has been placed on 'education as a central instrument for achieving rapid and inclusive growth'. Education can be used as an effective tool for enhancing the capabilities of all sections of the population, including women, poor, backward social groups, those living in unreachable terrains as well as slums, and the marginalized, by providing accurate and sufficient educational inputs. Enhancing capabilities through education, along with bridging the existing social, regional and gender gaps, forms the backbone of any human development effort.

In this chapter, along with studying trends and patterns in literacy, enrolment, school participation (measured by attendance) and schooling resources, we also attempt to review the existing evidence on quality and learning outcomes to assess how far the state of Maharashtra has come and how far it has to go in terms of ensuring educational outcomes of satisfactory quality for all school-going children. Given the importance being placed on the universalization of secondary education by the state, we have restricted our scope up to the level of secondary education. Data permitting, the disparities across regions, between cities and rural areas, boys and girls, and across social and income groups are analysed. The Report also takes stock of the progress made in education the last 10 years (since the MHDR in 2002) and outlines the challenges ahead.

Before embarking on a discussion of literacy and other educational attainments which are essential for capability enhancement, a brief demographic profile of the state is presented here. This would help to facilitate an initiation of the discussion on human development and capability enhancement, which is presented across three chapters (4, 5 and 6) touching upon education, health, housing, water and sanitation, which are imperative to human development

> The urbanization rate has been high, with the state accounting for 13.5 per cent of the urban population of the country.

Demographic Profile of Maharashtra

The enumerated population of Maharashtra based on Census 2011 figures is 112,372,972, which is approximately 9.3 per cent of India's population, making it the second most populous state in the country. Of this total population, 54.7 per cent resides in rural areas and 45.3 per cent in urban areas. The distribution of the state population has shown a remarkable shift towards urban areas (1951–2011) marking a population growth rate of 23.7 per cent, much higher than the 10.3 per cent population growth rate in rural areas (see Table 4.1 and Figure 4.1). The state also reports an increase in the number of villages, which has grown from 43,663 to 43,701 over 2001–11 and an increase in census towns by 152 over the same period.

The urbanization rate has been high, with the state accounting for 13.5 per cent of the urban population of the country (Government of India 2011b; see also Figure 4.2), which is also the highest amongst all the states (Uttar Pradesh, 11.8 per cent and Tamil Nadu, 9.3 per cent). Five metropolitan cities with a population greater than 10 million are located in Maharashtra, with the concentration of population near metro cities much higher than that nearer to smaller towns. The Konkan region, consisting of Mumbai and Thane districts, reports high urbanization with population increases in urban areas by 6 per cent during 1991 to 2011 while the Aurangabad, Nagpur and Pune divisions report an increase of 3 per cent in the same in the period under consideration.

TABLE 4.1
Total Population (1951–2011)

Census Year	Population of Maharashtra	Percentage of India's Population	Total Rural Population	Total Urban Population	Percentage of Urban Population
1951	32,002,564	8.9	22,801,551	9,201,013	28.8
1961	39,553,718	9.0	28,391,157	11,162,561	28.2
1971	50,412,235	9.2	34,701,024	15,711,211	31.2
1981	62,784,171	9.3	40,790,577	21,993,594	35.0
1991	78,937,187	9.3	48,395,601	30,541,586	38.7
2001	96,878,627	9.4	55,777,647	41,100,980	42.4
2011	112,372,972	9.3	61,545,441	50,827,531	45.2

Sources: Directorate of Census Operations Maharashtra (1951, 1961, 1971, 1981, 1991, 2001, 2011).

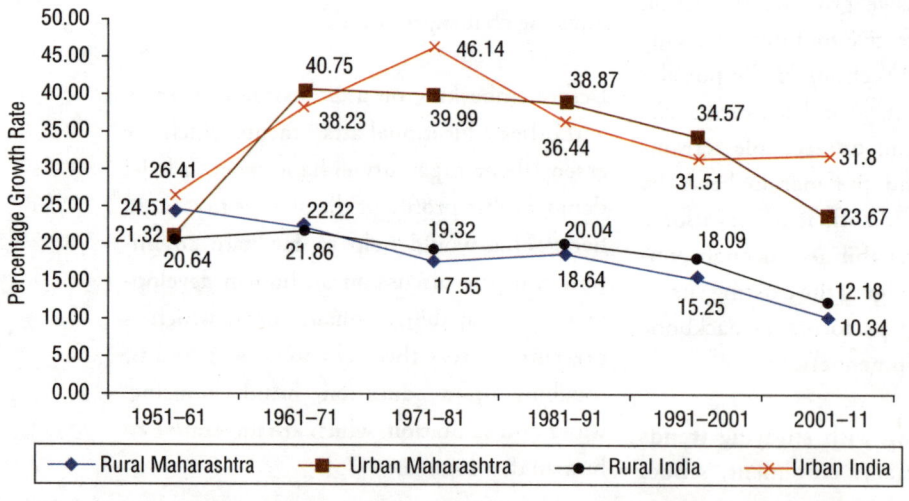

FIGURE 4.1 Decadal Population Growth Rate: India and Maharashtra (1951–61 to 2001–11)

Sources: Directorate of Census Operations Maharashtra (1951, 1961, 1971, 1981, 1991, 2001, 2011).

FIGURE 4.2 Trends in Urbanization: Maharashtra and India (1901–2011)

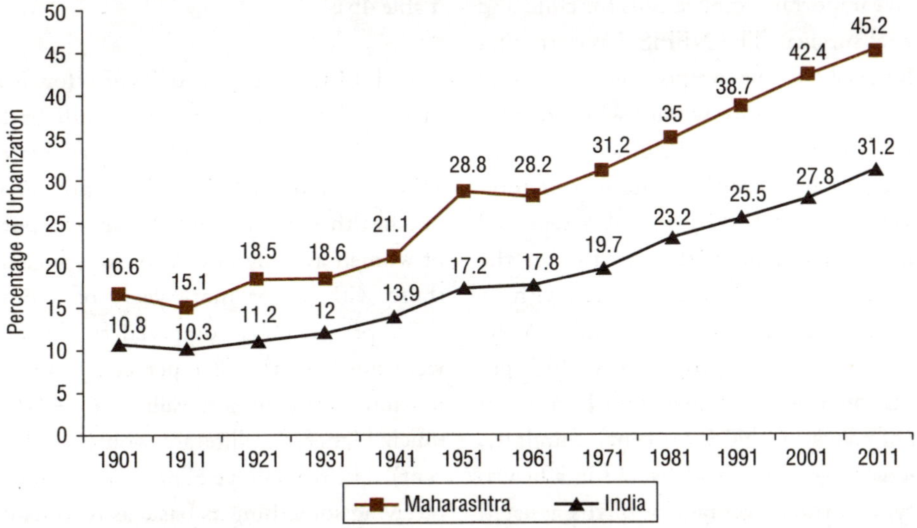

Sources: Directorate of Census Operations Maharashtra (1951, 1961, 1971, 1981, 1991, 2001, 2011).

Education and Its Interlinkages

Education is one of the principal means of improving the welfare of individuals through the myriad ways in which it exerts an influence on the socioeconomic, health and nutritional status of the populace as well as various other development-related outcomes. Female literacy and education has been shown to have far-reaching effects on child health and nutrition, participation of children in schooling as well as in the narrowing of the gender gap for various human development indicators. The data from NFHS-3 (2005–06) indicates that as we move up the wealth quintile ladder, the percentage of both men and women completing 10 or more years of education increases, implying that educational attainment and wealth status are possibly closely interlinked (see Figure 4.3). Besides the economic benefits that education brings to individuals, it also can be seen to be associated with enhancing individual ability to access and utilize various facilities.

The strong connection between female education and the effective usage of various maternal health infrastructural facilities is brought out lucidly by the NFHS as well as DLHS data for Maharashtra. The NFHS-3 data (2005–06) demonstrates clearly the link between infant mortality and maternal education. It is found that children born to women with no education are more than three times as likely to die before their first birthday as compared to children born to women who have completed 10 or more years of schooling. The risk of child mortality and under-five mortality is four or five times higher for children born to mothers with no education. The neonatal mortality is found to be three times more for mothers having no education as compared to those having completed 10 or more years of education (IIPS and Macro International 2008: Table 31).

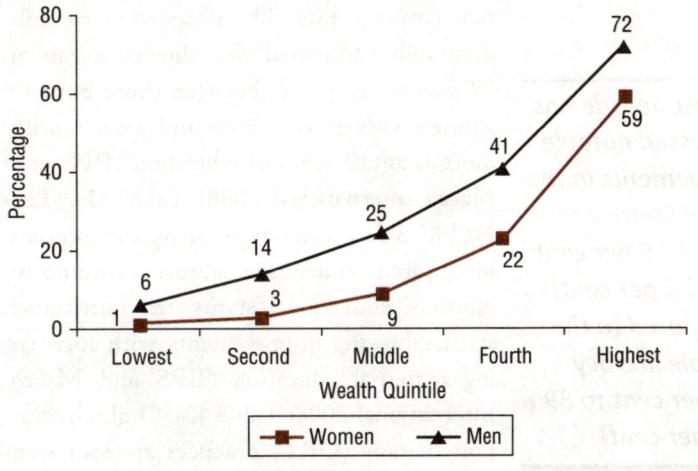

FIGURE 4.3 Percentage of Women and Men Aged 20–49 Who Have Completed At Least 10 Years of Education, by Wealth Quintile, NFHS-3: India

Source: Kishor and Gupta (2009).

Education 47

Access to and availing of assisted birth facilities have important implications for child and maternal survival. The NFHS-3 reports that in Maharashtra, the proportion of assisted births was far larger for women who had education of 10 years or more (unassisted births as low as 0.7 per cent). The number of antenatal check-ups (ANCs) was also reported to increase manifold with increases in the education levels of mothers. Women with no education were found to have availed of ANC visits in much lower proportions (46.3 per cent) as compared to women with 10 or more years of education (90.9 per cent). Similarly, the percentage of births delivered in a health facility, and the percentage of births assisted by health personnel showed sharp differentials according to female educational status, being much higher for women with 10 or more years of education. Also, the proportion of women undergoing postnatal check-ups was twice for those with 10 or more years of education when compared to women with no education (IIPS and Macro International 2008: Tables 35, 38). Thus, there clearly emerges a strong link between levels of female education and the utilization rates for various health facilities that impact maternal and child health.

Female education has a bearing on child vaccination rates. In 2005–06, while 8.1 per cent of children born to mothers with no education had not received any vaccination, those born to mothers with 10 or more years of education had a 100 per cent vaccination coverage rate. The proportion of children fully vaccinated also showed a gap of 22 percentage points between those born to women with no education and women with more than 10 years of education (IIPS and Macro International 2008: Table 41). The NFHS-3 data also reports sharp differentials in children's nutritional status, according to mothers' educational status, the nutritional status showing improvements with increasing maternal education (IIPS and Macro International 2008: Table 48). Oral rehydration therapy (ORT) practices are also seen to increase with increasing female education levels (IIPS and Macro International 2008: Table 45).

The DLHS-3 data (2007–08) for Maharashtra also supplements the findings from the NFHS-3 on the link between maternal education levels and the utilization of various health-related facilities. The proportion of women availing any ANC was higher for those with 10 or more years of education (97.9 per cent) as compared to those who were not literate (78.1 per cent). The proportion of women not availing any ANC was much higher for illiterate women (24.2 per cent). The percentage of pregnant women not receiving something as basic as tetanus injections was as high as 26.4 for illiterate women. Non-literate women were also reported to have had institutional deliveries in much lesser proportions (34.6 per cent) compared to women with 10 or more years of education (85.7 per cent). Full immunization rates of children were also reported to improve with maternal education (80.4 per cent for children born to women with 10 or more years of education vis-à-vis 48.9 per cent for those born to non-literate women). Thus the probability of women accessing and availing health facilities that have an important bearing on their as well as their children's health, longevity and safety is found to increase with their education.

Literacy Achievements

The literacy rate for Maharashtra has remained consistently higher than the national average. Maharashtra currently ranks 12th amongst all states, with a literacy rate of 82.9 per cent as per the Census 2011 (male literacy rate of 89.8 and a female literacy rate of 75.5), surpassing the national average by well over eight percentage points (Government of India 2011b). The state has shown good progress over the last 60 years, improving its literacy rate by almost 50 percentage points (see Figure 4.4). The last decade has witnessed notable improvements in the female literacy rate (from 67.5 per cent to 75.5 per cent) compared to the male literacy (86.3 per cent to 89.8 per cent).

The last decade has witnessed notable improvements in the female literacy rate (from 67.5 per cent to 75.5 per cent) compared to the male literacy (86.3 per cent to 89.8 per cent).

FIGURE 4.4   Trends in Male and Female Literacy: Maharashtra (1951–2011)[1]

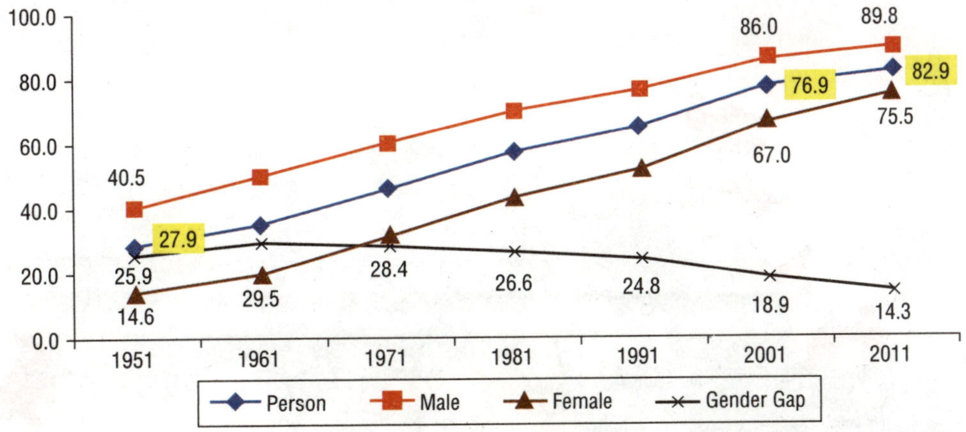

Year	Person	Male	Female	Gender Gap
1951	—	40.5	14.6	25.9
1961	—	—	—	29.5
1971	—	—	—	28.4
1981	—	—	—	26.6
1991	—	—	—	24.8
2001	—	86.0	67.0	18.9
2011	82.9	89.8	75.5	14.3

Highlighted: 27.9 (Person, early) and 76.9 (Person, 2001).

Source: Directorate of Census Operations Maharashtra (1951, 1961, 1971, 1981, 1991, 2001, 2011).
Note: Figures are indicated in percentage terms.

It appears that the male literacy rate is reaching a plateau while the female literacy rate is closing the gender gap. These changes are also reflected in improvements in the gender parity index (GPI)[2] for literacy, which has seen a rise from 0.4 in 1951 to 0.8 in 2011.

Literacy data from the Census 2011 shows that in rural areas the gender gap in literacy was approximately 19 percentage points vis-à-vis 8.4 percentage points in urban areas, showing the persistence of a female disadvantage in literacy achievements. The female literacy rate in rural areas continues to be low at 67.4 per cent. Although the state has witnessed an overall improvement in district-level literacy rates, inter-district variations in literacy exist. Nandurbar reports the lowest literacy rate at the aggregate level (63.0 per cent) as well as when disaggregated by gender (53.9 per cent for females) amongst all the districts while Mumbai Suburban reports the highest literacy rate at the aggregate level (90.9) as well as for females (86.9). Jalna retains its status of having the highest gender gap in terms of the literacy rate, although there has been a decrease in this gap over the decade 2001–11 (30.1 percentage points in 2001 and 23.9 percentage points in 2011, see Table 4A.1). Literacy data disaggregated further to the block-level highlights that 110 out of 357 blocks in the state report a literacy rate greater than the state average (see Figure 4.5). The cause for concern is, *first*, 13 blocks, which showcase literacy rates lower than the literacy rate of other backward states in India, and *second*, 57 blocks that report literacy rates less than the national average but higher than that of some backward states in India.

Variations in the literacy rate at the more disaggregated level of social groups can be studied using data from the 64th round of the NSS (2007–08). Amongst the social groups, at the aggregate level, the ST report the lowest literacy rate at 61.9 per cent (see Table 4A.2), with the literacy rate of the SC relatively higher at 77.8 per cent. When disaggregated by sector as well, the ST had the lowest literacy rate in rural Maharashtra (58.8 per cent) as well as in urban areas (79.4 per cent). The literacy status for males and females across all social groups was higher in urban areas of the state compared to their rural counterparts. This was also true for all the regions in the state. Inter-regional variations in the literacy rate across social groups can be seen (the ST report the lowest literacy

> Although the state has witnessed an overall improvement in district-level literacy rates, inter-district variations in literacy exist.

---

[1] Literacy Rate is calculated for 7+ population.
[2] Calculated as the ratio of the female literacy rate to the male literacy rate.

FIGURE 4.5 Block-Wise Literacy Rate

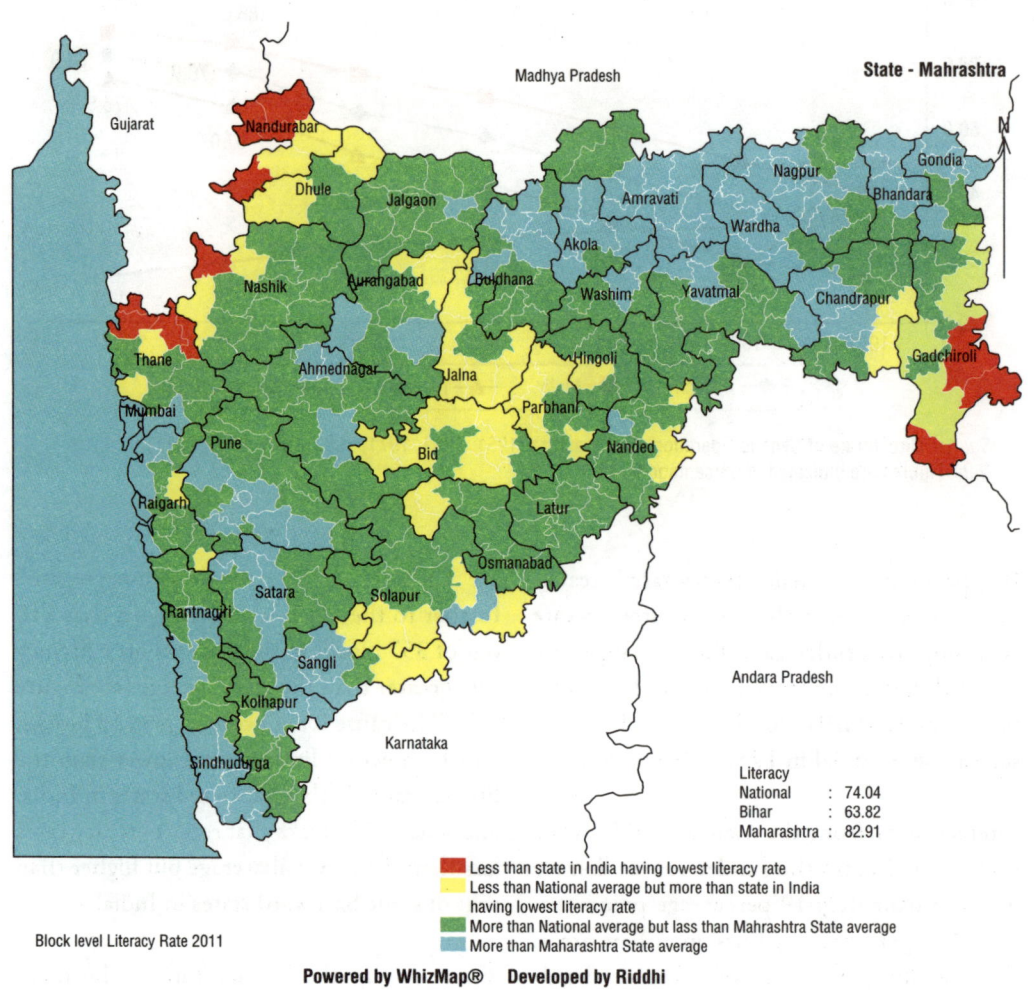

Source: Directorate of Census Operations Maharashtra (2011).

> *When the literacy rate for social groups was disaggregated by sex, the female literacy rate across all social groups was found to be well below the male literacy rate.*

rate in the Inland Northern region, while the Others category reports the highest in the Inland Eastern and Costal regions).

When the literacy rate for social groups was disaggregated by sex, the female literacy rate across all social groups was found to be well below the male literacy rate. Overall, the gender gap in literacy was found to be 24, 19, 15 and 11 percentage points respectively for the ST, SC, OBC and Others. When disaggregated by sector, in rural areas, the gender gap was quite high at approximately 25 percentage points for the ST, 22 percentage points for the SC and 17 percentage points for the OBC (see Table 4A.2). Similarly, in urban areas the gender gap for these social groups was 17, 13 and 11 percentage points respectively. Literacy rates for ST women were found to be low in rural areas across all regions (except in the Inland Eastern region), with the lowest being in rural parts of the Inland Northern region at 38.4 per cent. The Eastern region had the lowest urban literacy rate for ST women (44.6 per cent). The inter-regional variations in ST female literacy rates were also quite high. On the one hand, the Inland Northern region reported it to be as low as 39.7 per cent and on the other, literacy in the Inland Eastern region stood at 69.7 per cent. Similar variations within rural and urban areas were also found for female literacy rates for the ST/SC. Thus, literacy achievements in the state are yet to bridge the gap, especially for women residing in rural areas and belonging to backward social groups, especially the ST. 'Gender-sensitive inclusion' in literacy needs to be kept central to education policies in the state.

The adult (age 15+) literacy rate is a more useful indicator for development analysis as it has long lasting bearing on human development outcomes along with feedback effects. Research has shown that improvements in the adult male and female literacy rates have an encouraging effect on school attendance rates of children in the age group of 5–14 years, the same-sex effects being stronger than the cross-sex effects[3] (Jayachandran 2002). Data from the 64th round of the NSS analysed for adult literacy rates shows a gender gap of 18 percentage points at the aggregate level, which is higher at approximately 22 percentage points in rural areas (see Table 4A.3).

What is worth highlighting is that for the ST *first*, the adult female literacy rate is very low across a majority of regions; *second*, the rural–urban disparity in adult literacy rates is also quite prominent and *third*, there exist inter-regional variations in male and female adult literacy rates for this social group (see Tables 4A.3 and 4A.4). Thus the ST show up as the most deprived and marginalized groups in terms of adult literacy achievements in the state. While Maharashtra has made progress in overall improvements in the literacy rate, policy interventions need to take cognizance of the rural–urban, gender and social-group disadvantages that are still prevalent, especially for adult literacy rates.

Increasing Access and Rising Enrolment

The last two decades have witnessed increased school provisioning in Maharashtra, especially at the primary and secondary levels.[4] Primary school infrastructure, HR and enrolments have seen steady increases between 1970 and 2010–11. The number of primary schools has increased by more than 10 per cent in each decade over this period, the number of primary school teachers increasing by an average of 22 per cent, and the number of children in primary schools increasing by 27 per cent between 1990 and 2011.[5] Enrolment in primary classes has increased by 4.3 per cent between 2005–06 and 2011–12. On the other hand the enrolment for upper primary classes increased by 16.3 per cent (see Figure 4.6).

The rising enrolments could be attributed to increases in schooling facilities in the state. Data from DISE for the year 2010–11 (NUEPA 2011b) reveals that access to primary or upper primary schools is not an issue in most districts of Maharashtra as 72,353 (95.3 per cent) out of the total 75,884 habitations are served by primary schools (MPSP n.d.). Further for every two primary schools, an upper primary school is available in 26 districts and for every 2.5 primary schools an upper primary school is available in four districts of the state (see Figure 4.7). The ratio of schools having upper primary sections to the schools having secondary sections is found to vary from 3:8 in districts such as Ratnagiri to 1:4 in districts such as Dhule and Mumbai Suburb (see Table 4A.6).

> *The number of primary schools has increased by more than 10 per cent in each decade from 1970 to 2010.*

---

[3] Same-sex effect means that the positive effect of adult female literacy rate is higher for female child schooling, while the positive effect of adult male literacy is higher for male child schooling.

[4] For this section, data is used is primarily from three sources: statistics provided by the GoI and GoM (Ministry of Human Resource Development 2007; School Education Department 2001, 2002, 2003, 2004), District Information System for Education (DISE) data (Mehta 2004, 2005, 2006, 2007, 2008, 2009; NUEPA 2011b, 2012b), and ASER (Pratham 2005, 2006, 2007, 2008, 2009, 2010).

[5] See Ministry of Human Resource Development (2007), School Education Department (2001, 2002, 2003, 2004) and DISE data (Mehta 2004, 2005, 2006, 2007, 2008, 2009; NUEPA 2011b, 2012b). For figures, refer to Table 4A.5.

FIGURE 4.6 Primary and Upper Primary School Enrolment: Maharashtra (2005–11)

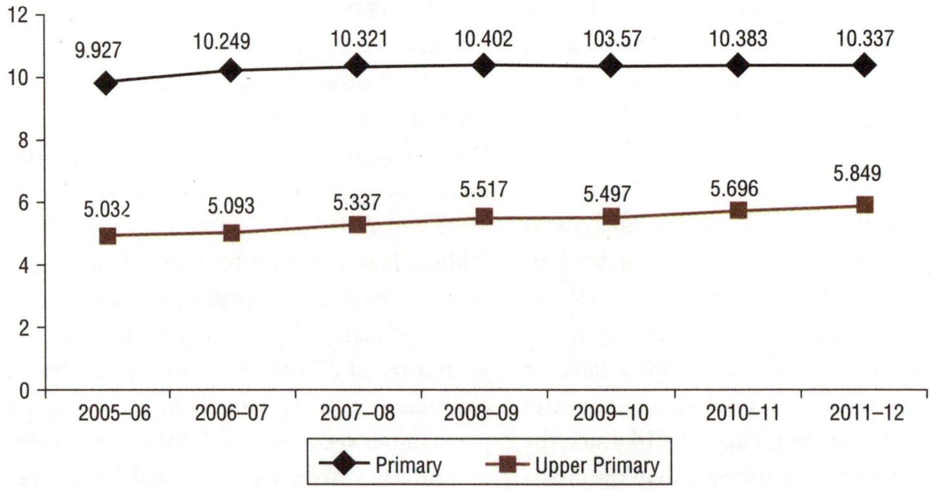

Year	Primary	Upper Primary
2005–06	9.927	5.032
2006–07	10.249	5.093
2007–08	10.321	5.337
2008–09	10.402	5.517
2009–10	103.57	5.497
2010–11	10.383	5.696
2011–12	10.337	5.849

Sources: Mehta (2007, 2008, 2009, 2011, 2012); NUEPA (2011b, 2012b).
Note: Enrolment figures are in lakhs.

Box 4.1 Human Development: Speaking to the People: School Enrolment

Universal enrolment was reported in primary schools by teachers, headmasters and government officers, except in the blocks of Soyegaon, Akkalkuwa and Kalamb. Some details reported on school enrolments include:

1. NGOs reported low child enrolments in Kalamb block, having a high concentration of the Pardhi community.
2. In the tribal Akkalkuwa block in Nandurbar, migration to Gujarat in search of livelihoods led to children either not enrolling or dropping out of school.
3. A similar situation was reported in Soyegaon (Aurangabad). Seasonal migration to other districts of Maharashtra for sugarcane cutting resulted in low school enrolments.

It was also reported that schemes such as free bus passes, midday meals (MDMs) and attendance allowance for girls enhanced female enrolments in school.

Source: Block-level consultations, YASHADA, December 2011.

In terms of provisioning, elementary education in Maharashtra is largely provided through government schools. Secondary education is mainly provided by privately aided institutions (see Figure 4.8) followed by private unaided schools and then by government secondary schools, which are relatively few in number (see Table 4A.7). The DISE data for various years indicates an increase in enrolments at the primary as well as upper primary levels in private schools in the state (NUEPA 2005 to 2011). As the IHDR indicates, "The phenomenal rise of private unaided institutions is of concern since enrolment in them is biased against girls and lower castes, leaving girls, SCs, STs to [sic] mostly in government schools" (Institute of Applied Manpower Research 2011).

As in the case of elementary schools, the number of secondary schools also increased by 63 per cent during 1980–90 and then by 48 per cent during the period 1990–2000, with the number of secondary school teachers increasing by an average of 47 per cent in each decade during 1970–2000. The number of children enrolled in secondary schools increased by a significant average of almost 60 per cent per decade across 1970–2000. During 2000 to 2001–12 the number of secondary schools increased by approximately 6,000 (46 per cent, Table 4A.5). Yet the number of teachers per school has actually fallen, especially so in the last 10 years. The reason may be the issues related to class VIII, which was initially treated as a part of secondary section, is included in the elementary section as per Right to Education Act 2009.

Female Enrolment in Education

The state witnessed an improvement in female participation in education (see Table 4A.8)

FIGURE 4.7 Ratio of Primary to Upper Primary Schools: Maharashtra (2010–11)

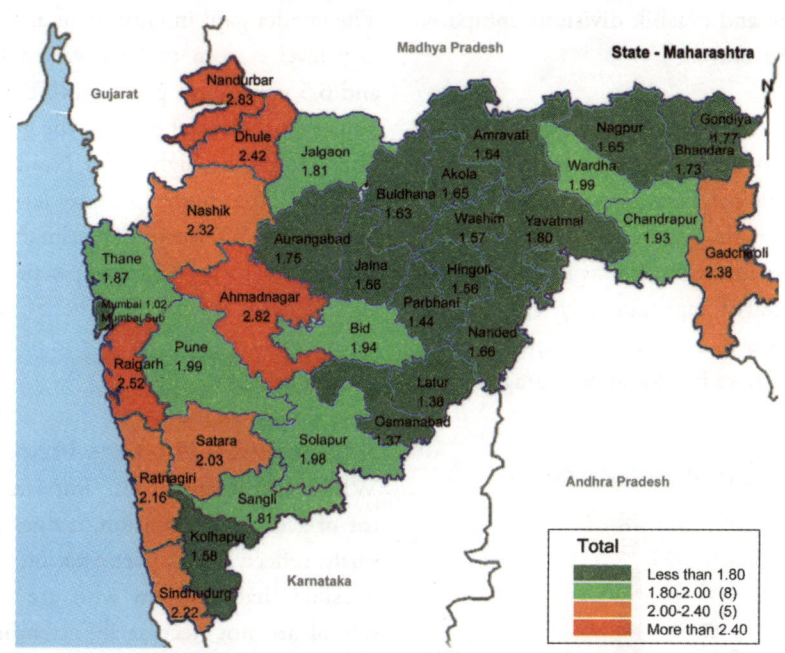

Source: Analysis by UNICEF based on DISE data for 2010–11 in NUEPA (2011b).

FIGURE 4.8 Types of Schools

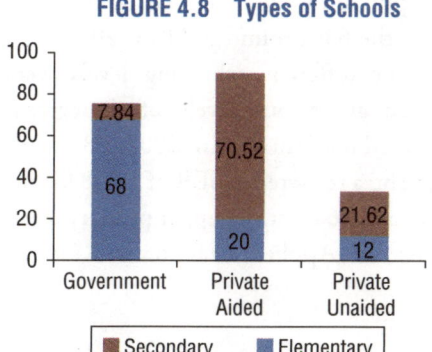

Sources: Mehta (2012); MPSP (2010, 2011, 2012); NUEPA (2011b, 2012b).

> **Box 4.2 Increasing Enrolment in Maharashtra: ASER[6] Survey**
>
> In 2011, almost every child in the age group of 6–13 years was enrolled in school, meeting a major Right to Education (RTE) goal for the state. For the age group of 6–13 years, it would be fair to say that across Maharashtra, for all regions, the state has reached universal enrolment. *Second*, a majority of children in the age group of 6–10 years were enrolled in government primary schools, and there was also an increase in the small proportion enrolled in private schools at the primary level (by two percentage points). *Third*, the provision of post primary education in Maharashtra has been in the private (often government-aided) domain. Over the last five years, a clear increase in private school enrolments in upper primary and secondary stages is observed.
>
> *Source:* Pratham (2011).

across the primary and secondary levels until 2008 and then slight decrease till 2011–12. Using DISE data for 2011–12 (NUEPA 2011b) it is found that female enrolment in primary and upper primary levels for the SC, ST and minorities ranges from 47 per cent to 51 per cent in all revenue divisions of the state (see Table 4.2). Female enrolment in

---

[6] The ASER is facilitated by Pratham, an NGO, and is carried out every year in every rural district in the country. It is the largest household survey of children in the country conducted outside the government domain. In each district, 30 villages are randomly selected and within each village, 20 households are also randomly selected for the survey. Every child in the age group of 3–16 years in the sampled households is covered. In 2011, the survey sample covered more than 300,000 households and 600,000 children in the country; in Maharashtra close to 20,000 households were surveyed covering 35,000 children.

elementary education is seen to be relatively low in Pune and Nashik divisions compared to the state average.

Block-level data[7] from DISE 2011–12 (NUEPA 2012b) shows that for 125 blocks and 8 municipal corporations (MNCs) in the state, female enrolment in the primary and upper primary levels was lower than the state average (of approximately 47 per cent) pointing towards the need for special interventions in these blocks to encourage female participation in schooling (see Table 4A.9). The gender gap[8] in enrolment at the elementary level is seen to have varied between 5 and 6.5 percentage points (NUEPA 2011b). Amongst the social groups, the gender gap is found to be the highest for Nomadic Tribes (NT) (10.6 at upper primary level) followed by the ST (7.7 for upper primary level) and *Vimukt Jati* (VJ) (7.2 for upper primary level) and General categories. The SC report the lowest gender gap (3.9 at the primary level) (see Figure 4.9).

Attendance Matters More

While enrolment is an important indicator of access to education, it does not necessarily reflect actual participation. It is quite possible that children who are enrolled in school are not necessarily attending school. Enrolment figures therefore may be much higher than actual attendance figures. Levels of actual participation in schooling are more aptly captured by the NAR. Using the dataset from the 64th round of NSS (2007–08), NARs for different schooling levels were calculated at various levels of disaggregation for Maharashtra.[9] In 2007–08, while Maharashtra reported a GER of 101.8 for the primary and 86.8 for the upper primary levels (Institute of Applied Manpower Research

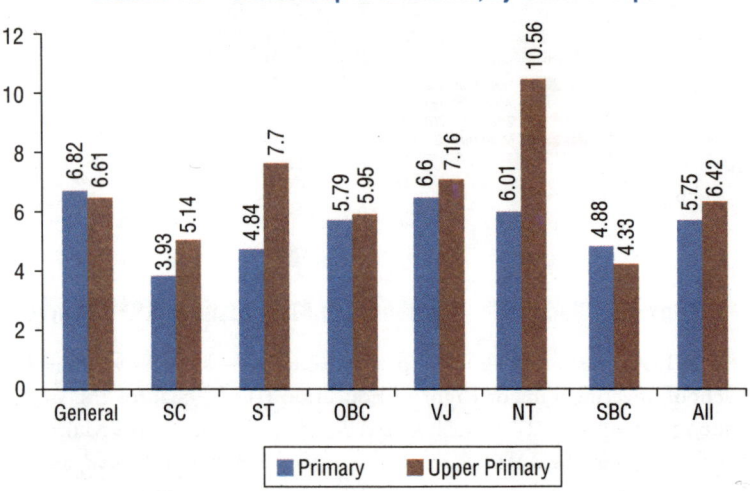

FIGURE 4.9 Gender Gap in Enrolment, by Social Groups

Source: NUEPA (2012b).
Note: SBC denotes Special Backward Class.

TABLE 4.2
Girls' Enrolment in Elementary Schools across Regions and Social Groups

Division	Total Children Enrolment in Primary and Upper Primary Schools	Percentage of Girls in All Children Enrolled in Primary and Upper Primary Schools (2011–12)			
		All	SC	ST	Minority
Nagpur	1,631,717	48	48	47	51
Amravati	1,706,752	47.4	48	48	50
Aurangabad	3,033,014	47.2	48	47	49
Pune	3,199,190	46.2	48	47	49
Konkan	3,771,150	47.2	48	47	49
Nashik	2,844,068	46.1	48	47	49
Maharashtra	16,185,891	46.9	48	47	49

Source: NUEPA (2012b).

---

[7] The source for all the data on GPI is DISE data for 2011–12 (NUEPA 2012b).
[8] Here, it refers to the difference between male and female enrolment rates.

2011), the NAR for the state was 90.8 per cent and 67.1 per cent respectively for these levels. Evidently, attendance has not kept pace with the high enrolments, especially at the upper primary levels. In terms of trends, the NAR at the primary and upper primary levels have seen an improvement across gender and sectors from 1995–96 to 2007–08 (see Table 4.3 and Figure 4.10). There has also been an evident narrowing of the gender gap in NARs at both these levels, in rural and urban areas of the state, and more so in rural areas, which needs mention..

At the primary level, the NAR for Maharashtra was about six percentage points more than the NAR for India (see Figure 4.10). The gender gap at primary level was negligible at the aggregate as well as for rural and urban areas. The upper primary NAR is 67.1 per cent, eight percentage points higher than the all-India average. The gender gap in upper primary NARs is also negligible around 0.2 percentage points, while in rural areas a female advantage is seen of two percentage points (see Figure 4.11).

TABLE 4.3
NAR at the Primary and Upper Primary Levels (1995–96 and 2007–08)

	Rural		Urban	
	1995–96	2007–08	1995–96	2007–08
Primary Level (Std I–V, 6–10 Years)				
Male	68.0	91.7	80.0	90.2
Female	56.0	91.3	77.0	89.2
Upper Primary Level (Std VI–VIII, 11–13 Years)				
Male	44.0	64.1	60.0	72.5
Female	32.0	66.5	57.0	67.7

Sources: Data for the NSS 52nd round (1995–96) from Institute of Applied Manpower Research (2011); information for the year 2007–08 is the author's calculations based on data from the 64th round of NSS (National Sample Survey Office 2009b).
Note: NAR is indicated in percentage terms.

Disaggregation by regions indicates highest NAR at aggregate level in Eastern region (which is a tribal belt) for both primary and upper primary level (see Table 4A.10). Interestingly the NAR figures for the Inland Northern region, which is also a tribal belt, are lowest.

The NARs at the primary and upper primary levels across MPCE quintiles do not show a

FIGURE 4.10 Primary-Level NAR: India and Maharashtra (2007–08)

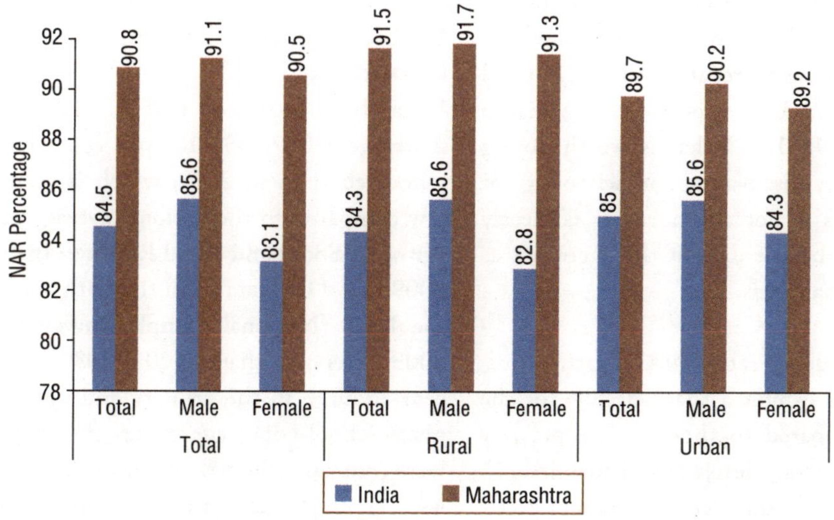

	Total			Rural			Urban		
	Total	Male	Female	Total	Male	Female	Total	Male	Female
India	84.5	85.6	83.1	84.3	85.6	82.8	85	85.6	84.3
Maharashtra	90.8	91.1	90.5	91.5	91.7	91.3	89.7	90.2	89.2

Source: Based on author's calculations using data from National Sample Survey Office (2009b).
Note: NAR is indicated in percentage terms.

---

[9] The 64th round (2007–08) of the NSS provides household- and individual-level data on the education particulars of persons in the 5–29 age group currently attending an educational institution at the primary level and above. Data disaggregated by age was extracted to suit the analysis presented here.

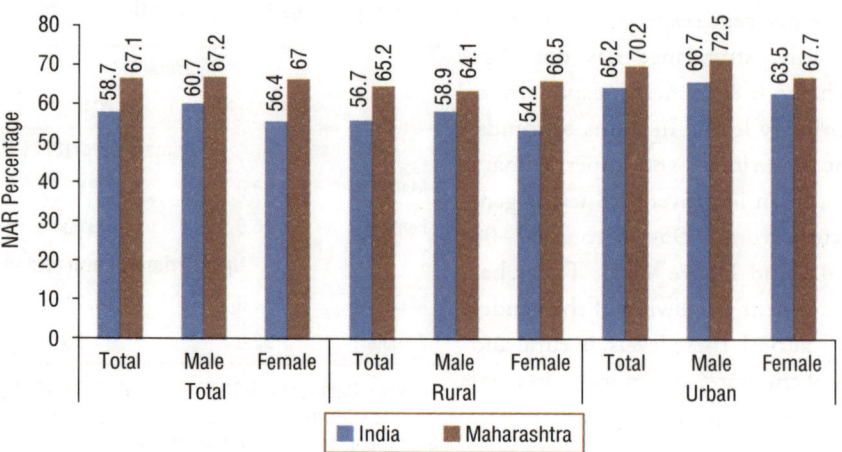

FIGURE 4.11 Upper Primary NAR: India and Maharashtra (2007–08)

Source: Based on author's calculations using data from National Sample Survey Office (2009b).
Note: NAR is indicated in percentage terms.

consistent rising pattern in school participation rates as we go up the MPCE ladder, both at the aggregate level and for rural and urban areas (see Table 4A.11).

Primary-level NARs for the SC, OBC and Others are higher than the state average at the aggregate level as well as when disaggregated by sex (see Figure 4.12, Table 4A.12). The ST still have a gap to breach, showing the lowest primary-level NARs at the state level (79.6 per cent). Social group disparities at the upper primary level again reveal the ST to be the most deprived group with the lowest NARs at the aggregate level and in rural areas, 55.4 and 52.3 respectively (see Figure 4.13, Table 4A.12). What is worth noting is that gender disadvantage in schooling for social groups is not the norm as is clearly brought out by the data at the aggregate as well as regional levels.

School attendance rates (NARs) at the secondary levels exhibit a sharp decline for the state as compared to those at the primary and upper primary levels (see Table 4A.13). At the state level the secondary school NAR was 59 per cent for boys and 52 per cent for girls. Rural NARs continued to be lower than their urban counterparts at the aggregate level as well as when disaggregated by gender. ST children showed a clear disadvantage, reporting the lowest NARs (33 per cent) which holds when disaggregated by gender as well (31.1 per cent for males and 35.7 per cent for females). The large rural–urban gap for ST NARs (approximately 25 percentage points, with NAR at 29.5 per cent in rural and 54 per cent in urban areas) reflects the wide intra-group disparity that exists in secondary school attendance. Within the social groups, a clear female advantage exists in school attendance amongst the STs and SCs.

Out-Of-School Children and Dropouts

It has been estimated that in Maharashtra there were 207,345 (1.3 per cent) out-of-school children in 2009, which is relatively low compared to the national average of 4.3 per cent (Social and Rural Research Institute 2009: 10–11). Data from the 64th round of the NSS (National Sample Survey Office 2009b) reports that in 2007–08, 11.6 per cent children in the primary and upper primary school-going age group (6–13 years) were out of school[10] in India (see Table 4A.14). In Maharashtra the corresponding proportion was 6.8 per cent (3.4 per cent who never enrolled and 3.4 per cent who had ever enrolled). Out-of-school children in the age group of 14–16 years (secondary level of

> *It has been estimated that in Maharashtra there were 207,345 (1.3 per cent) out-of-school children in 2009, which is relatively low compared to the national average of 4.3 per cent.*

---

[10] Out-of-school children can be taken to comprise those who have never enrolled in school and those who have enrolled in the past but are currently not attending school.

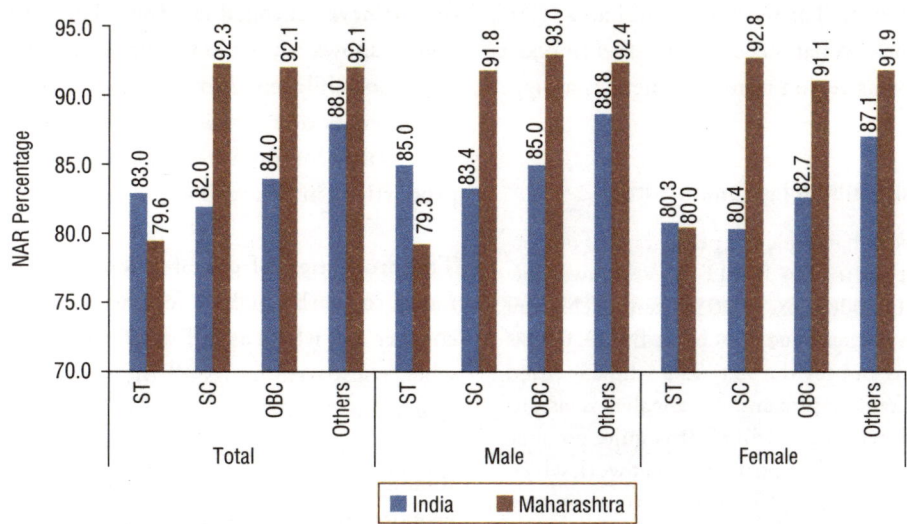

FIGURE 4.12 Primary-Level NAR, by Social Groups: Maharashtra (2007–08)

Source: Based on author's calculations using data from National Sample Survey Office (2009b).
Note: NAR is indicated in percentage terms.

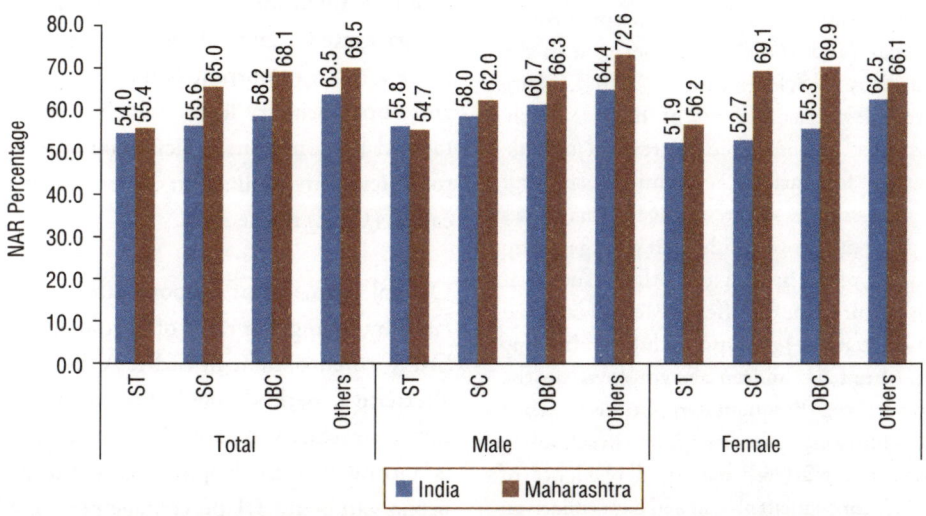

FIGURE 4.13 Upper Primary NAR, by Social Groups: Maharashtra (2007–08)

Source: Based on author's calculations using data from National Sample Survey Office (2009b).
Note: NAR is indicated in percentage terms.

schooling) are higher in proportion compared to those at the elementary level in the state. At the all-India level, 33 per cent of children in the secondary school going age were out of school in 2007–08 (see Table 4A.14). For Maharashtra, close to a fourth of the children's population in the same age group was out of school. There is no gender bias evident in the proportions of out-of-school children in the state, at the elementary level while a gender gap of 7.7 percentage points is evident at secondary level (see Table 4A.14).

A higher proportion of out-of-school children in rural areas is reported at elementary as well as at secondary level (see Table 4A.15). A closer look at the figures for out-of-school children at elementary reveals that children never enrolled were higher in proportion in the rural areas of the state (4.1 per cent) as compared to urban areas for elementary level (2.2 per cent). Regional disparities prevail, with the Inland Northern region (comprising Nandurbar, Dhule, Jalgaon and Nashik) having the highest proportion of

> *A higher proportion of out-of-school children in rural areas is reported at elementary as well as at secondary level.*

out-of-school children at the aggregate level (16.4 per cent) as well as in rural areas (20.2 per cent). What needs to be mentioned is that in this region non-enrolment is a bigger problem as reflected by the higher proportion of never-enrolled children. The Eastern region shows a very low proportion of out-of-school children, showcasing the possible effectiveness of education schemes for backward tribal communities that reside in large proportions in this region.

The proportion of out-of-school children is found to be the highest for the STs for the country as a whole as well as for Maharashtra when compared across all the social groups (see Table 4A.16). Social group disadvantage for ST children is again the norm with the Inland Northern region having the highest proportion of out-of-school children (53 per cent) and never-enrolled ST children (20.9 per cent). The Inland Central region had 43 per cent ST children in the ever-enrolled category, reflecting the need for strategies to promote retention (see Table 4A.16). The disaggregated data shows non-enrolment to be a more important issue at the primary and upper primary levels, which needs to be tackled by conscious policy making in order to achieve universalization of elementary education (UEE) in the state.

Official estimates of dropout rates are calculated by taking the ratio of enrolment in say Std V to enrolment in Std I. A more useful alternative methodology[12] to estimate dropout rates shows that in Maharashtra there is a rural bias in dropout rates, the rural–urban gap being 1.1 percentage points, while the gender gap is negligible at 0.2 percentage points (see Table 4A.17). Amongst the regions, the dropout rate is the highest in the

> **Box 4.3 Out-Of-School Children in Maharashtra**
>
> The ASER 2010 survey findings reveal that while the percentage of out-of-school children (in the age groups of 6–10 years and 11–13 years) was low in 2006, it further declined in 2010. In 2006, close to 10 per cent of children in the 14–15 years' age group were not enrolled in school. By 2010, this percentage dropped across all regions and for the state as a whole it stood at less than 5 per cent, with the Konkan, Nashik and Aurangabad divisions reporting higher proportions of children not in school. It is quite possible that as children get older there are pull as well as push factors at work which compel them to stay out of the schooling system.[11] The pull factors originate from increased opportunity costs to children's time as they are now able to engage in productive activities in or outside the home. The push factors constitute barriers to access to upper primary or secondary schools, thus impeding the child's ability to pursue education beyond the elementary level.
>
> Children enter the workforce in large numbers in the 16–17 years' age group and in 2006 the proportion of children in this age group not enrolled in school was 18 per cent for the state (and as high as 29 per cent in the Coastal region). It dropped substantially to 8.4 per cent in 2010. Despite high school-enrolment rates, there still persist pockets of 'hard-to-reach' children in both rural and urban areas. These children remain outside the purview of the education system for various economic, social and demographic reasons. Although the statute enforcing RTE mandates 'special training' for mainstreaming out of school children in the age group 6–14 children, a clearer understanding of the spatial and other issues that keeps these children out of school is required for the effectiveness of targeted interventions. Migration (intra- and interstate) disrupts a child's schooling cycle. In urban areas of cities like Mumbai, children are employed in the zari, embroidery and leatherworks industries. Frequent demolitions in urban slums are found to be another factor contributing to disruptions in schooling for children residing in these areas. The scattered nature of residence of these 'hard-to-reach' children and their consequent absence in data collection surveys (household- or school-based) makes it all the more difficult to plan interventions for their schooling.
>
> Sources: Pratham (2006, 2007, 2008, 2009, 2010).

---

[11] As children get older, there are two forces at work. There is a 'pull' factor—the opportunity cost of children's time begins to increase—children can now do other productive activities as well—such as working outside the home or in the home. And, there is a 'push' factor as well. There are often barriers or constraints to access—upper primary schools and secondary schools may be at a distance from the village or place of residence, making it not as easy to attend school as it was in the primary stage. It is not unusual to have substantial numbers of children, 14 years and above, who are not in school.

[12] Jayachandran (2007) states that official estimates of dropout rates are often unreliable as official enrolment data are often inflated for Std I (UNDP 1999) and unreliable. The alternative methodology uses the proportion of ever-enrolled children in the age group of 15–19 years who have not completed their primary level of education.

Inland Northern region (see Table 4A17). Within the social groups, the dropout rate is very high for children belonging to the ST, with female children facing a comparative disadvantage. As expected, the dropout rate is also seen to fall as households move up the MPCE ladder (see Table 4A.18) and this holds across gender and sectors.

Studying the reasons for never enrolling or discontinuing or dropping out of school makes for useful insights. In Maharashtra, parental as well as child disinterest in studies, financial constraints as well as education not being considered important are the four main constraints faced by never-enrolled or dropout children (National Sample Survey Office 2009b; see Table 4.4). In rural areas, parental disinterest in studies was reported as the major cause for children (especially girls) not enrolling or discontinuing their schooling, while in urban areas financial constraints faced by households contributed mainly to the same (again especially for girls). Child disinterest plays an important role in retention and the data shows it to be one of the four important reasons for children discontinuing or dropping out in the state. 'Lack of interest on part of the child is likely to reflect the dull or even hostile environment in the class room [sic] and points to a problem with the schooling system rather than with the parents, contrary to earlier interpretation' (Jayachandran 2010). Thus, making the schooling and classroom processes interesting to children comes forth as an important policy direction for retaining children in school.

The tracking of school cohorts using DISE data for various years indicates that during the years 2006–11, well over 96 per cent of children were retained in the schooling system in Maharashtra in the primary and the middle-school levels. The movement of cohorts through the primary school grades[13] (Std II to Std IV) and the movement of cohorts from the primary to upper primary stage (Std IV to Std VI) indicates that for the state as a whole for both cohort scenarios the school 'survival' rates were very high. Also, school survival patterns from Std IV to Std VI were marginally higher than for

TABLE 4.4
Reasons for Never Enrolling or Discontinuing or Dropping Out (2007–08)

Reason	India			Maharashtra			Maharashtra					
							Rural			Urban		
	Total	Male	Female	Total	Male	Female	Total	Male	Female	Total	Male	Female
Parents Not Interested	26.6	24	28.8	20.5	18.1	23.2	25.5	20.5	31.7	8.6	10.5	7.5
Financial Constraints	24.8	26.7	23.2	19.1	15.4	23.2	13.3	13	13.7	33.0	22.8	40.8
Education Not Considered Necessary	12.3	11.4	13.1	9.2	10.0	8.3	10.1	9.6	10.7	7.0	11.2	3.8
Child Not Interested	12.1	14.4	10.1	19.7	22.3	16.9	19.7	22.6	16.2	19.7	21.6	18.3
Non-availability of Lady Teachers (New)	0.1	0.0	0.1	–	–	–	–	–	–	–	–	–
Non-availability of Ladies' Toilets (New)	0.03	0.0	0.1	–	–	–	–	–	–	–	–	–
No Tradition in the Community	3.0	2.1	3.7	1.4	1.4	1.3	1.2	1.7	0.6	1.8	0.7	2.7
Unable to Cope or Failure	2.0	2.0	1.6	3.8	3.7	3.9	2.9	2.8	3.1	5.8	7.0	5.3

Source: Author's calculations based on data from National Sample Survey Office (2009b).
Note: Findings are presented in percentage terms.

[13] We do not include Std I for the analysis as the underlying assumption is that schools 'settle down' in terms of steady enrolments by Std II. It is possible that in Std I children are enrolled in several schools but eventually they attend only one of them.

those in lower grades. The cohort-tracking exercise also indicates substantial inter-district variations in school survival rates at the elementary level. It was found that about a third of all districts had school survival rates that were below 80 per cent. Also, a little less than a third of all districts found themselves in the 90 per cent and above range in terms of school survival (see Table 4A.19).

Amongst the set of children currently not attending school, it is possible that some are engaged in work (child labour) while others are not. Child labour or workforce participation by children in the age group of 6–13 years can be measured by the usual principal activity status of those currently not attending school. In Maharashtra, 18.8 per cent children who were currently not attending school were found to be engaged in work[14] in 2007–08. WPRs were higher for male children (24.7 per cent) vis-à-vis female children (11.5 per cent). Male child labour was also found to be the highest in rural areas (27.1 per cent). Casual labour in 'other types of work' absorbed a large proportion of male and female children, especially in the rural parts of the state (see Table 4A.20).

Schooling Incentives

In 2007–08 children attending government schools in Maharashtra were found to be availing free education in highest proportions (92.6 per cent) in the state. It was in the private unaided institutions where children availed of free education in the smallest proportions (33.6 per cent rural and 3.4 per cent urban; see Table 4.5).[15] A clear advantage for children attending school in rural areas in terms of access to free education compared to their urban counterparts (38 percentage points approximately) is also seen. The, female children who attended elementary school availed of free education in larger proportions compared to male children in the state, across both rural and urban areas and in all the six regions of the state (see Table 4A.21). At the aggregate level, children belonging to ST households who were attending elementary school were availing free education in larger proportions amongst all the backward social groups and such a pattern also held across sectors, that is, in both rural and urban areas (see Table 4A.21).

Box 4.4 Human Development: Speaking to the People: School Attendance and Dropout

1. Despite significant improvements in enrolment figures, issues related to attendance and dropout in primary schools were reported as persistent in the blocks selected for the consultation.
2. Seasonal migration was cited as the most common reason for non-attendance and dropping out.
3. Irregular attendance was reported as the norm during December to April as well as July to August (season for agricultural activities).
4. In Gevrai block of Beed district, children were reported as being engaged in work in cotton farms between October and November, which told on their school participation.
5. An interesting solution suggested by the stakeholders was management of water resources and making available livelihood opportunities in local areas. This would help in arresting migration as well as enhance family incomes, thus releasing children for schooling.
6. Migration in search of livelihoods was reported to lead to a dropout rate in excess of 50 per cent in Chikhaldara block of Amravati. Here, parents reported a preference for residential ashram schools to enable their children to continue their studies when they migrated in search of livelihoods.

Source: Block-level consultations by YASHADA, December 2011.

---

[14] The NSS' definition of work under the usual principal activity status includes those who have worked in household enterprises (own-account worker, employer and as a helper in household enterprises), worked as regular or salaried wage employee, worked as casual labour in public works or other types of work.

[15] Education is free of tuition fee in government schools in most the states and also in private schools in some states up to certain levels of education. There are some schools where students up to a certain level are not required to pay tuition fees. Nevertheless, a fixed sum of money has to be paid such as development fee, library fee, etc. Education in such schools is still considered to be free. This applies to the institution as a whole and not to the specific situation obtaining for the student (National Sample Survey Office 2009a).

TABLE 4.5
Proportion of Children (6–13 years) Attending School and Receiving Free Education, by Type of Institution Attended (2007–08)

	Total	Government	Local Body	Private Aided	Private Unaided	Other
India	70.3	91.4	88.9	43.7	6.2	16.8
Maharashtra	76.5	92.6	91.4	71.4	6.4	38.6
Rural India	78.7	92.5	90.9	53.5	9	23.1
Urban India	41.6	83.5	80.4	33.6	3.1	10.5
Rural Maharashtra	91.4	96.4	92	85.2	33.6	100
Urban Maharashtra	53.5	82.6	88.8	59.3	3.4	0

Source: Author's calculations based on data from National Sample Survey Office (2009b).
Note: Findings are presented in percentage terms.

In a study of the best practices in Mid Day Meals (MDM), in government primary and upper primary schools in Maharashtra, Chugh (2008) highlights the beneficial impact of MDMs in schools. Implemented through the Panchayati Raj system in the state, MDMs were reported to be an effective schooling incentive, which helped children overcome caste and class prejudices, and sit together and eat food served in school, bringing a "spirit of togetherness and cohesiveness" among them. A study of 7,742 schools conducted by YASHADA in 2008–09 found that in 86 per cent of schools surveyed, all children availed of the MDM. In the remaining 14 per cent of schools, 10–15 children did not eat food in the school. The Report finds that children belonging to higher income classes generally did not partake of MDM in schools, more so in private and English medium schools. The study also highlights the contribution that MDMs make in increasing attendance as well as retaining children in school for the entire duration of the school day.

The Quality of Education

While plenty of data and information is available on access and enrolments, inputs and infrastructure, there is a dearth of evidence on the outcomes of the education system, especially in terms of what children are actually learning. Traditionally, pass rates in examinations have been used as a measure of the 'quality' of schooling. But these examinations are conducted only at the end of the school year. There is hardly any information about student learning and achievements in the primary and upper primary school levels. For Maharashtra, the issue of whether children are learning anything in school and what their competency levels are in different grades can be studied by examining data from ASER (Pratham 2006, 2007, 2008, 2009, 2010, 2011, 2012) and state government board examination results for Std X.

The ASER survey figures for various years show that reading and arithmetic abilities of children in Std I and Std II have shown some improvement over the period between 2006 and 2010 but declined in 2011, whereas the performance of children in Std III and Std IV in the same subjects has shown a decline (see Figures 4.14 and 4.15). The reading ability data for higher grades reveals that in rural Maharashtra around 75 per cent of children in Std V were able to fluently read Std II level textbooks. Thus, one out of every four children in Std V is still unable to read textbooks of the Std II level.[16] While Maharashtra performs much better than the India average

> *Reading and arithmetic abilities of children in Std I and Std II have shown some improvement over the period between 2006 and 2010 but declined in 2011, whereas the performance of children in Std III and Std IV in the same subjects has shown a decline.*

---

[16] The ASER reading test is a very simple test: the tasks are basic—ability to recognize letters, read simple words, read a basic four-sentence paragraph (at Std I level of difficulty) and a longer paragraph at Std II level of difficulty. It is useful for distinguishing between poor readers and fluent readers up to the Std II level.

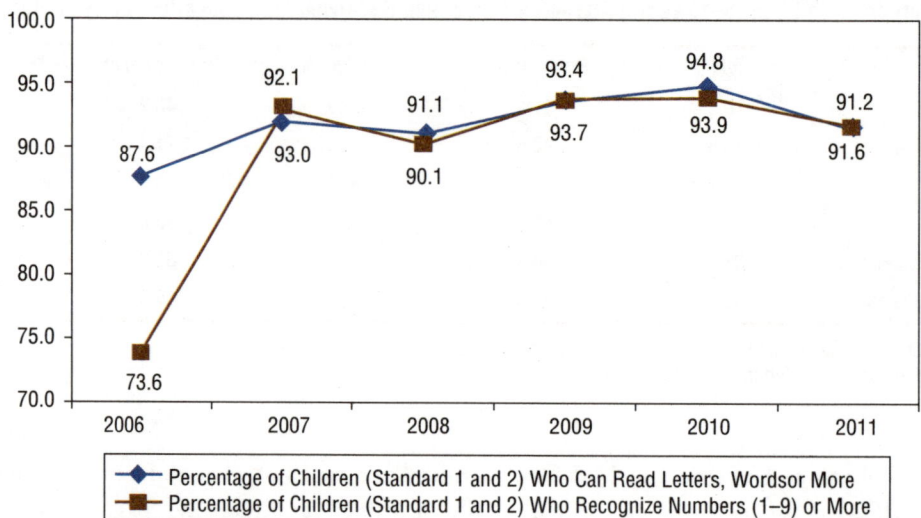

FIGURE 4.14 Reading and Arithmetic Ability of Children in Std I and Std II: Maharashtra (2006–11)

Source: Pratham (2012).

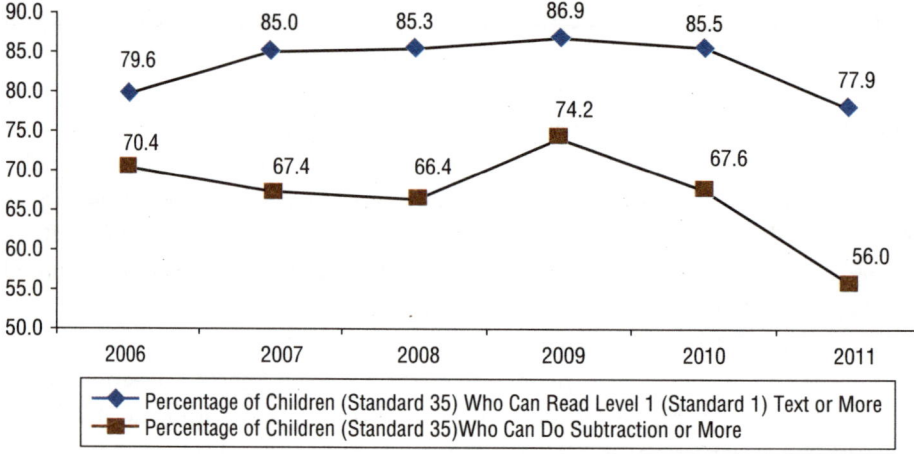

FIGURE 4.15 Reading and Arithmetic Ability of Children in Std III and Std IV: Maharashtra (2006–11)

Source: Pratham (2012).

on reading ability (nationally about 50 per cent of children in Std V are unable to read textbooks of the Std II level), it is important to keep in mind that 25 per cent of children in Std V will leave primary school without being completely competent at reading. There are also clear regional variations reported in children's abilities to read. While in the Pune division some improvements are visible in reading fluency, in the Konkan and Nashik divisions there has been deterioration of the same (see Table 4A.22). Such findings point clearly towards the need to ensure that all children are not only literate, but are also fluent according to their grade levels

The ASER also reports strong regional differences in children's proficiency in mathematics[17] (see Table 4A.22). In most regions of the state, more than 50 per cent of children

---

[17] For arithmetic, ASER asks children to do a series of simple tasks. These include recognizing numbers from one to nine, recognizing numbers from 11 to 100, two-digit subtraction problems using the borrowing method (this is expected of children in Std II) and a division problem (three

in Std V were unable to do a simple three-digit-by-one-digit division problem. When compared to what is expected of children based on their regular school textbooks for Std V, the problem that emerges is even more acute. Thus, despite being well above the all-India average in terms of success in basic reading and division problems in Std V, Maharashtra has still to achieve satisfactory standards of achievements. Everyday Maths,[18] another mathematics proficiency test for children, reveals large learning deficits in Std V and Std VIII, with children unable to cope with simple everyday-related maths problems (see Table 4A.22). The limited evidence that is available on children's abilities to apply knowledge to real-life problems suggests that much more research is needed to understand the current levels of knowledge, skills and application abilities that children obtain in elementary school. This is particularly important in rapidly urbanizing states such as Maharashtra where there are a wide variety of non-agricultural work opportunities that are available to young people. The education component of a person's human capital must ensure that the skills and the knowledge that he/she accumulates in school are at an appropriate level to translate well into jobs and productivity.

The exit exams from the schooling system are one of the most important elements of the entire education process. Each state via its 'board exams' sets the benchmark of what a 'successful' candidate is expected to know. The proportion of children who successfully complete the board examination is a reflection of how well the system is able to prepare its students to measure up to the examination standards. The data shows that overall female candidates fared better than males in the Std X board examinations (see Table 4.6). The pass percentage for children belonging to the SC and ST categories is lower than that for the state; the children belonging to the OBC category were doing better than the state average.

TABLE 4.6
Percentage of Students Who Passed in Board Examinations: 2010–11

	Gender	SC	ST	OBC	Others	Total
Students Passing Std X Board Exams	Boys	74.5	77.9	82.6	84.2	81.9
	Girls	76.0	78.9	85.4	87.2	84.5

Source: Author's calculations based on data from National Sample Survey Office (2009b).

School Resources

Teachers

DISE data for 2011–12 (NUEPA 2012b) reveals that Maharashtra had 544,265 teachers in its elementary schools of which nearly half (45.2 per cent) are female teachers. The proportion of female teachers varies across districts, with five districts including Mumbai, Mumbai (Suburban), Thane, Pune and Nagpur reporting it to be more than 60 per cent, while in Hingoli and Gadchiroli it was less than 25 per cent. Out of a total of 100,084 schools in the state, 67.2 per cent schools had female teachers, while the remaining 32,857 (32.8 per cent) did not have even a single female teacher. There still remained 2,274 schools that are functionary with single teacher.

The pupil-teacher ratio (PTR) at the primary level saw a decline between 2004–05 and 2008–09, but increased and reached 30 in 2011–12 (see Figure 4.16). It was seen to vary across districts: six districts with a PTR of less than 25 (Wardha, Gadchiroli,

> *The pupil-teacher ratio (PTR) at the primary level saw a decline between 2004–05 and 2008–09, but increased and reached 30 in 2011–12.*

---

digits by one digit), which is usually expected of children in Std IV. The ASER set of tasks for arithmetic is very basic. By Std V children in Maharashtra are expected to have knowledge of numbers and do operations at a much more advanced level.

[18] The tasks include calculations with a menu, using a calendar, computing area of a field and estimation. According to state textbooks, many of these competencies are expected of children by Std IV.

> Buildings were in place in almost all schools in the state, certain other schooling support infrastructure facilities are still lacking in many schools.

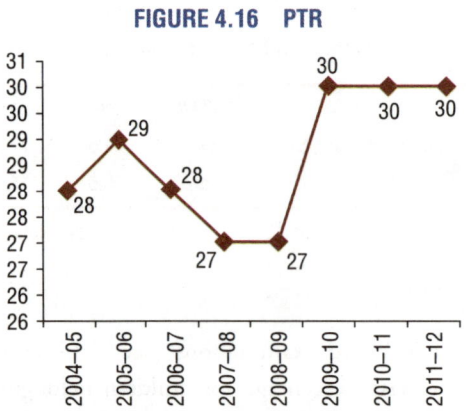

FIGURE 4.16 PTR

Source: Mehta (2005, 2006, 2007, 2008, 2009, 2011, 2012) and NUEPA (2011b, 2012b).

Raigarh, Satara, Ratnagiri and Sindhudurg) and six others with a PTR of more than 33 (Jalgaon, Washim, Hingoli, Jalna, Thane and Mumbai [Suburban]). There has also been a decline in schools with PTRs greater than 60, from 6.4 per cent in 2006–07 to 2.7 per cent in 2010–11 (Mehta 2005, 2006, 2007, 2008, 2009, 2011, 2012; NUEPA 2011b, 2012b).

The proportion of trained teachers is a useful indicator for assessing teacher competency. Nearly all regular teachers in schools in Maharashtra are professionally trained while 87 per cent of contractual teachers are trained (2.4 per cent of the total teachers are those on contract). When in-service training of teachers is considered, 25.1 per cent of teachers were trained in the year 2010–11 (Mehta 2005, 2006, 2007, 2008, 2009, 2011, 2012; NUEPA 2011b, 2012b). Teachers need to be physically present in classrooms to enable learning achievements amongst the students. The percentage of teachers involved in non-teaching work has shown an increase over the years (1.9 per cent in 2009–10 to 3.7 per cent in 2010–11, and further to 5.3 per cent in 2011–12) (NUEPA 2012a).

Education Infrastructure

An analysis of infrastructure in elementary schools by UNICEF based on DISE 2010–11 in NUEPA (2011b) indicates that while buildings were in place in almost all schools in the state, certain other schooling support infrastructure facilities are still lacking in many schools. Nearly 24 per cent of schools do not have separate toilets for girls, 35 per cent of schools lack ramps, 38 per cent lack play grounds and 41 per cent do not have any boundary wall (see Figure 4.17). On the flip side, what is encouraging is that the student-classroom ratio (SCR) has shown a sharp decrease from 41 in 2004–05 to 31 in 2010–11.[19] It is reported to be high in private aided, upper primary and urban schools. Jalgaon, Thane and Mumbai (Suburban) districts have SCRs of more than 35.

With respect to secondary school infrastructure, 98 per cent the schools are shown to have drinking water facilities. However, many of them do not possess the necessary infrastructure such as laboratories, computer facilities, etc. (see Figure 4.18). Integrated science laboratories are needed in 43 per cent of schools, 59 per cent of schools need buildings, 82 per cent of schools lack computer laboratories and 72 per cent do not have Internet facility.

Education for the Katkari Tribe

Based on an in-depth field case study of the Katkari tribe, carried out in Jawhar taluka, Thane district, R. Mutatkar (2007) reported the socioeconomic and cultural constraints faced by these communities in accessing education and makes some very useful policy recommendations. He found the educational status of the Katkari population to be very low, with the majority of children in the school-going age group not attending school. Those children who do attend school were found to be enrolled in the village government primary schools, and not in the residential ashram schools meant for tribal children. This was mainly attributed to the sociocultural constraints and discrimination that Katkari children faced in accessing

---

[19] Based on analysis of DISE data.

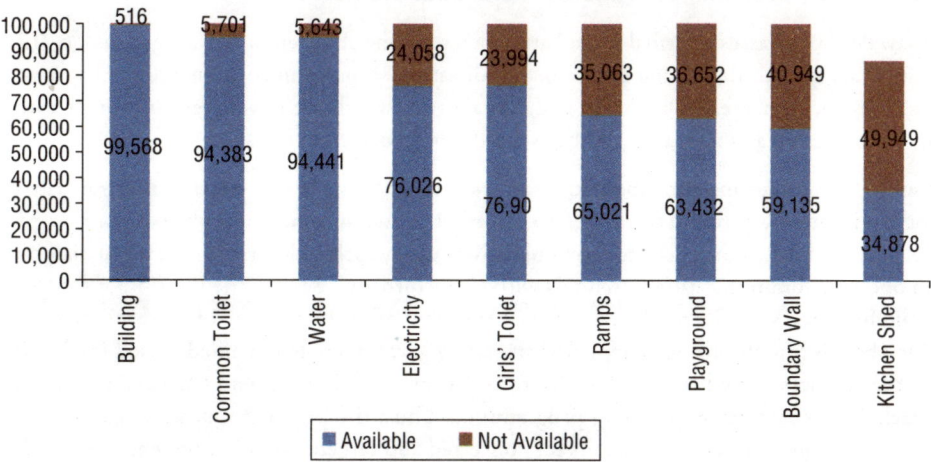

Source: Analysis done by UNICEF based on DISE data for 2010–11 in NUEPA (2011b).

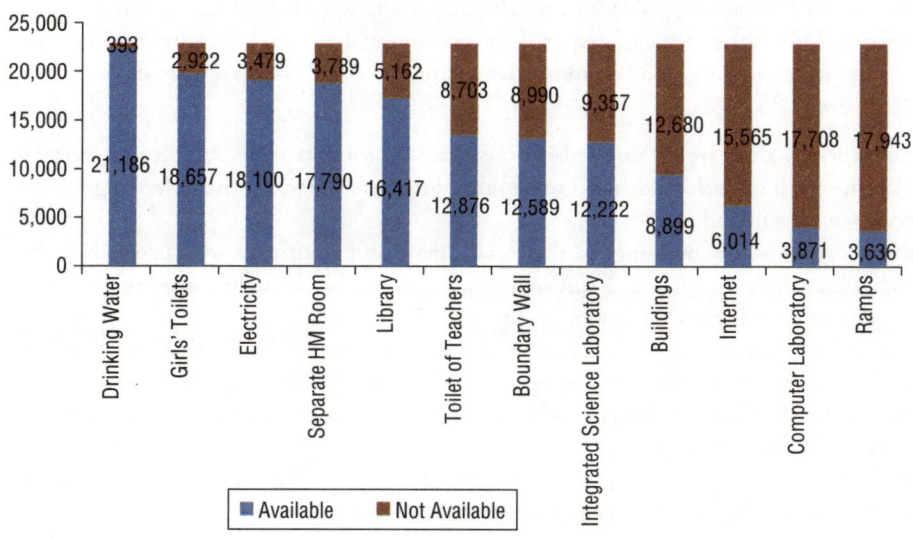

Source: MPSP (2012).

ashram schools. The opportunity cost of child labour, drop out due to seasonal migration, peer group, neighbourhood effects and structural issues related to government primary schools were some of the other factors hindering school enrolment and attendance for children belonging to this tribe.

The highest educational level in most households was found to be below the middle-school level. Katkari perceptions about education also had an important bearing on their low levels of participation and attainments, as well as being directly linked to their livelihood concerns. Education was looked upon as an instrument for getting a job and ensuring a fixed monthly income. Given their ascribed status of wage labour, they were unable to overcome their assumptions of the futility of education. They were unable to relate education to their immediate survival concerns. There was also a dearth of any success story within their cultural setting, of educational attainments as instruments for upward mobility and improvements in earning capacity.

> **Box 4.5 Primary Schooling for Tribals in Nandurbar District**
>
> A study by Chattopadhyay and Durdhawale (2009) assesses tribal school attendance among children in the age group of 6–12 years and the reasons for non-attendance, along with describing the primary education scenario in some selected villages of Nandurbar district. Six villages[20] from two blocks, namely, Dhadgaon and Akkalkuwa (which are lowest on the literacy rate scale and highest on tribal population) were selected and a total of 183 households were covered in the survey.
>
> Their qualitative findings bring out some very useful insights about the factors that lead to the non-participation of tribal children in schooling. *First*, the concept of education was found to be alien to the tribal population and hence they were reported to not realize the relevance of the same. The medium of instruction in schools is Marathi, which is different from tribal dialects like Bhilli, Pawri, etc., and "resulted in one-way communication in schools with no reciprocity". *Second*, the location of schools as well as the hilly and inaccessible terrain hindered school attendance. *Third*, 40 per cent of the population of these villages was found to migrate to Gujarat during October to March raising school absenteeism. *Fourth*, schools remained closed for 5–10 days in a month (besides Sundays) as the teachers visited the block office to collect their salaries, attend teachers' meetings, supply school statistics to block research offices and attend training programmes. Thus, the primary education scenario in terms of access, infrastructure and participation in such tribal areas calls for concerted and targeted policy interventions.

Source: Chattopadhyay and Durdhawale (2009).

> **Box 4.6 Planning for Improvements in Education in Rural Maharashtra**
>
> In a study conducted by the Indian Institute of Education (2004) on the schooling scenario in three backward districts of Maharashtra (Nandurbar, Jalna and Yavatmal), the basic elements required for promoting quality school education in rural areas of the state are lucidly spelt out. The major findings and recommendations of the study also make for useful policy guidelines for the state today. Some of them are:
>
> 1. Certain schooling norms do not work in the case of tiny habitations. Factors such as climatic patterns, varying agricultural seasons and migration in search of livelihoods need to be taken into consideration when planning for the school year so as to ensure universal enrolment and attendance.
> 2. Measures such as remedying the design of school buildings to the local climate and culture, as well as ensuring the availability of drinking water facilities, toilets for girls and sufficient play area would certainly contribute towards increasing attendance, promoting retention and arresting dropping out.
> 3. The education curriculum needs to be planned using a bottom-up methodology for rural and tribal areas, where communities in partnership with local NGOs design and develop apt curriculums for school-going children.
> 4. Examinations that bring forth the analytical abilities of children and help in assessing how they organize and understand what they have learnt in the classroom are recommended.
> 5. Teacher-pupil ratios of 1:40 calculated using the district as a unit could be misleading. Each school should be looked at as an individual unit along with class strength before fixing a commensurate teacher-pupil ratio.
> 6. Teachers belonging to the local community, even if lesser qualified, go a long way in promoting participation in schooling as they enjoy the confidence of the community and have good knowledge of the local geography, culture, terrain and the aspirations of the community and its people.
> 7. Effective implementation of the MDM scheme would go a long way in stopping dropping out from school.
>
> The community needs to accept the school and the schooling processes as a first step towards community involvement. The village community could involve itself in household surveys for assessing and enumerating enrolment, out-of-school children and dropouts, and further conduct discussions with families of such identified children.

Source: Indian Institute of Education (2004).

Education Budget: Allocations and Achievements[21]

India's education budget (centre and states) has more than doubled in the last five years, increasing from ₹835,640 million in the financial year (FY) 2004–05 to ₹1,919,460 million in FY 2009–10. As a proportion of the GDP, it has actually fallen from 3.1 per

---

[20] Dhadgaon, Bijary, Molgi, Toranmal, Khuntamodi and Khadki.
[21] See Accountability Initiative (2011a).

cent to 2.9 per cent during the same period. Within the education budget, elementary education is a priority. In FY 2011–12, elementary education constituted over 50 per cent of the total expenditure on education.

Expenditures under the SSA are on a centre–state sharing basis in the ratio of 65:35 (RTE Act), with the central government bearing the bulk of the financial responsibility for the same. Over the period from 2006–07 to 2009–10, the SSA expenditures in Maharashtra showed a 12 per cent increase in comparison to Bihar and Rajasthan, which showed an increase in the same of 78 per cent and 79 per cent respectively (see Figure 4.19). Such an increase in the SSA budget in Bihar and Rajasthan could be because of substantial amounts of pending expenditures on education infrastructure, teacher recruitment and training and the need to still bring in large numbers of out-of-school children into schools.

It was seen that in 2007–08, Maharashtra was able to effectively utilize 86 per cent of its SSA funds while in 2012–13, only 63 per cent of the allocated SSA funds was utilized (Accountability Initiative 2013).

The state spent 1.3 per cent of the State Domestic Product on education in 2007–08 (Institute of Applied Manpower research 2011). State-level trends in education expenditures can best be understood when examined on a per-child basis.[22] The Government of India releases ₹950 per elementary school going child per year under the SSA and there exist interstate variations in expenditures on the same. Rajasthan and Chhattisgarh spend ₹1,300 per child while Maharashtra spends ₹875 per child on average (see Figure 4.20). However, when computed by taking the state budgetary allocations for elementary education into account, the per-child expenditure in Maharashtra rises substantially to ₹9,635, which is much higher than that in West Bengal (₹3,604), Madhya Pradesh (₹4,023) and Rajasthan (₹7,025).

Summing Up

The literacy rate in Maharashtra has shown an improvement over the decade 2001 to 2011, moving up from 76.9 per cent to

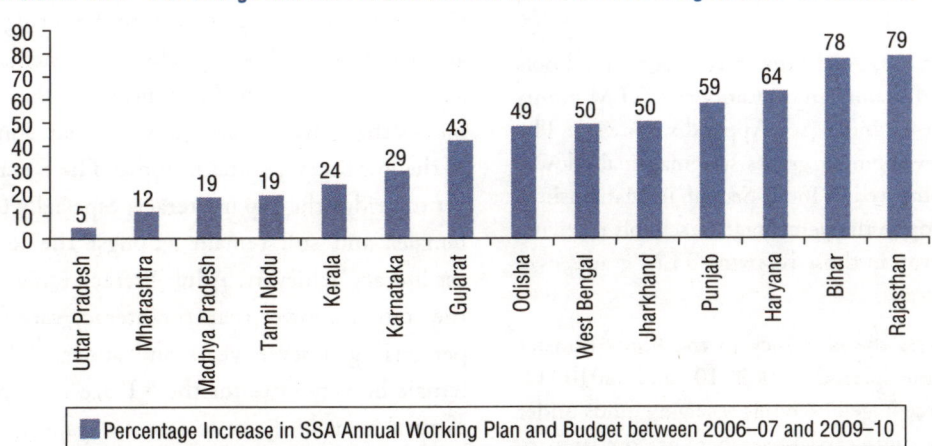

FIGURE 4.19 Percentage Increase in SSA Annual Work Plan and Budget: 2006–07 and 2009–10

Source: Accountability Initiative (2011a).

[22] The per-child expenditure calculation consists of total expenditure on elementary education divided by the total enrolment in schools under government management. More specifically, it includes state budgets (including state share of SSA and GoI funds release for SSA), aggregating to total funds for elementary education, which is divided by the sum of enrolments in government managed schools (Std I to Std V) and enrolment in government-managed schools (Std VI to Std VIII), that is, enrolments in Std I to Std VIII.

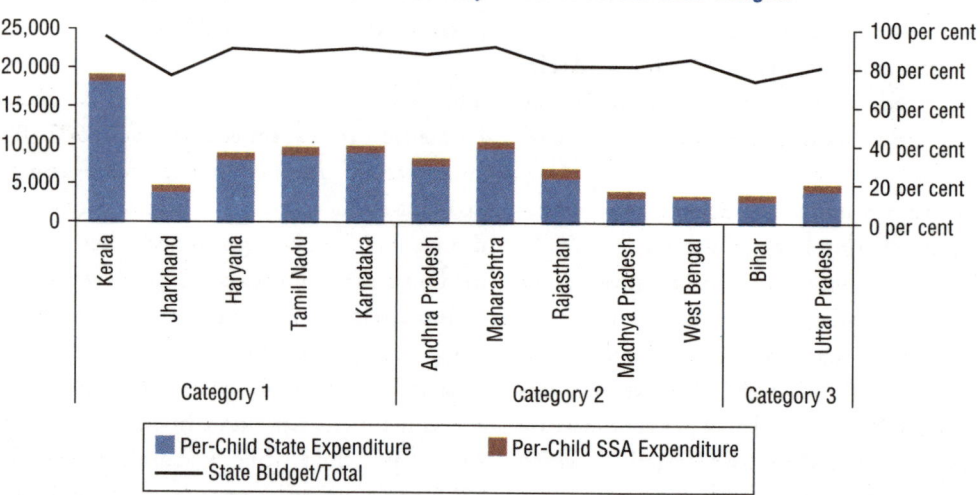

FIGURE 4.20 Per-Child Expenditures versus State Budgets

Source: Mehta (2012).
Note: States have been clubbed into three categories based on enrolment proportions relative to the country as a whole.

Box 4.7   The PAISA Survey (2011)

The PAISA survey is conducted annually under the aegis of ASER-Rural, with the main aim of tracking public expenditure in education at the India and state levels. The survey investigates school grants under the SSA umbrella as these grants have an important bearing on the functioning of primary and upper primary schools. The PAISA survey tracks schooling grants under three heads namely, maintenance grants, development grants and teacher grants (TLM grants). What this survey helps to understand is whether schools receive their money on time and whether they receive their entire entitlements. Data from PAISA 2011 survey brings forth some useful findings:

First, in both FYs 2009–10 and 2010–11, the percentage of schools receiving funds under the heads of maintenance grants and TLM grants was greater for Maharashtra vis-à-vis India (see Appendix 4A.23). The percentage of schools receiving development grants was marginally lower for Maharashtra in 2010–11 as compared to India. *Second,* in Maharashtra in particular, there was a sharp drop in the percentage of schools receiving development grants and a small drop in those receiving TLM grants over the two time periods being considered.

The timely arrival of grants reflects the efficiency in the funds transfer mechanisms. Over the two time periods 2009–10 and 2010–11, Maharashtra reported a higher percentage of schools receiving funds under all the three heads considered, by mid-year (November) as compared to India (see Appendix 4A.23). What is to be noted is that the timing of grant receipts has shown a worsening for the state for development grants and TLM grants. By November 2009, while 64 per cent of schools reported receiving development grants on time, this dropped to 58 per cent by November 2010. Similarly, the percentage of schools receiving TLM grants by mid-year also showed a drop from 69 to 66 over the same time period.

82.9 per cent. There have also been considerable improvements in the female literacy rate during the last decade, approximately eight percentage points, which is also reflected in the improvements in the GPI (0.8) in 2011. Maharashtra, with a literacy rate of 82.9 per cent in 2011, has a persistent gender gap of 19 percentage points in rural areas and 8.4 percentage points in urban areas. Disparities in literacy achievements exist across regions; the rural–urban gap is yet to be bridged and rural female literacy calls for immediate attention. The cause for concern is the 13 blocks that have literacy rates less than some of the low literacy states in India. The ST are yet to bridge the gap in literacy, especially for females and still remain amongst the lowest literacy achievers. Adult literacy rates for the state are lower than the literacy rate for persons aged seven years and above. Adult female literacy rates for the ST are very low in rural areas of the state across a majority of regions. Despite progress made by the state, which is reflected in overall improvements in the literacy rate, inclusion in literacy achievements by gender and social groups, especially for adult literacy, needs to be the focus of policy interventions.

Maharashtra has made considerable progress in enrolments and has achieved near-universal enrolment in the primary school going age, showcasing the effectiveness of access in the state. The enrolment rate at the upper primary is more than that at the primary level. Increasing female enrolment is a highlight. In 2007–08, the NAR for the state was 90.8 per cent for the primary and 67.1 per cent for the upper primary level, attendance in the latter not having evidently kept pace with the former. The NARs at the primary and upper primary levels have seen an improvement across gender and sectors over 1995–96 to 2007–08. A narrowing in the gender gap in primary and upper primary NARs in both sectors, especially rural, is also a highlight. Primary-level NARs do not show much inter-regional variation.. Primary-level NARs for the SC, OBC and Others are higher than the state average at the aggregate level, as well as when disaggregated by sex, indicates a move towards social inclusion.

The NARs for the upper primary level are much lower at 67.1 per cent. There is marginal gender gap at the aggregate level, and across most regions. Rural upper primary NARs are lower than urban NARs in Maharashtra with a gap of five percentage points at the aggregate level. Even though ST children continue to face a disadvantage in upper primary school attendance and the gap to be breached is quite large, gender advantage in school attendance for female children at the regional level showcases gender and social inclusion in educational processes in the state.

In 2007–08, what is worth noting is that amongst female children availed of free education in higher proportions than their male counterparts across all regions of the state. ST children too availed of this schooling incentive in larger proportions compared to all other social groups in rural as well as urban areas.

The coverage of MDMs for children attending school, an important schooling intervention which aims mainly at promoting attendance and retention, was around 86 per cent of schools in 2008–09.

The proportion of out-of-school children in the elementary school going age was 6.8 per cent in 2007–08. While there was no gender bias evident in the proportions of out-of-school children at the aggregate level, at the sectoral level there were higher proportions of out-of-school children in rural areas. Never-enrolled children formed a larger proportion of out-of-school children in rural areas, flagging the need to address this proportion of children to achieve universal enrolment in the state. Regional concentration of out-of-school children in the Inland Northern region (comprising Nandurbar, Dhule, Jalgaon and Nashik), especially in the rural sector, with a high proportion of never-enrolled out-of-school children reiterates such a finding. On the other hand, the presence of out-of-school children in small proportions in the tribal Eastern region brings to fore the possible effectiveness of education and schemes that promote schooling in this pocket of the state.

Out-of-school children in the age group of 14–16 years group (secondary level of schooling) were reported to be higher in proportion compared to those at the elementary level. For Maharashtra, a quarter of the child population in the same age group was out of school, with a clear disadvantage for female children and children belonging to the ST. For the secondary school age group, the proportions of never-enrolled children were much smaller than those enrolled but currently not attending school, clearly highlighting that at the secondary level of schooling retention is more of a problem.

Dropout rates calculated using an alternative methodology (to overcome the enrolment-related issues that the official dropout rate has) show an evident rural bias and a negligible gender gap and show that they are quite uniform across sector and gender. Within the social groups, the dropout rate was high for children belonging to the ST, with female children facing a comparative disadvantage. As expected, the dropout rate was also seen to fall as households moved up the MPCE ladder. While parental disinterest in studies was the major cause for children (especially girls) not enrolling or discontinuing their schooling in rural areas, financial constraints faced by households in urban areas dissuaded school participation (again especially for girls). At the aggregate level, child disinterest was found to play an important role in school retention, pointing towards the need to make schooling and classroom processes interesting for retaining children in school.

Given the advances made in the provisioning of schooling as well as high rates of enrolments at the elementary level, the need for the state is to go beyond access, infrastructure and enrolments and look at educational outcomes. Learning achievements in the primary and upper primary school levels are important indicators of competency gained. ASER data underscores the low competency and achievement levels of school-going children in the state. It reports that 25 per cent of children graduate from primary school without complete reading competency. It also finds no improvements in basic reading abilities of children, coupled with clear regional variations with the Konkan and Nashik divisions showing a deterioration, which flags the need for policy attention. Despite being well above the India average for success in basic reading and division problems in Std V, Maharashtra still has a long way to go in terms of learning achievements at the primary and upper primary levels. Thus, the challenge now is to provide and ensure learning commensurate to the grade levels in which the children are enrolled. An extra year of schooling does not necessarily ensure improvements in learning in the context of Maharashtra as it is found that children enrolled at the elementary level fall well short of the competency levels expected from the grades they are enrolled in, raising concern about the teaching and learning mechanisms in practice.

Over the period from 2006–07 to 2009–10, the SSA expenditures in Maharashtra showed an increase of 12 per cent. The utilization of SSA funds has increased between 2005–06 and 2009–10. The PAISA survey finds that in Maharashtra approximately 90 per cent of schools reported receiving the maintenance, development and TLM grants in 2009–10 and 2010–11. It also highlights the timely arrival of grant funds in the state with a majority of primary schools reporting receipt of maintenance grants by mid-year, which is much higher than for schools in India.

Thus, the state has made considerable progress in access of education but has to strive for equity and quality issues.

5
Health and Nutrition: Imperative for Capability Enhancement

Motivation

"The *health* of a nation is an essential component of development, vital to the nation's economic growth and internal stability" (Planning Commission 2008). Ill health and morbidity contribute to losses in the productivity of individuals and keep them from earning a decent living. Ensuring the good health of a country's populace by providing them with accessible, affordable and good-quality health care could go a long way in contributing towards their productive capabilities. One of the major objectives of the Eleventh Plan was to achieve good health for the populace with special focus on the poor, the underprivileged and those living in remote rural regions. To ensure access to good health care, the Eleventh Plan envisaged a more comprehensive approach, which included individual and public health care, provisioning of clean drinking water, sanitation facilities, knowledge of hygiene and good feeding practices.

Adequate and proper nutrition has important implications for the health and well-being of children as well as adults. Conceptually, malnutrition reflects poor food intake when in utero and eventual poor feeding practices in early infancy and childhood. Malnutrition leads to poor cognitive and social development, inability to concentrate and participate in the schooling process, low energy levels and hence low productivity in adult life. It also disables a person from recovering fast from illnesses and increases his/her susceptibility to infections. The Eleventh Five Year Plan elucidates the nutrition challenges that need to be addressed and these include high levels of adult malnutrition, inappropriate infant feeding and caring practices, high rates of under-nutrition, especially amongst women and children, micronutrient deficiencies, diet-related diseases and inadequate access to health care. To enhance the capabilities of children as well as adults, it therefore becomes essential to ensure that their intake of nutrients is balanced, is in sufficient quantities and the requisite prenatal and postnatal care is provided to mothers as well as infants.

Improvement in the health and nutrition status of mothers and their children enhances learning abilities in school on the one hand and leads to higher resistance and lower incidence of diseases on the other (Institute of Applied Manpower Research 2011: Figure 5.1). Good health facilitates capability enhancements for individuals, helping them access income-generating opportunities. In addition to its inherent value in improving human well-being, good health also contributes to reduction in poverty, hunger and malnutrition as well as improving access to basic amenities such as housing, water and sanitation, leading to better standards of living. Such feedback loops between health inputs, education and health-related outcomes work towards generating interconnected synergies that help in overcoming capability deprivation and lead to improvements in the standard of living of the populace.

Health: Outcome Indicators

The Eleventh Five Year Plan marked out seven measurable health targets to be achieved by the end of the plan period, namely, increase in the child sex ratio for the age group of 0–6 years, reduction of the IMR, the MMR, the total fertility rate (TFR), under-nutrition among children and anaemia among women and girls and the provision of safe and clean drinking water for all. Available data on these and other vital indicators reveals that Maharashtra has achieved progress in outcome indicators at the aggregate level. However, there are a few shortfalls in achievements that get accentuated when disaggregated by gender, rural–urban sectors and social groups.

The CBR for the state, which indicates the number of live births occurring during the year, per 1,000 population and estimated at mid-year, experienced a decline between 2001 and 2011, from 20.7 to 16.7 (Office of the Registrar General 2012). The CBR for Maharashtra in 2011 was also lower than the national figure of 21.8. Sector-wise comparisons show the birth rate to be slightly higher in rural areas (17.3) vis-à-vis urban areas (15.8) Inter-district variations exist in rural CBR, ranging from as low as 11.1 in Sindhudurg to as high as 20.1 in Nandurbar. It is reported to be less than 15 in Chandrapur, Gondia, Raigarh, Ratnagiri, Sindhudurg and Wardha, while it is more than 20 in Nandurbar (State Bureau of Health Intelligence and Vital Statistics 2010).

The CDR, which is measured as the number of deaths per 1,000 persons, has also shown a decline from 7.1 in 2001 to 6.3 in 2011 and is lower than the national average of 7.1. The CDR is higher in rural areas (7.3) as compared to urban areas (5.3) (Office of the Registrar General 2012). The CDR is the lowest in Thane district (4.9). Inter-district variations in the CDR show it to be less than 5.5 in Pune and Thane, while it is higher than 8 in Gadchiroli, Gondia, Ratnagiri, Sangli, Satara, Sindhudurg and Wardha (State Bureau of Health Intelligence and Vital Statistics 2010).

Progress made with respect to demographic outcomes reveals that nine major states in the country have reached replacement fertility levels and Maharashtra is one of them (as cited in Institute of Applied Manpower Research 2011). The TFR of the state has shown a decline from 4.9 in 1971 to 1.9 in 2010 (see Figure 5.1) (Office of the Registrar General 2012).

The TFR in both rural and urban areas of the state has seen a steady decrease, reaching near-replacement levels in the former (2.0) and well below replacement levels in the latter (1.7) in 2010. There is a slight disparity in TFRs of rural and urban areas, with the former reporting higher fertility rates than the later (2.0 and 1.7 respectively).

Sex ratio of Maharashtra has shown a small improvement, as reflected by a sex ratio of 925 in 2011 vis-à-vis 922 in 2001 (Appendix 5A.1). Mumbai and Mumbai suburb districts have very low sex ratio and Ratnagiri and Sindhudurg districts have very good sex ratio. The possible explanation is that a sizable proportion of men in the productive age group from Ratnagiri and Sindhudurg districts are working in and around Mumbai.

What is alarming is the drop in the child sex ratio (0–6 years) from 913 in 2001 to 883 in 2011. Beed district reported the lowest child sex ratio (801) and Gadchiroli the highest (956). While in 2001, not a single district had reported a child sex ratio below 830, in 2011 two districts reported a child sex ratio below 830: Jalgaon (829) and Beed (801). Almost

> *Maharashtra has achieved progress in outcome indicators at the aggregate level. However, there are a few shortfalls in achievements that get accentuated when disaggregated by gender, rural–urban sectors and social groups.*

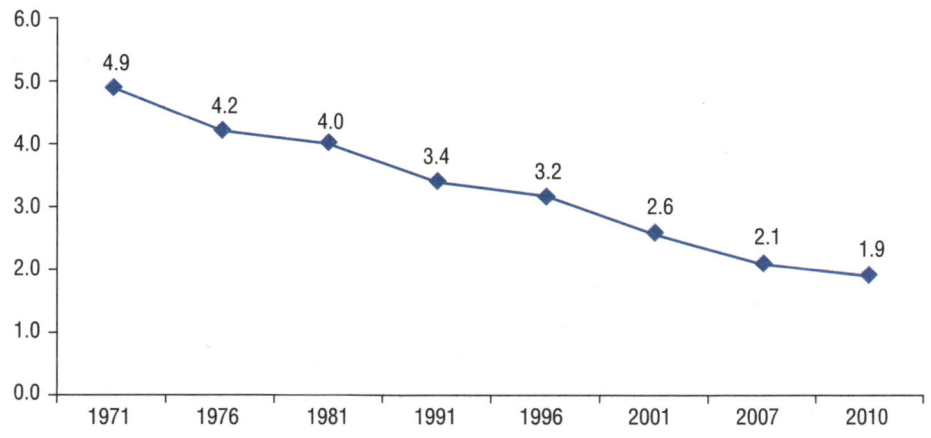

FIGURE 5.1   Trends in TFR: Maharashtra

Source: Office of the Registrar General (2003, 2004, 2005, 2006, 2007, 2008, 2009, 2010, 2011, 2012).

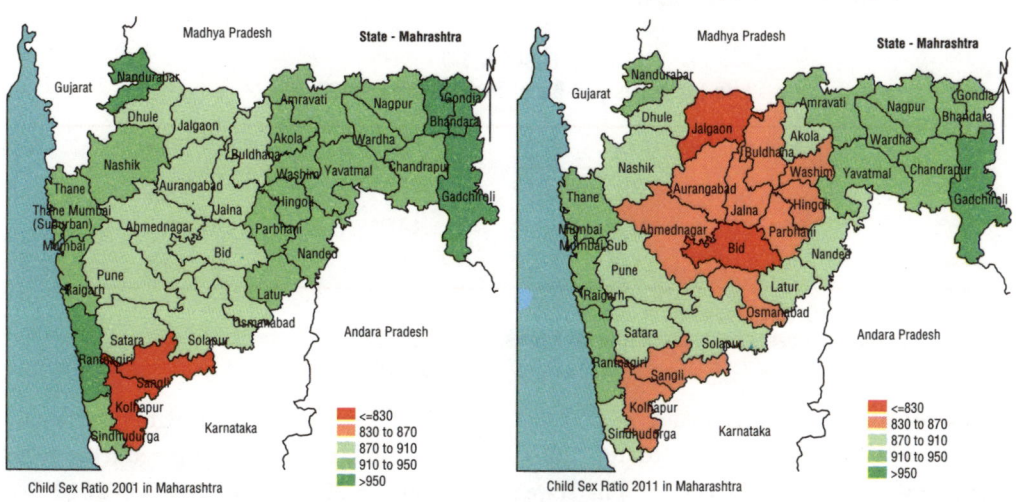

FIGURE 5.2   District-Wise Child Sex Ratio: Maharashtra (2001 and 2011)

Source: Based on data from Census 2001 and Government of India (2011a).

every district in Maharashtra shows a worsening child sex ratio over 2001–11, the exceptions being Satara, Chandrapur, Kolhapur and Sangli (where it improved by 3, 6, 6 and 11 points, respectively). Wardha experienced the lowest decline in the child sex ratio of 12 points vis-à-vis Beed where the decline was 93 points over the decade under consideration (see Table 5A.1 and Figure 5.2). The declining child sex ratio is not only a reflection of preference for male children but may also reflect the quality of care given to the girl child.

The life expectancy of any individual, which is a component of the HDI and reflects the number of years a person can be expected to survive, given the current age-specific mortality rate of the age group to which he/she belongs. Life expectancy for Maharashtra's population was only 53.8 years during 1970–75, but has increased to 67.2 years during 2002–06 (see Figure 5.3), which is also higher than the national average (63.5 years). Females reported an advantage of over two years in life expectancy over males in both the rural and the urban areas of the state. The life expectancy of the urban population is also significantly higher (by six years) in urban areas compared to rural areas (Registrar General, India [2009: Table 11]).

The IMR captures the number of deaths in the first year of life per 1,000 live births. The

Health and Nutrition

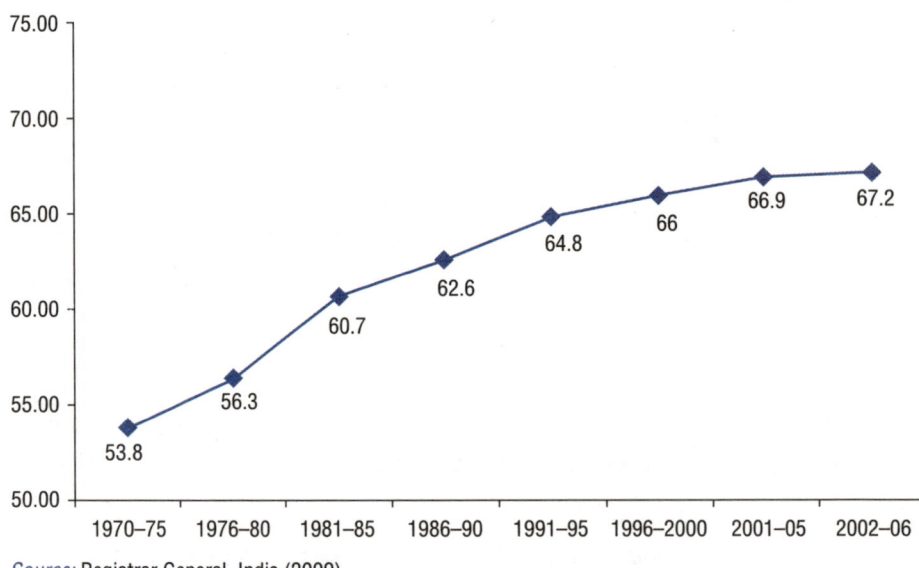

FIGURE 5.3 Life Expectancy at Birth: Maharashtra

Source: Registrar General, India (2009).

TABLE 5.1
Life Expectancy at Birth: Maharashtra (2002–06)

	Total	Rural	Urban
Total	67.2	65.2	71.2
Male	66.0	64.0	69.6
Female	68.4	66.3	72.8

Source: Registrar General, India (2009: Table 11).
Note: Computations based on 2002–06 average figures.

> The state has shown considerable progress in terms of reduction in the IMR experiencing a marked drop of 22 points over the decade 2001–11.

causes of infant mortality could vary from poor maternal or child health to the non-availability of health-care facilities. The state has shown considerable progress in terms of reduction in the IMR[1] experiencing a marked drop of 22 points over the decade 2001–11 (47 in 2001 to 25 in 2011).[2] In both 2001 and 2011, the IMR was reported to be higher in rural areas, although the rural–urban gap has narrowed from 27 points in 2001 to 13 points in 2011. The IMR remains higher for female children with the gender gap reducing from five points in 2000 to two points in 2010 (see Table 5.1).

The trends in IMR by social groups (available from reports of NFHS-2, 1998–99 and NFHS-3, 2005–06[3]) reveal an improvement, but its distance from the state average still remains large. There has nevertheless been a

---

[1] The source of data on IMR in this section are the SRS bulletins of April 2002, October 2002, April 2011 and December 2011 released by the Registrar General & Census Commissioner of India.

[2] The IMR in 2001 was 47 (as per the census of 2001) and decreased to 44 in 2007–08 as per DLHS-3 (refer to Chapter 2). Please note that three sources of data are used in the MHDR 2012 with regard to IMR figures. The sources used in this chapter are the SRS bulletins. In Chapter 2, to for the purpose of calculating district-wise HDI for 2001 and 2011, the sources of IMR are Census 2001 and DLHS-3. For an explanation about using IMR figures from different sources, see Chapter 2.

[3] See IIPS and ORC Macro (2011) for NFHS-2 data and IIPS and Macro International (2008) for NFHS-3 data.

striking drop in the IMR for the ST (22 points), which has not been matched by the drop in IMR for the SC (seven points) and OBC (two points) over the two time points under consideration. The need for the state now is to focus essential interventions aimed at reduction in the IMRs of the socially and economically disadvantaged groups. There are marked interdistrict variations in the IMR, with variations in the IMR between districts found to be associated with district economic development (see Figure 5.4; note that the size of the circle denotes district per capita income). That is, if a district is economically well off as evidenced by a high per capita income, it is highly likely that the district has a low IMR. Special attention needs to be given to five districts, namely, Nandurbar, Washim, Yavatmal, Wardha and Bhandara, where the IMR in rural areas exceeds 35 (see Figure 5.5). Another interesting fact borne out by the NFHS-3 data is that IMR varies inversely with the mother's age, being higher for younger mothers (IIPS and Macro International 2008).

The U5MR measures the probability of children born in a certain year not surviving until the age of five and is the number of child deaths per 1,000 live births. In Maharashtra, the U5MR[4] has shown a consistent decline over the years from 58.1 in 1998–99 to 46.7 in 2005–06, and further to 36 in 2008. The U5MR for Maharashtra in 2009 was relatively lower at 36 compared to the national U5MR of 64 (Office of the Registrar General 2011). Also, the rural–urban gap in this indicator was 17 points for the state while it was higher at 30 points for India as a whole. A gender gap of eight points in the U5MR points towards a clear female disadvantage (see Figure 5.6). Social group disparities in child mortality rates exist with the ST reporting the highest IMRs and U5MRs amongst the social groups and the SC showing a similar disadvantage for the NMR (see Figure 5.7). It is useful to point out here that 65.6 per cent of the U5MR deaths are neonatal deaths, which is the number of neonates dying before reaching 28 days of age, per 1,000 live births (Office of the Registrar General 2011).

Child survival indicators such as the IMR and the U5MR are closely linked to the

> *In Maharashtra, the U5MR[4] has shown a consistent decline over the years from 58.1 in 1998–99 to 46.7 in 2005–06, and further to 36 in 2008.*

FIGURE 5.4 IMR and PCDDP: Maharashtra

Association between Infant Mortality and PCDDP

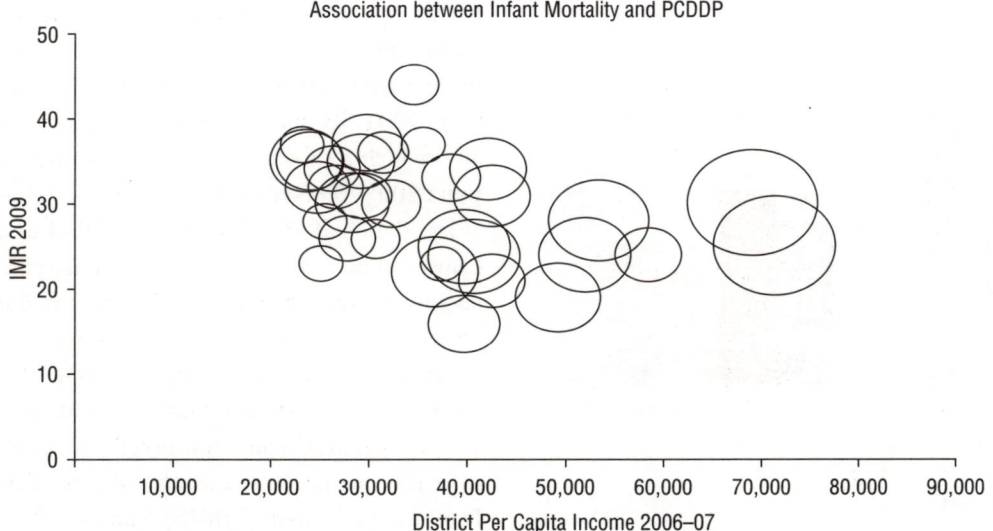

Sources: SHSRC (2009) for IMR and Planning Commission (2007) for PCDDP 2006–07.

---

[4] The sources of data on U5MR are NFHS-2 (IIPS and ORC Macro 2001), NFHS-3 (IIPS and Macro International 2008), and SRS statistical reports and SRS bulletins published by the RGI, cited in Institute of Applied Manpower Research (2011).

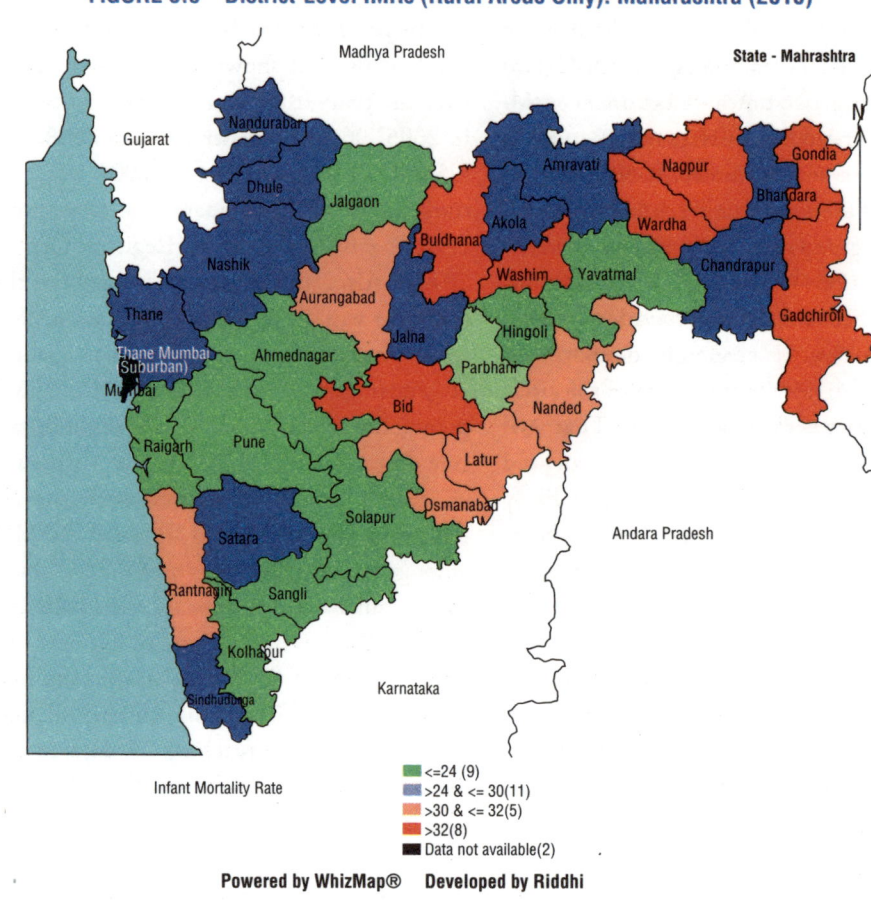

FIGURE 5.5 District-Level IMRs (Rural Areas Only): Maharashtra (2010)

Source: State Bureau of Health Intelligence and Vital Statistics (2010).

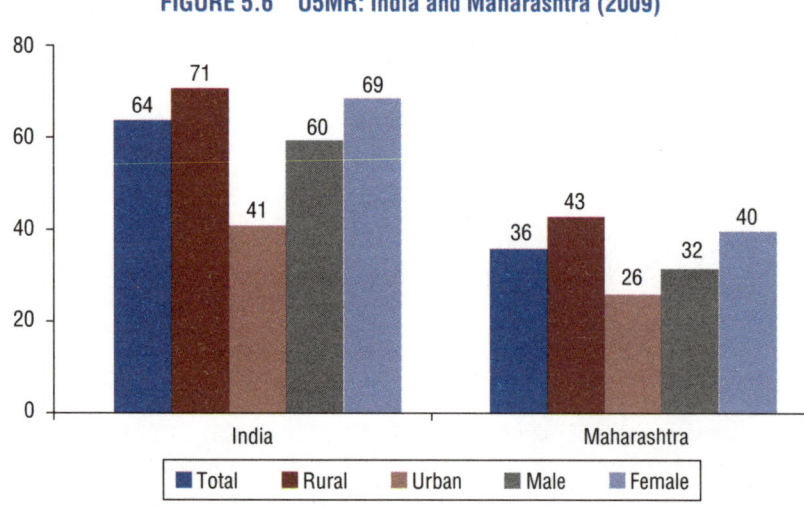

FIGURE 5.6 U5MR: India and Maharashtra (2009)

Source: Office of the Registrar General 2011.

MMR, which is the number of women who die during pregnancy and childbirth, per 100,000 live births The National Population Policy, 2010 aims at achieving less than one maternal death per 1,000 live births. The MMR has always remained below the all-India average in Maharashtra. It has shown a decline from 166 in 1997–98 to 149 in the years 2001–03 and 130 in 2004–06, eventually reducing substantially to 104 during the years 2007–09 (see Figure 5.8) and standing at less than half of the national MMR of 212. Causes of maternal mortality reveal marginal success by the state in reducing deaths due to postpartum haemorrhage, toxaemia of pregnancy and puerperal sepsis. Along with these causes, anaemia is found to contribute to maternal deaths amongst pregnant women in rural areas (see Health Management Information System (HMIS) data for 2007–10 in Government of Maharashtra [n.d.]).

Adolescent pregnancy could also be a factor contributing to maternal deaths. The NFHS-3 (2005–06) data shows that at the time of the survey, 13.8 per cent of girls between the ages of 15 and 19 were already mothers or were pregnant (9.3 per cent in urban areas and 18.9 per cent in rural areas) (IIPS and Macro International 2008). Overall, 13.8 per cent of adolescent pregnancies were reported, with 19.4 per cent among the SC, 23.1 per cent among the ST and 7.5 per cent among the OBC. The disparity in adolescent pregnancies by economic status was glaring, with 22.6 per cent of adolescent pregnancies reported for the lowest and 5.7 per cent for the highest wealth index categories respectively.

Health: Input Indicators

Public Spending on Health

For a deeper and better understanding of health-related outcomes it is useful to study various health input and process indicators in greater detail. Public spending on health is the first input indicator that has an important bearing on health outcomes. The availability of commensurate state allocations for health has a direct bearing on the provisioning of infrastructure, effective health-care services and health outcomes.

State Health Expenditure

Public provisioning of health care in India is a responsibility shared by the state, central and local governments. However, since health is a 'state' subject, the primary responsibility of financing and provisioning of public health services rests with the state governments.

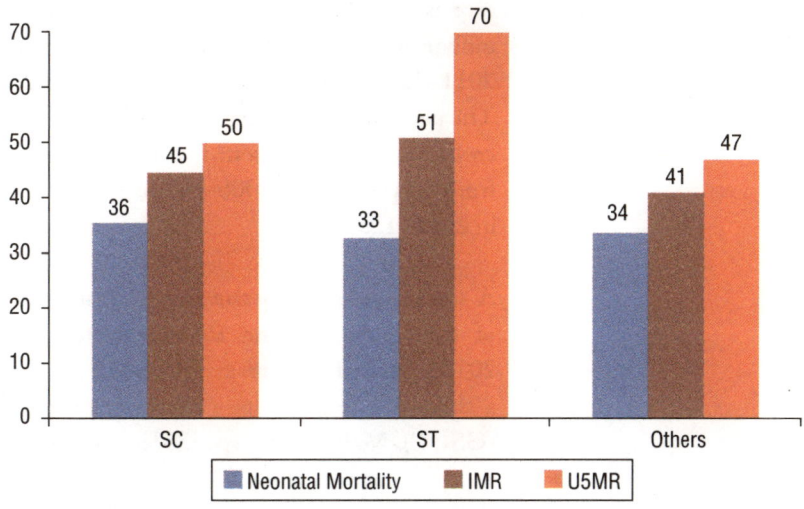

FIGURE 5.7 NMR, IMR and U5MR, by Social Groups: Maharashtra

Sources: IIPS (1995); IIPS and ORC Macro (2001); IIPS and Macro International (2008).

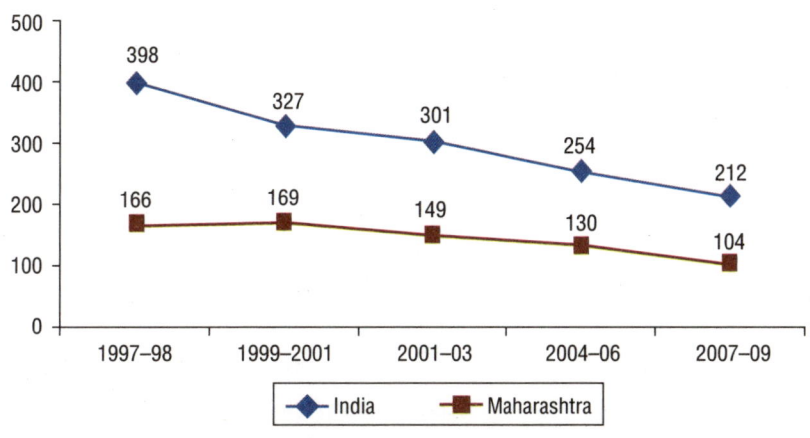

FIGURE 5.8 MMR: India and Maharashtra (1997–98 to 2007–09)

Sources: Office of the Registrar General (2000, 2003, 2005, 2008, 2011).

Box 5.1 Human Development: Speaking to the People: Some Sociocultural Factors Affecting IMR and CMR

1. The most common reasons cited for high IMRs and CMRs are child marriage and early pregnancy.
2. The hilly areas of Jawhar, Soyegaon, Akkalkuwa, Kelapur, Taloda, Chikhaldara, Dharni and Charmoshi are inaccessible for setting up PHCs and hence 10–20 per cent of deliveries here are conducted at home by experienced women.
3. In some communities pregnant women are dissuaded from eating more to avoid high birth weight of the child, which is believed to lead to difficulties during delivery.
4. Migration leads to pregnant women going unrecorded in areas such as Chikhaldara and Dharni. Further, infants are looked after by older female siblings when the mother goes to work, leading to incorrect nurturing of the child.
5. Low literacy levels, addiction among women and unclean atmosphere in their habitations are cited as some of the causes of high IMRs in the Pardhi community in Kalamb. Also, the reluctance of this community to take advantage of the nearby medical facilities leads to higher CMRs.

Source: Block-level consultation by YASHADA, December 2011.

The expenditure of the government on health care is seen have increased from ₹13,278.8 million in 2006–07 to ₹28,044.6 million in 2011–12 in absolute terms (see Table 5.2). The percentage of the total expenditure (Plan and Non-Plan) also seems to be increasing, from 92 per cent in 2006–07 to 98 per cent in 2011–12.

A study conducted by the National Institute of Public Finance and Policy (NIPFP) in 2010 reveals that in terms of per capita and a share of the gross state domestic product (GSDP), Maharashtra spends less on health (Sen et al. 2010). Public expenditure on health and family welfare was 0.6 per cent of GSDP for Maharashtra while Kerala allocated 0.8 per cent of their GSDP to these two sectors. As a proportion of total budgetary expenditure, the state spent 3.7 per cent on health and family welfare, which is lower than the target of 7–8 per cent mandated by the National Health Policy, 2002. A study by NIPFP in 2012 indicate that in 2008–09, the per capita expenditure on health was ₹351 in Maharashtra, while it was ₹507 in Kerala and ₹421 in Tamil Nadu (Govindarao et.al. 2012). In 2008–09, the proportion of state

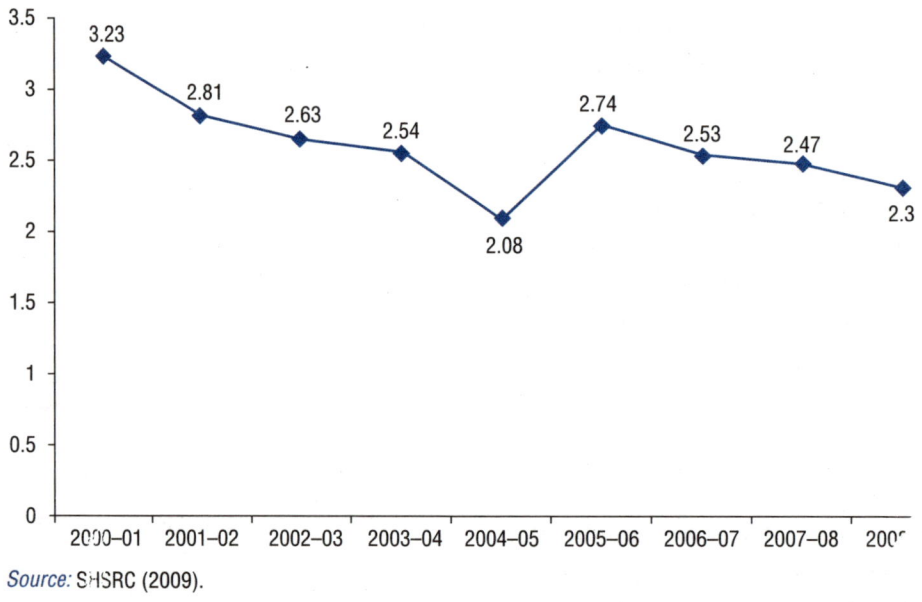

FIGURE 5.9 Percentage of Health Budget to State's Total Budget: Maharashtra (2000–01 to 2008–09)

Source: SHSRC (2009).

TABLE 5.2
Public Health Expenditure: Maharashtra

	Plan			Non-Plan			Total		
	Grant Received	Expenditure	Percentage of Expenditure	Grant Received	Expenditure	Percentage of Expenditure	Grant Received	Expenditure	Percentage of Expenditure
2006–07	4,183.7	2,775.7	66	10,209.6	10,503.1	103	14,393.2	13,278.8	92
2007–08	6,347.8	4,635.7	73	11,075.6	11,145.7	101	17,423.4	15,781.4	91
2008–09	7,353.7	5,512.1	75	12,541.6	13,248.2	106	19,895.3	18,760.3	94
2009–10	8,294.5	4,826.5	58	16,853.4	16,744.2	99	25,148.0	21,570.7	86
2010–11	6,700.8	6,283.1	94	20,038.4	19,823.1	99	26,739.2	26,106.2	98
2011–12	5,804.7	5,701.3	98	22,855.5	22,343.3	98	28,660.2	28,044.6	98

Source: Government of Maharashtra (2012b).
Note: Amounts are indicated in Rupees (millions).

budget allocated to health alone was less than 2.5 per cent (see Figure 5.9). The percentage utilization of the budgeted outlay for the state-level plan scheme has shown a trend of increase since 2006–07 (see Figure 5.10).

The National Health Policy, 2002 suggests that a state allocate and spend 55 per cent, 35 per cent and 10 per cent, respectively on the primary, secondary and tertiary health care sectors. In 2005–06, the share of the tertiary health care services sector was substantially high at 26 per cent, with the expenditure on primary health care much lower than mandated, at 35 per cent. Also, a substantial part of the tertiary health care expenditure was for Mumbai alone along with a sizeable concentration of tertiary health care facilities (Sen et al. 2010). In 2008–09 the distribution of total resources available for health and family welfare showed that *first*, the state's budgetary allocation constituted more than 70 per cent of the total resources available, and *second*, NRHM contributions in terms of approvals were relatively smaller constituting 28 per cent of total available funds (Sen et al. 2010). An important component of the NRHM is the allocations made under the Mission Flexible Pool as it encompasses all new initiatives. Approximately 50 per cent of the funds under this head go towards improvements in health infrastructure facilities including medicines, equipment and untied funds.

Per Capita Health Expenditure

Using disaggregated budget data accessed from the districts from 2001–07, it is possible to understand the relative priority given

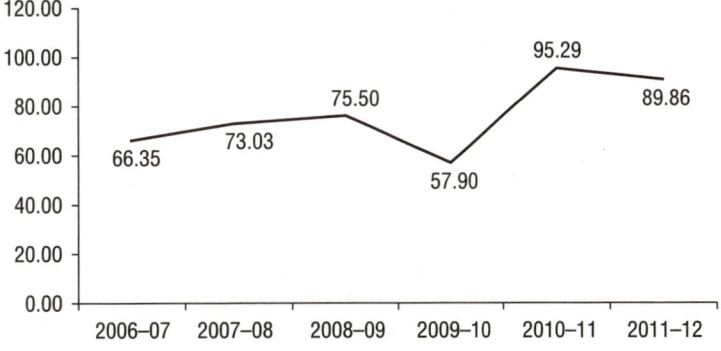

FIGURE 5.10 Percentage of Utilization of Budgeted Outlay (State-Level Plan Scheme): Maharashtra (2006–07 to 2011–12)

Source: Government of Maharashtra (2012b).

to investments in public health.[5] A large number of districts were reported to have high per capita health expenditures in rural areas and interestingly these are mostly districts which did not have a government medical college (Thane, Raigarh, Nashik, Nandurbar, Akola and Chandrapur). At the same time, districts which had a government medical college such as Nagpur, Sangli, Solapur, Aurangabad, Beed, etc., had a higher urban per capita health expenditures (Pune being the exception). Per capita health expenditure for rural and urban populations between 2001–02 and 2006–07 across districts, indicated that it was higher for the urban population per se than for the rural population. Further, rural per capita health expenditure shows that 15 districts have per capita health expenditures lesser than the state average (see Tables 5A.2 and 5A.3).

Health Infrastructure and Facilities

Health infrastructure and facilities are the second important input indicators that help

---

[5] The source of district level expenditure data is the Indian Audit & Accounts Department, Office of the Accountant General (AG), Maharashtra. The sum of all districts' treasury health expenditure data will not match with the sum total of the state health expenditure (the differences are not huge) as there are some other expenses that are not categorized as district level. This district-level expenditure is routed through the treasury and is captured by the AG's office through the vouchers received for the same. Using disaggregated budget data from districts we have tried to understand the relative priority given to investment in public health across districts. However, to gain a comprehensive picture of district health service expenditure, local government's (municipal corporation) own contributions to such services should also incorporated in this analysis. We limit our analysis to the district treasury data because of non-availability of the health expenditure by urban local bodies (ULBs).

FIGURE 5.11 Public Health Care Infrastructure: Maharashtra (2012)

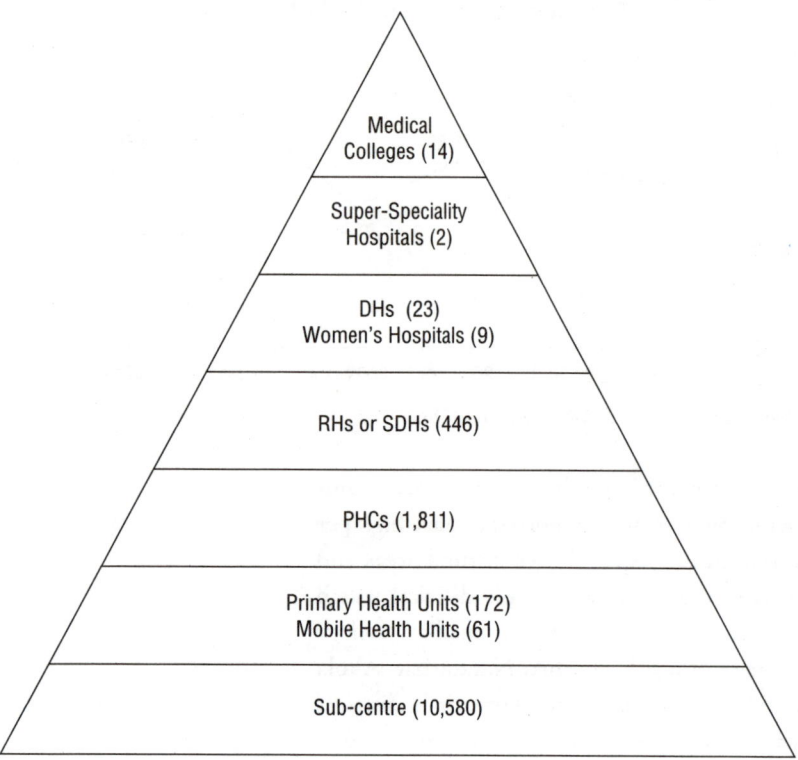

Source: Public Health Department, GoM, Annual Report, 2011–12.

When studying and assessing the provisioning of health facilities in the state it needs to be mentioned right at the start that in Maharashtra there are 15 districts that have a sizeable population of different tribal communities which constitute almost 10 per cent of the population of the state. The State Health Systems Resource Centre (SHSRC) report (SHSRC 2009) points towards an important feature arising from the data of the 2001 census, namely, that there were 22,383 small villages with a population of less than 1,000 which accounted for about 50.5 per cent of the total number of villages in the state. Also, amongst these villages, 2,942 had a population of less than 200, which made it difficult to extend the outreach of medical facilities to these pockets of the populace.[6]

The sub-centre is the lowest rung of public health infrastructure and covers services such as maternal and child health care, treatment of minor ailments, referrals as well as health education services. Government norms stipulate a sub-centre to be made available for a population of 3,000 in tribal areas and a population of 5,000 in non-tribal areas. Currently, the average population served per sub-centre in tribal areas of the state is 4,340 while that for rural areas is 6,179.[7] However, there exist wide variations in the district-wise availability of sub-centres (see Table 5.3). Interestingly, what we find is that the average population served by sub-centres in the tribal districts of Gadchiroli, Gondia and Nanded is well below the norm, reflecting good coverage. On the other hand in Jalgaon the coverage of this health facility is poor given the scattered nature of the tribal population in one block. The non-tribal rural

in assessing the available provisioning of effective and timely health care to the population. Maharashtra has an extensive network of health-care delivery institutions, infrastructure and manpower, reaching out to some of the remote areas in the state (see Figure 5.11). There is basically a three-tier public health system that includes community health centres (CHCs), PHCs and sub-centres, RHs, district hospitals (DHs), sub-district hospitals (SDHs) in rural and semi-urban areas. In addition to the public health institutions, private nursing homes and NGOs also are involved in providing health-care services in the state.

---

[6] The norms consider population as the only criteria which may not do justice to some areas with highly varying densities of population and it was therefore realized that to enhance the quality of healthcare the following parameters were taken into account to prepare the proposed plan of action by Government of Maharashtra: (a) increase in population, (b) distance between village and public healthcare facility (c) irregular land terrains. Based on the above parameters the government of Maharashtra has proposed establishment and upgradation of need based healthcare facilities.

[7] The data about sub-centres is reported at http://www.maha-arogya.gov.in/ and the data for population is from ORGI, 2011, Primary Census Abstract.

areas of Ratnagiri, Sindhudurg and Nagpur (low population districts) show reasonably good population sub-centre coverage while Nandurbar, Thane and Gondia (high population districts) show poor coverage of this health facility, indicating that population norm based shortfalls still prevail in the state.

PHCs play a crucial role in the provisioning of public health services. This is because of their important functional role in prevention and control of epidemics, facilitation of vaccination, water quality testing and management of malnutrition, health education and provision of services such as outpatient department (OPD), in-patient department (IPD), laboratory and minor operations. As per government norms, a PHC needs to be made available for a population of 20,000 in tribal areas and a population of 30,000 in non-tribal areas. The average population covered per PHC in tribal areas was 28,591 and in rural areas of the state it was 35,174.[8] Inter-district disparities in the coverage of PHCs however exist. While on the one hand the coverage of PHCs based on population norms is very good in the tribal districts of Gondia, Gadchiroli and Nanded, on the other, the coverage is poor in tribal Jalgaon where the tribal population is scattered in one block (see Table 5.4).

In an attempt to upgrade all PHCs in the state to make them functional and accessible to the community at all times, from a total of 1,811 PHCs, 419 PHCs have been upgraded as 24×7 First Stage Referral Units (FRUs) until 2011–12 (Government of Maharashtra 2012c).

RHs are 30-bedded referral hospitals which provide specialized services, including advanced medical and surgical care and cases from PHCs are usually referred here. Government norms require one RH for every five PHCs. The average population served by RH is 177,533.[9] Population ratios for RHs have improved slightly, particularly during the last decade across all regions of the state, with the Western Maharashtra region showing the highest improvement for this indicator (see Table 5A.4). What is also noticed is a decrease in inter-district inequities in this health facility (see Figure 5.12), which could be a result of the recent upgrading of various RHs across the state.

TABLE 5.3
Average Population per Sub-Centre: Maharashtra (2011)

Districts with Lowest Population		Districts with Highest Population	
Average Tribal Population per Sub-Centre			
Gadchiroli	1,059	Jalgaon	33,567
Gondia	1,615	Raigad	14,251
Nanded	2,627	Nagpur	7,698
Average Rural Population per Sub-Centre			
Ratnagiri	3,525	Nandurbar	23,210
Sindhudurg	2,970	Thane	8,769
Nagpur	4,395	Gondia	7,988

Source: http//:www.mahaarogya.gov.in and Directorate of Census Operations (2011).

TABLE 5.4
Average Population per PHC: Maharashtra (2011)

Districts with Lowest Population		Districts with Highest Population	
Average Tribal Population per PHC			
Gadchiroli	8,850	Nagpur	50,039
Gondia	10,727	Raigad	90,225
Nanded	17,265	Jalgaon	37,496
Average Rural Population per PHC			
Bhandara	17,751	Thane	47,419
Sindhudurg	19,385	Beed	61,942
Ratnagiri	19,889	Gondiya	44,733

Source: http//:www.mahaarogya.gov.in and Directorate of Census Operations (2011).

---

[8] The data about PHC reported is taken from http://www.maha-arogya.gov.in/ and the data for population is from ORGI, 2011, Primary Census Abstract.

[9] The data about RH reported from http://www.maha-arogya.gov.in/ and the data for population is from ORGI, 2011, Primary Census Abstract.

The availability of hospitals and beds per 100,000 of population has shown a constant increase in the state since 1981 (see Figures 5.13 and 5.14). The total number of hospital beds also showed an urban bias with urban areas having close to 20 times more hospital beds vis-à-vis rural areas. Many districts also reported an increase in the population per hospital bed in the public sector over the last decade (see Table 5A.5), indicating the need to improve the ratio of such services on a priority basis.

Health Personnel

HR for public health care form the backbone of effective functioning of the existing health infrastructure in the state and are the third input indicator. Adequate health personnel is an important precondition for making health facilities accessible to the populace, especially

FIGURE 5.12 District-Wise Trends in Population per RH: Maharashtra

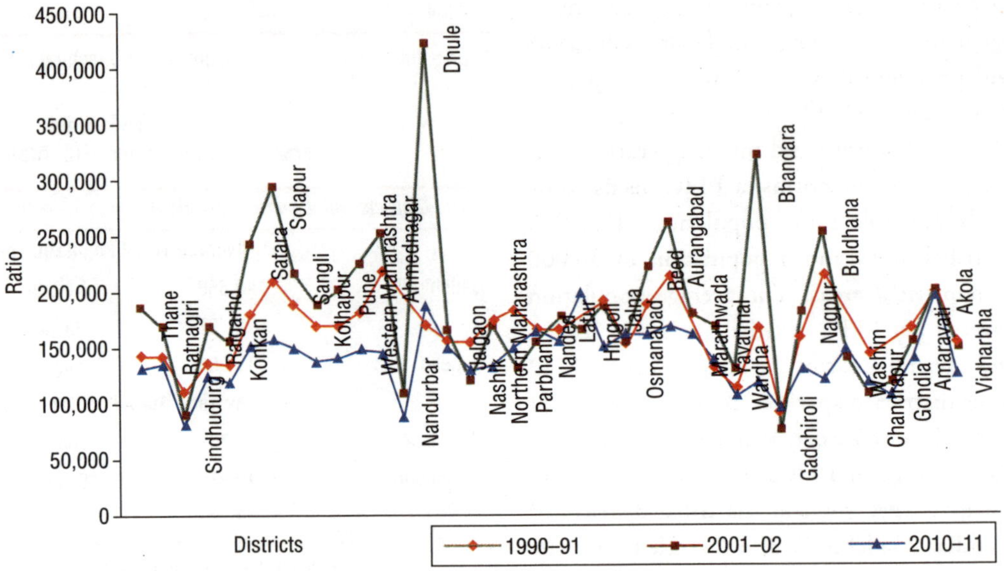

Source: Government of Maharashtra (n.d.).
Note: For the year 2011, we have also taken into account the SDHs that were actually RHs earlier so that comparability is maintained. Many RHs were upgraded in the last decade into SDHs of 50 as well as 100 beds.

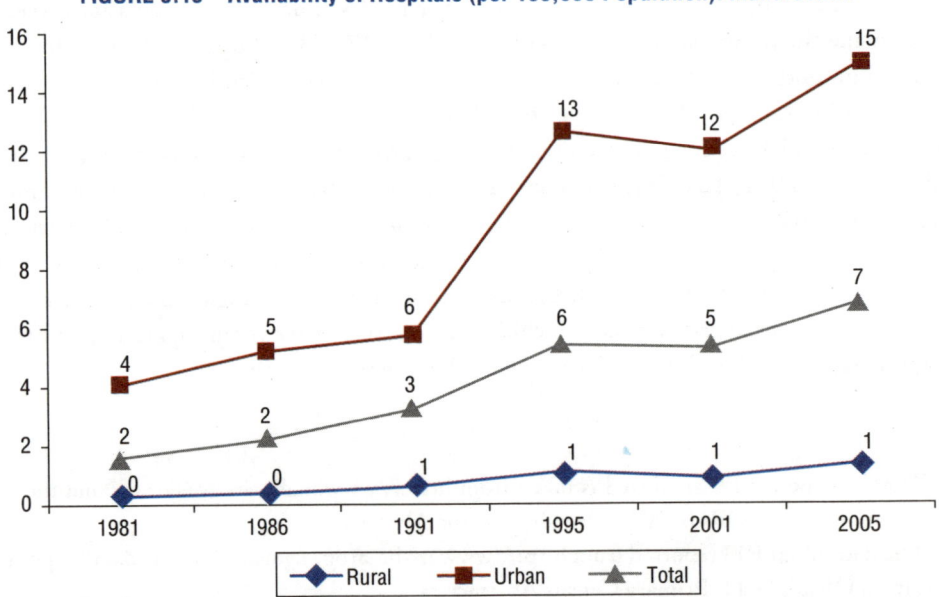

FIGURE 5.13 Availability of Hospitals (per 100,000 Population): Maharashtra

Source: SHSRC (2009).

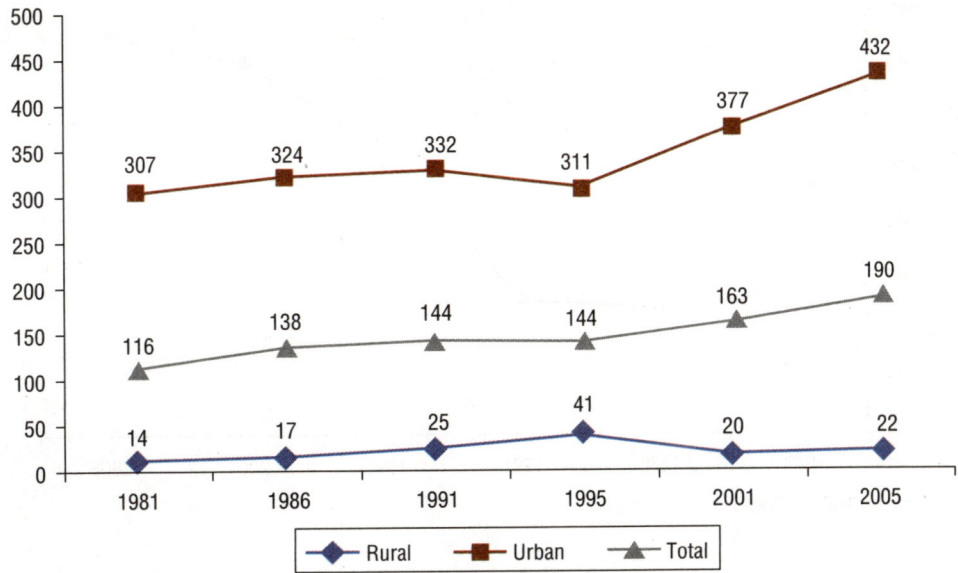

FIGURE 5.14 Availability of Beds (per 100,000 Population): Maharashtra

Source: SHSRC (2009).

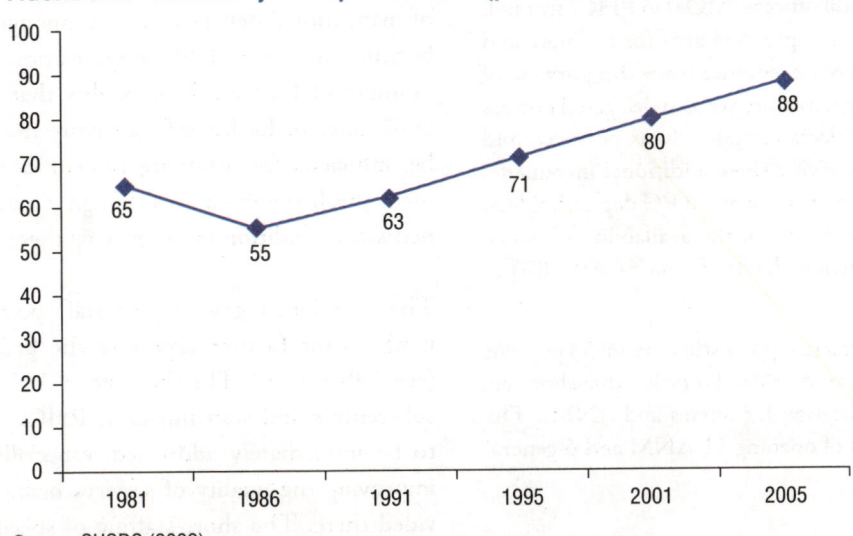

FIGURE 5.15 Availability of Allopathic Doctors (per 100,000 Population): Maharashtra[10]

Source: SHSRC (2009).

in rural and far-flung tribal-inhabited areas. In Maharashtra, for the public and private sectors taken together, the availability of allopathic doctors and nurses per 100,000 population has seen a steady increase over 1981–2005, with the growth rate in the nurse population being higher (see Figures 5.15 and 5.16). Despite such overall improvements in health manpower, there exist apparent inter-regional variations in these indicators. While the Vidarbha region had the best population-per-doctor and nurse ratios in the public sector in 2009 (SHSRC 2009), the Konkan region exhibited a poor population-per-doctor ratio and the Marathwada region reported poor population-per-nurse ratios.

Intra-regional disparities exist in the availability of HR. Within the Vidarbha region, where the doctor population ratio is 7,340,

---

[10] As on April 2012 (Annual Report of Public Health Department), 6,281 allopathic doctors and 1,023 ayurvedic doctors are working in rural areas of Maharashtra.

FIGURE 5.16 Availability of Nurses (per 100,000 Population): Maharashtra

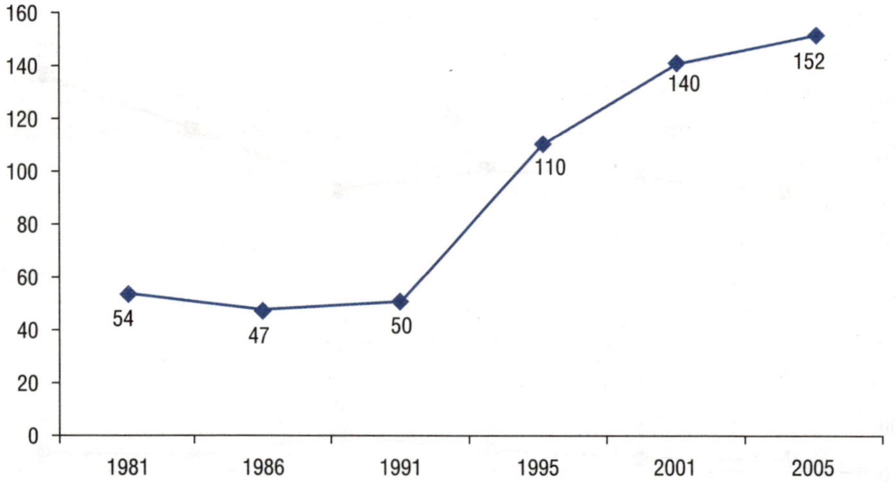

```
160
140                                                    140    152
120
100                                    110
 80
 60
 40   54        47        50
 20
  0
     1981     1986      1991      1995    2001    2005
```
Source: SHSRC (2009).

Box 5.2 Availability of Health Personnel

Maharashtra has taken some positive initiatives to address the issue of HR for health care. The availability of medical officers (MOs) in PHCs through the Public Service Commission has been a problem area for the state and to overcome this the MO's post has been exempted from the purview of the Commission. The Regional Deputy Directors are also delegated powers to appoint Specialists and Medical Officers temporarily as per need and vacancy. In addition, goverment is also giving three additional increments to PG diploma holders and six additional increments to PG degree holders. This has resulted in significant improvements in the availability of MOs. Currently, 7,419 posts of MOs are sanctioned, out of which 6,419 (87 per cent) posts have been filled.

However, a large number of vacant contractual posts still remain: 53 per cent for staff nurses and 46 per cent for urban ANMs. To tackle this shortage, the state has stepped up preservice education for nurses and ANMs. The state government is now in the process of opening 11 ANM and 6 general nursing and midwifery schools.

Source: NRHM (2011a).

---

wide inter-district variations exist. Within this region, districts such as Buldhana, Washim and Yavatmal show much lower doctor population ratios at 14,458, 13,915 and 12,790 respectively (Government of Maharashtra 1991–2011). Paradoxically, Gadchiroli district in the Vidarbha region has the best population-per-doctor ratio combined with very low actual utilization rates of health care reflected in the very low percentage of institutional deliveries (23.5 per cent) and inadequate coverage of child immunization (46.4 per cent).[11] It ranks the last amongst all the districts for percentage of institutional deliveries and is amongst the bottom three for child immunization. The example of Gadchiroli highlights that mere availability of health infrastructure may not be sufficient for attaining human development (health) outcomes, although it may be a necessary condition for improving them.

The sanctioned government staff positions lying vacant further aggravate the problem (see Table 5A.6). The shortage of ANMs at sub-centres and staff nurses at PHCs needs to be immediately addressed, especially for improving the quality of services being provided there. The short-staffing of specialists in IPHS hospitals is also a cause for concern (NRHM 2011c). The unavailability of such specialists in the public health-care system has implications for the well-being of the poor, with them having to either forgo specialized health care or incur high out-of-pocket expenditure for the same.

Health: Process Indicators

The provisioning of health-care facilities captured by various input indicators should ideally be translated into health outcomes

---

[11] Data for institutional deliveries and child immunization for Gadchiroli is from IIPS (2010).

through their effective utilization. Data on indicators which form part of the health care provisioning processes, such as population proportions utilizing IP and OP care, the proportion of institutional deliveries, maternal and antenatal care and child immunizations under the aegis of the reproductive and child health (RCH) programmes, disaggregated by social groups, sectors and wealth classes help in understanding how effectively the health infrastructure and services provided have been utilized, the progress made and the gaps that need to be bridged. Data from various rounds of DLHS and NFHS have been utilized to facilitate such an analysis for Maharashtra. Variations in various process indicators across districts, rural–urban sectors, social and income groups are observed and are reported in the sections below.

Utilization of Health Care

Population proportions accessing and utilizing IP and OP health care are an important process indicator of the effectiveness of the available health-care infrastructure in the state. According to estimates from the 60th round of the NSS (January–June 2004), only 11 per cent of urban OP care, 16 per cent of rural OP care and about 28 per cent of rural and urban IP care were being taken care of by the public health facilities in Maharashtra (National Sample Survey Organisation 2006). There was a large dependence on the private sector, especially for OP care and hospitalization. Private IP and OP utilization showed an increase by around 15 percentage points between 1986–87 and 2004 (see Figure 5.17).

Although overall the provisioning of health services in the state is dominated by the private sector it does not necessarily imply inadequacy of the public sector. A substantial proportion of patients from the lower socioeconomic levels choose to access public health care in Maharashtra. In many districts, a large proportion of women still access government facilities for pregnancy- and childbirth-related services, reflected by the proportion of institutional deliveries (IIPS 2010; see also Table 5A.7). Also, in districts such as Sindhudurg, Gadchiroli, Nagpur,

In many districts, a large proportion of women still access government facilities for pregnancy- and childbirth-related services, reflected by the proportion of institutional deliveries.

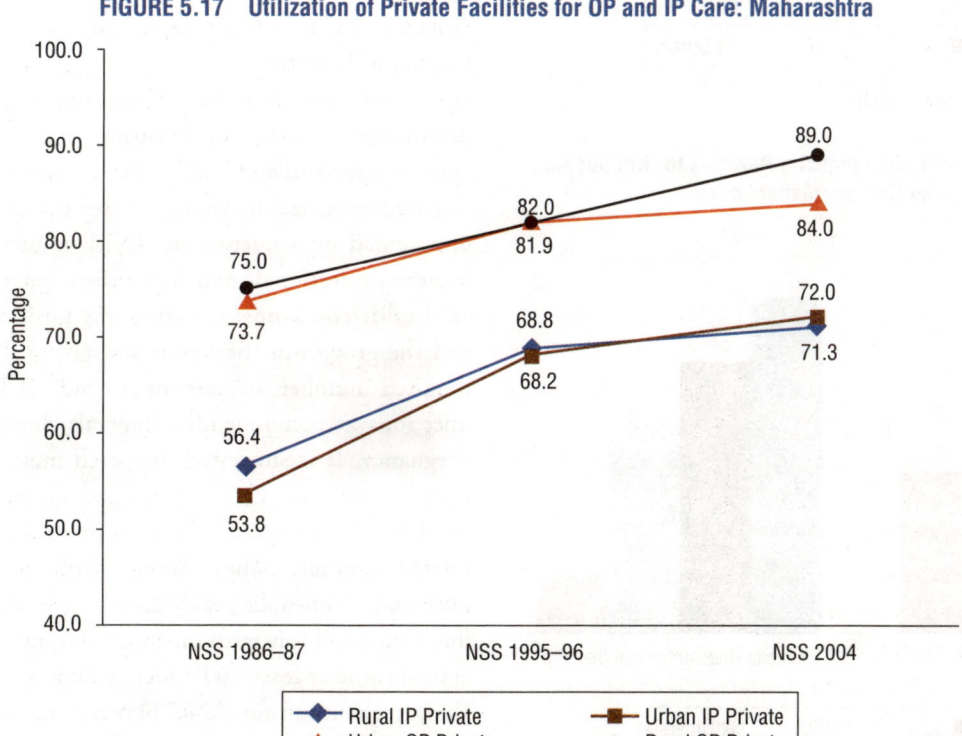

FIGURE 5.17 Utilization of Private Facilities for OP and IP Care: Maharashtra

Sources: National Sample Survey Organisation (1998, 2006, 2012).

Chandrapur, Gondia, Sangli, Thane and Ratnagiri more than 50 per cent of women choose to access public facilities for ANCs (IIPS 2010; see also Table 5A.8). It needs to be noted here that the government and private health care system operate on different philosophies. The government provides publicly financed and managed curative and preventive health services, from the primary to tertiary level, throughout the state and free of cost to the consumer. A fee-levying private sector on the other hand plays a dominant role in the provision of individual curative care.

Data from the NSS 60th round, when disaggregated by social groups points towards a caste disparity in the utilization of health facilities (National Sample Survey Organisation 2006). Figure 5.18 shows that as a proportion of total care accessed, the SC, ST and OBC depend more on the public sector for health care as compared to the Others category. The cause for concern is the low utilization of public health facilities by the ST population as compared to other social groups. Since tribal districts are also areas where the private health sector is poorly developed, the potential role that an effective public health system can play as an equalizer of socioeconomic disparities cannot be stressed enough.

Financial constraints are an important cause for not accessing health care and it is found that those belonging to the backward social groups predominantly cite this as a reason for not accessing health care (National Sample Survey Organisation 2006). A small proportion of the population belonging to the Others category cites financial reasons (11 per cent) as a reason for not accessing health care showcasing the degree of inequity (see Figure 5.19).

Antenatal Care: An Imperative for Maternal Health

Antenatal care is a crucial component of health-care services for ensuring maternal and child survival and is also a determinant of the quality of health services. Antenatal care is provided by a doctor, an ANM or other health professional and comprises physical health check-ups, checking the position and the growth of the foetus and giving the required number of tetanus toxoid (TT) injections at recommended intervals during pregnancy. It is suggested that each mother have at least three check-ups as part of antenatal care to safeguard her from pregnancy-related complications. Along with good nutrition, iron–folic acid tablets are also important and it is recommended that mothers consume at least 100 tablets before term. Early registration for ANC between 12 and 16 weeks of pregnancy is crucial for ensuring a healthy pregnancy, screening and treatment

FIGURE 5.18 Use of Public Facilities, by Social Groups: Maharashtra

Source: National Sample Survey Organisation (2006).

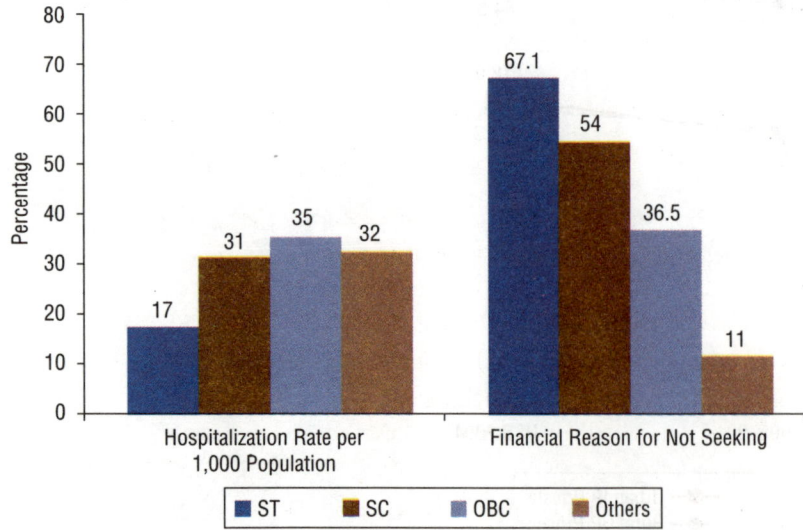

FIGURE 5.19 Hospitalization Rates and Financial Reasons for Not Seeking Treatment, by Social Groups: Maharashtra

Source: Based on data from NSSO, 2006, cited in Mishra et al. (2008).

for high-risk pregnancies, treatment of the mother and initiating the continuum of mother care and childcare.

Data from DLHS-3 reveals the following (IIPS 2010): *First*, a third of the women in Maharashtra received full antenatal care[12] in 2007–08. (32.6 per cent in rural and 37.1 per cent in urban areas) (see Table 5A.7). There existed inter-district disparities in percentage of full ANC from lowest in Aurangabad (14.1 per cent) to highest in Satara (55.5 per cent) (see Table 5A.8). The percentage is improved to 70 per cent in rural area and 61 per cent in urban area (Government of Maharashtra 2012c).

Second, the educational and economic status of women had a bearing on their access to antenatal care (see Table 5A.7). The percentage of women availing antenatal care went up as we moved up the wealth index and education ladder. Across social groups there was not much variation in this health indicator. The place of residence did seem to matter with women residing in urban areas availing antenatal care in higher proportions.

Third, place of accessing ANCs revealed that close to half the women belonging to the SC and the ST categories availed it from government health facilities (see Table 5A.7).

Fourth, the preference for private health clinics for ANCs during pregnancy was higher in urban areas (59.8 per cent) as compared to rural areas (40.2 per cent) (see Table 5A.7).

Fifth, inter-district variations also existed in terms of place of accessing ANCs. In Gondia, Gadchiroli, Bhandara and Sindhudurg more than 65 per cent of women accessed ANCs from government facilities (see Table 5A.8). On the other hand, accessing ANCs from government facilities was less than 28 per cent in districts such as Satara, Hingoli and Washim.

Box 5.3 Human Development: Speaking to the People: Perceptions on Health Issues: Sarpanch's Speak

1. A group of sarpanchs of the Bramhapuri block in Chandrapur reported an increase in HIV and AIDS cases.
2. Since the block is a remote area, they also stressed the need for more maternity home facilities.
3. The Taloda block in Nandurbar highlighted the imperative need to tackle malnutrition and sickle-cell anaemia, which was reported as common in the area. Although the health department does provide primary aid for this, the pressing need for more interventions to combat this disease was highlighted.
4. A group of sarpanchs of the Zari Jamani block in Yavatmal mentioned snake bite as a major cause of death in the area and the need for snake-bite antidotes for immediate relief action.
5. Non-vegetarian diets, a tradition of child marriage, isolated residences, decision-making in the Jat Panchayat (a body of influential people in the community) and delinquency were cited as the root causes of all health- and education-related problems of the Pardhi community in Kalamb (Osmanabad).

Source: Block-level consultation by YASHADA, December 2011.

Sixth, the proportion of women not availing any antenatal care visit was approximately 10 per cent for the state with it being highest for illiterate women (24.2 per cent), women belonging to the ST (20.7 per cent) and those belonging to the lowest wealth index category (26.0 per cent) (IIPS 2010: Table 4.5[A]). Such differentials in maternal health-care coverage have implications given that almost two-thirds (65 per cent) of women in Maharashtra have had at least one delivery complication like obstructed labour, premature or prolonged labour.

Seventh, access to sonographs during pregnancy is low in rural areas, for women belonging to ST those belonging to lowest wealth index category.

Eighth, more than three-fourths of pregnant women received the required dose of two or more TT injections, the proportion being higher for urban areas (85.7 per cent) vis-à-vis rural areas (74 per cent). A little over a third of ST women did not receive this important maternal care input, access to

---

[12] At least three visits for ANC, at least one TT injection and 100 or more iron–folic acid tablets or syrup.

which also showed an improvement over the wealth index classes from lowest to highest. The proportion of women receiving iron–folic acid tablets or syrup for at least three months was 34 per cent for the state, again higher in urban areas as compared to rural areas (42 per cent and 36.8 per cent respectively). SC women showed the lowest coverage for this indicator, which also showed an increase for classes with a higher standard of living.

Finally, a large proportion (73 per cent) of women used 'other' means of transportation for delivery and only 22.7 per cent used an ambulance, jeep or car. Less than one tenth (8.3 per cent) received government financial assistance for delivery care through the JSY (IIPS 2010: Table 4.8). This points to the pressing need for the state to make available maternal health services through the JSY and referral transport systems.

A comparison of the data from DLHS-2 (2002–04) and DLHS-3 (2007–08) brings forth that *first*, the percentage of pregnant women who had at least three or more ANCs[13] has increased from 72.0 per cent to 74.4 per cent, showing an increase in rural areas of four percentage points vis-à-vis 1.4 percentage points in urban areas. *Second*, the proportion of SC and ST women receiving three or more ANCs has also shown an improvement by approximately eight and four percentage points respectively over the two DLHS time points considered. *Third*, while the proportion of women accessing any antenatal care has gone up for both government and private health facilities, it has been greater for the latter (the increase being 3.7 and 8 percentage points respectively). *Fourth*, progress has also been made in the proportion of women receiving full antenatal care coverage in the state from 23 per cent to 33.9 per cent over the DLHS years considered. *Fifth*, the coverage of two or more TT during pregnancy has seen a small drop of two percentage points over the two DLHS time periods considered, while the proportion of women receiving iron–folic acid tablets or syrup for three months (100 days) reports an improvement of 10 percentage points over the same time period. Thus, what emerges is that for the state to achieve complete antenatal care coverage, mothers who are illiterate, economically disadvantaged, belong to the ST and at the aggregate level are from rural areas need to be reached with adequate and improved antenatal care services.

Institutional Births and Safe Deliveries

The place of delivery is one of the main determinants of maternal and neonatal survival. It is also a key indicator of the demand for public health facilities for maternal health. Under the Eleventh Plan, the basic social interventions needed to encourage institutional deliveries under the NRHM included the need for providing training to traditional birth attendants (TBAs) and reductions in travel time to two hours for emergency obstetric care. To achieve reductions in infant and neonatal mortality, home-based neonatal care was also sought to be encouraged.

The NFHS-3 (2005–06) data (IIPS and Macro International 2008) shows an improvement in the proportion of institutional births in the state, from 45 per cent in 1992–93 to 66 per cent in 2005–06. There is also seen a distinct urban bias in the percentage of institutional births. High educational as well as economic status show a positive association with the percentage of institutional births. Data from the DLHS also reiterates the NFHS-3 findings of an improvement in institutional deliveries from 57.1 per cent in DLHS-1 (1998–99) (IIPS 2001) to 57.9 per cent in DLHS-2 (2002–04) (IIPS 2006) and further to 63.5 per cent in DLHS-3 (2007–08) (IIPS 2010) and 81.8 per cent in 2009 (CES 2009).[14] The Public Health Department of GoM reports that 96 per cent deliveries are in the institution

> *The NFHS-3 (2005–06) data (IIPS and Macro International 2008) shows an improvement in the proportion of institutional births in the state, from 45 per cent in 1992–93 to 66 per cent in 2005–06.*

---

[13] ANCs done at home or outside the home.
[14] UNICEF (2011), Fact Sheet of Maharashtra State, Coverage Evaluation Survey, 2009.

in 2012-13 (Government of Maharashtra 2012c). Although there exists an urban bias, the increase in the same has been higher for rural areas over the period from 2002–04 to 2007–08. District-wise data for 2007–08 shows institutional births varying from 93.5 per cent in Mumbai (Suburban) to as low as 23.5 per cent, 25.4 per cent and 41.5 per cent, respectively, in Gadchiroli, Nandurbar and Hingoli (see Table 5A.9). Between DLHS-2 and DLHS-3, Nandurbar shows a decline in the proportion of institutional deliveries by three percentage points while Gadchiroli reports an improvement by three percentage points.

At the aggregate level, the percentage of safe deliveries saw an improvement in both rural and urban areas over DLHS-2 DLHS-3 (see Table 5.5). In 2007–08, at the more disaggregated level of the district, the percentage of safe deliveries was again found to be the lowest in Nandurbar (34.0 per cent), Gadchiroli (34.6 per cent) and Hingoli (47.3 per cent) (see Table 5A.9). The proportion of safe deliveries was found to be less than the state average (69.2 per cent) in 12 districts out of 35. As per Public Health Department of GoM the safe 98 per cent are the safe deliveries in the state with Nandurbar (Rural) having the least per cent of safe deliveries (78 per cent) (Government of Maharashtra 2012).

Access to maternity care services studied across class and caste shows that *first*, the proportion of population not accessing basic health care such as ANCs and postnatal check-ups (PNCs) was higher for the lower MPCE classes (see Figure 5.20), who also reported a larger proportion of deliveries at home. *Second*, when studied by social groups, the SC and ST accessed ANCs and PNCs in much lower proportions and had a higher home delivery rate compared to the OBC and Others (see Figure 5.21). Thus, in spite of the large and extensive health network in the state, access and utilization of maternity care showed the need for better inclusion of the poor and social groups such as the SC and ST. To this end, the involvement of ASHAs in improving the coverage and participation in various mother and childcare programmes in the state needs to be enhanced on a priority basis.

Child Immunization and Postnatal Care

Efforts aimed at improving the CSRs and reducing infant mortality under the NRHM

FIGURE 5.20 Access to Maternity Services across MPCE Classes: Maharashtra

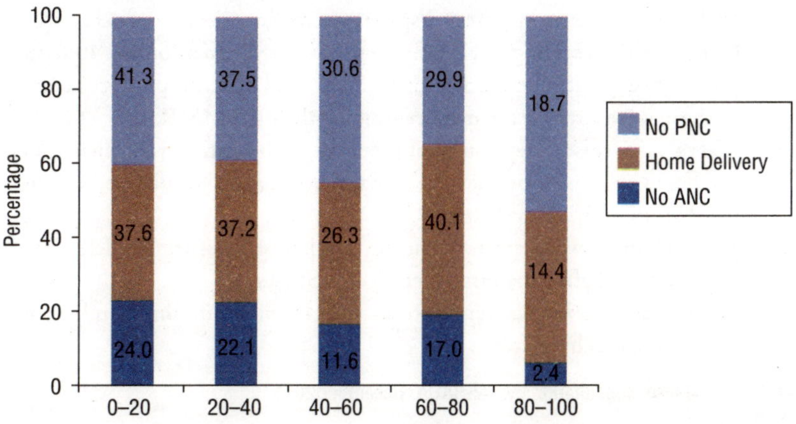

MPCE Class	No ANC	Home Delivery	No PNC
0–20	24.0	37.6	41.3
20–40	22.1	37.2	37.5
40–60	11.6	26.3	30.6
60–80	17.0	40.1	29.9
80–100	2.4	14.4	18.7

Source: Based on data from National Sample Survey Organisation (2006) cited in Mishra et al. (2008).

TABLE 5.5
Maternal Health Indicators as per Targets: Maharashtra

Indicators	National Population Policy Target (By 2010)	DLHS-3 (2007–08)			GoM (2012–13)		
		Total	Rural	Urban	Total	Rural	Urban
Full Antenatal Care Coverage (Percentage)	–	33.9	32.7	37.1	22.5	21.3	24.8
Institutional Deliveries (Percentage)	80	63.6	54.1	87.3	96	96	96
Safe Deliveries (Percentage)	–	69.4	61.1	90.1	98	98	98
Fully Immunized Children (12–23 Months) (Percentage)	100	69.1	67.8	72.7	95	96	90

Sources: IIPS (2006, 2010); Sen et al. (2010).

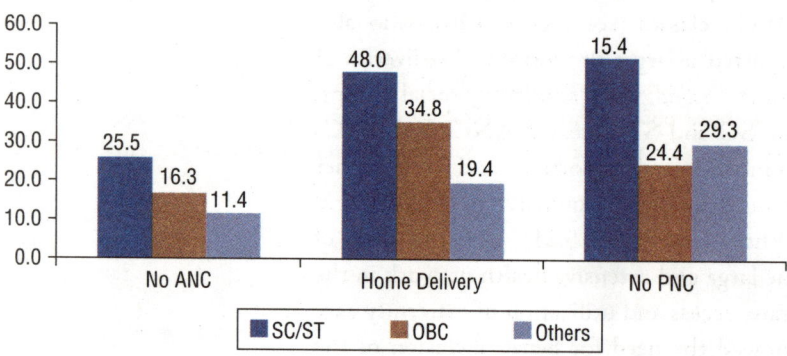

FIGURE 5.21 Access to Maternity Services, by Social Groups: Maharashtra

Source: Based on data from National Sample Survey Organisation (2006) cited in Mishra et al. (2008).

> **Box 5.4 Human Development: Speaking to the People: Institutional Deliveries**
>
> 1. Absence of safe delivery facilities in PHC sub-centres and inaccessible PHCs due to bad road conditions in the hilly areas of Peth, Akkalkuwa, etc., were cited.
> 2. The Korku community residing in Dharni and Chikhaldara still showed faith in the local sadhus, *buva*s and *dasi*, who are usually untrained.
> 3. Traditionally, in tribal areas, the girls select their life partner at the early age of 13–16 years, leading to early pregnancies and maternal and child health related issues.
> 4. Traditionally, if the first child to a woman is born at home, the family finds it unnecessary to access dispensaries for the second delivery.
> 5. Communities residing in Kalamb keep women in isolation for 40 days post-delivery without much nourishment, and cultural practices such as these were cited as the main reason for the high MMR.
> 6. There is a misconception that doctors in hospitals will insist on caesarean deliveries or that the newly born infants would be kept in incubators in the dispensaries.
> 7. In Parbhani, it was reported that the number of institutional deliveries had improved after the introduction of ASHAs.
> 8. Almost all the blocks reported an improvement in the number of institutional deliveries.
>
> Source: Block-level consultation by YASHADA, December 2011.

mainly focus on newborn care, breastfeeding practices, adequate food supplementation and complete immunization for newly born children. To this end, the DLHS-3 reports that in 2007–08 in Maharashtra (IIPS 2010):

1. A high proportion of newborns in urban areas (87.8 per cent) received care within 24 hours of their birth. More than half the women initiated breastfeeding within one hour of delivering their child. Such a practice was seen to be the least amongst women in Nandurbar (37.8 per cent) and most widely practised in Sindhudurg (74 per cent) (IIPS 2010: Table 5.5) (IIPS 2010: Table 5.1).
2. More than two-thirds of children in the 12–23 months' age group received their full immunization dosage. Only 1 per cent of children did not receive any vaccine (see Table 5A.10). There was no significant gender gap in full immunization rates for children (69.9 per cent for boys and 68 per cent for girls).
3. There were inter-district variations in coverage of full immunization of children. It was below 50 per cent in the three districts of Nandurbar (17.0 per cent), Dhule (35.0 per cent) and Gadchiroli (46.4 per cent) and more than 85 per cent in districts such as Satara (92 per cent), Nagpur (90.5 per cent), Sangli (87.5 per cent), Gondia (87.8 per cent), Pune (86.1 per cent) and Ahmednagar (85.3 per cent) (IIPS 2010: Table 5.7). Public Health Department of GoM reports that 95 per cent of the children are fully immunised (Government of Maharashtra 2012–13).
4. Class-based inequalities in vaccination coverage reveal ST children having the lowest coverage at 52.2 per cent. Income (MPCE) class-based inequalities reveal that for the lowest wealth quintile the coverage was just 43.2 per cent while for the highest wealth quintile it was 80.7 per cent. Also, higher birth order and lack of maternal education constrain improved immunisation coverage in the state.

Cost of Health Care

Data from the NSS 60th round (2004) facilitates an in-depth analysis of the cost of health care to households in the state (National Sample Survey Organisation 2006). The main findings are from an analysis of the data are: *first*, sale of assets or borrowing to fund IP care was lower for the State than all India for rural as well as urban areas and the proportion of households forced to borrow or sell assets to seek health care shows a rural bias.[15] *Second*, for IP as well as OP care, a higher percentage of socially backward households (among the SC, ST and OBC) had to resort to sale of assets or borrowings (see Figure 5.22). With increased medical indebtedness amongst these backward socio-economic categories of people, the possibility of their lapsing into a downward spiral of poverty and ill health becomes greater.

Availability and Pricing of Essential Drugs

Linked to the issue of the accessibility of health care is the availability of essential drugs within the public health system. Expenditure on medicines generally constitutes 50 to 80 per cent of the total cost of treatment, over and above which is the added cost of various tests. In Maharashtra, approximately 62 per cent of the IPD expenditure for medical treatment in public hospitals is on the purchase of medicines (about 60 per cent in rural and 63 per cent in urban areas) (National Sample Survey Organisation 2006). The Fourth Common Review Mission (CRM) (NRHM 2011a, 2011b) reports that the financial allocation for medicines per PHC in the state is a mere ₹120,000 per year, which amounts to 4 per person, highlighting the need for immediate revision. Along with the availability of essential medicines, drug pricing is a related issue of concern. The National List of Essential Medicines covers 348 drugs, of which the prices of only 37 medicines are controlled by the National Pharmaceutical Pricing Authority. Regulation in drug pricing is closely linked to government spending on essential drugs and demands immediate attention.

New Government Initiatives

NRHM

With health being a state subject in India, the NRHM, launched in 2005, aims at providing support to the states for strengthening health care in rural areas through provisioning of physical infrastructure, HR, equipment, emergency transport, drugs, diagnostics and other support. As per the Maharashtra state report (NHRM 2009) the main achievements have been the improved performance of the JSY, community mobilization by ASHAs, increases in institutional deliveries and OPD care. The highlight achievement of

Box 5.5 HIV Prevalence in the State

Maharashtra ranks fourth highest amongst the states for AIDS prevalence (IIPS and Macro International 2008). The AIDS incidence data for 2007 shows more positive cases in the state than the country (see Table 5.6). However, HIV prevalence has significantly decreased amongst female sex workers from 54.3 per cent to 18 per cent over the years between 2003 and 2007 (NACO 2008). There has been an increase in the availability of infrastructure to combat the disease in terms of establishing centres, recruiting HR or the supply of medications. Maharashtra has 190,083 people registered as living with HIV/AIDS and 107,886 patients ever started on antiretroviral therapy.

TABLE 5.6
Percentage of HIV/AIDS Prevalence: Maharashtra (2007)

State	Antenatal Clinic, HIV Prevalence	Sexually Transmitted Diseases Clinic, HIV Prevalence	Injection Drug Users, HIV Prevalence	Female Sex Worker, HIV Prevalence
Maharashtra	0.5	11.6	24.4	17.9
India	0.5	3.6	7.2	5.1

Source: NACO (2008).

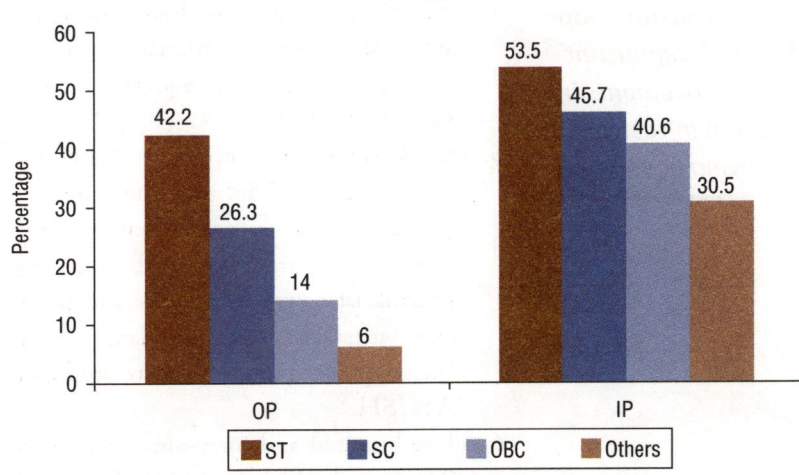

FIGURE 5.22 Borrowings and Sale of Assets for Accessing Health Care: Maharashtra

Source: Based on data from National Sample Survey Organisation (2006), cited in Mishra et al. (2008).

---

[15] GoM, Report on Morbidity and Health Care, NSS 60th Round, Volume I and Volume 2.

a significant increase in institutional deliveries has been facilitated by putting into place several incentive packages including cash incentives to PHC staff for increasing the institutional delivery rate by three times over the previous year, hardship allowances to staff in tribal and Naxalite areas and incentives to staff in low performing areas to encourage institutional deliveries.

In quantitative terms the main achievements under the NRHM in Maharashtra include:

Infrastructure and Manpower Augmentation

1. Four hundred and nineteen PHCs have been made operational as FRUs on a 24×7 basis.
2. One hundred and ten RHs and seventy-four SDHs (including nine women's hospitals) are also functional in the state on a 24×7 basis.
3. Fifty eight thousand eight hundred and thirty-one ASHAs have been appointed.
4. Ten thousand five hundred and eighty sub-centres are functional with an ANM, while 6,617 are equipped with a second ANM.
5. Six hundred and seventeen Ayurveda, yoga, Unani, Siddha and homoeopathy (AYUSH) doctors with seven hundred and eleven paramedic staff including pharmacists, yoga nature therapists and massagists-cum-attendants have been appointed under mainstreaming of AYUSH.
6. Five hundred and forty-nine specialists, 923 lady health visitors (LHVs) and 809 staff nurses have been appointed on a contractual basis, providing a boost to manpower availability in various health facilities.

Service Enhancement

1. Substantial improvement in institutional deliveries from 11.0 lakhs in 2006–07 to 13.5 lakhs in 2007–08, to 15.5 lakhs in 2008–09, and further to 16.3 lakhs in 2011–12.
2. Increase in JSY beneficiaries from 1.8 lakhs in 2006–07 to 2.2 lakhs in 2007–08 to 2.2 lakhs in 2008–09 and to 4.4 lakhs in 2012–13.
3. Implementation of the Integrated Management of Neonatal and Childhood Illness by 33 districts, with 84,795 personnel having received training.
4. Operationalization of the first phase of CBM.
5. The state has initiated certain programs specific to the health needs of the people particularly the children and tribal in the remote villages in Maharashtra. Sickle Cell Programme, Telemedicine program, Health Advisory Call Center, School Health Program are unique programs to name a few which are specific to the state.

The Fourth CRM Report (NRHM 2011a, 2011b) states that Maharashtra is close to achieving the goals in infrastructure gaps, with significant improvements in health infrastructure having been made. The establishment of an infrastructure development wing in 2007–08 has contributed towards progress in total infrastructure works taken up in the state. ASHAs are the most visible face of the NRHM in Maharashtra.

Demand-Side Financing in Maharashtra

The Rashtriya Swasthya Bima Yojna (RSBY) was introduced in 2008, whereby hospitals were empanelled in large numbers across Maharashtra to offer IP health care benefits to the people below poverty line (BPL). While it was visualized to be a scheme where both public and private providers participated, in Maharashtra's case more than 99 per cent of hospitals empanelled belonged to the private sector. Quoting SHSRC, it was reported by the press that Nagpur, Jalgaon and Thane districts had only 1 per cent, 13.6 per cent and 18.6 per cent coverage of potential beneficiaries under the scheme respectively (Isalkar 2011).

The GoM recently launched the Rajiv Gandhi Jeevandayee Arogya Yojana (RGJAY) to

> *Maharashtra is close to achieving the goals in infrastructure gaps, with significant improvements in health infrastructure having been made.*

facilitate access to medical facilities for BPL (yellow-card holders) as well as APL (orange-card holders) families in the state. The main objective of the RGJAY is to provide quality medical care through certain speciality services that call for hospitalization for surgeries, therapies and consultations through a network of health-care providers. The RGJAY is to be implemented in the state in a phased manner over three years with insurance coverage spanning eligible beneficiary families in eight districts of the state, namely, Amravati, Dhule, Gadchiroli, Nanded, Raigarh, Solapur, Mumbai and the suburbs (RGJAYS 2013). Given the learning from RSBY, it will be prudent for the government to tread a more cautious path, rather than scaling up insurance-based schemes hoping that the poor will be able to access private health care.

Health Concerns of Tribals: A Case Study of the Katkari Tribe

Inclusive growth and human development needs to address the multiple dimensions of deprivation faced by primitive tribal communities. R. Mutatkar (2007) details in his case study of the Katkari tribe (Jawhar block, Thane district) the various constraints faced by this socially backward tribal community in accessing health care. The Katkaris are regarded as the lowest in the social hierarchy among the ST ethnic groups and the demographic composition of the village they live in shows their hamlets to be excluded, with limited interaction with other groups. The living conditions of the Katkari are found to be very simple and minimal, comprising either *pucca* dwellings or *kutcha* houses constructed through government schemes, with no sanitation facilities in their hamlets and dependence on wells or public taps for drinking water. They are mainly landless, and dependent largely on wage labour for their livelihoods. Seasonal migration along with women and children is found to take place between the cultivation and harvesting seasons and in the post-agricultural season. Their food consumption patterns highlight the extreme deprivation faced by them. Food purchases are made in piecemeal quantities just before every meal. The Katkaris depend mainly on the public distribution system for foodgrains. To cope with food shortages they

> **Box 5.6 CBM of Health Services**
>
> One of the mechanisms under the NRHM that has shown good results for monitoring the right to health in the state is CBM.[16] Launched in Maharashtra in mid-2007 and implemented in five districts covering 23 blocks and 510 villages, the CBM initiative has proven to be an effective method in involving the community to monitor health rights. This initiative has been extended to cover an additional eight districts during 2010–11 and the budget for the same has been approved in the project implementation programme (PIP) for 2012–13. From ensuring availability and attendance of health professionals, questioning corruption, raising issues of non-availability of drugs, the CBM initiative has resulted in increased utilization of public health services.
>
> According to the Fourth CRM Report, Maharashtra is one of the only two states in the country that has successfully implemented community monitoring and which has had a demonstrable positive impact on health services (NRHM 2011a, 2011b). According to the report, data collected during the three CBM rounds in the five districts covered show that *first*, there has been a positive impact of CBM on health services. In the first round of data collected around 48 per cent of villages rated their health facilities as 'good' and this proportion increased to 66 per cent by the third round of the CBM, with improvements in specific indicators such as immunization, *anganwadi* facilities, use of untied funds and PHC facilities. *Second*, there has been an additional increase in PHC utilization in CBM areas. The impact in terms of higher utilization was marked in both OP and IP services from 2007–08 to 2009–10. *Third*, stopping informal charges in PHCs and external prescriptions as well as increased availability of medicines, increased visits of staff to remote villages and habitations and the reopening of previously closed sub-centres have been some of the qualitative improvements through this initiative. finally, there is also a need to replicate the CBM experience in other districts and its inclusion in the National Urban Health Mission to facilitate the involvement of communities in urban areas (small towns and cities) in monitoring their health-rights.
>
> *Sources:* NRHM (2011a, 2011b).

---

[16] The process of CBM consists of recording the status of health services as experienced by community members. Information about various services including PHCs and CHCs are collected through group discussions. A pictorial village report card is used to indicate a service as good, partly satisfactory or bad, reflecting the availability, quality and regularity of health services. Such findings are presented in jan sunwais (public hearings) along with suggestions for improvement.

resort to liquefying and grinding the food, consuming wildly grown food or borrowing food. Anthropometric indicators reveal severe under nourishment among Katkari children (aged 0–6 years). Morbidity is found to be the highest in the monsoon period, which is also the agricultural season when absence from work due to any illness results in loss of daily wages. Work-related injuries due to labour-intensive stone breaking also lead to a vicious cycle of ill health and loss of wages. There are no health-care facilities in the region studied, especially in terms of specialized care for women and children.

Nutrition: Essential for Health and Education

Nutrition is a key determinant of good health and is critical for survival, good quality of life and well-being. Nutrition is an everyday phenomenon, extending through a human being's life cycle starting from conception and foetal development in utero, through infancy, childhood and adolescence to adulthood and old age. It is critical for growth and development as it directly influences physical and mental development, thus having an important bearing on the issue of human development. In a research study by Sood (2010) it is reported that in India, early childhood malnutrition can be related to shortfalls in the cognitive development of children, which persisted in children through the schooling years, and which in turn resulted in lower learning capacities. Stunting was found to postpone school enrolment and also lead to the possibility of grade repetition and dropping out at the primary schooling level. Malnourished children were also reported to display behavioural issues. Insufficient intakes of essential micronutrients such as iron, iodine and zinc were found to be linked with lower attention span, poor memory, mental retardation and poor school achievements in children.

Under-Nutrition in Maharashtra

The NFHS-3, 2005–06 (IIPS and Macro International 2008) reports an improvement in all the three nutrition indicators[17] for Maharashtra for the period following 1998–99 (NFHS-2) with a significant reduction in the proportion of underweight children (see Figure 5.23). Some of the observations of malnutrition reported include: higher prevalence of malnutrition in rural areas vis-à-vis urban areas for all three malnutrition characteristics; higher prevalence amongst slum children in urban areas (especially the stunting and underweight attributes); gender disadvantage for female children with respect to the underweight attribute; and children belonging to the SC, ST and the lowest wealth category reporting stunting and being underweight in higher proportions (see Table 5.7). SAM, which is the most extreme form of acute under-nutrition, is reported to afflict 5.2 per cent of children in Maharashtra. The percentage of children suffering from SAM is slightly higher in rural areas, in Mumbai slums, amongst the SC and in the population belonging to the second lowest wealth index category.

To fully understand and evaluate the impact of interventions such as the RJMCHNM (Phase I) the Comprehensive Nutrition

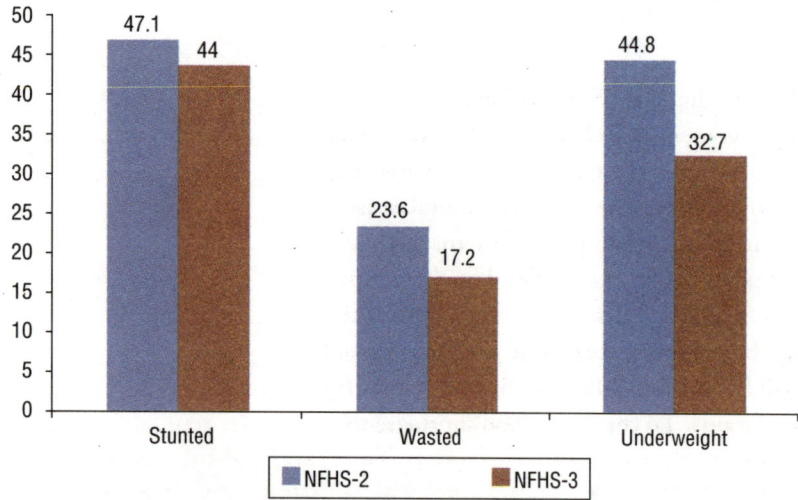

FIGURE 5.23 Prevalence of Under-Nutrition among Children: Maharashtra

Sources: IIPS and ORC Macro (2001); IIPS and Macro International (2008).
Note: Prevalence is indicated in percentage terms.

---

[17] Stunting—too short for age, wasting—too thin for height and underweight—too thin for age.

TABLE 5.7
Prevalence of Under-Nutrition, by Place of Residence, Sex, Social Group and Wealth Index: Maharashtra

Characteristics	Height for Age (Percentage)		Weight for Height (Percentage)		Weight for Age (Percentage)	
	Stunting (Standard Deviation [SD] < –2)	Severe Stunting (SD< –3)	Wasting (SD< –2)	Severe Wasting (SD< –3)	Under-weight (SD< –2)	Severe Under-weight (SD< –3)
All-India	48.0	23.7	19.8	6.4	42.5	15.8
Maharashtra	46.3	19.1	16.5	5.2	37.0	11.9
Residence						
Rural	49.1	21.0	18.2	5.6	41.6	13.9
Urban	42.2	16.4	14.1	4.6	30.7	9.1
Mumbai (Slum)	47.4	16.1	16.1	4.0	36.1	11.6
Mumbai (Non-Slum)	41.5	15.7	16.4	2.5	25.8	6.9
Gender						
Male	47.3	20.3	17.5	5.2	36.7	12.6
Female	45.1	17.7	15.4	5.2	37.3	11.1
Social Group						
SC	55.2	23.4	20.2	6.6	41.7	13.5
ST	57.8	30.0	18.9	5.6	53.2	21.1
OBC	40.6	14.4	15.7	5.2	33.0	10.0
Others	42.5	16.9	14.6	4.4	32.6	9.6
Wealth Index						
Lowest	63.2	32.9	18.2	5.9	51.8	18.8
Second	55.1	25.1	21.8	6.8	46.4	20.0
Middle	53.6	25.3	19.4	5.3	48.2	13.4
Fourth	45.1	16.4	16.1	5.8	32.4	10.2
Highest	28.9	7.2	10.8	3.3	20.9	4.5

Source: IIPS and Macro International (2008).

Box 5.7 RJMCHNM

The RJMCHNM was launched in Maharashtra in March 2005 as a pioneering government initiative with the primary objective of reducing grade III and grade IV malnutrition in children in the age group of 0–6 years. The main interventions under the RJMCHNM include: ensuring provision of neonatal care to pregnant women, newborn care, nutrition and complete immunization of children aged 0–3 years, education of adolescent girls to reduce the incidence of child marriage, promotion of awareness about spacing between children and community participation for nutrition management.

The database created by the RJMCHNM shows quite clearly that under-nutrition begins early in the life cycle. There is only a 1,000-day 'window of opportunity' (of –9 months, that is, beginning of pregnancy, to 24 months after the child is born) available to make a lasting difference in the lives of young children. Backed by this evidence, the GoM constituted the second phase of the RJMCHNM in 2011 with a renewed focus on the first 1,000 days of life. The primary focus is the prevention and reduction of under-nutrition among children below two years of age, using an evidence-based, high-impact package of essential interventions providing a continuum of care. Special attention is to be provided to the most vulnerable, youngest, poorest, socially excluded and severely undernourished children residing in the hard-to-reach areas. The RJMCHNM also gives priority to the nutrition and well-being of adolescent girls, pregnant women and breastfeeding mothers. With the help of the Mission, the GoM launched a campaign on Information Education and Communication (IEC) on 2 October 2011 named the Rajmata Jijau Malnutrition-Free Village Campaign aimed at exploring community participation to curb malnutrition in the state.

Maharashtra is now well positioned to achieve the MDG, with the creation of strong alliances and partnerships for scaling using cost-effective models for improved nutrition outcomes amongst young children and their mothers.

Source: Health Education to Villages (n.d.).

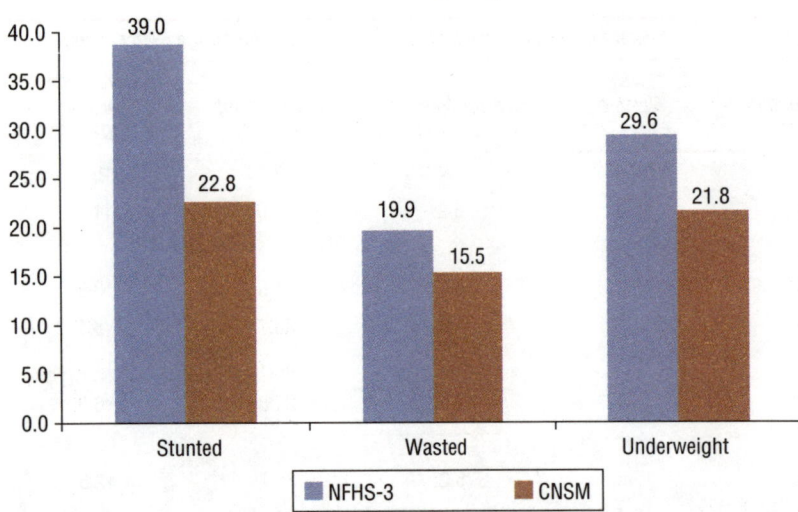

FIGURE 5.24 Trends in Nutritional Status of Children below Two Years: Maharashtra (2012)

Source: IIPS 2012.
Notes: Prevalence indicated in percentage terms. Below −2 SD units from the median of the World Health Organization (WHO)'s 2006 global database on child growth and malnutrition.

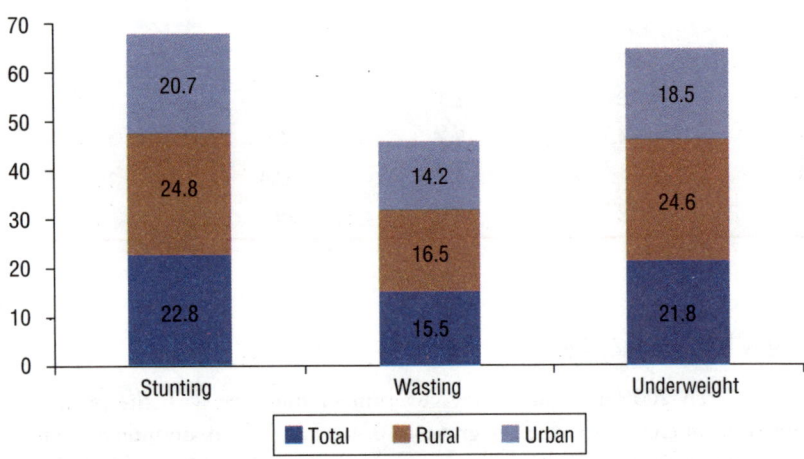

FIGURE 5.25 Prevalence of Under-Nutrition in Children (0–23 Months): Rural and Urban Maharashtra

Source: IIPS 2012.
Note: Prevalence is indicated in percentage terms.

(stunting, wasting and underweight). While there was hardly any decline reported in the prevalence of stunting between NFHS-2 and NFHS-3, the CNSM report finds a significant reduction in these indicators over the period 2006–2012, which is noteworthy (see Figure 5.24). Child malnutrition continues to be higher in rural areas and amongst SC and ST children for all three indicators (see Figures 5.25 and 5.26). Region-wise data shows disparities in the prevalence of the three nutrition indicators. The Nashik division, where the tribal population is higher in proportion, reports higher prevalence of children with stunting (32.3 per cent) compared to the Pune and Nagpur divisions (16.7 per cent and 15.3 per cent, respectively, see Table 5.8). Higher proportions of underweight children are reported in the Amravati and Nashik divisions (29.3 per cent and 30.6 per cent respectively) while Nagpur has the highest proportion of children afflicted by wasting (21.9 per cent). These first findings from the CNSM report highlight the concerted efforts that are being made to tackle child under-nutrition in the state through various interventions targeted specifically at enhancing maternal care and childcare. These findings for Maharashtra also bring forth the vital relevance of the need to provide an essential continuum of care during the first 1,000-day window of life to bring about reductions in the prevalence of under-nutrition in children below two years of age.

Under-nutrition in childhood persists through adolescence and adulthood. Although the prevalence of under-nutrition is less among adults as compared to children, overall, one-third of the women in Maharashtra have low BMI (less than 18.5) and a little less than half are anaemic (based on haemoglobin levels) according to NFHS-3 (IIPS and Macro International 2008). The percentage of women low BMI

Survey (CNSM) in Maharashtra (IIPS 2012)[18] was undertaken. The CNSM is a pioneering initiative in the country, focused on children below two years of age and their mothers. Comparisons of the preliminary results from this survey with NFHS-3 data (for under-two-year-olds) reveals an improvement in all three nutrition indicators

[18] CNSM 2012 is the first-ever state-specific nutrition survey with a focus on infants and children under the age of two and their mothers. The survey was a joint endeavour of the Department of Women and Child Development, GoM, IIPS and UNICEF.

shows disparities between rural and urban areas, with women in rural areas facing a disadvantage (see Figure 5.27).

Amongst the social groups, a higher proportion of women belonging to the ST report low BMIs (see Figure 5.28). It is also found that more than half the women belonging to the lowest two wealth quintiles had a low BMI (see Table 5A.11). Nutritional status of women in the age group of 15–49 years as measured by anaemia (haemoglobin levels) also shows clear disadvantages for rural areas, backward social groups and lower wealth quintiles. Although females are seen to face a disadvantage, the nutritional status of males is not that much better either in rural areas, amongst the social groups and the lower wealth quintiles.

Overweight and Obesity in Maharashtra

Along with under-nutrition, Maharashtra is also faced with the challenge of obesity. Obesity itself is a risk factor for diabetes and atherosclerosis. The NFHS-3 data indicates that in Maharashtra about one-fourth of urban women may be at risk of obesity, whereas in rural areas, the prevalence of obesity is higher amongst men (see Figure. 5.29).

Anaemia

In the Eleventh Plan, targets were set for reducing the prevalence of anaemia among children and women. Data on anaemia from

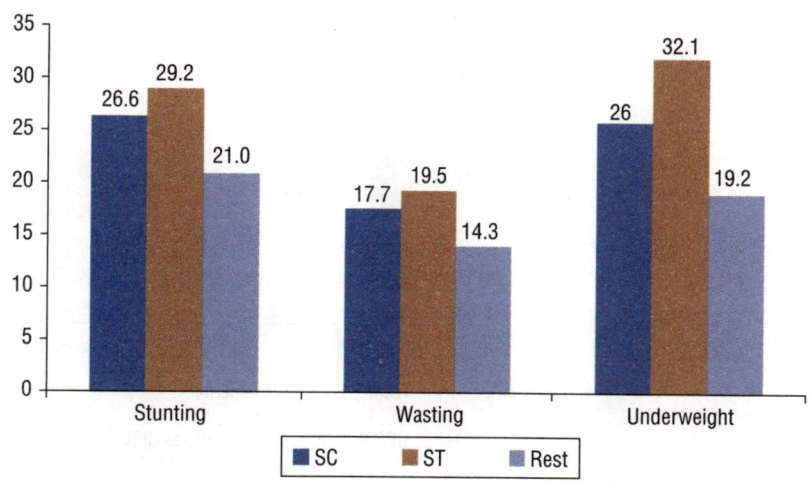

FIGURE 5.26 Prevalence of Malnutrition among Children below Two Years, by Social Groups: Maharashtra

Source: IIPS 2012.
Notes: Prevalence indicated in percentage terms Below –2 SD units from the median of the WHO's 2006 global database on child growth and malnutrition.

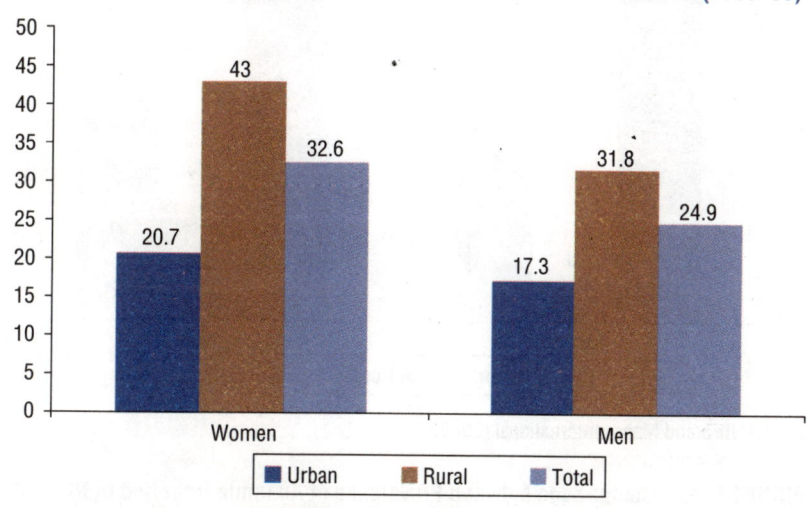

FIGURE 5.27 Adult Males and Females with Low BMI: Maharashtra (2005–06)

Source: IIPS and Macro International (2008).

TABLE 5.8
Prevalence of Malnutrition among Children (0–23 Months), by Administrative Divisions: Maharashtra

	Stunting		Wasting		Underweight	
Division	Severe Stunting (SD < –3)	Stunting (SD < –2)	Severe Wasting (SD < –3)	Wasting (SD < –2)	Severe Underweight (SD < –3)	Underweight (SD < –2)
Pune	4.3	16.7	3.7	13.9	4.3	17.3
Nashik	14.9	32.3	6.6	19.1	13.1	30.6
Nagpur	3.2	15.3	4.6	21.9	4.7	22.7
Konkan	8.6	23.4	4.4	15.2	5.0	20.5
Aurangabad	7.9	24.5	4.9	14	7.4	19.7
Amravati	6.8	23.5	4.2	18.6	6.5	29.3

Source: IIPS (2012).
Note: Prevalence indicated in percentage terms.

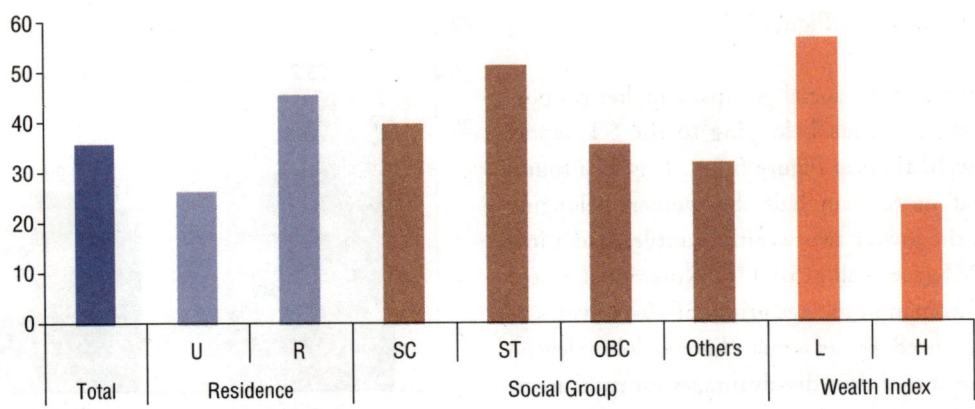

FIGURE 5.28 Percentage of Women (15–49 Years) Having BMI Less than 18.5: Maharashtra (2005–06)

Source: IIPS and Macro International (2008).

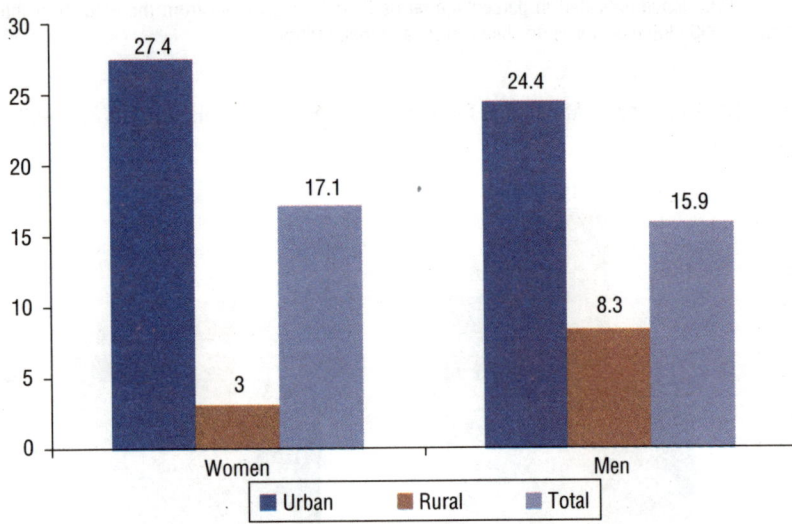

FIGURE 5.29 Prevalence of Overweight and Obesity: Maharashtra

Source: IIPS and Macro International (2008).

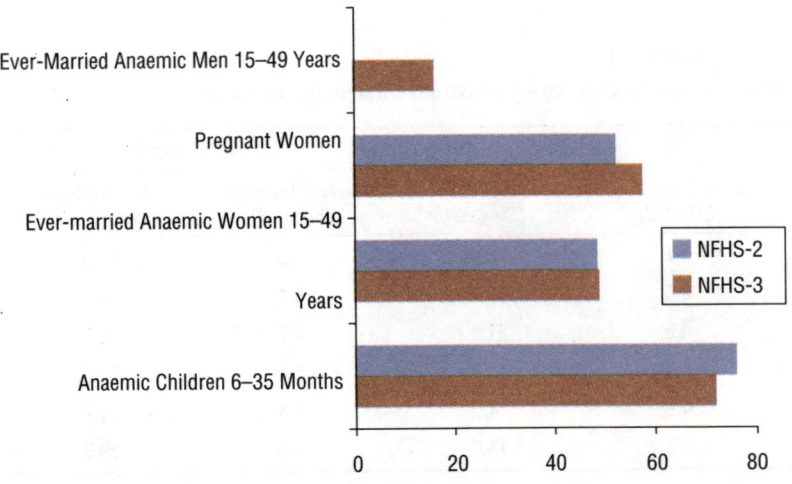

FIGURE 5.30 Comparison between Prevalence of Anaemia Reported in NFHS-2 and NFHS-3: Maharashtra

Sources: IIPS and ORC Macro (2001); IIPS and Macro International (2008).

NFHS-2 and NFHS-3 for Maharashtra shows the following (IIPS and ORC Macro 2001; IIPS and Macro International 2008):

1. The prevalence of anaemia among children is slightly lower than that for the country as a whole (Table 5A.12).
2. Close to 49 per cent of women in the state are anaemic, with 33 per cent reporting mild anaemia, 14 per cent moderate and 2 per cent severe anaemia.
3. Approximately 58 per cent of pregnant women and 54 per cent who were breast-feeding are anaemic.
4. There has been an increase in the prevalence of anaemia amongst pregnant women, with no evident reduction in its occurrence amongst adult women and a small decrease in its occurrence amongst children of 6–35 months of age over the two NFHS surveys (see Figure 5.30).
5. Children below five years of age suffer from anaemia in larger proportions in rural areas, as well as among ST households (see Table 5A.13).

Vitamin A Coverage

Vitamin A plays an important role in child survival and its deficiency ultimately results in blindness. The state has been implementing the vitamin A prophylaxis programme, but is yet to reach complete coverage for a single dose of the vitamin A supplement (see Table 5A.14). Coverage is influenced by the age of the child and it is found that higher birth order, belonging to backward groups (Muslims, ST) and poverty are associated with lower coverage. Given the debilitating lifelong disability caused by vitamin A deficiency, coverage combined with awareness generation needs to be strengthened.

Childhood Diarrhoea

One of the immediate causes of under-nutrition in children is diarrhoea and in Maharashtra around 20 per cent of children suffered from diarrhoea in 2007–08 (IIPS 2010). Less than half (44.2 per cent) of the children were given ORS while 77.9 per cent sought other treatment. A majority (two-thirds) of the children suffering from diarrhoea, even in rural areas, sought treatment in private health facilities. The DLHS-3 data (IIPS 2010) shows that only one-third of mothers were aware of the use of ORS, although half the women were aware of homemade salt-and-sugar solution as a cure for diarrhoea. Knowledge and practices related to diarrhoea management were influenced by the mother's age and education, place of residence, social group and wealth index category that the household belonged to (see Table 5A.15). In 15 of the 35 districts, prevalence of diarrhoea was higher than the state average (19 per cent) and in 10 out of 35 districts less than one-third of mothers knew about ORS. Other practices such as continuity of normal feeding, continuation of breastfeeding and administering plenty of fluids were also found to be less prevalent. Less than 6 per cent of mothers reported that breastfeeding should be continued and less than 4 per cent felt the need to give plenty of fluids during diarrhoea, across all the population categories considered. If diarrhoea and the resultant under-nutrition and mortality (and related health-care costs) are to be reduced, useful diarrhoea-management practices need to be spread more widely through education and intensive IEC.

> **Box 5.8 ICDS Scheme**
>
> The ICDS is the largest national flagship programme targeted at improving child nutrition, growth and development. The ICDS is also the primary channel for educating mothers about childcare and nutrition practices. The Evaluation Report on ICDS by Planning Commission reveals the following for the State of Maharashtra:[19]
>
> - As far as the proportion of days when the supplementary nutrition (SN) was actually available for the children are considered Maharashtra is a 'good performing State' (SN available to children for 80 per cent of days)
> - Maharashtra ranks third as far as infrastructure of Anganwadis are considered as observed by the Infrastructure/facility index
> - In health checkups, AWC in Maharashtra, performed the best with implementation in more than 90 per cent of AWC
> - In providing immunisation, Maharashtra did exceptionally well with implementation in more than 90 per cent of AWC as part of KSY
> - In providing referral service, Maharashtra was one of the States that did the best
> - Maharashtra was performing above the national average in the performance indicators related to children such as percentage of children weighed at birth, percentage of children getting weighed once in every month, percentage of children started deworming, percentage of children consumed iron and folic acid tablets, percentage of mothers who initiated breastfeeding within one hour of child birth,
> - Maharashtra ranked second on overall performance of ICDS with an Performance Index of 0.716 (with Kerala at first rank, Performance Index 0.728)
>
> *Source:* Planning Commission (2011).

Childcare and Feeding Practices

Breastfeeding as a feeding practice has the largest potential to bring about reductions in child mortality. Early initiation of breastfeeding reduces neonatal mortality. The initial six months of exclusive breast feeding could have a significant effect on the reduction of child mortality from its two biggest precipitators, namely, diarrhoea and pneumonia (Black et al. 2008).

The NFHS-3 data (IIPS and Macro International 2008) indicates that in Maharashtra 52 per cent of children were breastfed within one hour of birth compared to 24.5 per cent children at the all-India level. Also, 53 per cent of infants (0–5 months of age) were exclusively breastfed, which is higher than the national average of 46.4 per cent. The data

---

[19] Evaluation Report on Integrated Child Development Services, Planning Commission, GoI, March 2011.

also shows that one-third of children received pre-lacteal feeds. Pre-lacteal feeds are a common cultural practice and lead to various infections for newborns, against which awareness generation is essential on a regular basis.

The DLHS-3 survey (IIPS 2010) shows no significant differences between rural and urban areas as far as breastfeeding practices are considered (see Table 5A.17). A little over half the children were exclusively breastfed, with children from SC families and children of illiterate mothers showing a disadvantage in terms of breastfeeding practices. Further, only 77.5 per cent of infants below two months of age were exclusively breastfed. It is widely recommended that children not be given any solids before the age of six months as their gastrointestinal tract is not developed enough. However, it is found that 10.4 per cent of children aged below six months were being fed with semi-solid and/or solid foods (1 per cent of them were less than two months of age).

There is tremendous scope for improvement in feeding practices in the state, with the most important intervention being spreading awareness amongst mothers about appropriate complementary feeding practices in order to check malnourishment in children.

Summing Up

Maharashtra witnesses improvement in the outcome indicators of health. The State finds a place amongst the set of nine states that have reached replacement fertility levels in the country with a TFR of 1.9 in 2010.

For Maharashtra the IMR has shown a considerable drop of 20 points (from 47 in 2001 to 25 in 2011) with the rural–urban gap in IMR also narrowing from 27 points to 13 points over the period under consideration. There is an evident female disadvantage, with IMRs for female children higher than those for male children by five points in 2000, which reduced to two points in 2010. The trends for IMR by social groups reveal an improvement, the ST reporting a considerable reduction in IMR of 22 points over 2000–09; the state still has a long way to go though when it comes to this IMR converging with the state average. Districts that call for immediate intervention with respect to IMR are Nandurbar, Washim, Yavatmal, Wardha and Bhandara because here the IMRs in rural areas exceed 35. The U5MR on the other hand has shown a consistent

---

Box 5.9 Malnutrition and Child Health amongst Tribals in Maharashtra: A Case Study

To investigate and study the causes of persistent malnutrition amongst children, especially tribal children, in Maharashtra, an in-depth analysis of the impact of the sociocultural and economic environment of tribals on the nutritional status and health of children was carried out by Sonowal (2010).

Some of the main inferences from this study which have important policy lessons are highlighted here. The loss of right to access forests and forest produce (fruits, green shoots, tubers, etc., which are the main source of natural nutrients for tribals) and the degradation of forest land coupled with rising population have led to changes in the dietary composition of tribals as well as their economic condition. Seasonal migration of tribal families to neighbouring states such as Gujarat for wage labour is found to have a debilitating effect on the health and nutritional status of tribal children. The study clearly states that the number of households with malnourished children increases sharply when wage labour is the primary source of income. With both parents working, the smaller children and babies are found to be exposed to dust, heat, insects and dirt. Breastfed babies are reported to be more prone to infections and illness as mothers are unable to feed them often whilst working. The study reports a strong negative relationship between mother's work participation and a child's health and nutrition, which is an important finding as it is contrary to general belief that higher family incomes should lead to better child health.

Female literacy, age at marriage, small gap between two births and poor diets of pregnant mothers are found to have an important bearing on children's health and nutrition. The study finds that low female literacy amongst tribals (as low as 21 per cent in Gadchiroli for the sample households studied) could be a possible reason for programmes related to health awareness not being very successful. With as many as 80 per cent of girls getting married before the age of 17 in the households surveyed, and subsequent early pregnancies, the study finds a negative relationship between age at marriage and child malnourishment. The close relation between the treatment of diseases and the sociocultural perceptions of tribals influences the extent of health care availed by them. Reasons found for the low utilization of available PHC facilities for antenatal care and childbirth practices include long distances from PHCs and the inability to rush expectant mothers there, loss in household work and wages due to regular visits required to PHCs, the need to stay away from home when engaging in contract work even during pregnancy and the need to observe some religious rites during pregnancy and delivery.

Source: Sonowal (2010).

decline in the state, from 58.1 in 1998–99 to 36 in 2009, which is much lower than the national U5MR of 64. There does exist a clear female disadvantage with a gender gap in U5MR of eight points in 2009. The MMR for Maharashtra has dropped from 166 in 1997–98 to 104 in 2007–09, which is also well below the India average of 212.

The sex ratio has shown an improvement over the years 2001–11 from 922 to 925. What is cause for concern is the drop in the child sex ratio (0–6 years) from 913 in 2001 to 883 in 2011, with Beed district reporting the lowest ratio at 801 in 2011. Such a declining child sex ratio reflects not only male child preference but also the poor quality of care given to female children.

Public spending on health has important implications for health-related outcomes, including the provisioning of infrastructure and effective health-care services. A study conducted by NIPFP reveals that in both per capita terms as well as a share of GSDP, Maharashtra spends lesser on health. In 2008–09, per capita expenditure on health was ₹351 in Maharashtra, while it was ₹507 in Kerala and ₹421 in Tamil Nadu. As a proportion of total budgetary expenditure, the state spent 3.7 per cent on health and family welfare which is much lower than the target of 7–8 per cent as mandated by the National Health Policy, 2002. In 2008–09, the proportion of state budget allocated to health alone was less than 2.5 per cent.

Provisioning of health facilities in the state of Maharashtra needs to be understood in the context of the sizeable tribal population spread across 15 districts. Difficulties in outreach of health facilities based on population norms are faced when the size of the villages is less than 1,000 and sometimes even less than 200 people. The SHSRC (2009) report clearly brings out the existence of wide inter-district variations in the provisioning of sub-centres, PHCs and RHs in the state. On the one hand, tribal districts such as Gadchiroli, Nanded and Gondia fare well in terms of population per sub-centre and PHC, while on the other, high-population tribal districts such as Jalgaon, Raigad, Nagpur, Nandurbar, Thane and Gondia show poor coverage in terms of these health facilities.

HR is one of the pillars of any effective and fully functioning health infrastructure set-up, essential for reaching health facilities to rural and far-flung areas inhabited by tribal communities. In Maharashtra, there exist inter-regional as well as inter-district disparities in the availability of HR. Gadchiroli district (Vidarbha region) on the one hand shows the best population-per-doctor ratio and on the other very low utilization rates of health-care facilities, with very low proportion of institutional deliveries (23.5 per cent) and low coverage of immunization of children (46.4 per cent). Such a scenario clearly highlights that mere availability of health infrastructure may not be sufficient for attaining health-related human development outcomes, although it may be a necessary condition for improving them. Variations in population-per-doctor and per-nurse ratios across districts, sanctioned staff positions lying vacant in public hospitals, shortage of ANMs in sub-centres and the shortage of specialists in IPHS hospitals have important implications, especially for the poor, who either have to forgo essential health care or incur high out-of-pocket expenditure to access the same.

Improvements in utilization rates are reflective of inclusive human development. Utilization rates captured by the proportions of population accessing IP and OP care in Maharashtra shows some interesting trends: *first*, there is a large dependence on the private sector especially for OP care and hospitalization. Only about 11 per cent of urban OP care, 16 per cent of rural OP care, and 28 per cent of rural and urban IP care are sought through public health facilities (National Sample Survey Organisation 2006). Private IP and OP utilization has increased by around 15 percentage points from 1986–87 to 2004. *Second*, in many districts (Sindhudurg, Gadchiroli, Nagpur,

Chandrapur, Gondia, Sangli, Thane and Ratnagiri) it is found that a substantial proportion of women still choose to access government facilities for pregnancy and childbirth related services (IIPS 2010). *Third*, the SC, ST and OBC are found to depend more on the public sector for health care. The low share in utilization of public health facilities by the ST is a cause for concern. Data on the proportion of households (50 per cent) forced to borrow or sell assets to seek health care shows a strong rural bias.

Access to maternity care shows the existence of a large and extensive network in the state, despite which access and utilization of such facilities remain out of reach for large proportions of the population. Western Maharashtra reports a higher coverage of antenatal care compared to other parts of the state (IIPS 2010). Inter-district variations prevail in the proportion of women availing full antenatal care. The educational status of women and place of residence had a large bearing on their access to antenatal care. Proportions of women availing no antenatal care visits was highest for illiterate women, those belonging to the ST and to the lowest wealth classes.

The place of delivery is an important indicator of inclusion and during the period from 2002–04 to 2007–08 (DLHS-2 and DLHS-3) an improvement has been reported in the proportion of institutional deliveries in the state over 2002–04 to 2012 (CES 2009). While there is an urban bias in the same, the increase has been more in rural areas which is an indication of progress made in the provisioning of this essential maternal health facility. Inter-district variations in this indicator reveal the proportion of institutional births to range from 93.5 per cent in Mumbai (Suburban) to as low as 23.5 per cent, 25.4 per cent and 41.5 per cent respectively in Gadchiroli, Nandurbar and Hingoli. Proportions of the population not accessing ANC and PNC is higher for the lower MPCE classes, those belonging to the ST and SC, who also report higher proportions of deliveries at home. The proportion of safe deliveries has also seen a rise in both rural and urban areas (between DLHS-2 and DLHS-3), although it is the lowest in Nandurbar and Gadchiroli. The thrust areas that emerge for maternal and childcare include improvements in antenatal coverage as well as increases in the outreach and participation of ASHAs to facilitate further successes in the maternal- and child-health programmes operating in the state. This would also facilitate improved inclusion of socially backward groups and low-income categories in this important maternal care and childcare imperative. In terms of child immunization, a clear advantage is seen in full immunization coverage for urban residents and interdistrict variations. The percentage is less in STs and low MPCE quintile.

The NRHM, launched in 2006, is a flagship programme of the government with the main aim of strengthening health care in rural areas. The NRHM (2009) report for Maharashtra lists the three main achievements of this programme as: increases in institutional deliveries and OPD care; improved performance of the JSY through increases in the JSY beneficiaries and community mobilization by ASHAs. The highlight accomplishment of this programme has been the significant increase in institutional deliveries in rural areas of the state which are attributable to various incentive packages, such as cash incentives to PHC staff, hardship allowances to staff located in tribal and Naxalite areas and incentives to staff in low institutional delivery areas. The Fourth CRM Report 2010 (NRHM 2011a, 2011b) states that significant advances have been made in health infrastructure and Maharashtra is close to bridging all the health infrastructure gaps that exist.

The report cites Maharashtra as one of the two states in the country that has successfully implemented community monitoring in the health sector along with demonstrating its positive effects on the availability and utilization of health services (including increases in immunization, improvements in *anganwadi* facilities, improved usage of PHC facilities, etc).

Maharashtra has made progress in the area of health and related services, reflected in the various health-related vital statistics, with input as well as process indicators also showing improved inclusion in terms of gender, sectors and socioeconomic groups. However, many gaps have to be breached, especially for the socially and economically backward groups, to enable them to reach the state level averages. What emerges is that for the health system in Maharashtra to be successful in fulfilling public health goals, some of the imperative policy action areas are addressing regional disparities in infrastructure availability in primary, secondary and tertiary health care services; strengthening rural infrastructure along with making it accessible to highly disadvantaged groups; stepping up state allocations to the health sector coupled with better utilization of available resources; improved drug availability in hospitals as well as increased transparency in the procurement systems; enhancing manpower especially in rural and tribal areas through financial and non-financial incentives; expansion of CBM of the NRHM, which has proved successful in some districts of the state, to all the districts; well-organized referral systems with sufficient manpower and a focus on primary health care in urban areas of the state.

Nutrition is a key determinant of good health and is critical for survival, good quality of life and well-being. In Maharashtra, the proportion of children suffering from stunting has reduced significantly between the years 2006 and 2012, which is noteworthy. Malnutrition amongst children is seen to have a rural bias; children belonging to SC and ST populations show stunting and low weight in larger proportions and inter-regional disparities exist in the same. Progress is being made under the RJMCHNM in tackling the various forms of undernutrition in children below two years of age, with the provision of a continuum of interventions targeted at children and their mothers during the first 1,000-day window of life.

One-third of the women in Maharashtra are found to have BMI < 18.5 kg/m^2 and a little less than half reported being anaemic (haemoglobin levels < 12 g/dL). There is a reported increase in the occurrence of anaemia amongst pregnant women in the state (standing at 58 per cent in 2005–06). Low coverage of vitamin A supplements for children was found to be associated with higher birth order, belonging to the ST and Muslim community, and poverty. The state also faces the challenge of obesity. NFHS-3 shows that about one-fourth of women residing in urban areas may be at risk of obesity.

Diarrhoea is one of the main causes of undernutrition in children and ORS is critical to combating it. Less than half of the children suffering from diarrhoea in the state were found to have been administered ORS. In 15 of the 35 districts, prevalence of diarrhoea was higher than the state average of 19 per cent and in 10 out of 35 districts less than one-third of mothers knew about ORS. Knowledge of other practices such as continuation of normal feeding and breastfeeding and administering plenty of fluids were also found to be poor.

Although more than half the children in the state (52 per cent) were found to have been breastfed within one hour of birth, one-third received pre-lacteal feeds, which could lead to various infections in newborns and eventually under-nutrition. Factors that adversely influence exclusive breastfeeding were found to be maternal illiteracy and belonging to the SC.

The five priority areas for the state in its efforts to improve the nutrition status of women and children include the implementation of early initiation into breastfeeding practices, colostrum feeding and exclusive breastfeeding practices, initiation of complementary foods at the age of six months for infants, addressing micronutrient deficiencies and anaemia in the first years of life, addressing anaemia and micronutrient deficiencies in adolescent girls and women, and finally, the provision of quality care for children suffering from severe under-nutrition along with encouraging simple home-based protocols. Strengthening capacity building, IEC, community participation, monitoring and evaluation, coordination and convergence to achieve results in these priority areas are the way forward.

6

Housing, Water and Sanitation: Interlinked with Capability Enhancement

Motivation

Along with adequate nutrition and health care, the availability of *pucca* housing, clean and safe drinking water and sanitation facilities (including drainage and garbage disposal) is fundamental for reducing morbidity and improving the health of the population. The Eleventh Plan reiterates (Planning Commission 2008: 162):

> Lack of covered toilets nearby imposes a severe hardship on women and girls. Also, provision of clean drinking water without at the same time provision for sanitation and clean environment would be less effective in improving health. The two should be treated together as complementary needs.

The availability of these facilities has a direct bearing on the health and educational attainments of the population (directly or indirectly) and thus impinges on their capabilities too.

Recognizing the importance of housing as a bundle of amenities is important to any study of human development. The set of housing amenities that needs to be considered includes structure of the dwelling, condition of structure, size (area) of the dwelling, tenure type, separate kitchen, adequate ventilation, source of safe drinking water, availability of drinking water, bathroom facility, sanitation (toilet) facility, drainage facility, garbage disposal facility and electricity. Cooking fuel also needs to be considered as part of housing amenities in light of concerns about indoor air pollution.

Interlinkages with Health and Well-Being

"Health risks arise from poor sanitation, lack of clean water, overcrowded and poorly ventilated living and working environments and from air and industrial pollution" (UNFPA 2007: 16). A household with inadequate housing amenities is more likely to be prone to ill health and morbidity. Goal 4 of the MDG aims at reductions in child mortality while goal 5 of the MDG aims at improving maternal health. It is an empirically proven fact that child mortality and infant mortality are higher where housing amenities are inadequate (Agha 2000; Nayar 1997). Data on the wealth index that captures housing amenities and ownership of assets in India (IIPS and Macro International 2008) also reveals that early childhood mortality rates are highest in households belonging to the lowest wealth quintile (see Table 6.1). The U5MR in households belonging to the lowest wealth quintile is nearly 3.5 times that of households in the highest wealth quintile.

The researches on child mortality reveal that IMRs and CMRs in the slums of Chennai, Delhi, Meerut, Indore and Nagpur are seen to be higher than in their non-slum urban counterparts (see Table 6A.1). The nutrition status of children residing in slums measured by height for age (stunting), weight for height (wasting) and weight for age (underweight) is seen to be lower than in non-slum areas (see Table 6A.2).

Amongst the targets specified in goal 6 of the MDG is the reduction in 'incidence and death rates associated with malaria'. Prevalence of malaria is higher where living conditions are far from sanitary. Two targets specified in goal 7 of the MDG also cannot be achieved without addressing the issue of housing amenities namely, 'reductions by half in the proportion of people without sustainable access to safe drinking water and basic sanitation' and 'achieving significant improvements in the lives of at least 100 million slum dwellers, by 2020'. Progress in achieving the health-related targets of the MDG needs to therefore be assessed by the pace and extent to which the issue of housing poverty and lack of housing amenities are being addressed.

Urbanization and the Proliferation of Slums

For any discussion on the availability of housing facilities and other amenities, which are important elements of human development, it is essential to start with a look at the housing rentals scenario as well as the implications of rapid urbanization. This is also very pertinent for a state such as Maharashtra which has been experiencing rapid urbanization as well as facing a lot of in-migration. Traditionally, the poverty line in India does not make any allowance for incorporating housing rents. This fact was acknowledged in the Report of the Expert Group on Estimation of Proportion and Number of Poor. In its report the expert group recognized the limitations of the poverty line,

> the proportion of non-food expenditures on essentials (rent, fuel, clothing, health care, etc.) is not normative but empirical and likely to be seriously inadequate with reference to normative standards. Poverty lines derived from personal consumption patterns and levels do not take into account items of social consumption such as basic education and health, drinking water supply, sanitation, environmental standards, etc. in terms of normative requirements or effective access.
>
> (Government of India 1993: 11)

Any discussion on poverty that does not highlight the issue of urbanization of poverty is incomplete. The urbanization of poverty, that is, a decrease in the number of rural poor accompanied by an increase in number of urban poor, is evident in India. The latest household census data of 2011 for Maharashtra reveals an increase in the number of households from 8.0 million in 2001 to 25.6 million in 2011, showing a decadal increase of 31.1 per cent (25.6 per cent for rural and 37.7 per cent for urban parts of the state) (Government of India 2011c). Such a high level of urbanization

TABLE 6.1
Early Childhood Mortality Rates, by Wealth Quintiles: Maharashtra

	Neonatal	Post-Neonatal	Infant	Child	Under-Five
Lowest	71.6	24	95.6	23.5	116.8
Second	32.5	4.6	37.1	6.3	43.1
Middle	41.3	10.9	52.3	6.2	58.1
Fourth	26.7	9.7	36.4	5.6	41.8
Highest	22.9	4.5	27.4	6.4	33.6

Source: IIPS and Macro International (2008).

has implications for poverty in general and housing poverty in particular. The NSS in 2008–09 estimates that there were a total of 48,994 slums in India, with Maharashtra accounting for nearly 35 per cent of the notified and non-notified slums in the country. A comparison between NSS data (58th and 65th rounds) reveals that the total number of slums in Maharashtra has seen an increase from 16,662 in 2002 to 17,019 in 2008–09 (National Sample Survey Organisation 2003; National Sample Survey Office 2010a).[1] The Committee on Slum Statistics reveals that Maharashtra accounts for 19.5 per cent of individuals living in slums or slum-like conditions (Government of India 2010). Figure 6.1 depicts the projected slum population for Maharashtra and India. It shows that by 2017, over 20.5 million individuals will be living in slums in Maharashtra.

Migration: Implications for Support Infrastructure and Amenities

The Magnitude of Migration

In the context of a state such as Maharashtra, which attracts a large number of people from all over the country as well as experiences a lot of inter-district population movement, migration[2] becomes an important subject vis-à-vis the demands that it makes on various development-related amenities and subsequently on various human development outcomes. The census of 2001[3] reported nearly 8 per cent of the state's population to be migrants from other states and 34 per cent as inter- and intra–district migrants. Migration into the state was seen to be a lot higher than migration out of the state (see Table 6.2), with an increase in the state's population by

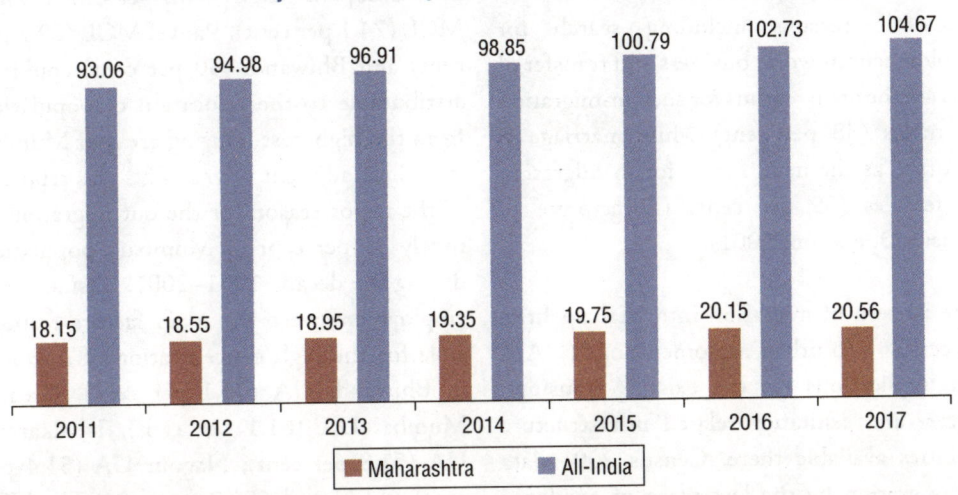

FIGURE 6.1 Projected Slum Population: Maharashtra and India (2011–17)

Source: Government of India (2010).
Note: Figures are in millions.

[1] The Committee on Slum Statistics/Census in its report points out that the "UN-HABITAT definition is based on the conditions prevailing at a particular household, while the approach to be followed in the Indian context would be area-based, which would have a cluster of households lacking of basic amenities" (Government of India 2010: 24). In India, different organizations and different state governments use different definitions of slums (see Annexure 6.1 for the definition used in Maharashtra).

[2] In India, a migrant is a person who, at the time of census enumeration, is found at a place different from his/her place of birth or place of last residence.

[3] The census of India uses two concepts to define a person as migrant, namely, place of birth and last place of residence. Based on place of enumeration and place of last residence, four types of movement can be identified—rural to rural migration, rural to urban, urban to urban and urban to rural migration.

TABLE 6.2
Inter-District and Interstate In- and Out-Migrants: Maharashtra (1991–2001)

Type of Migration	In-Migrants			Out-Migrants		
	Total	Male	Female	Total	Male	Female
Inter-District						
Rural to Rural	28.6	24.6	31.9	28.6	24.6	31.9
Rural to Urban	28.3	31.1	26.0	28.3	31.1	26.0
Urban to Urban	33.7	35.0	32.6	33.7	35.0	32.6
Urban to Rural	7.5	7.4	7.6	7.5	7.4	7.6
Total Migrants	5,054,759	2,278,720	2,776,039	5,054,759	2,278,720	2,776,039
Interstate						
Rural to Rural	16.6	14.8	19.3	26.2	21.1	30.2
Rural to Urban	49.7	54.5	42.7	24.0	26.3	22.1
Urban to Urban	28.1	25.5	32.0	35.6	36.4	35.0
Urban to Rural	3.5	3.3	3.8	12.2	14.1	10.7
Total Migrants	3,231,612	1,922,629	1,308,983	896,988	393,097	503,891

Source: Directorate of Census Operations (2001).

2.3 million over 1991–2001, mainly attributable to inward migration from other states. Economic reasons including search for employment or work, business and transfer of jobs are the main reasons for such in-migration by males (38 per cent) while marriage is reported as the main factor for in-migration by females (59 per cent) (Directorate of Census Operations 2001).

The pattern of migration into Maharashtra, especially into urban agglomerations (UAs), has implications for the existing housing-, water- and sanitation-related infrastructure facilities available there. Census 2001 data on migration by the last place of residence for each UA city for Maharashtra reveals that approximately 67 per cent of urban migration into the state was directed towards class I cities (having a population of more than 100,000), where the availability of employment and business opportunities were large, putting a lot of pressure on the available amenities and services there. High concentrations of migrants in districts adjacent to Mumbai such as Thane and Raigarh and also in various municipal councils (MCLs) such as Nalasopara MCL (84.2 per cent), Virar MCL (74.1 per cent), Panvel MCL (69.7 per cent) and Bhiwandi (50 per cent) could be attributable to the relocation of population from the high-cost housing areas of Mumbai into these adjacent towns. This was reported as the major reason for the out-migration of nearly 31 per cent of Mumbai's population during the decade 1991–2001. Business and employment were the main factors responsible for the high concentration of migrants in Bhiwandi UA (75.1 per cent), Greater Mumbai UA (61.1 per cent), Ichalkaranji UA (51.8 per cent), Nagpur UA (51.4 per cent) and Nashik (50.2 per cent). The NSS data for 2007–08 shows that male migrants preferred million-plus population cities while female migrants were more concentrated in rural areas and smaller towns (see Figure 6.2) (National Sample Survey Office 2010c).

Effects of Rising Urbanization

The immediate implication of higher levels of urbanization is higher rents.[4] An analysis of rental figures from NSS data reveals

---

[4] There are two sources of data on housing rents: NSSO's survey of household consumption expenditure and NSSO's survey of housing condition and amenities.

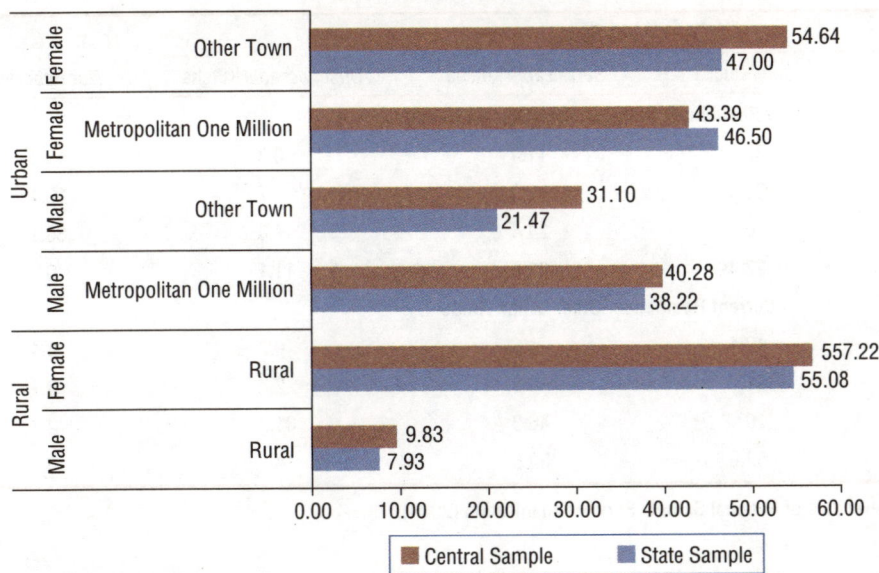

FIGURE 6.2 Percentage of Migrants into Million-Plus Cities, Other Towns and Rural Areas of Maharashtra (2007–08)

Source: National Sample Survey Office (2010c).

that by very conservative estimates, housing rents in urban India have increased by nearly 2.7 times in the last decade, during the period between 1999–2000 and 2009–10. Data from household consumption expenditure surveys reveals that in 1999–2000 the per capita monthly housing rent was ₹143.8 while it stood at ₹386.9 in 2009–10 (Government of India 2001a; National Sample Survey Office 2011). Assuming an average household size of five, the average monthly rent in urban areas has thus increased from ₹718.8 to ₹1,934.6. The NSS of 2008–09 reports the average monthly rent for hired accommodation with a written contract in urban India to be ₹1,878 while it was ₹1,006 for those without a written contract (National Sample Survey Office 2010b). Amongst the major states, the average urban rent per month was ₹1,997 in Karnataka, ₹1,502 in Delhi, ₹1,371 in Kerala, ₹1,209 in Andhra Pradesh, ₹974 in Tamil Nadu and ₹1,225 in Maharashtra.

In the absence of affordable housing in cities, the immediate outcome is an increase in squatter settlements and a proliferation of slums. The average monthly rent paid for slum dwellings after 1995 has been quite high at ₹435 (National Sample Survey Organisation 2004). There is compelling evidence to suggest that households moving into slums are moving down the ladder of dwelling quality. Evidence suggests that one of the compromises that individuals have to make when moving into cities is in their housing conditions. The distribution of households, by dwelling structure, before and after they moved into urban areas shows that only 41 per cent of households currently residing in *pucca* structures in slum and squatter settlements reported living in pucca structures earlier too (see Table 6.3). In contrast, 46.5 per cent of the current slum resident population had moved down the housing ladder from *pucca* structures to semi-*pucca* structures. Similarly, 32 per cent had moved from *pucca* structures to living in serviceable *kutcha* houses in slum and squatter resettlement areas. The proportion of households not reporting any change in structure of dwelling is reflected by the shaded cells in Table 6.3. Thus, with increases in housing rents, urban boundaries tend to expand and populations inhabiting peripheral urban areas also tend to increase. These areas are characterized by lower rents (compared to the cities) and poor housing and sanitation facilities.

> one of the compromises that individuals have to make when moving into cities is in their housing conditions.

Housing, Water and Sanitation

TABLE 6.3
Distribution of Households, by Type of Dwelling Structure: India

Present Structure	Last Structure				
	Pucca	Semi-Pucca	Serviceable Kutcha	Unserviceable Kutcha	Not Reported
Current Residence: Slum and Squatter Settlements					
Pucca	41	32	11.4	0.3	15.3
Semi-Pucca	46.5	30.5	8.3	1.7	13.1
Serviceable Kutcha	31.8	0	24.4	7.6	36.1
Unserviceable Kutcha	4.6	22.4	61.8	11.1	0
Current Residence: Other Urban Areas					
Pucca	79.7	12.4	4.2	0.3	3.4
Semi-Pucca	43	41.7	10.3	2	3.1
Serviceable Kutcha	7.8	10	46.3	31.2	4.7
Unserviceable Kutcha	0.5	52.9	32.5	14	0

Sources: Author's calculations based on unit level data of National Sample Survey Organisation (2004).
Note: Row totals add up to 100.

Housing Amenities in Maharashtra: Trends and Patterns

Traditionally, the NSSO in its reports focuses on three main housing amenities: drinking water within the household premises, electricity for domestic use and the availability of toilets. According to the data from 65th round of surveys by the NSS in (2008–09) (National Sample Survey Office 2010b), in rural Maharashtra, 21.1 per cent of households had all three facilities while 14 per cent had none of them. In urban Maharashtra, 61.8 per cent of households had all three facilities while 0.7 per cent had none of the same (see Figure 6.3), showing a clear urban advantage. When compared to similar average figures for 2002, a significant improvement is seen in the availability of these amenities in rural and a marginal improvement in urban Maharashtra (the figures for urban Maharashtra lag behind the all-India average in 2008–09, see Figure 6.3). This is of concern in light of the high rates of urbanization in the state as discussed earlier.

The NSS data from the 65th round also provides information on whether there has been a

FIGURE 6.3 Proportion of Households with Drinking Water within Their Premises, Electricity for Domestic Use and Toilets: Maharashtra and India (2008–09)

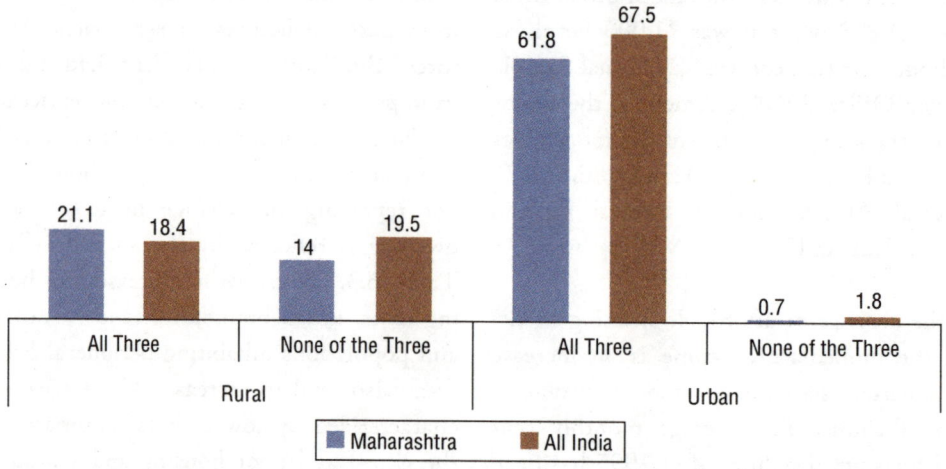

Source: Author's calculations based on unit level data from the 65th round of NSS.

change (classified as improvement, no change, deterioration) in certain useful indicators for slums and some of the main inferences for Maharashtra include: *first*, among the notified and non-notified slums, more than 50 per cent reported no change in the condition of roads, water supply, electricity (72 per cent), street lights, toilet facilities, drainage, sewerage and garbage disposal. *Second*, while 70.2 per cent reported no improvements in the condition of education facilities, 74.2 per cent marked no change in medical facilities. What is also of concern is the proportion of slums reporting a deterioration in available amenities (in the five years preceding the survey). The condition of water supply, drainage and garbage disposal was reported as having deteriorated in 6 per cent, 4 per cent and 6.4 per cent of the slums respectively. On the other hand, 5 per cent of slums marked complete absence of certain facilities including drainage, garbage disposal, medical and educational facilities, while over 15 per cent reported no street lights and sewerage facilities.

Condition of Dwellings

Using data from the household census of 2011 (Government of India 2011c), it is found that there has been a substantial rise in the proportion of 'houses' with good housing conditions during the decade 2001–11. There also exists an urban bias of approximately 17 percentage points in the same (see Table 6.4).

The data from Census 2011 also shows an increase in the proportion of households living in dwellings in good condition is also observed for both the SC (44 per cent in 2001 vis-à-vis 57 per cent in 2011) and ST households (37 per cent in 2001 compared to 48 per cent in 2011).

Districts in the Vidarbha and Marathwada region were found to have a lower proportion of households living in dwellings that are in good condition (see Table 6.5).

TABLE 6.4
Percentage of Households, by Condition of Structure Occupied: Maharashtra (2001–11)

	2001			2011		
	Total	Rural	Urban	Total	Rural	Urban
Good	52.6	43.3	62.6	64.1	56.5	73.1
Livable	42.4	48.4	34.3	31.6	37.2	25.0
Dilapidated	5.0	6.3	3.1	4.3	6.3	1.9

Source: Author's calculations based on Government of India (2011c).
Notes: (i) Good means those houses which do not require any repairs and in good condition.
(ii) Livable means those housed which require minor repairs.
(iii) Dilapidated means those houses which are showing signs of decay or those breaking down and require major repairs.
(iv) The table excludes institutional households.

The condition of dwelling structures can also be assessed from data provided on roof, wall and floor materials used for constructing them. Data from census 2011 reveals that there has been an improvement in dwelling structures, with households moving towards galvanized iron (GI), metal, asbestos sheets or concrete for roofs, burnt bricks and stone for walls and stone, cement and mosaic tiles for flooring materials (see Tables 6A.3). Such trends clearly indicate improvements in housing quality over the decade from 2001 to 2011 in the state.

The classification of households by ownership status[5] indicates that there has been negligible change over the years 2001–11 in rural and urban areas (see Figure 6.4). The district-wise classification of households by their ownership status in urban areas indicate that in 12 districts (including Pune) less than 70 per cent of houses were owner-occupied, while in only two districts namely, Washim and Amravati, more than 80 per cent houses were owner-occupied. Land prices, construction costs, migration, availability of housing loans, etc. could possibly be the different factors affecting ownership status (see Table 6.6).

The analysis of the ownership status by social groups does not show a very encouraging picture of the state. The proportion of owner-occupied houses has remained the same for

Housing, Water and Sanitation

TABLE 6.5
Classification of Districts Based on Proportion of Households Living in Dwellings in Good Condition: Maharashtra (2011)

Proportion of Households Living in Dwellings in Good Condition	Districts
40–50	Buldhana, Washim, Yavatmal, Nanded, Hingoli, Parbhani
50–60	Nandurbar, Akola, Amravati, Wardha, Bhandara, Gondia, Gadchiroli, Chandrapur, Jalna, Beed, Latur, Osmanabad
60–70	Dhule, Jalgaon, Nagpur, Aurangabad, Nashik, Ahmednagar, Solapur, Satara, Ratnagiri, Sindhudurg, Sangli
Above 70	Thane, Mumbai (Suburban), Mumbai, Raigarh, Pune, Kolhapur

Source: Government of India (2011c).

TABLE 6.6
Classification of Districts Based on Proportion of Urban Households Residing in Owner-Occupied Houses: Maharashtra (2011)

Percentage of Households Residing in Owner-Occupied Houses	Districts
50–60	Pune
60–70	Gadchiroli, Chandrapur, Nanded, Aurangabad, Nashik, Thane, Raigarh, Ahmednagar, Satara, Ratnagiri, Sindhudurg
70–80	Nandurbar, Dhule, Jalgaon, Buldhana, Akola, Wardha, Nagpur, Bhandara, Gondia, Yavatmal, Hingoli, Parbhani, Jalna, Mumbai (Suburban), Mumbai, Beed, Latur, Osmanabad, Solapur, Kolhapur, Sangli
Above 80	Washim, Amravati

Source: Government of India (2011c).

the SC and ST during 2001–11 (80.4 per cent in 2001 and 80.3 per cent in 2011 for the SC, and 85.2 per cent and 85.8 per cent for the ST, respectively).

The relationship between the quality of dwelling and consumption expenditure (captured by MPCE classes) in Maharashtra comes forth quite clearly using data from 65th round of the NSS (National Sample Survey Office 2010b). In 2008–09, the proportion of households living in dwellings in bad condition was the highest amongst the lowest MPCE households in both rural and urban areas of the state (20.5 per cent and 21.3 per cent respectively). The condition of dwellings showed an improvement with increase in the MPCE for both rural and urban areas. Access to financial resources, especially for slum dwellers to undertake improvements in their dwelling structures, was reported to be a major constraint. While findings from the NSSO surveys suggest that formal institutions such as banks were less likely to finance repairs of dwellings, slum dwellers were also not able to provide the necessary documents to access loans from the formal sector.

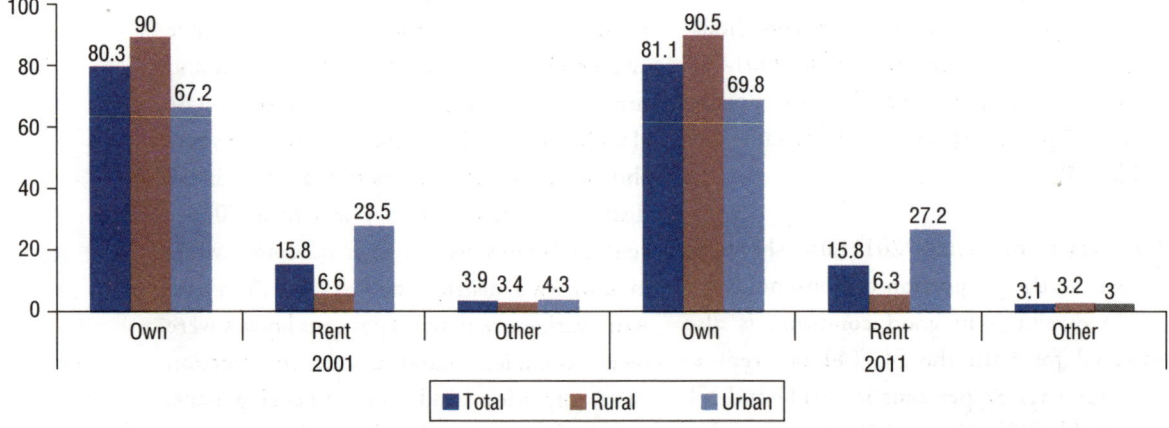

FIGURE 6.4 Classification of Households by Ownership Status: Maharashtra (2001–11)

Source: Government of India (2011c).

[5] At the time of the census survey, if a household is occupying a house it owns and is not making any payments in the form of rent to anyone, then the household may be considered as living in a owned house. A housing unit is rented if rent is paid or contracted for by the household in cash or even in kind, for example, rented accommodation provided by an employer, such as government quarters or similar accommodation. The category 'any other' comprises situations where the household lives in a house which is neither owned nor rented.

Housing Programmes

There have been various state interventions to facilitate housing for LIGs and for those living in slums. The three important centrally sponsored schemes for housing are the JNNURM, AHP and RAY. Launched in 2005, the JNNURM has two components, namely, the BSUP and the IHSDP, which focus on providing shelter and basic services to the urban poor. While the BSUP is being implemented in Mumbai, Pune, Nagpur, Nashik and Nanded, the IHSDP covers all other cities that do not come under the purview of the BUSP. Box 6.1 lists the admissible components under the sub-mission on BSUP under the JNNURM.

To improve the living conditions in slums the state government has put in place various policy interventions. Between 1995 and 2010, the Slum Rehabilitation Authority rehabilitated 141,016 slum families. The Shivshahi Punarvasan Prakalp Ltd has been working towards acceleration of slum rehabilitation since its inception in 1995. A total of 105 buildings comprising 10,056 tenements have been constructed while construction work is ongoing in 617 tenements in 6 buildings. Under the decade-old Beedi Kamgar Gharkul Yojana, houses have been constructed at Solapur, Nashik, Pune, Kolhapur, Garkheda in Aurangabad, Nanded and Kamtee in Nagpur, for beedi workers (Government of Maharashtra 2011).

The AHP programme aims to construct one million houses for the EWS, LIGs and middle income groups (MIGs) with at least 25 per cent for the EWS. This scheme is to be implemented in partnership with urban local bodies and developers (Government of India 2011). Under the aegis of the RAY, a sum of ₹12,700 million was allocated for the year 2010–11 towards the preparatory phase. Funds from this were to be released to the states "for undertaking slum surveys, mapping of slums, developing slum information systems, undertaking community mobilization, preparation of slum-free city/ state plans, etc." The number of houses built under

> **Box 6.1 Admissible Components: BSUP under JNNURM**
>
> 1. Integrated development of slums, that is, housing and development of infrastructural projects in the slum in identified cities.
> 2. Projects involving development, improvement and/or maintenance of the BSUP.
> 3. Slum improvement and rehabilitation projects.
> 4. Projects on water supply, sewerage, drainage, community toilets, baths, etc.
> 5. Houses at affordable costs for slum dwellers, urban poor, economically weaker sections (EWS) and lower income group (LIG) categories.
> 6. Construction and improvement of drains and storm-water drains.
> 7. Environmental improvement of slums and solid waste management.
> 8. Street lighting.
> 9. Civic amenities like community hall, child care centres, etc.
> 10. Operation and maintenance of assets created under the component.
> 11. Convergence of health, education and social security schemes for the urban poor.
>
> *Source:* MHADA (2008).

the Indira Awas Yojana (IAY) for homeless BPL families in rural areas has shown a steady increase in the state from 70,336 in 2005–06 to 125,214 in 2007–08 to 205,149 in 2009–10 (Government of Maharashtra 2012a). Box 6.1 details the state government's initiatives in the context of housing.

Water: An Important Resource for Human Development

Access to clean drinking water and sanitation has far-reaching implications for health outcomes as well as for the MDGs relating to health. In this context, focus needs to be placed on the source of drinking water, its availability in sufficient quantities and the right to the water source. Data on the access to water and its availability from the household census of 2011 reveals that in Maharashtra, tap water was the major source of drinking water for approximately two-thirds of the households (67.9 per cent) while wells (14.4 per cent), hand pumps (9.9 per cent) and tube wells (5.7 per cent) were others. In urban areas a larger proportion of households accessed drinking water from taps (89.1 per cent) than those in rural areas, where only half the households accessed taps for drinking water. Also, while in urban areas hand pumps and tube wells were the next main source of drinking water for the households (6.6 per cent) well water

> In Maharashtra 59.4 per cent of households had the source of drinking water within their premises, showing an increase from 53.4 per cent in 2001.

was the next main source for rural households in the state (Government of India 2011c).

Inter-district variations in access to tap water existed, with households in Mumbai and Mumbai (Suburban) availing of it in highest proportions (97.8 per cent and 96.5 per cent respectively). In Jalgaon, Kolhapur, Dhule, Thane and Pune, over 80 per cent of households had tap water as their main source of drinking water. At the other extreme were districts such as Gondia, Gadchiroli and Sindhudurg where less than approximately a third of households had access to tap water. It needs to be mentioned here that in Sindhudurg well water was the major source of drinking water.

Districts such as Raigarh, Wardha and Ratnagiri have shown improvements in the proportion of households having access to tap water by over 10 percentage points over the decade 2001–11 while in districts such as Akola, Jalna, Nanded and Mumbai (Suburban), there has been a marginal decrease in the same between two and three percentage points (see Table 6A.4).

Additionally, there has been an improvement in the proportion of households having tap water within their premises over the decade 2001–11 by approximately six percentage points for Maharashtra as compared to 7.6 percentage points for India as a whole (see Figure 6.5).

Distance to the source of drinking water has important implications for women and children. Census 2011 data indicates that in Maharashtra 59.4 per cent of households had the source of drinking water within their premises, showing an increase from 53.4 per cent in 2001. There existed a clear urban advantage for this indicator (79.3 per cent of households) compared to its rural counterpart (42.9 per cent of households). Further, while in urban areas, 5.2 per cent of households had to fetch water from a source located within a distance of 100m; in rural areas on the other hand 19.6 per cent of households had to fetch water from a distance of 500m or more. District-level data for this indicator shows wide inter-district variations. In 9 out of the 35 districts, less than 40 per cent of the households reported that the source of drinking water was within their premises (see Figure 6.6). In Gondia and Gadchiroli, not even a third of households had this facility while in Washim and Yawatmal, just about a third of households enjoyed this facility. When studied by social groups, the proportion of SC households having their source of drinking water within the premises reported an increase over the decade 2001–11 from 44 per cent to 54.8 per cent, while it has shown only a marginal increase for ST households from 32 per cent to 33.9 per cent (Government of India 2011c).

The NSS data from the 65th round (2008–09) (National Sample Survey Office 2010b) provides data on the availability of drinking water in sufficient quantities for households, which is a useful indicator as it helps us look beyond access. In rural areas, 25 per cent of households reported unavailability of sufficient drinking water from the first source throughout the year compared to 12 per cent of urban households. We also find that in urban Maharashtra, nearly 70 per cent of households reporting insufficient drinking water belonged to the bottom 60 per cent of

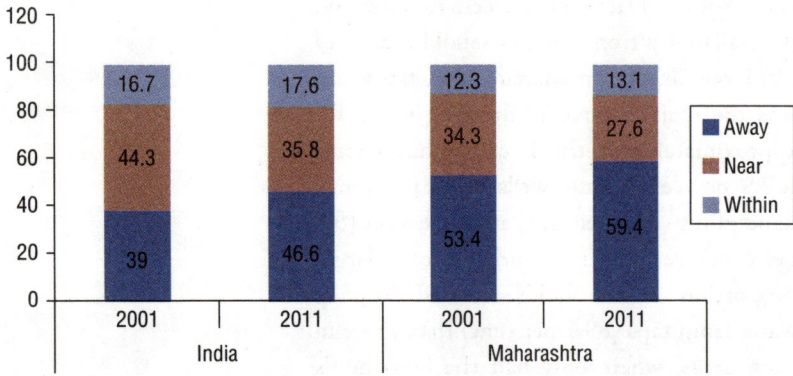

FIGURE 6.5 Distance of Tap Water Source from Households: Maharashtra and India (2001–11)

Source: Government of India (2011c).
Notes: (i) Near means within a distance of 500 metres (m) from the household in rural areas and within 100m in urban areas.
(ii) Away means at a distance of 500m or beyond from the household in rural areas and 100m or beyond in urban areas.

FIGURE 6.6 Percentage of Households Having Drinking Water Facility within Their Premises, by Districts: Maharashtra (2001–11)

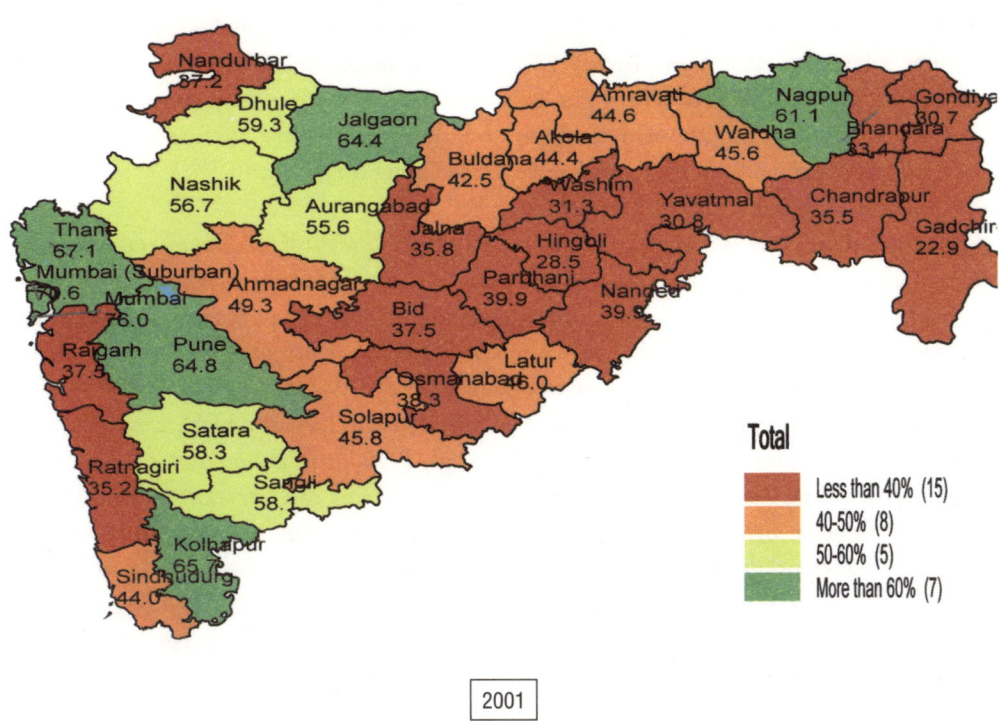

2001

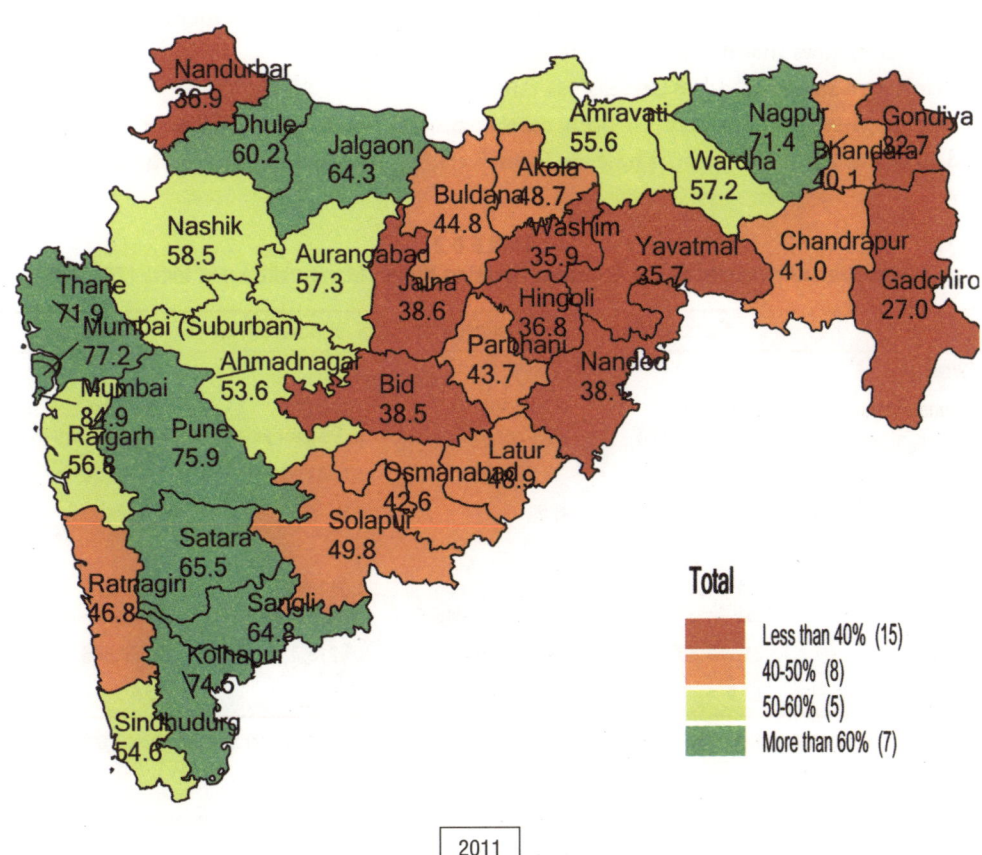

2011

Housing, Water and Sanitation

> Mumbai is reported to have the highest average water supply (200 lpcd); although the supply in different areas of the city varies widely.

the MPCE groups. Across the social groups, in rural areas, predominantly SC and OBC households reported insufficiency of drinking water while in urban areas largely SC households faced a shortage. The right to water source is an important human development dimension and in 2008–09 about 7 million rural and 1.5 million urban households reported community use as their water source (56.9 per cent and 15.6 per cent respectively, see Table 6.7). In both rural and urban areas, richer households were found to have larger exclusive access to their water source as compared to poorer households who were mostly relegated to community use. In rural as well as urban areas the OBC were reported as having exclusive use of drinking water facilities in higher proportions (39 per cent and 62.5 per cent respectively). The ST relies mainly on community use drinking water facilities in both rural and urban areas (75 per cent and 42 per cent respectively).

Interestingly, the data from the 65th round of the NSS shows that distance to the source of drinking water is found to decrease as one moves up the MPCE ladder, in both rural and urban areas of the state. The data from DLHS-3 also reveals that access to safe and improved drinking water by wealth quintiles is much higher for the top two quintiles whereas nearly one-fifth of the bottom most sections of the population are still dependent on unimproved and surface water sources (see Figure 6.7).

In urban parts of Maharashtra, there are more than 245 urban centres with piped drinking water supply schemes, although the supplied water is inadequate as per the standards laid down by the GoI.[6] Mumbai is reported to have the highest average water supply (200 lpcd); although the supply in different areas of the city varies widely. In the slum areas of Mumbai city, the availability is 90 lpcd whereas those living in well-off areas receive as much as 300–350 lpcd. In 12 municipal corporations except Mumbai, the water supply is below the norm. In 15 A-class MCLs, 39 B-class MCLs and 81 towns in C-class MCLs water supply is again reported to be below the norms mentioned by NEERI (MPCB 2007).

Besides inadequacy of water supply, other critical issues that need to be addressed by

TABLE 6.7
Distribution of Households, by Access to Drinking Water: Maharashtra and India (2008–09)

	Exclusive Use	Common Use	Community Use	Others
Rural				
Maharashtra	3,685,516 (29.9 per cent)	1,118,836 (9.1 per cent)	7,009,084 (56.9 per cent)	495,443 (4.0 per cent)
India	49,199,922	13,102,037	89,860,425	5,989,120
Share of Maharashtra	7.5	8.5	7.8	8.3
Urban				
Maharashtra	5,455,615 (55.4 per cent)	1,933,145 (19.6 per cent)	1,537,815 (15.6 per cent)	917,382 (9.3 per cent)
India	31,242,807	16,415,150	15,215,711	3,578,646
Share of Maharashtra	17.5	11.8	10.1	25.6

Source: Author's calculations based on unit level data on housing conditions in National Sample Survey Office (2010b).

[6] The water supply standards and norms in rural and urban areas recommended by the National Environmental Engineering Research Institute (NEERI) in 2002 are cited in a report by the Maharashtra Pollution Control Board (MPCB). The norms prescribed are 40 litres per capita per day (lpcd) for rural areas, 125 lpcd for A-class MCLs, 100 lpcd for B-class MCLs and 70 lpcd for C-class MCLs. The norm is higher for corporations (135–150 lpcd) (MPCB 2007).

FIGURE 6.7 Access to Drinking Water, by Wealth Quintiles: Maharashtra (2007–08)

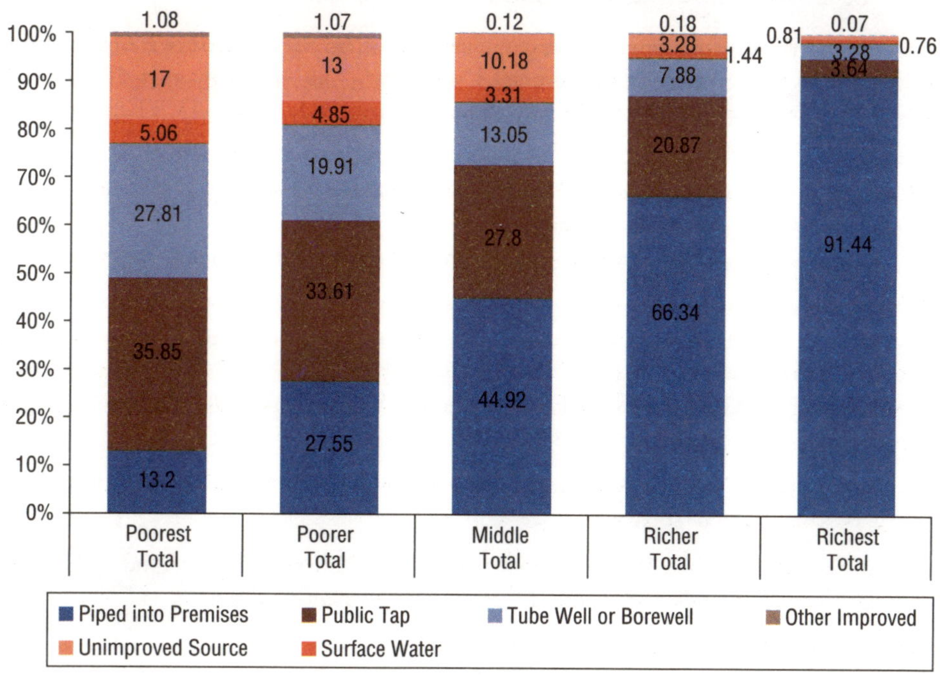

	Poorest Total	Poorer Total	Middle Total	Richer Total	Richest Total
Piped into Premises	13.2	27.55	44.92	66.34	91.44
Public Tap	35.85	33.61	27.8	20.87	3.64
Tube Well or Borewell	27.81	19.91	13.05	7.88	3.28
Other Improved	5.06	4.85	3.31	3.28	0.07
Unimproved Source	17	13	10.18	1.44	0.81
Surface Water	1.08	1.07	0.12	0.18	0.76

Source: IIPS 2010.

the state are: water pollution due to municipal sewage and industrial activities, unsatisfactory sanitation, management of available water resources and the depletion of ground water. In an effort to address such issues, in the year 2005, the GoM, under the World Bank-assisted Jalswarajya project, conducted a very detailed study across the districts for five chemical parameters, namely, nitrate, fluoride, iron, chloride and total dissolved solids. Both government and private agencies were engaged in this exercise, wherein about 278,939 water sources were sampled and checked, covering 35,049 villages. All the details were put in simple geographical information system software. Out of 35,049 villages, 9,845 villages were found to be chemically affected. The districts severely affected by chemicals included Yavatmal, Wardha, Nagpur, Bhandara, Chandrapur, Jalgaon, Nanded, Beed, Osmanabad and Thane. The least affected districts were Dhule, Buldhana, Akola, Hingoli, Jalna, Gadchiroli, Pune, Latur, Solapur, Satara, Kolhapur and Sangli. Fluoride contamination above acceptable levels was found most frequently in Chandrapur, Yavatmal, Nagpur, Washim, Nanded, Parbhani and Beed and to a lesser extent in some other districts. Nitrate contamination was seen predominantly in Jalgaon, Wardha, Chandrapur and Yavatmal and to some extent in other districts. Sustainability of the water sources during summer months was also a problem faced by a majority of the districts in the state. As on 1 April 2012, 16,570 habitations were partially covered, with less than 40 lpcd of water (see IMIS information on www.indiawater.gov.in).

Box 6.2 details some initiatives implemented by the government for improving access to water.

In 2012–13, 87.5 per cent of habitations in rural areas had complete (100 per cent) population coverage of drinking water supply (see Table 6.8).

Sanitation Conditions

The GoI's TSC seeks to "ensure sanitation facilities in rural areas with the broader goal to eradicate the practice of open defecation". It is found that in 2011, in Maharashtra, approximately 85.4 per cent households had a bathing facility within their premises, showing an increase of 24.3 percentage points over

> *Nitrate contamination was seen predominantly in Jalgaon, Wardha, Chandrapur and Yavatmal and to some extent in other districts.*

> **Box 6.2 Government Initiatives for Improving Access to Water**
>
> The GoI-sponsored National Rural Drinking Water Programme is being implemented in Maharashtra since 1 April 2009. Of the targeted 6,502 habitations for 2011–12, 6,364 habitations were reported as covered. The Action Plan for 2012–13 and 2013–14 includes coverage of 13,237 habitations, out of which 5,940 habitations are targeted for 2012–13. The achievement up to July 2012 is 668 habitations (see IMIS report on www.indiawater.gov.in).
>
> The Rural Water Supply Project, Aaple Pani, being implemented in Pune, Aurangabad and Ahmednagar, aims at improving health and sanitation standards through sustainable water supply, development of watershed areas, exhaustive planning of ground water, etc. As of 31 March 2011, a total 840 habitations in 235 village panchayats had been provided with water supply through this initiative.
>
> The Jalswarajya programme seeks to improve the quality of rural water supply and environmental sanitation services. It has reported a coverage of 461 village panchayats in the Amravati region, 790 in the Aurangabad region, 317 in the Konkan region, 641 in the Nagpur region, 286 in the Nashik region and 471 in the Pune region, all of whom now have regular water supply (Government of Maharashtra 2011).
>
> The primary objective of the Maharashtra Sujal and Nirmal Abhiyanis overcoming water scarcity and growing demand for water by providing potable water and good sanitation facilities to all citizens.
>
> The Nagri Dalit Vasti Water Supply and Sanitation Scheme (under Maharashtra Sujal and Nirmal Abhiyan) and the Shivkalin Pani Sathvan Yojana are two other programmes that aim at water and sanitation improvements in the state.

Source: Information provided by the Water and Sanitation Department, GoM.

TABLE 6.8
Statistics on Rural Drinking Water Supply: Maharashtra (2012–13)

Number of Districts: 33
Number of Blocks: 351
[Semi-Critical: 7 per cent, Critical: 0 per cent, Over-Exploited: 2 per cent]
Number of Panchayats: 27,961
Rural Population as on 1 April 12 (In Millions): 65.0 [SC: 7.1(11.0 per cent), ST: 8.5(13.1 per cent), General: 49.4 (75.9 per cent)]
Population Managing Water Supply Scheme:[7] 76.8 per cent
Stage of Ground Water Development: 48 per cent

Coverage Status of Habitation as on 21 August 2012:

Total Number of Habitations	Number of Habitations with Partial Population Coverage	Number of Habitations with 100 per cent Population Coverage
100,683	12,568 (12.5 per cent)	88,115 (87.5 per cent)

Coverage of SC, ST, Minority Habitations (Coverage as on 21 August 2012):

Particulars	Total Habitations	Coverage	Percentage of Coverage
SC-Concentrated Habitations	4,763	4,243	89.1
ST-Concentrated Habitations	17,964	16,379	91.2
Habitations in Minority Concentrated Districts	3,875	3,067	79.2
Liquid Water Equivalent Concentrated Habitations	3,756	3,357	89.4

Source: Ministry of Drinking Water and Sanitation (2011).

---

[7] Evaluation studies carried out at different levels reveal that although after the promulgation of the 73rd constitutional amendment, responsibility for operation and maintenance of water supply system lies with the PRIs, in many states the responsibility in this context is poorly defined and not supported by transfer of adequate funds and trained manpower by state governments to PRIs. The inadequacy of the existing operations and maintenance systems, and the reluctance of PRIs to take responsibility for maintaining these systems, particularly the regional water supply schemes, are well documented. It is a well-known fact that the PRIs and the VHSCs are not willing to take over completed schemes in which they were not involved at the planning and implementation stages. Inadequate water resource investigation, improper design, poor construction, substandard materials and workmanship and lack of preventive maintenance also lead to rapid deterioration of the water supply systems. Accordingly

2001 (Government of India 2011c). There were 64.3 per cent of households having bathrooms with covered roofs, while 14.6 per cent of households had no facility and used open spaces. The corresponding figures at the national level were 42 per cent and 41.6 per cent respectively, showing that Maharashtra has fared much better in provisioning on this front (see Table 6.9). In urban areas, 86 per cent of households reported having bathrooms within their premises, although in rural areas it was much lower at 46.2 per cent. Only 4.6 per cent of households in urban and 22.9 per cent in rural areas did not have any type of bathroom.

The district-level data for 2011 reveals that in Mumbai, Mumbai (Suburban), Raigarh, Thane and Kolhapur, more than 85 per cent of households reported a bathing facility in their homes. At the other extreme, in Beed, Nandurbar and Gadchiroli, less than a third of households had this facility. The data also shows that in Nandurbar and Beed districts, of the remaining two-thirds of households, a third had an enclosure without a roof for a bathroom while the remaining third did not have a bathing facility at all. In Gadchiroli, the proportion of households not having a bathing facility was higher, at 42.5 per cent, which is also the highest amongst all the districts of the state.

The NSS data from the 65th round (2008–09) (National Sample Survey Office 2010b) reveals that the availability of bathrooms shows an improvement as households moved up the MPCE ladder in both rural and urban areas of the state.

Census data also facilitates a look at the proportion of households having a latrine facility and it is found that in 2011, 53 per cent of households in Maharashtra had a latrine facility within their premises. This is an improvement of 18 percentage points over 2001 for the state vis-à-vis 10.5 percentage points for the country as a whole (see Figure 6.8). The sector-wise data shows that 38 per cent of households in rural areas had a latrine facility within their premises, which was far less than the proportion in urban areas where close to three-fourths of households had the same. Such a fact flags the presence of a disparity in the access to sanitation facilities in rural areas vis-à-vis urban areas of the state. Inter-district variations in this essential sanitation facility show that the proportion of households having latrines within the premises to vary from as low as 25 per cent in Beed to approximately 76 per cent in Sindhudurg and Nagpur (see Table 6A.5). Data at the district level brings forth wide variations in the proportion of households having latrine facility within their premises. While in nine districts including Mumbai, Mumbai (Suburban), Kolhapur, Raigarh, Thane, Nagpur, Pune, Sindhudurg and Ratnagiri close to three-fourths of the households had latrine facilities within their premises, at the other extreme were districts such as Beed, Gadchiroli and Nandurbar where less than a third of households had access to the same. Around 56 per cent of rural and 7.7 per cent of urban households in the state used open

TABLE 6.9
Percentage of Households and Bathroom Facility: Maharashtra and India (2011)

	Percentage of Households and the Bathroom Facility within Their Premises		
	Have Facility		
	Bathroom	Enclosure without Roof	Do Not Have Facility
India	42.0	16.4	41.6
Maharashtra	64.3	21.1	14.6

Source: Government of India (2011c).

> *The sector-wise data shows that 38 per cent of households in rural areas had a latrine facility within their premises, which was far less than the proportion in urban areas where close to three-fourths of households had the same.*

---

to encourage the states to ensure that the PRIs operate and maintain the water supply schemes, weightage has been provided for 'rural population managing rural drinking water supply schemes' under the revised criteria for fund allocation under the Rural Water Supply Programme and Advanced Rural Water Supply Programme. Under the demand-oriented and beneficiaries-responsive approach envisioned for the sector, communities will have access to relevant information, and will exercise their decision at each stage of planning (Ministry of Rural Development 2009).

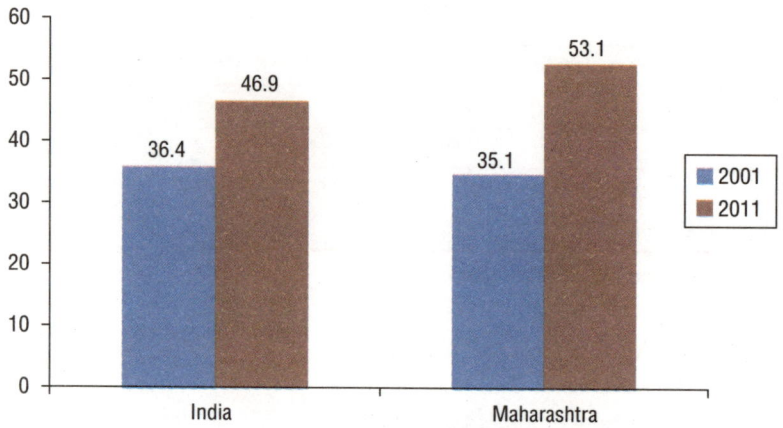

FIGURE 6.8 Percentage of Households Having Latrine Facility within Their Premises: India and Maharashtra (2001–11)

Source: Government of India (2011c).

spaces for defecation. Districts where such a practice was high included Beed (73.2 per cent), Gadchiroli (71.9 per cent), Parbhani (70.1 per cent) and Osmanabad (68.9 per cent) (Government of India 2011c). What is worth noting is that in certain districts where the proportion of households having a latrine facility within the household's premises was low, the usage of public facilities for the same was also high. Dhule and Jalgaon are two such examples where 21.6 per cent and 17.6 per cent of households, respectively, used public latrine facilities. Mumbai (Suburban) also reported equal proportions of households with a latrine facility within their premises and those using public facilities (43 per cent) pointing towards a useful way in which such facilities could be made available for common use as well as to promote cleanliness, hygiene and sanitation in the state.

Access to latrine facilities within the household premises has shown an improvement by social groups for the state, which is an important development as it points towards inclusion in the availability or provisioning of sanitation amenities. During the decade 2001–11 it was found that the proportion of SC households having a latrine facility within the household premises increased from 28.4 per cent to 44.7 per cent. The proportion of ST households availing the same had also risen from 20.2 per cent to 30.1 per cent during the same period, implying a move towards better sanitation conditions and a proportionate decrease in open defecation in the state. Among the households having a latrine facility within their premises, around 35 per cent had latrines connected to a piped sewer system. Disaggregated by sector, the scenario becomes quite lopsided with only 5.8 per cent of households in rural areas having a piped sewer system as against 53 per cent of households in urban areas.

A study carried out by UNICEF (2012) finds a strong correlation between the percentage of households having a latrine facility and the availability of drinking water facility within the households premises, per capita income and literacy rate. In households having drinking water within premises, irrespective of the type, the adoption of toilets was found to be twice more likely as compared to households with drinking water near or away from their premises.

The details of Nirmal Gram Puraskar are provided in Box 6.3. The status of TSC is set out in Table 6.10. Box 6.4 profiles the success story of a village in Ahmednagar.

The availability of appropriate drainage facilities has important implications for the cleanliness and sanitation conditions of households. It is found that in 2011, approximately 33.2 per cent of households had closed drainage facilities, 34.2 per cent had open drainage while 32.5 per cent households did not have any appropriate drainage facilities (compared to 48.9 per cent for India) (Government of India 2011c). The drainage scenario in the state has shown a marginal improvement of around seven percentage points over the decade 2001–11 (see Figure 6.9).

There was also a clear urban bias in this indicator with 8.8 per cent of households in urban areas and 52.2 per cent of households in rural areas lacking drainage facilities. In rural areas, the open drainage system was found to be more prevalent (39.1 per cent households) while in urban areas closed drainage was present in a higher proportion

> Access to latrine facilities within the household premises has shown an improvement by social groups for the state, which is an important development as it points towards inclusion in the availability or provisioning of sanitation amenities.

of households (62.7 per cent). In the districts of Nandurbar, Gondia, Gadchiroli and Ahmednagar, approximately two-thirds of households reported not having any drainage facility and for those who did have the same, open drainage was the system in greater proportions.

The garbage disposal arrangement in rural areas of the state is a matter of concern. While in rural areas only a fourth of households had a garbage disposal system in place, in urban areas approximately 78 per cent of households had it (National Sample Survey Office 2010b). Further, in urban areas, the local municipal corporation was mainly responsible for garbage disposal (62 per cent of households) while 21 per cent households made their own arrangement (and half of these households belonged to the bottom 40 per cent MPCE classes). Thus, the lower MPCE classes lived in poor housing and sanitation conditions and also lacked proper garbage disposal facilities.

Summing Up

There is a strong link between good health and the availability of clean drinking water, well-ventilated and uncongested housing and good sanitation facilities. Households having inadequate access to housing and various related amenities can be expected to be more susceptible to ill health and morbidity and this in turn has important implications for the achievement of the various MDGs. Thus, the importance of housing as a bundle of amenities becomes important when studying human development. With urbanization comes the added problem of proliferation of slums, where the housing conditions and availability of various amenities are markedly worse. In Maharashtra too, rapid urbanization has been accompanied by an increase in the number of slums with the state accounting for nearly 35 per cent of notified and non-notified slums in the country. Maharashtra's progress in achieving health-related targets needs to therefore be assessed in the light of urbanization and the existing conditions of housing and other amenities.

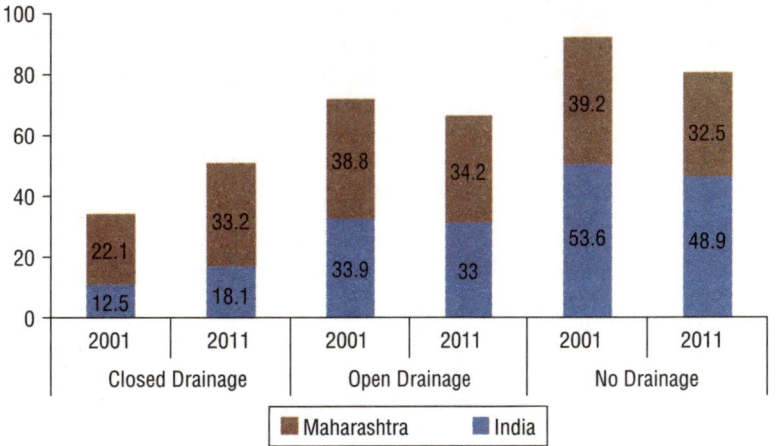

FIGURE 6.9 Percentage of Households Having Different Types of Drainage Facility: India and Maharashtra (2001–11)

Source: Government of India (2011c).

TABLE 6.10
Report Card Status of TSC as on 14 March 2012: Maharashtra

Components	Project Objective	Project Performance	Percentage of Achievement
Individual Household Latrines BPL	3,623,439	2,657,183	73.3
Individual Household Latrines APL	6,104,904	4,415,104	72.3
Individual Household Latrines Total	9,728,343	7,072,287	72.7
School Toilet	87,452	88,190	100.8
Sanitary Complex	8,210	6,024	73.4
Anganwadi	60,076	58,555	97.5
Rural Sanitary Marts	329	771	234.4

(Funds in ₹ Lakhs)

Share	Approved	Funds Received	Utilization	Percentage of Utilization against Release
GoI	97,771.8	56,251.3	51,669.1	91.9
State Share	36,414.5	28,066.8	21,783.5	77.6
Beneficiaries Share	14,782.8	12,573.9	6,917.5	55.0
Total	148,969.0	96,891.9	80,370.0	83.0

Source: Government of India (2012b).

The first by-product of rapid urbanization is a rise in rentals and in Maharashtra the average monthly rent for hired accommodation in urban areas in 2008–09 was ₹1,225. Unaffordable housing leads to the emergence of squatter settlements and slums. Evidence from the NSS data (2008–09) clearly suggests that the main compromise that individuals have to make when moving into cities is in their housing conditions. Households moving into slums find themselves moving

> **Box 6.3 Nirmal Gram Puraskar (NGP)**
>
> The TSC is a comprehensive programme to ensure sanitation facilities in rural areas with the broader goal to eradicate the practice of open defecation. To add vigour to the TSC, in October 2003, the GoI initiated an incentive scheme named the NGP. The NGP is given to 'open defecation-free' Nirmal village panchayats, blocks and districts which have become fully sanitized. The incentive provision is PRIs as well as individuals and organizations that are the driving force for full sanitation coverage.
>
> A *nirmalgram* is an open defecation-free village where all houses, schools and *anganwadis* have sanitary toilets and the community is aware of the importance of maintaining personal and community hygiene as well as a clean environment.
>
> In Maharashtra during 2005–12, a total of 9,523 village panchayats and 11 panchayat samitis were awarded the NGP. Satara housed the highest number of gram panchayats receiving the NGP (1,435).
>
> *Source:* Government of India (2012b).

> **Box 6.4 A Success Story: Borban, A '*Hagandari Mukt Gaon*'**
>
> Borban is a small community of about 185 families in Sangamner block, Ahmednagar district, in Maharashtra. Today, the villagers have an air of achievement and confidence about them as all households have constructed individual household toilets. This transformation started with the village actively taking part in the Sant Gadge Baba sanitation campaign and ranked second in the district-level competition. However, the practice of open defecation made the village lose valuable points.
>
> The villagers therefore decided to adopt the challenge of ending open defecation in their village. Each household decided to construct a toilet. Since it was the lean period, the villagers had no financial resources available to buy even the basic material required for a low-cost toilet. The sarpanch of the village immediately agreed to stand guarantee for supply of construction material, thus making it possible for the people to purchase it on credit from the local market. The district administration educated them about low-cost technology toilets so that everyone could construct toilets according to their financial capacity. The lack of any prescriptive technologies led to different types of toilets being constructed at varying costs.
>
> In fact, the village now imposes a fine if anyone is seen to continue the traditional practice. The community solidarity and status of this village has become a model for the entire district.
>
> *Source:* Government of India (2012a).

down the dwelling-quality ladder (from *pucca* structures to semi-*pucca* or serviceable *kutcha* structures). With increasing urbanization and rising rents, there is an expansion in urban boundaries and areas peripheral to cities. Here lower rents are combined with poor housing and sanitation facilities. Although there has been an improvement in the three main housing facilities, namely, households with drinking water within their premises, electricity for domestic use and the availability of toilets over the period 2002–09 the improvement was seen to be larger in rural areas and marginal in urban areas, which is a cause for concern, given the fast paced urbanization in the state. Also, the proportion of households living in dwellings in bad conditions was highest among the poorest households with the condition of dwellings improving with rising MPCE, in both rural and urban areas of the state. In 2008–09, data on housing amenities for slums reveals the deterioration in the condition of water supply, drainage and garbage disposal. Five per cent of slums lacked drainage, garbage disposal, medical and educational facilities while over 15 per cent did not have street lights and sewerage facilities.

In general the state reports improvements in the quality of housing. The household census data for 2011 indicates that there has been a substantial increase in the proportion of houses in good condition during the decade 2001–11, with the increase being significant in rural areas. There has been an improvement in household quality with households moving towards GI, metal or asbestos sheets or concrete for roofs, burnt bricks and stone for walls and stone, cement and mosaic tiles for flooring materials. The districts in the Vidarbha and Marathwada regions continue to have lower proportions of households having good condition.

Availability and access to clean and safe drinking water is imperative for human development. The household census of 2011 shows that in urban areas larger proportions of households access drinking water from taps, while the proportion is much lower in rural areas. Districts such as Raigarh, Wardha and Ratnagiri have shown improvements in household access to tap water by over 10 percentage points over the decade 2001–11 while in districts such as Akola, Jalna, Nanded and Mumbai (Suburban), there has been a marginal decrease in the same by around two to three percentage points. NSS data shows that the right to a water source in terms of exclusivity is higher for households belonging to the higher wealth quintiles.

As far as the distance of the water source from the household is considered, there is seen an improvement in the percentage of households having tap water as the source of drinking water within the premises during 2001–11 with SC households reporting a significant increase and ST households showing a marginal improvement. There were still 19.6per cent of rural households who had to fetch water from a source which is 500m or more away. The situation is of concern in nine districts of Nandurbar, Jalna, Beed, Washim, Hingoli, Nanded, Yavatmal, Gondia and Gadchiroli where less than 40 per cent of households had a drinking water source within the premises.

Sanitation data from Census 2011 indicates that in Maharashtra 85.4 per cent households had a bathing facility within their premises, showing an increase of 24.3 percentage points over 2001 (Government of India 2011c). The rural–urban disparity for the same indicator is prominent, close to 40 percentage points, making the urban advantage quite evident. In the districts of Mumbai, Mumbai (Suburban), Raigarh, Thane and Kolhapur, more than 85 per cent of households reported a bathing facility in their homes, while in Beed, Nandurbar and Gadchiroli, less than a third of households had this facility. Only 38 per cent households in rural areas had latrine facilities within their premises, which was less than in urban areas where close to three-fourths of households had the same. In nine districts including Mumbai, Mumbai (Suburban), Kolhapur, Raigarh, Thane, Nagpur, Pune, Sindhudurg and Ratnagiri, close to three-fourths of households reported having latrine facilities within their premises. At the other extreme are districts such as Beed, Gadchiroli and Nandurbar where less than a third of households had access to the same. In certain districts where the proportion of households having a latrine facility within the premises was low, the usage of public facilities was found to be high, pointing towards a useful way in which open defecation can be discouraged with the provisioning of public sanitation facilities.

Drainage facilities are an important component of sanitation and the state shows a marginal improvement of around seven percentage points over the decade 2001–11. The rural–urban disparity was quite pronounced, with 52.2 per cent rural and only 8.8 per cent urban households lacking drainage systems. In the districts of Nandurbar, Gondia, Gadchiroli and Ahmednagar, approximately two-thirds of households reported not having any drainage facility.

To summarize, while there have been improvements in dwelling conditions of households, the source of and distance to drinking water as well as sanitation conditions in Maharashtra, their provisioning being above the all-India averages during 2001–11, there is still a gap to bridge in terms of rural–urban, social group as well as inter-district disparities in the provisioning and utilization of these amenities, pointing towards the need for improved inclusion in these human development imperatives.

Annexure 6.1
Definition of Slums in Maharashtra

There is no definition of 'slums' in the Maharashtra Slum Areas (Improvement, Clearance and Redevelopment) Act, 1971. However, section 2(ga) defines a 'Slum Area' as:

Slum area means any area declared as such by the Competent Authority under sub-section (1) of section 4;

As per the provisions of sub-section (1) of section 4, to declare an area as slum area, it must satisfy the following conditions:

1. It must be an area that is or may be a source of danger to the health, safety or convenience of the public of that area or of its neighbourhood, by reasons of the area having inadequate or no basic amenities, or being insanitary, squalid, overcrowded or otherwise.
2. It must be an area having buildings, used or intended to be used, for human habitation that are, in any respect, unfit for human habitation or that are, by reasons of dilapidation, overcrowding, faulty arrangement and design of such buildings, or narrowness or faulty arrangement of streets, or lack of ventilation, light or sanitation facilities or any combination of these factors, detrimental to the health, safety or convenience of the public of that area.
3. To decide whether the buildings are unfit for the purpose of human habitation, the following conditions should be considered:
   + repairs;
   + stability;
   + freedom from damp;
   + natural light and air;
   + provision for water supply;
   + provision for drainage and sanitary services;
   + facilities for disposal of waste water.

Source: Government of India (2010).

7

Inclusive Human Development: Looking Ahead

Progress towards inclusiveness is more difficult to assess, because inclusiveness is a multi-dimensional concept. Inclusive growth should result in lower incidence of poverty, broad based and significant improvements in health outcomes, universal access for children to school, increased access to higher education and improved standards of education, including skill development. It should also be reflected in better opportunities for both wage employment and livelihoods and in improvement in provision of basic amenities like water, electricity, roads, sanitation and housing. Particular attention needs to be paid to the needs of the SC, ST and OBC population, women and children as also minorities and other excluded groups. To achieve inclusiveness in all these dimensions requires multiple interventions and success depends not only on introducing new policies and government programmes, but on institutional and attitudinal changes, which takes time.

(Planning Commission 2011: 2)

The Approach to the Twelfth Five Year Plan document rightly states, "Progress towards inclusiveness is more difficult to assess, because inclusiveness is a multi-dimensional concept" (Planning Commission 2011). Nevertheless, in this SHDR an attempt has been made to study and analyse the progress that Maharashtra has made with respect to human development in some of its dimensions. To assess the extent of 'inclusiveness' of the growth and human development processes in the state, a five-way lens has been used, which covers in its spectrum disparities in various dimensions of human development across regions and districts, income groups, social groups, and spatially, between rural and urban areas, and gender (subject to data availability). Such an analysis facilitates an understanding of inclusion across these crosscutting themes, highlights progress made and brings to the fore the gaps that need to be bridged, all of which has been presented in depth in the various preceding chapters of this Report. Here, we make an attempt to look at the way forward by giving some suggestions for the formulation of policy interventions for the state, based on an analysis of human development related issues presented in various chapters.

To begin with, attempts at making suggestions for the formulation of human development policy need to keep certain key principles in mind: *first*, the need to differentiate between the most crucial and the peripheral gaps or areas that policy guidelines need to address; *second*, broad guidelines applicable to the state that need to be considered rather than issues related to micromanagement, which could be dealt with through institutional frameworks; *third*, issues for which a credible commitment of budgetary resources is required, need to be effectively addressed. Based on these principles, certain broad policy guidelines could be suggested initially which could then be followed by sector-specific recommendations. In the course of this chapter, an attempt is also made to differentiate amongst three types of policy frameworks within which the various human development related policy imperatives for Maharashtra can be categorized. These are: *first*, areas where larger policy prescriptions are not the need of the hour; rather, it is business as usual and what is needed is improvement in service delivery through incentives to enhance the performance of HR. *Second*, areas those require actual policy reforms supplemented by specific action plans. *Third*, the small focussed delivery of particular policy programmes in specific areas in a time-bound manner (having a limited geographical boundary) to facilitate processes as well as output in the short run. This implies implementation of programmes and interventions in the mission mode.

Human Development Policy Imperatives

The HDI is a dynamic development indicator (see Chapter 2). The first and foremost intervention required for achieving district-level improvements in the HDI is adopting a mission mode. After the identification of low-HDI districts, their specific needs must be identified and assessed, after which the mission mode could be applied.

The premier issue that arises from the HDI analysis is that the district-specific policies need to be evolved in order to explore each district's potential for enhancing its income. Working through feedback loops, gainful employment of individuals leads to better access to food and nutrition and therefore health, and promotes participation in education, for all members of the working individual's household. Hence the availability of employment opportunities is important, not only for economic well-being, but also for enhancing human capabilities. The National Rural Livelihood Mission (NRLM) is a good opportunity in this direction. Here, the second kind of policy imperative described earlier comes into play. Vocational and skill development at the district level could be assessed through the NRLM or through the National Skill Development Corporation as a way forward. Given such a scenario, what is of policy consequence is the local specific creation of gainful employment opportunities, which could lead to enhancement in capabilities. The synergies which would come into play through various feedback loops, with the availability of larger employment opportunities through skill formation, can be expected to facilitate the broader goal of inclusive growth.

In terms of consumption deprivation, the incidence of rural poverty in Maharashtra relative to its all-India counterpart has tended to decline over time while the corresponding estimate for urban Maharashtra has increased. For rural areas of the state, one of the main policy imperatives that emerges is the need for improved connectivity of villages to enhance income-generation capacities and to bridge the gap between the rural and urban sectors. The increase in urban poverty, as brought out by the NSS data analysis, is a reality that needs to be acknowledged and addressed. Urban areas of a state such as Maharashtra are high growth centres and attract the poor with income-earning opportunities. What is of importance is the need to provide support services such as health, education, housing, water and sanitation for the urban poor (it has also been demonstrated in Chapter 6 that access to water and sanitation conditions, for example, worsen as one moves down the MPCE ladder). Better targeting of the poor is possible by interventions such as direct cash transfers for essential health and education expenditures, etc. The whole problem of urban poverty needs to be dealt as rigorously as that of rural poverty. For the effective provisioning of health care and education services in the state, performance

> *The premier issue that arises from the HDI analysis is that the district-specific policies need to be evolved in order to explore each district's potential for enhancing its income.*

assessments of districts which reflects the proportions of poorest and socioeconomically disadvantaged population covered emerges as a policy imperative.

Population norm based shortfalls in the provisioning of basic health and education infrastructure still persist in rural and urban areas of the state. The geographical distribution of public health and education facilities play an important role in the equitable addressing of the health-care and education needs of the population and in alleviating disparities between rural and urban areas as well as within districts. In addition, the availability of commensurate state allocations for health and education has a direct bearing on the provisioning of infrastructure, effective services and outcomes. It is found that in Maharashtra, the distribution of resources in districts is based exclusively on 'supply-side considerations' (that is, the existing supply of infrastructure and personnel), without taking into account any equity-based considerations that are driven by the need or demand for services. The state is yet to achieve the population norms for health and immediate steps need to be taken to remove regional imbalances and to maintain inter-district equity while making provisions for health services. The most important policy prescription is that resource distribution should be based on gaps rather than existing supply- or demand-based norms. More resources should be allocated to those sectors and regions where the outcome indicators are poor. The capacity of district planning committees should be built so as to make them able to identify gaps in the services.

Disparities in literacy achievements exist across regions, the rural–urban gap is yet to be addressed and rural female literacy calls for immediate attention. The ST are yet to bridge the gap in terms of literacy, especially for females, and still remain amongst the lowest literacy achievers. 'Gender sensitive inclusion' in literacy needs to be kept central to education policies in the state. For literacy rate enhancements the need of the hour is adopting the mission mode in 13 blocks, where the literacy rate is lower than other backward states in India, with the focus on literacy achievement in Jalna and Nandurbar, especially for ST females. The TSP budget for education needs to be better utilized and the need of the hour is better prioritization of TSP funds for education-related interventions in ST dominated areas or pockets. Application of mission mode is also required to encourage the participation of female children in schooling in the Pune and Nashik divisions and in 135 blocks where female enrolment is below the state average. Ashram schools as well as *anganwadi*s are important institutions to ably address the multiple dimensions of tribal socioeconomic development, including education, and need to be strengthened as nodal agencies at the hamlet and village levels. Micromanagement via mission mode could be brought into play for improving NARs at the upper primary level, for ST children at the primary, upper primary and secondary levels, and in the rural areas at the secondary level. District HDRs could also facilitate identification of areas or pockets with low NARs and suggest policy interventions for them.

Going beyond attendance, no evident gender bias is found in the proportions of out-of-school children at the aggregate level for primary schooling, although at the sectoral level there are higher proportions of out-of-school children in rural areas. For policy interventions to be effective in bringing these children into the purview of education, a greater understanding of the economic, social, demographic and cultural reasons that hinder policy outreach to these groups is needed. Some of these are the scattered nature of their residence, migration, and not getting covered in data collection surveys.

Improvement in the quality of education is an issue of utmost importance. ASER data (2006–10) underscores the low competency and achievement levels of school-going

> *The most important policy prescription is that resource distribution should be based on gaps rather than existing supply- or demand-based norms.*

> The challenge now is to provide and ensure learning levels commensurate to the grade levels in which children are enrolled.

children in the state and raises concerns about the teaching and learning mechanisms currently in practice. Thus, the challenge now is to provide and ensure learning levels commensurate to the grade levels in which children are enrolled. The main agent of change is the teacher and teachers need to provide all the support required to enhance learning achievements. District-specific action plans need to be evolved through consultation with the stakeholders. Mobilizing the community for monitoring learning in schools could ensure improvement in the quality of teaching in schools. Achievement-based rankings of schools also could contribute towards motivating them to perform better.

Without good health, it is next to impossible for individuals to enhance their capabilities and access livelihood-generating opportunities. Data on child survival, malnutrition and maternal mortality clearly show rural areas falling short of urban areas, females still at a disadvantage compared to males when it comes to something as basic as survival and social groups still lagging behind in vital statistics. Performance assessments of districts need to include provisions for quality of health-care services provided in terms of the proportions of the poorest and socio-economically disadvantaged communities that have received these services. Nevertheless, achieving faster and more inclusive growth and human development by the state calls for immediately addressing child and maternal survival and malnutrition through appropriate policies to tackle and impact these outcomes. What is needed is an improvement in the quality of antenatal care and referral services for high-risk women to achieve reductions in the IMR and MMR. This is required especially in the districts of the Marathwada region and in the districts of Nashik, Dhule and Jalgaon, with the focus on ST women. While improvements in the IMR and MMR can be achieved through various state interventions, it is more difficult to tackle issues such as anaemia, which require spreading of awareness and information more than direct state interventions.

The figures on child sex ratios (0–6 years) clearly highlight the need for the state to aggressively implement, preferably in mission mode, the Pre-Conception and Pre-Natal Diagnostic Techniques (Prohibition of Sex Selection) Act, 1994 (PCPNDT Act) by creating accountability at all levels, involving all stakeholders, and ensuring that a strong legal system is in place. Although there are policies and statutes already in place, there is a need to seriously consider and develop strategies and programmes involving males that will enable and empower girls and women to exercise their rights. There is a need to develop and establish a support mechanism through the existing delivery systems, to help girls have access to health, education and employment. Coupled with this is the urgent need to intensify strategies to prevent adolescent marriages and early pregnancies, more prevalent among SCs and STs. The situation calls for mapping, identifying vulnerable and high-burden divisions, districts and blocks and developing customized plans of action tailored to deal with the socioeconomic and cultural milieu in these regions. Along with implementation, there is a need for concurrent, inbuilt monitoring, evaluation linked to self-correction for coverage and quality of services and possibly to include frequent assessments by institutions outside the public sector, in a systematic manner based on scientific approaches.

The six most pressing health-sector development imperatives that Maharashtra needs to immediately address across the five cross-cutting themes of rural–urban, income groups, social groups, regions and districts and gender (wherever applicable) are disparities in infrastructure availability in primary, secondary and tertiary health care services, shortages in HR for health care (ASHAs being an important resource for rural areas), complete child immunization, enhancements in institutional deliveries, increased coverage of antenatal care and reduction in child malnourishment. Also, for the poorest in the state, ST mothers and those from rural areas, there is considerable scope for improvement in terms of creating demand for essential maternal and health-care services through ASHAs and also ensuring that services are in place and are provided equitably. It is to be remembered that people belonging to the SC, ST and LIG category depend more on public health facilities; hence, improving their access, especially in tribal and poor districts is imperative.

What is of essence now is the need to immediately address regional disparities in the availability of primary, secondary and tertiary health-care services in the state. To enable equitable distribution of doctors and medical staff in rural and urban areas, specific directives making rural postings for doctors (with MBBS and postgraduate degrees) compulsory and non-negotiable; financial and non-financial incentives for placements in rural and tribal areas; setting up more nursing colleges and improved incentives for the same are three specific interventions that need to be implemented and monitored. Drug availability in hospitals as well as increased transparency in procurement systems are needed for improved efficiency and access. It is not possible to replicate in urban areas health facility models similar to PHCs, CHCs, etc. that are present in rural areas. To enable access to health facilities in urban areas, policy reforms are necessary to facilitate access to private health care for the poor through interventions such as cash transfers and coupons. Linkages with the unique identification number (Aadhaar) would enable effective tracking of poor beneficiaries, but would require policy reform. Alternatively, planned expansion of private institutions to enhance their outreach is required. What is also needed is a convergence of central and state funds in the health sector, with a high-ranking public official overseeing and coordinating it.

A few priority recommendations for the health sector as a way forward are: *first*, strengthening of health facilities by way of improved infrastructure, skilled HR and use of standard protocols for patient management; *second*, expanding the network of special care newborn units at facilities with high institutional deliveries to treat sick newborns with standard treatment protocols; *third*, home-based newborn care to be provided by ASHA workers following standard protocols for early diagnosis of illness and subsequent referral to health facilities; *fourth*, special focus on developing action plans to reach the unreached pockets, *padas*, and villages; *fifth*, regular audits of infant and maternal deaths in high-burden blocks for improved programming to reduce mortality. *Finally*, all these policy interventions need to be accompanied by an increase in public expenditure on health by the state. Underutilization of resources reflected in the low level of spending in the health sector, along with the underutilization of available funds, is a matter of concern. State expenditure on health needs to be stepped up with an increase in expenditures under the Special Components Plan.

The data and analysis on nutrition as an essential vehicle for capability enhancement presented in Chapter 5 clearly highlights the need to provide nutrition education to the masses, with special focus on mothers. This can be achieved through well-trained AWWs as well as the implementation of sound IEC packages. The interventions need to have inbuilt components for situation assessment, with emphasis on interim evaluations and formative research in areas where information is limited such as (*a*) complementary feeding practices, (*b*) the diets of children aged 6–23 months, (*c*) prevalence of anaemia in age groups not addressed previously and (*d*) knowledge, attitudes, practices and social norms related to feeding of infants and young children. Building capacities combined with supportive supervision and on-the-spot guidance to *anganwadi* and health workers on key maternal and child health issues needs to be an integral component of interventions rather than just monitoring alone. In a nutshell, there is a vital need to improve all childcare practices in the state and to accelerate programming to improve infant and young child nutrition through capacity enhancements of various agents as well as putting in place immediate interventions for change.

> *To enable access to health facilities in urban areas, policy reforms are necessary to facilitate access to private health care for the poor through interventions such as cash transfers and coupons.*

Two other important ways in which the nutrition needs of the population can be met are: *first*, encouraging the cultivation of fruits and vegetables by households to help supplement the diets of children in particular and the family in general. To enhance complementary feeding of children, the need is to educate and counsel households on the benefits of using locally available fruits and vegetables. Supplementation at best is a short-term strategy. *Second*, to improve maternal and child health along with nutrition, all relevant programmes and interventions need to focus on the first 1,000 days of its population's life cycle. Addressing maternal and child under nutrition is a long-term investment that the state needs to urgently make to reap larger benefits in the medium and long term. Finally, in Maharashtra, the need of the hour is a public health statute such that all laws governing public and private health care (Medical Termination of Pregnancy Act, 1971, PCPNDT Act, Bombay Nursing Home Registration Act, 1949, etc.) are brought under one umbrella to increase efficiency as well as effectiveness. This would ensure simplified procedures, better compliance and stricter monitoring. The state needs to work towards this goal through consultative processes involving various stakeholders.

Lack of clean drinking water and sanitation facilities is known to lead to a myriad waterborne diseases which, through various feedback loops, are found to impinge on the ability of individuals to engage competently in productive activities. Health outcomes are also directly linked to solid waste management, which needs to have universal coverage, irrespective of constraints such as rural–urban, rich–poor divides. The increase in the number of households living in slum-like conditions in a rapidly urbanizing state such as Maharashtra calls for addressing the issue of housing poverty on a priority basis. Some recommendations to this end are detailed below.

As a first step, it is important to make adequate allowances for housing rents while setting the poverty line. Given that it is unlikely that the poverty line would be revised upwards to reflect adequate housing needs, it is important that housing programmes are not targeted only at those below the poverty line. Many housing amenities are private goods and without an increase in income and a reduction in poverty it is unlikely that there will be a reduction in housing poverty. Small-ticket loans can be used by households for upgrading and improving dwelling structures. Making available finances to upgrade housing does provide one route for promoting inclusion in urban areas.

Urban reforms are integral to tackling housing shortages in an increasingly urbanizing Maharashtra. In the context of reforms in urban areas, under JNNURM, two of the six mandatory reforms required at the level of the ULB or municipal corporation are: (*a*) internal earmarking within the local body budgets for providing basic services to the urban poor and (*b*) provision of basic services to the urban poor, including security of tenure at affordable prices, improved housing, water supply, sanitation and ensuring delivery of other already existing universal services provided by the government for education, health and social security. Two mandatory reforms required at the state level are the enactment of the community participation law, which would lead to institutionalization of citizens' participation and introduction of the concept of the area *sabha* in urban areas. An optional reform could be earmarking at least 20–25 per cent of developed land in all housing projects (both public and private agencies) for EWS and LIG categories with cross-subsidization.

Recognizing the importance of the provisioning of basic services in slums, the Committee on Slum Statistics/Census (Government of India 2010) has stressed the importance of developing an urban information management system on slums and urban poverty, housing and construction. This would facilitate the identification of slum clusters for interventions and the time period within which targets could be achieved. The Committee has also stressed the need for developing a methodology for inclusion of new slums and the need to geospatially match expanded urban boundaries with census information in order to reflect city growth and increases in population in peripheral urban areas. The recommendations of the Committee on Slum Statistics/Census need to be implemented.

Special focus is required to provide drinking water within the household premises for rural and ST households. More attention is required in 15 districts where less than 40 per cent of households have a source of drinking water within their premises. Also water and sanitation programmes in the state need to work closely, given the high correlation that is found between households having water in their premises and households having latrine facilities. Although Maharashtra has shown progress in terms of the spread of the TSC, sanitation conditions in the state are still far from satisfactory. A possible solution could be found by taking a relook at the IEC programmes that are currently in place. The objective of goal 7 of the MDG is to 'halve, by 2015, the proportion of the population without sustainable access to safe drinking water and basic sanitation' compared to 1990. If Maharashtra has to achieve this goal and improve the health coordinates of its people, it needs to urgently address the regional disparities and inequities that exist in respect of access to and utilization of water and sanitation facilities. Dedicated efforts need to be made to develop integrated IECs focusing on the critical importance of sanitation and water quality and the impact these two have on individual, family and community health. It is also important to ensure inclusion and equity with regard to access to water and sanitation. District-level action plans need to be conceived and implemented to improve not only access to drinking water but also to prevent pollution and contamination of drinking water. The emphasis at block, district and state levels needs to be on viewing water as a valuable resource and to work towards water management for sustainable development. Greater focus should be on districts and blocks with high numbers of open defecators and water quality problems. Communication strategies also need to address improvements in local knowledge, using evidence-based examples of better performing villages.

Recommendations for Data Collection and Management

1. Comprehensive institutional capacity must be set up to generate periodic statistical information on human development related indicators like life expectancy, IMR, CMR and child enrolment rates at the district level.
2. Similar capacity needs to be set up at decentralized local levels to realize attempts aimed at publishing human development profiles at the block level.
3. Human development indicators could also be monitored at different levels of disaggregation, and capacity developed for the publication of reports at regular intervals. For instance, a website could be created for publishing such information and the public, including experts and different stakeholders, could be invited to participate in analysis and policy reviews, which would also be beneficial to the process.
4. Periodic newsletters on issues and statistical information pertaining to different indicators of human development and their determinants at different levels of disaggregation could be brought out. Academic institutions could be co-opted by provisioning periodic internships and fellowships to research scholars and academic experts.

Comprehensive institutional capacity must be set up to generate periodic statistical information on human development related indicators like life expectancy, IMR, CMR and child enrolment rates at the district level.

APPENDIX A

Maharashtra Human Development Report, 2012: Preparation Process

Work on the MHDR 2012 commenced in April 2011 with the passing of a government resolution[1] by the GoM. The MHDR is the outcome of various consultations held with many stakeholders, workshops with experts, explorations of various related research studies, innumerable brainstorming sessions of the core team and a meticulously carried out exercise of data analysis and background paper writing. The above-mentioned resolution clearly states the purpose of the SHDR as a foundation for the implementation of human development based schemes and interventions in the state. The government resolution assigned the responsibility of preparing the MHDR to YASHADA, the GoM's apex research academy.

A State Steering Committee under the chairmanship of the Principal Secretary, Planning Department, GoM, was instituted to overview the process of SHDR preparation. A working group was formed in the DES to provide data support. The various processes through which the SHDR 2012 for Maharashtra evolved to its current stage are elaborated below:

MHDR Preparation: Process and Partners

Number	MHDR Process	Participants
1	Preparatory workshops for deciding methodology and indicators	YASHADA, UNDP representatives, background paper writers
2	Consultations on human development issues in the selected blocks	Block development officer, block education officer, taluk health officer, ASHA, MO of PHC, ANM, AWW, headmasters and teachers of primary schools, local women folk in the villages
3	Background paper writing, conceptualization, planning the structure and editing the background papers to prepare the draft SHDR	YASHADA, writers, editor, officers in the Departments of Planning, Women and Child Development, Tribal Development, Rural Development, Urban Development, Water and Sanitation Development, Public Health Development and School Education Development
4	Consultation meetings and workshops to discuss and debate the draft SHDR	Planning Department, YASHADA, district collectors and chief executive officers of zilla panchayats, district- and block-level officers of health and education, district planning officers, etc.
5	Finalizing the SHDR	State Steering Committee, YASHADA

[1] Government Resolution, State of Maharashtra, Number MMAVI-2011/Pra.Kra. 21/KA 1498, dated 13 April 2011.

MHDR Preparation: Flow Chart

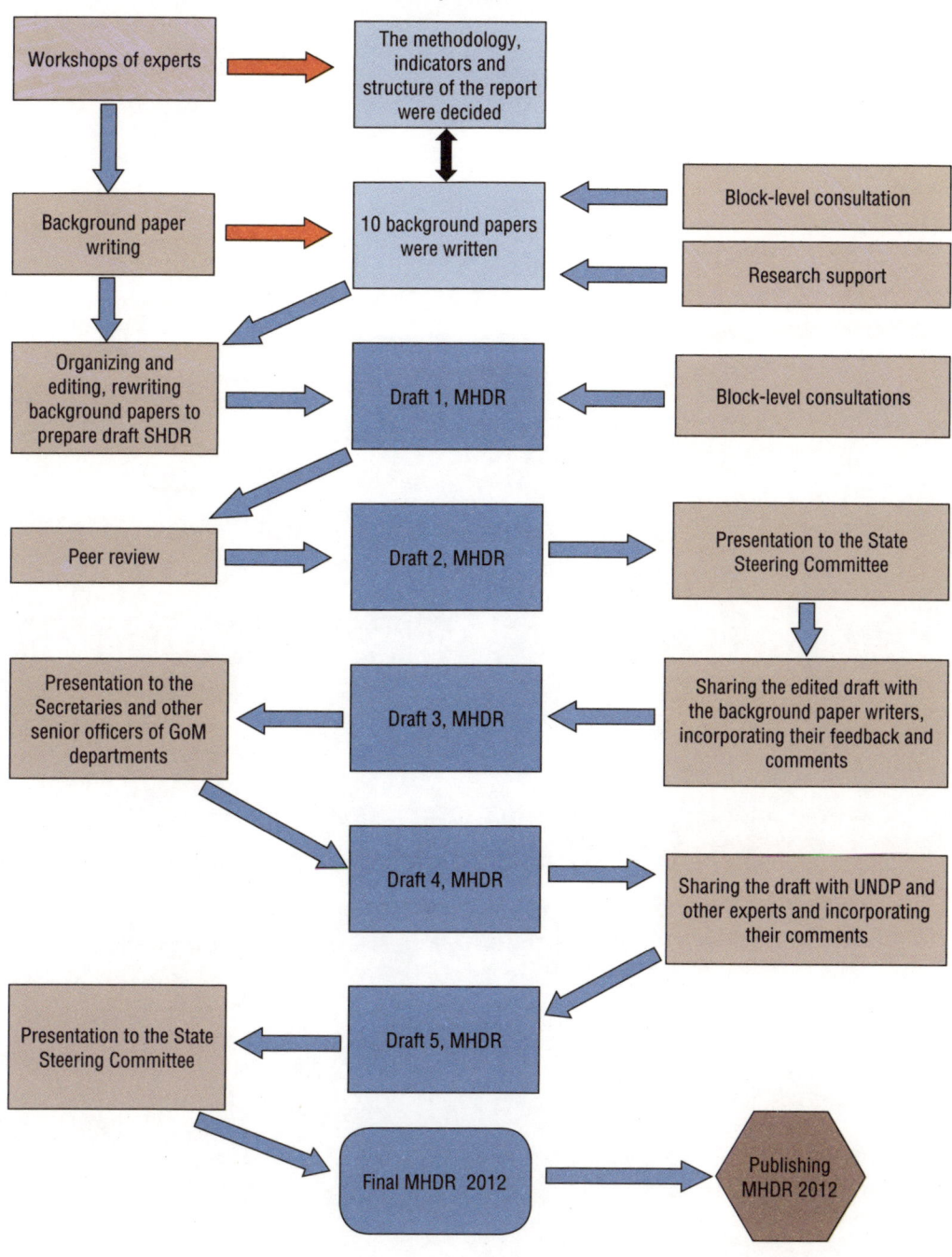

Appendix A 133

APPENDIX C

Further Data

Tables from Chapter 2

TABLE 2A.1
Classification of Districts by HDI: 2001

District	Literacy Index	GER Index	Combined Education Index	ISR Index	Income Index	HDI	HDI Status
Nandurbar	0.558	0.558	0.558	0.939	0.043	0.513	Low
Gadchiroli	0.601	0.691	0.631	0.925	0.059	0.538	
Jalna	0.644	0.719	0.669	0.944	0.050	0.554	
Washim	0.734	0.663	0.710	0.948	0.006	0.554	
Nanded	0.678	0.730	0.695	0.943	0.036	0.558	
Hingoli	0.663	0.764	0.696	0.946	0.042	0.561	
Buldana	0.758	0.654	0.723	0.951	0.026	0.567	
Parbhani	0.661	0.748	0.690	0.950	0.095	0.578	
Dhule	0.717	0.642	0.692	0.944	0.102	0.579	
Osmanabad	0.690	0.757	0.712	0.953	0.097	0.588	Medium
Yavatmal	0.736	0.703	0.725	0.939	0.113	0.592	
Latur	0.715	0.894	0.775	0.950	0.061	0.595	
Beed	0.680	0.822	0.727	0.957	0.135	0.606	
Gondiya	0.785	0.738	0.770	0.927	0.155	0.617	
Bhandara	0.785	0.710	0.760	0.932	0.176	0.623	
Jalgaon	0.754	0.697	0.735	0.950	0.187	0.624	
Solapur	0.713	0.741	0.722	0.957	0.194	0.624	
Ahmednagar	0.753	0.718	0.741	0.956	0.181	0.626	High
Ratnagiri	0.751	0.724	0.742	0.963	0.182	0.629	
Akola	0.814	0.670	0.766	0.956	0.169	0.631	
Amravati	0.825	0.697	0.782	0.939	0.178	0.633	
Wardha	0.801	0.673	0.758	0.949	0.195	0.634	
Chandrapur	0.732	0.736	0.733	0.933	0.245	0.637	
Aurangabad	0.729	0.801	0.753	0.949	0.247	0.650	
Nashik	0.744	0.666	0.718	0.949	0.290	0.652	

District							
Satara	0.782	0.735	0.766	0.968	0.249	0.661	Very High
Sindhudurg	0.803	0.746	0.784	0.965	0.252	0.667	
Sangli	0.766	0.762	0.765	0.968	0.277	0.670	
Kolhapur	0.769	0.754	0.764	0.962	0.308	0.678	
Nagpur	0.840	0.765	0.815	0.946	0.313	0.691	
Raigarh	0.770	0.727	0.756	0.958	0.437	0.717	
Thane	0.807	0.737	0.783	0.961	0.419	0.721	
Pune	0.805	0.713	0.774	0.968	0.425	0.722	
Mumbai	0.868	0.744	0.826	0.960	0.482	0.756	
Maharashtra	0.769	0.728	0.755	0.953	0.289	0.666	

Source: Author's calculations based on data in Table 2.1.

TABLE 2A.2
Classification of Districts by HDI: 2011

District	Literacy Index	GER Index	Combined Education Index	ISR Index	Income Index	HDI	HDI Status
Nandurbar	0.630	0.677	0.646	0.926	0.240	0.604	Low
Gadchiroli	0.706	0.807	0.739	0.937	0.148	0.608	
Washim	0.817	0.880	0.838	0.955	0.147	0.646	
Hingoli	0.760	0.787	0.769	0.951	0.223	0.648	
Osmanabad	0.763	0.819	0.782	0.950	0.214	0.649	
Nanded	0.769	0.803	0.780	0.970	0.220	0.657	
Jalna	0.736	0.837	0.770	0.952	0.266	0.663	
Latur	0.790	0.911	0.831	0.948	0.210	0.663	
Dhule	0.746	0.837	0.776	0.956	0.282	0.671	
Beed	0.735	0.904	0.791	0.967	0.274	0.678	Medium
Parbhani	0.752	0.863	0.789	0.950	0.310	0.683	
Buldana	0.821	0.876	0.839	0.966	0.246	0.684	
Yavatmal	0.807	0.849	0.821	0.953	0.325	0.700	
Gondiya	0.854	0.872	0.860	0.934	0.309	0.701	
Amravati	0.882	0.860	0.875	0.942	0.288	0.701	
Bhandara	0.851	0.893	0.865	0.940	0.349	0.718	
Chandrapur	0.814	0.889	0.839	0.926	0.390	0.718	
Ahmednagar	0.802	0.879	0.828	0.959	0.372	0.720	High
Akola	0.876	0.856	0.869	0.972	0.324	0.722	
Wardha	0.872	0.879	0.874	0.939	0.355	0.723	
Jalgaon	0.797	0.882	0.826	0.952	0.392	0.723	
Aurangabad	0.804	0.822	0.810	0.956	0.414	0.727	
Solapur	0.777	0.895	0.817	0.977	0.391	0.728	
Ratnagiri	0.824	0.890	0.846	0.975	0.376	0.732	
Satara	0.842	0.857	0.847	0.974	0.405	0.742	

Sangli	0.826	0.879	0.844	0.967	0.414	0.742	Very High
Nashik	0.810	0.822	0.814	0.955	0.468	0.746	
Sindhudurg	0.865	0.875	0.869	0.966	0.424	0.753	
Raigarh	0.839	0.889	0.855	0.965	0.456	0.759	
Kolhapur	0.829	0.884	0.847	0.988	0.475	0.770	
Nagpur	0.895	0.926	0.905	0.961	0.493	0.786	
Thane	0.862	0.785	0.836	0.967	0.597	0.800	
Pune	0.872	0.882	0.875	0.973	0.595	0.814	
Mumbai	0.903	0.855	0.887	0.982	0.654	0.841	
Maharashtra	0.829	0.854	0.837	0.956	0.463	0.752	

Source: Author's calculations based on data

TABLE 2A.3
Status of Districts (Dimension-Wise): 2001 and 2011

Education Index 2001	ISR 2001	Income 2001	HDI 2001	Education Index 2011	ISR 2011	Income 2011	HDI 2011	
Nandurbar	Gadchiroli	Washim	Nandurbar	Nandurbar	Nandurbar	Washim	Nandurbar	Low
Gadchiroli	Gondiya	Buldhana	Gadchiroli	Gadchiroli	Chandrapur	Gadchiroli	Gadchiroli	
Jalna	Bhandara	Nanded	Jalna	Hingoli	Gondiya	Latur	Washim	
Parbhani	Chandrapur	Hingoli	Washim	Jalna	Gadchiroli	Osmanabad	Hingoli	
Dhule	Amravati	Nandurbar	Nanded	Dhule	Wardha	Nanded	Osmanabad	
Nanded	Nandurbar	Jalna	Hingoli	Nanded	Bhandara	Hingoli	Nanded	
Hingoli	Yavatmal	Gadchiroli	Buldana	Osmanabad	Amravati	Nandurbar	Jalna	
Washim	Nanded	Latur	Parbhani	Parbhani	Latur	Buldhana	Latur	
Osmanabad	Dhule	Parbhani	Dhule	Beed	Parbhani	Jalna	Dhule	
Nashik	Jalna	Osmanabad	Osmanabad	Aurangabad	Osmanabad	Beed	Beed	Medium
Solapur	Hingoli	Dhule	Yavatmal	Nashik	Hingoli	Dhule	Parbhani	
Buldana	Nagpur	Yavatmal	Latur	Solapur	Jalgaon	Amravati	Buldana	
Yavatmal	Washim	Beed	Beed	Yavatmal	Jalna	Gondia	Yavatmal	
Beed	Aurangabad	Gondiya	Gondiya	Jalgaon	Yavatmal	Parbhani	Gondiya	
Chandrapur	Nashik	Akola	Bhandara	Ahmednagar	Nashik	Akola	Amravati	
Jalgaon	Wardha	Bhandara	Jalgaon	Latur	Washim	Yavatmal	Bhandara	
Ahmednagar	Jalgaon	Amravati	Solapur	Thane	Aurangabad	Bhandara	Chandrapur	
Ratnagiri	Latur	Ahmednagar	Ahmednagar	Washim	Dhule	Wardha	Ahmednagar	High
Aurangabad	Parbhani	Ratnagiri	Ratnagiri	Chandrapur	Ahmednagar	Ahmednagar	Akola	
Raigarh	Buldhana	Jalgaon	Akola	Buldana	Nagpur	Ratnagiri	Wardha	
Wardha	Osmanabad	Solapur	Amravati	Sangli	Raigarh	Chandrapur	Jalgaon	
Bhandara	Ahmednagar	Wardha	Wardha	Ratnagiri	Sindhudurg	Solapur	Aurangabad	
Kolhapur	Akola	Chandrapur	Chandrapur	Satara	Buldhana	Jalgaon	Solapur	
Sangli	Beed	Aurangabad	Aurangabad	Kolhapur	Thane	Satara	Ratnagiri	
Akola	Solapur	Satara	Nashik	Raigarh	Beed	Aurangabad	Satara	

Satara	Raigarh	Sindhudurg	Satara	Gondiya	Sangli	Sangli	Sangli	Very High
Gondiya	Mumbai	Sangli	Sindhudurg	Bhandara	Nanded	Sindhudurg	Nashik	
Pune	Thane	Nashik	Sangli	Sindhudurg	Akola	Raigarh	Sindhudurg	
Latur	Kolhapur	Kolhapur	Kolhapur	Akola	Pune	Nashik	Raigarh	
Amravati	Ratnagiri	Nagpur	Nagpur	Wardha	Satara	Kolhapur	Kolhapur	
Thane	Sindhudurg	Thane	Raigarh	Amravati	Ratnagiri	Nagpur	Nagpur	
Sindhudurg	Pune	Pune	Thane	Pune	Solapur	Pune	Thane	
Nagpur	Sangli	Raigarh	Pune	Mumbai	Mumbai	Thane	Pune	
Mumbai	Satara	Mumbai	Mumbai	Nagpur	Kolhapur	Mumbai	Mumbai	

Source: Author's findings based on data in Tables 2.1 and 2.2.

TABLE 2A.4
Radar Scores for Human Development Indicators: 2011

| District | Dimension Index | | | | Radar Scores | | | |
	Total Literacy	GER	Infant Survival	Per Capita Income	Total Literacy	GER	Infant Survival	Per Capita Income
Ahmednagar	0.63	0.81	0.60	0.28	3.153	4.05	3.000	1.379
Akola	0.90	0.72	0.36	0.14	4.499	3.589	1.800	0.724
Amravati	0.92	0.73	0.44	0.16	4.624	3.664	2.200	0.821
Aurangabad	0.64	0.58	0.28	0.43	3.186	2.898	1.400	2.131
Beed	0.39	0.91	0.24	0.09	1.925	4.550	1.200	0.426
Bhandara	0.81	0.87	0.36	0.14	4.057	4.326	1.800	0.693
Buldana	0.70	0.80	0.24	0.04	3.497	4.002	1.200	0.219
Chandrapur	0.67	0.85	0.36	0.26	3.361	4.259	1.800	1.288
Dhule	0.42	0.64	0.33	0.19	2.124	3.203	1.658	0.948
Gadchiroli	0.28	0.52	0.12	0.02	1.378	2.607	0.600	0.102
Gondiya	0.82	0.78	0.20	0.07	4.106	3.907	1.000	0.363
Hingoli	0.48	0.44	0.92	0.00	2.386	2.201	4.600	0.002
Jalgaon	0.61	0.82	0.44	0.28	3.064	4.113	2.200	1.413
Jalna	0.39	0.64	0.64	0.08	1.940	3.214	3.200	0.423
Kolhapur	0.73	0.83	0.68	0.52	3.645	4.162	3.400	2.601
Latur	0.59	0.94	0.28	0.13	2.935	4.700	1.400	0.628
Mumbai	1.00	0.71	0.36	1.00	5.000	3.571	1.800	5.000
Nagpur	0.97	1.00	0.20	0.52	4.860	5.000	1.000	2.584
Nanded	0.51	0.50	0.32	0.06	2.551	2.519	1.600	0.305
Nandurbar	0.00	0.00	0.36	0.00	0.000	-0.001	1.800	0.000
Nashik	0.66	0.58	0.52	0.43	3.289	2.912	2.600	2.158
Osmanabad	0.49	0.57	0.28	0.08	2.439	2.841	1.400	0.411
Parbhani	0.45	0.75	0.20	0.12	2.236	3.738	1.000	0.586
Pune	0.89	0.82	0.80	0.90	4.433	4.111	4.000	4.477
Raigarh	0.77	0.85	1.00	0.69	3.827	4.245	5.000	3.448
Ratnagiri	0.71	0.85	0.28	0.30	3.559	4.273	1.400	1.487
Sangli	0.72	0.81	0.76	0.33	3.594	4.054	3.800	1.638
Satara	0.78	0.72	0.52	0.33	3.884	3.612	2.600	1.637
Sindhudurg	0.86	0.79	0.36	0.33	4.314	3.971	1.800	1.662

Solapur	0.54	0.88	0.64	0.27	2.695	4.382	3.200	1.361
Thane	0.85	0.43	0.56	0.90	4.247	2.168	2.800	4.478
Wardha	0.89	0.81	0.00	0.21	4.438	4.047	0.000	1.040
Washim	0.69	0.82	0.04	0.09	3.425	4.077	0.200	0.429
Yavatmal	0.65	0.69	0.72	0.08	3.242	3.457	3.600	0.395
Maharashtra	0.73	0.71	0.44	0.47	3.647	3.546	2.200	2.332

Source: Author's findings based on data in Tables 2.1 and 2.2.
Note: The radar scores are calculated by first finding the index of each of the four indicators, using the maximum and minimum in the series as the goalposts. The index is then multiplied to find radar scores.

TABLE 2A.5
District-Wise Radar Graphs for Human Development Indicators in Maharashtra: 2011

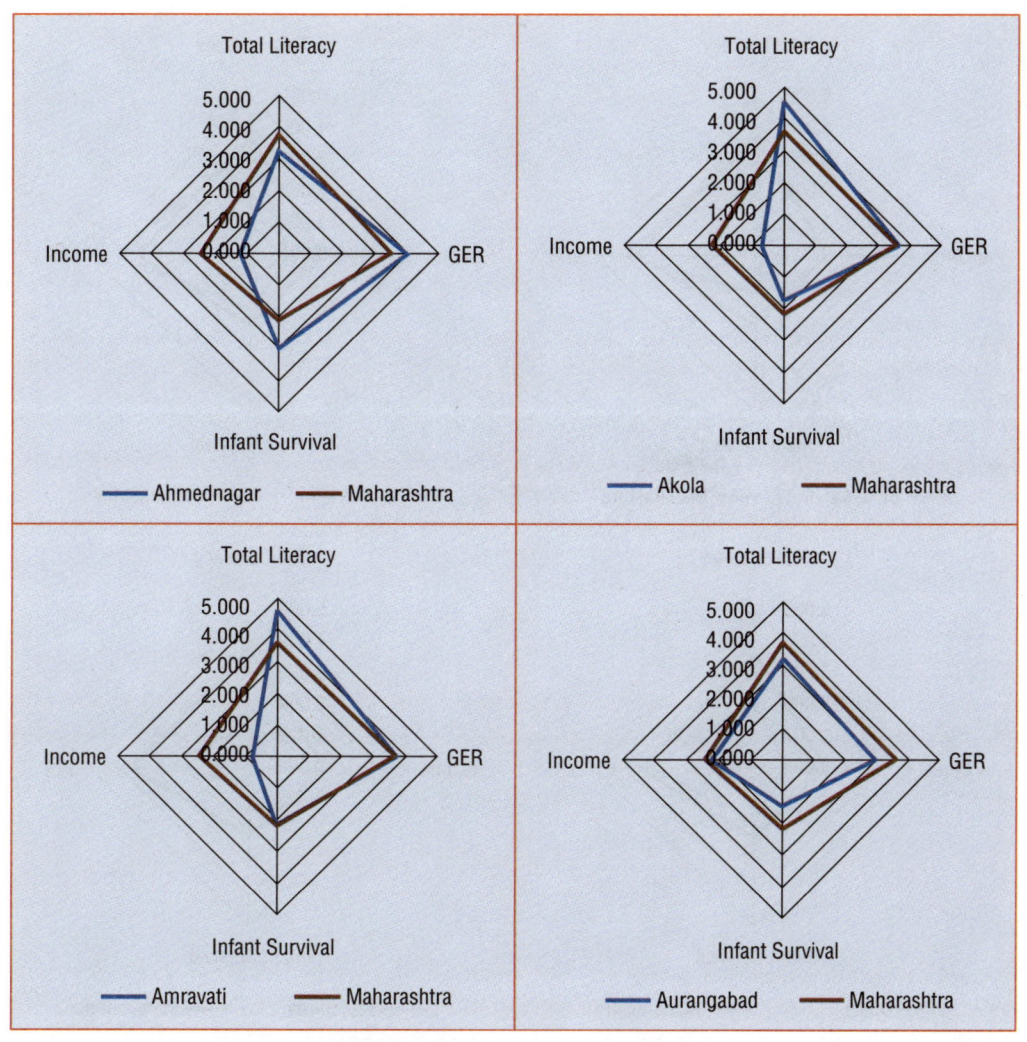

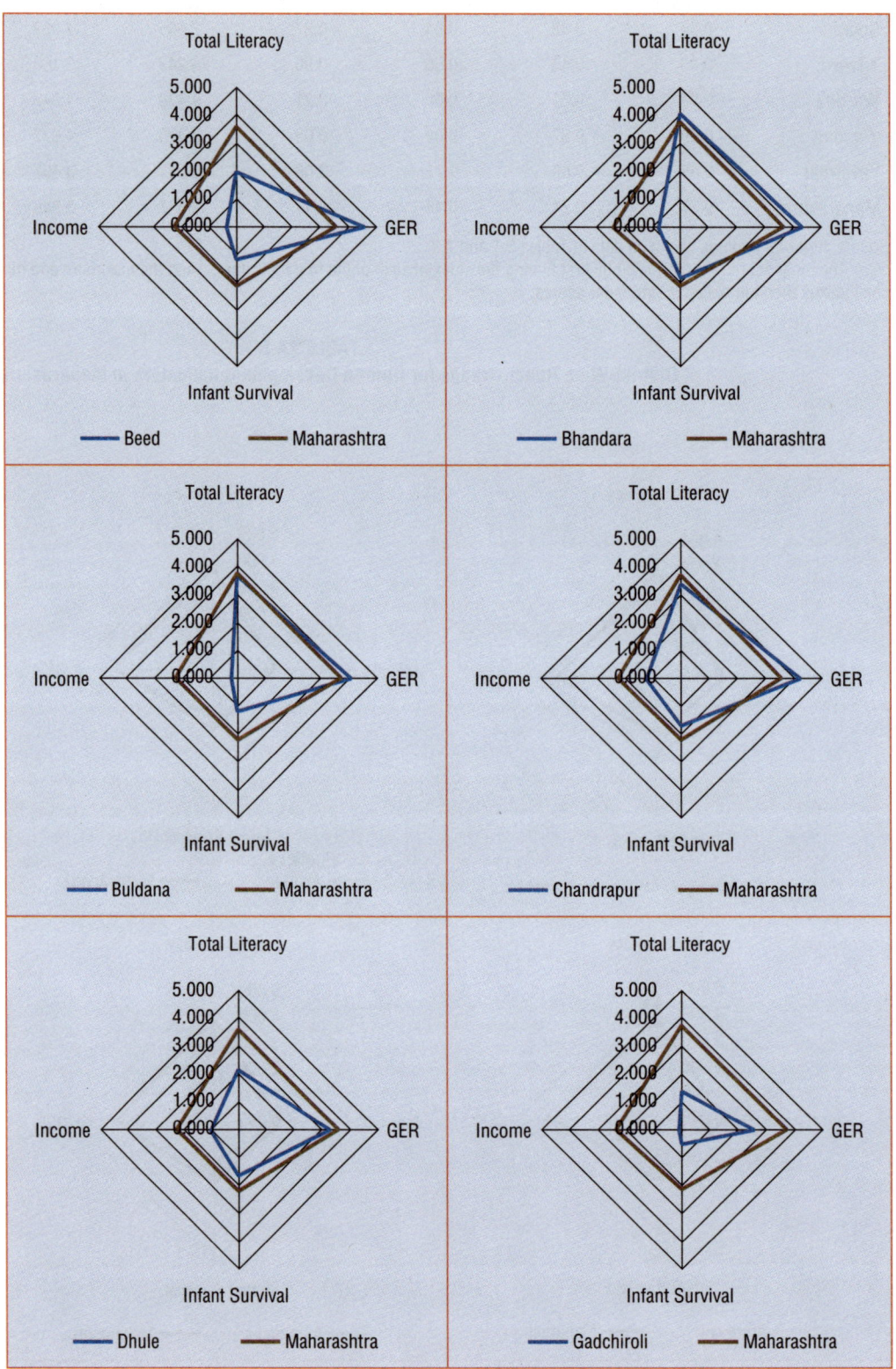

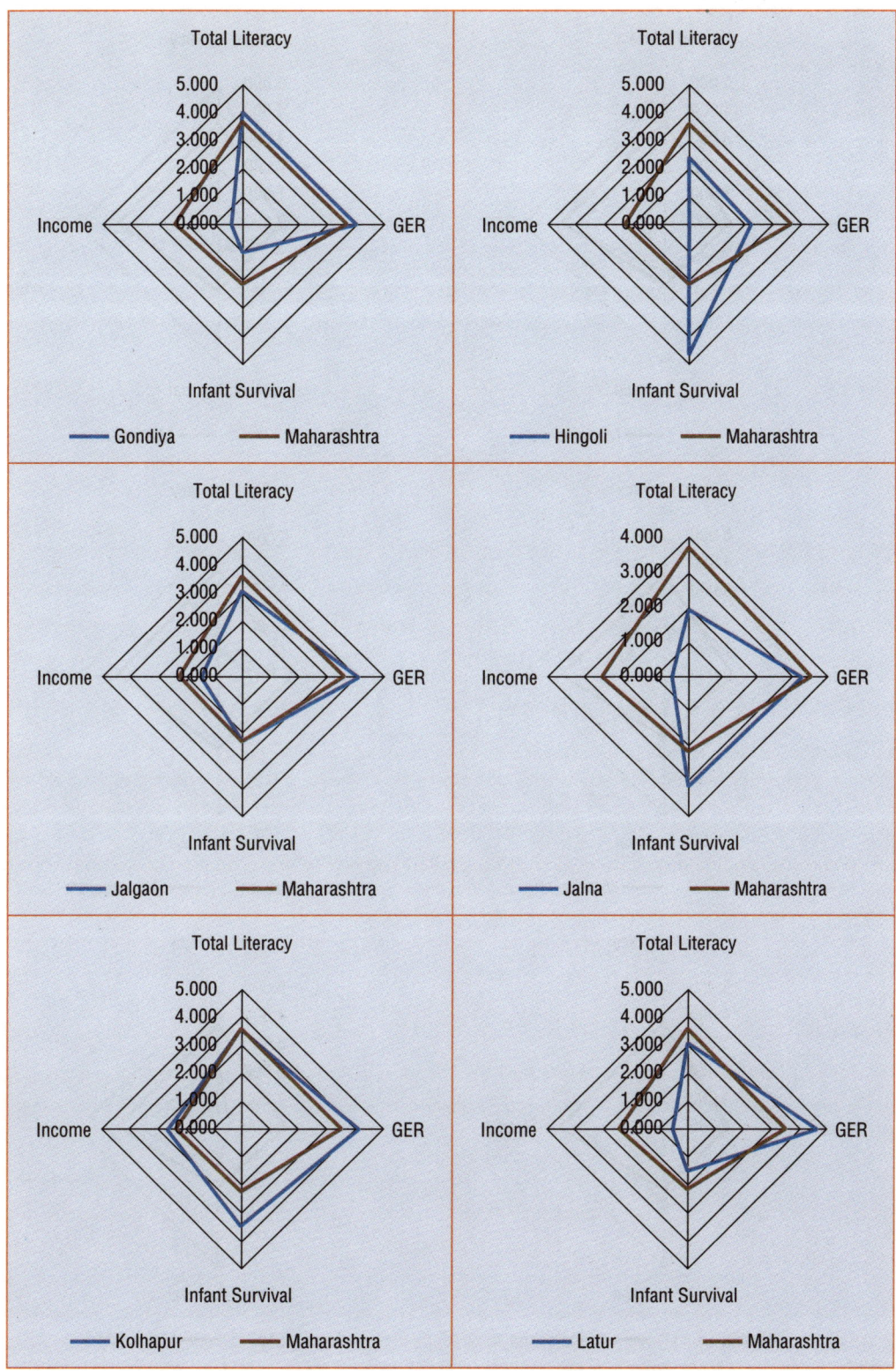

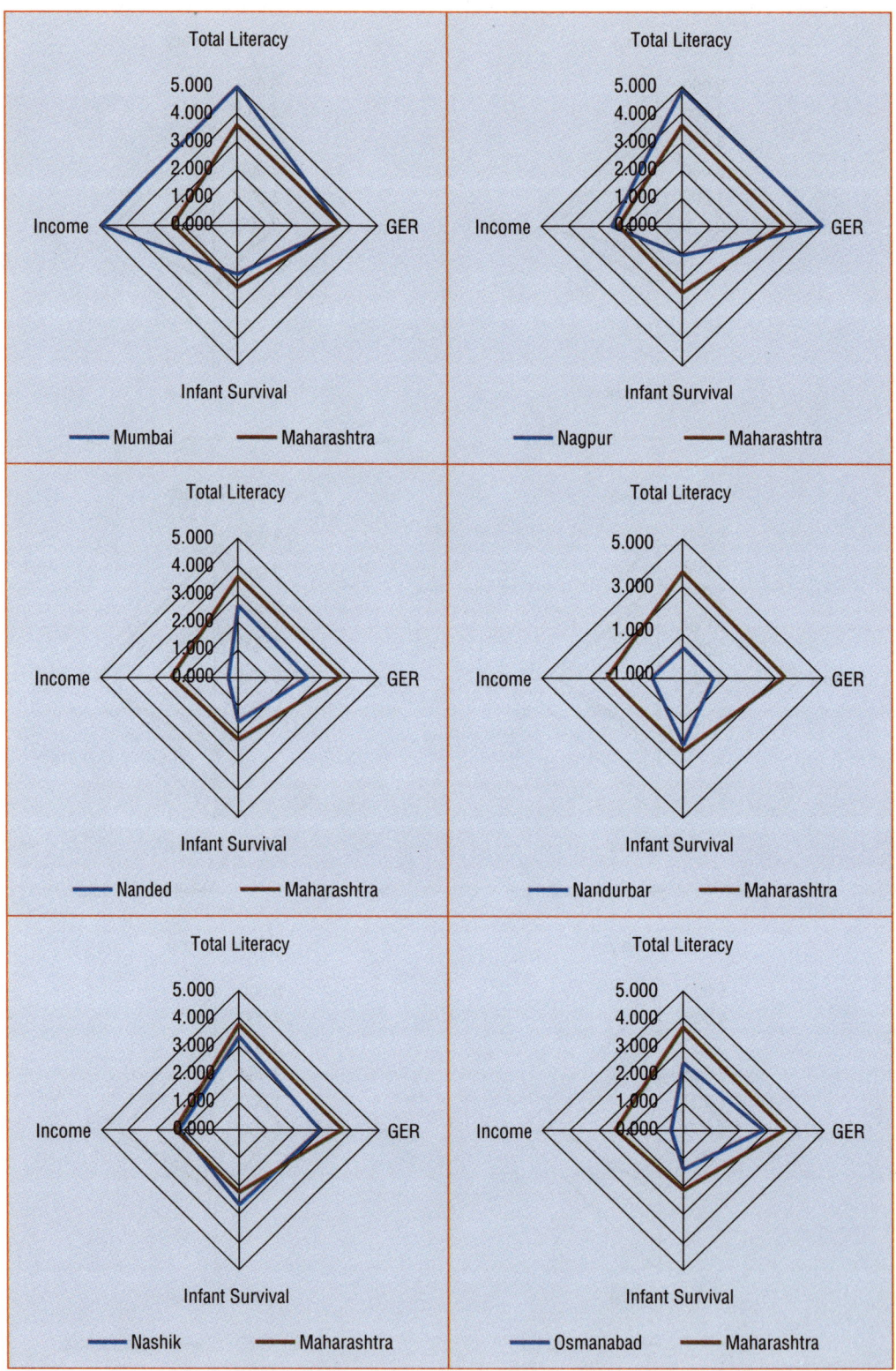

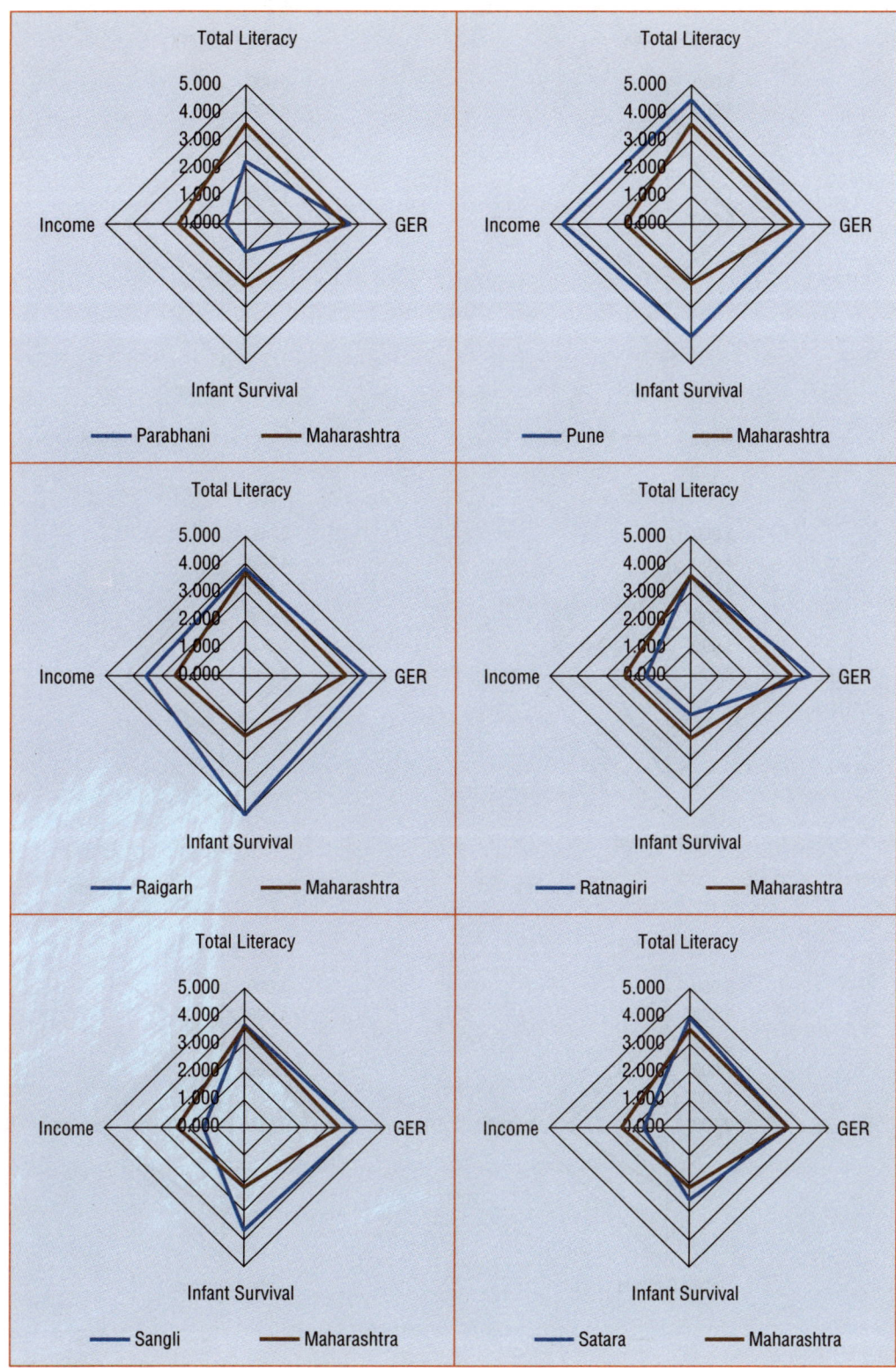

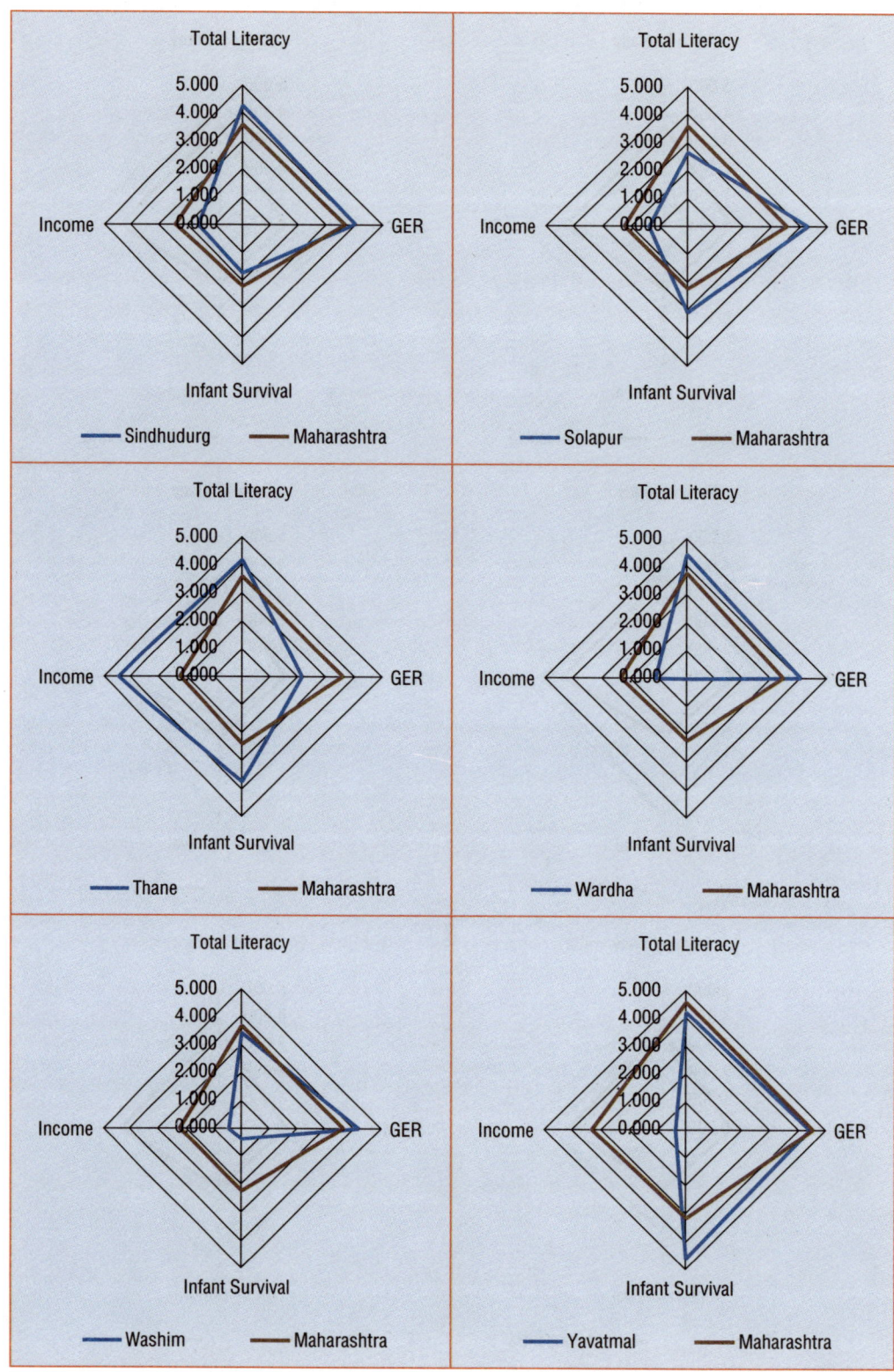

Source: Author's representation of findings.

TABLE 2A.6
Estimates of Sub-Indices by Dimension, With and Without Adjustment for Inequality: 2010–11

State	Income (x)		Education (y)		Health (z)	
	I_x	I_{Ix}	I_y	I_{Iy}	I_z	I_{Iz}
Andhra Pradesh	0.467	0.397	0.347	0.192	0.703	0.479
Assam	0.442	0.404	0.392	0.258	0.616	0.379
Bihar	0.398	0.364	0.34	0.187	0.658	0.411
Chhattisgarh	0.420	0.356	0.358	0.202	0.601	0.343
Gujarat	0.484	0.413	0.403	0.243	0.698	0.475
Haryana	0.513	0.445	0.432	0.244	0.731	0.485
Himachal Pradesh	0.499	0.433	0.468	0.287	0.744	0.527
Jharkhand	0.421	0.363	0.361	0.196	0.658	0.411
Karnataka	0.461	0.387	0.396	0.226	0.717	0.503
Kerala	0.535	0.449	0.534	0.410	0.854	0.764
Madhya Pradesh	0.431	0.366	0.355	0.194	0.601	0.343
Maharashtra	0.489	0.398	0.453	0.279	0.747	0.562
Odisha	0.400	0.341	0.345	0.199	0.627	0.380
Punjab	0.523	0.455	0.452	0.265	0.782	0.572
Rajasthan	0.462	0.409	0.333	0.179	0.665	0.400
Tamil Nadu	0.486	0.405	0.454	0.278	0.731	0.550
Uttar Pradesh	0.444	0.384	0.365	0.195	0.633	0.384
Uttarakhand	0.474	0.417	0.454	0.256	0.633	0.384
West Bengal	0.468	0.396	0.397	0.238	0.71	0.494
India	0.465	0.389	0.400	0.229	0.688	0.452

Source: Suryanarayana et al. (2011).

Notes: (i) The three dimensions, namely, income, education and health are respectively denoted by x, y, and z respectively.
(ii) The symbol I_j denotes the dimension index for jth dimension and I_{Ij} denotes the corresponding inequality-adjusted index.
(iii) The scores presented above are normalized with reference to the international goalposts defined in UNDP (2010).

Tables from Chapter 3

TABLE 3A.1
Sector-Wise Growth Performance across Districts: Maharashtra (1999–2000 to 2008–09)

Serial Number	District	Primary	Secondary	Tertiary	Total Gross DDP	Per Capita NDDP
1	Raigarh	−1.0 (9.2)	4.0** (42.9)	2.6** (47.8)	2.9** (100.0)	1.6
2	Gadchiroli	−3.3 (47.7)	9.0*** (9.3)	7.3*** (43.0)	3.9*** (100.0)	2.9**
3	Amravati	−4.4** (40.4)	9.7*** (11.8)	8.4*** (47.8)	4.9***	3.4***
4	Sangli	−0.5 (34.2)	6.8*** (16.1)	9.4*** (49.7)	6.2*** (100.0)	4.4***
5	Chandrapur	1.4 (38.1)	8.5*** (18.1)	8.9*** (43.8)	6.4*** (100.0)	4.9***
6	Wardha	0.1 (29.9)	9.5*** (18.4)	8.3*** (51.7)	6.5*** (100.0)	5.1***
7	Akola	4.2 (27.9)	6.4*** (17.9)	7.8*** (54.2)	6.8*** (100.0)	5.2***
8	Mumbai	−1.9 (2.0)	6.1*** (32.8)	8.7*** (65.3)	7.8*** (100.0)	5.2***
9	Aurangabad	7.7*** (17.6)	8.4*** (34.6)	6.0*** (47.8)	7.1*** (100.0)	5.5***
10	Washim	2.0 (38.3)	8.5*** (10.6)	9.2*** (51.1)	6.8*** (100.0)	5.5***
11	Nanded	2.7 (28.4)	7.3*** (16.2)	8.5*** (55.3)	6.9*** (100.0)	5.6***
12	Beed	2.7* (42.7)	8.1*** (12.4)	9.5*** (44.91)	6.9*** (100.0)	5.6***
13	Osmanabad	1.5 (38.1)	7.8*** (13.0)	9.6*** (48.9)	6.9*** (100.0)	5.6***
14	Pune	3.1*** (12.3)	9.2*** (34.3)	7.4*** (53.4)	7.7*** (100.0)	5.7***
15	Kolhapur	−0.4 (26.36)	7.6*** (21.83)	9.9*** (51.81)	7.3*** (100.0)	5.8***
16	Satara	2.1* (30.7)	7.6*** (19.8)	9.1*** (49.5)	7.0*** (100.0)	5.8***
17	Nagpur	1.6 (15.7)	9.8*** (27.0)	8.5*** (57.3)	8.0*** (100.0)	5.8***
18	Gondia	−4.6 (30.8)	8.9*** (22.6)	10.6*** (46.6)	7.0*** (100.0)	5.9***
19	Latur	1.0 (32.0)	8.6*** (16.1)	9.5*** (51.9)	7.3*** (100.0)	5.9***
20	Dhule	8.2*** (13.9)	5.6*** (23.5)	7.7*** (62.6)	7.3*** (100.0)	5.9***
21	Ratnagiri	−0.6 (17.3)	7.4*** (29.6)	9.4*** (53.1)	7.4*** (100.0)	6.2***
22	Thane	1.6 (4.0)	6.7*** (33.0)	9.3*** (63.0)	8.4*** (100.0)	6.2***
23	Sindhudurg	3.1 (30.9)	9.4*** (16.2)	9.2*** (53.0)	7.4*** (100.0)	6.3***
24	Bhandara	2.2 (29.5)	9.8*** (21.7)	9.4*** (48.8)	7.6*** (100.0)	6.7***

Serial Number	District	Primary	Secondary	Tertiary	Total Gross DDP	Per Capita NDDP
25	Buldhana	6.4** (33.4)	8.5*** (13.0)	8.3*** (53.6)	7.8*** (100.0)	6.5***
26	Jalgaon	5.5*** (34.1)	9.4*** (17.6)	9.0*** (48.3)	7.9*** (100.0)	6.5***
27	Nashik	7.6*** (23.1)	8.5*** (28.2)	8.1*** (48.7)	8.2*** (100.0)	6.5***
28	Yavatmal	5.4** (40.9)	9.6*** (12.6)	9.1*** (46.5)	7.9*** (100.0)	6.6***
29	Parbhani	7.0*** (36.8)	8.0*** (12.8)	8.8*** (50.4)	8.1*** (100.0)	6.6***
30	Ahmednagar	6.0*** (26.7)	7.0*** (2094)	9.3*** (52.36)	8.0*** (100.0)	6.7***
31	Jalna	7.3*** (33.5)	6.1** (17.7)	9.8*** (48.8)	8.4*** (100.0)	7.1***
32	Hingoli	5.3** (37.8)	10.1*** (10.4)	10.5*** (51.8)	8.5*** (100.0)	7.3***
33	Solapur	6.5*** (25.3)	7.6*** (21.0)	10.4*** (53.7)	8.7*** (100.0)	7.4***
34	Nandurbar	8.2** (40.8)	9.4*** (9.5)	11.6*** (49.7)	10.3*** (100.0)	9.0***
	Quartile 1					5.5
	Quartile 2					5.9
	Quartile 3					6.5

Source: Author's estimates based on information provided by DES.
Notes: (i) Figures in parentheses indicate percentage shares in total district NDP in the base year 1999–2000.
(ii) The growth rates are estimated from fitted semi-log trend functions.
(iii) Districts are arranged in ascending order of growth performance in terms of per capita NDDP.
(iv) *** indicates statistical significance at 1 per cent level; ** indicates statistical significance at 5 per cent level; * indicates statistical significance at 10 per cent level.

TABLE 3A.2
Sector-Wise Annual Growth Performance in Maharashtra

Sector	2000–01	2001–02	2002–03*	2003–04*	2004–05*	2005–06*	2006–07*	2007–08*	2008–09+	CAGR
1.1 Agriculture	−4.8	5.6	2.88	11.1	−6.6	8.9	11.6	10.4	−21.2	1.4
1.2 Forestry	−7.1	1.7	−4.1	−2.6	−11.7	−0.4	8.2	−0.4	−5.2	−2.5
1.3 Fishing	−5.2	4.3	−3.4	3.0	−11.5	12.1	−1.3	−0.9	−12.2	−1.9
1. Agriculture and Allied Activities	−5.0	5.6	2.4	10.3	−6.8	8.7	11.2	9.9	−20.6	1.2
2. Mining and Quarrying	6.2	4.8	6.6	9.4	6.3	3.6	6.0	8.5	−14.1	3.9
Primary Sector	−4.5	5.6	2.6	10.3	−6.2	8.4	11.0	9.8	−20.3	1.3
3.1 Registered	−20.4	−6.7	13.1	14.3	10.8	8.3	11.1	7.1	−0.1	3.4
3.2 Unregistered	7.7	−3.0	6.8	5.2	7.3	7.3	10.7	8.2	−1.6	5.3
3. Manufacturing Total	−13.5	−5.6	11.1	11.6	9.8	8.0	11.0	7.4	−0.6	4.0
4. Electricity, Gas and Water supply	17.0	−20.3	20.4	3.6	17.5	7.2	−3.2	15.8	2.6	6.0
5. Construction	−12.2	11.3	−0.1	8.9	1.7	6.3	40.2	24.8	28.0	11.1
Secondary Sector	−11.2	−3.1	9.0	10.3	8.5	7.6	16.1	12.4	7.8	6.1
Industry Sector	−10.8	−2.9	8.9	10.3	8.4	7.5	15.8	12.3	7.2	6.0
6.1 Railways	7.3	12.4	3.0	18.4	10.8	5.3	9.5	9.8	1.4	8.6

Sector	2000–01	2001–02	2002–03*	2003–04*	2004–05*	2005–06*	2006–07*	2007–08*	2008–09+	CAGR
6.2 Transport by Other Means and Storage	5.2	–7.4	1.9	2.4	10.1	3.3	–5.0	0.9	–13.8	–0.5
6.3 Communication	33.0	10.1	–4.4	22.4	13.2	10.7	6.7	15.8	18.3	13.5
6.4 Trade, Hotels and Restaurants	–0.8	6.1	11.2	7.3	18.0	9.0	19.8	10.4	2.2	9.1
6. Trade, Hotels, Transport, Storage and Communication	4.0	4.7	7.4	8.9	16.1	8.4	14.9	10.2	3.0	8.5
7.1 Banking and Insurance	–8.1	12.4	10.1	5.2	14.1	18.7	17.8	10.3	10.9	9.9
7.2 Real Estate, Ownership of Dwelling, business services, public administration and other services.	11.7	6.5	6.4	8.7	12.2	11.4	9.4	11.8	11.4	9.9
7. Finance, Insurance, Real Estate and Business Services	0.1	9.6	8.5	6.8	13.2	15.5	14.2	11.0	11.1	9.9
8.1 Public Administration	–5.1	–1.8	4.0	–0.4	16.2	0.7	–15.1	12.2	14.4	2.3
8.2 Other Services	1.1	2.0	6.0	–1.9	2.8	6.2	–0.9	–3.4	4.4	1.8
8. Community and Personal Services	–1.2	0.6	5.3	–1.4	7.5	4.1	–6.1	1.7	8.0	2.0
Tertiary Sector	1.3	5.7	7.4	6.0	13.3	10.5	11.0	9.3	7.3	7.9
9. NSDP	–3.1	3.5	6.9	7.7	8.7	9.5	12.2	10.2	3.3	6.5
Population (Thousands)	1.9	1.8	1.5	1.6	1.6	1.6	1.5	1.5	1.5	1.6
Per Capita Income (₹)	–4.9	1.7	5.3	6.0	7.0	7.8	10.5	8.5	1.8	4.8

Source: Author's estimates based on information provided by DES.
Notes: (i) CAGR means Compound Annual Average Growth Rate (in percentage), from the geometric mean of $(1+g_i)$ where 'g' refers to annual growth rate of sector 'i'. These estimates are lower than the corresponding estimates in Table 3.1 but are realistic since they are not derived from parametric exponential specification.
(ii) * indicates provisional estimates.
(iii) + indicates preliminary estimates.

TABLE 3A.3
District-Wise Shares in Growth Performance

| Serial Number | District | Annual Growth Rates Weighted by Base Year Shares in NSDP at 1999—2000 Prices | | | | | | | | | Base Year Weighted Average Annual Growth Rate in 2008–09 over 1999–2000 |
		2000–01	2001–02	2002–03	2003–04	2004–05	2005–06	2006–07	2007–08	2008–09	
1	Gadchiroli	–0.1	0.1	–0.0	0.0	–0.0	0.1	0.1	0.0	–0.0	0.0
2	Washim	–0.0	0.2	–0.1	0.0	0.0	0.1	0.1	0.1	–0.1	0.0
3	Hingoli	0.1	0.1	0.0	0.1	–0.1	0.1	0.1	0.10	–0.0	0.0
4	Osmanabad	0.0	–0.1	0.1	–0.1	0.1	0.2	0.1	0.1	–0.1	0.0
5	Nandurbar	0.0	0.0	0.0	0.3	–0.0	0.2	0.1	0.1	–0.1	0.1
6	Gondia	0.0	0.0	0.0	0.0	–0.0	0.2	0.1	0.1	–0.0	0.1
7	Sindhudurg	0.1	–0.1	0.2	0.1	–0.1	0.1	0.1	0.1	0.0	0.1
8	Bhandara	0.0	0.0	0.1	0.1	0.00	0.2	0.1	0.1	–0.0	0.1
9	Wardha	–0.0	0.1	0.1	0.1	–0.0	0.1	0.1	0.1	0.0	0.1
10	Raigarh	0.1	–0.4	0.5	0.3	0.3	–0.5	0.3	0.2	–0.2	0.1

Serial Number	District	Annual Growth Rates Weighted by Base Year Shares in NSDP at 1999—2000 Prices									Base Year Weighted Average Annual Growth Rate in 2008–09 over 1999–2000
		2000–01	2001–02	2002–03	2003–04	2004–05	2005–06	2006–07	2007–08	2008–09	
11	Latur	0.0	0.0	0.1	0.1	0.0	0.3	0.1	0.2	–0.1	0.1
12	Jalna	–0.0	0.1	0.1	–0.1	0.0	0.3	0.2	0.1	0.0	0.1
13	Dhule	–0.0	0.2	–0.0	0.1	0.0	0.1	0.1	0.1	–0.0	0.1
14	Akola	–0.0	0.0	0.2	0.0	–0.1	0.2	0.3	0.1	0.0	0.1
15	Parbhani	–0.0	0.1	0.1	0.0	–0.1	0.2	0.1	0.3	0.1	0.1
16	Beed	0.0	–0.1	0.1	0.0	0.1	0.3	0.3	0.1	–0.0	0.1
17	Amravati	–0.1	0.0	–0.1	0.1	0.00	0.3	0.3	0.2	0.0	0.1
18	Buldhana	–0.1	0.2	0.1	0.1	–0.1	0.2	0.2	0.2	0.0	0.1
19	Ratnagiri	–0.1	0.1	0.2	0.1	–0.0	0.2	0.2	0.1	0.1	0.1
20	Nanded	–0.1	0.2	0.1	0.1	0.0	0.2	0.2	0.2	0.0	0.1
21	Chandrapur	–0.1	0.1	0.1	0.2	0.0	0.2	0.2	0.1	–0.0	0.1
22	Yavatmal	–0.1	0.1	0.1	0.1	–0.1	0.3	0.2	0.3	0.1	0.1
23	Sangli	0.0	0.0	0.0	–0.0	0.2	0.3	0.3	0.2	0.1	0.1
24	Satara	–0.1	0.0	0.1	0.1	0.2	0.4	0.3	0.2	–0.0	0.1
25	Aurangabad	–0.2	–0.1	0.2	0.2	0.4	0.1	0.3	0.3	0.1	0.2
26	Ahmednagar	–0.2	0.1	0.1	0.2	0.3	0.6	0.5	0.3	0.0	0.2
27	Jalgaon	–0.3	0.3	0.1	0.2	0.2	0.6	0.4	0.2	0.2	0.2
28	Solapur	0.1	0.1	0.0	0.2	0.3	0.6	0.5	0.2	0.1	0.2
29	Kolhapur	–0.1	0.2	0.2	0.0	0.3	0.7	0.5	0.3	0.1	0.2
30	Nagpur	–0.1	0.2	0.4	0.4	0.2	0.6	0.6	0.5	0.3	0.3
31	Nashik	–0.0	0.4	0.3	0.7	0.6	0.6	0.6	0.4	–0.0	0.4
32	Pune	–0.6	0.2	0.9	1.1	1.8	0.1	1.4	1.0	0.4	0.7
33	Thane	0.06	0.1	1.1	1.0	1.3	1.1	1.5	1.4	0.7	0.8
34	Mumbai	–1.1	1.2	1.5	2.2	2.9	0.3	2.6	2.4	1.8	1.5
	Maharashtra	–3.1	3.5	6.9	7.7	8.7	9.5	12.2	10.2	3.3	6.4

Source: Author's estimates based on information provided by DES.
Note: Districts are arranged in ascending order of average growth performance during the period.

TABLE 3A.4
Ordinal Distribution of Districts in Terms of Per Capita NSDP (at 1999–2000 Prices)

Rank	1999–2000	2000–01	2001–02	2002–03	2003–04	2004–05	2005–06	2006–07	2007–08	2008–09
1	Hingoli	Washim	Nandurbar	Washim	Osmanabad	Washim	Washim	Gadchiroli	Gadchiroli	Washim
2	Washim	Buldhana	Latur	Nandurbar	Washim	Hingoli	Gadchiroli	Washim	Nanded	Gadchiroli
3	Nandurbar	Nanded	Nanded	Gadchiroli	Jalna	Gadchiroli	Buldhana	Nanded	Washim	Latur
4	Latur	Hingoli	Buldhana	Latur	Gadchiroli	Buldhana	Nanded	Buldhana	Latur	Osmanabad
5	Jalna	Nandurbar	Osmanabad	Buldhana	Nanded	Jalna	Hingoli	Latur	Buldhana	Nanded
6	Nanded	Jalna	Hingoli	Hingoli	Latur	Latur	Latur	Hingoli	Hingoli	Hingoli
7	Buldhana	Gadchiroli	Jalna	Nanded	Buldhana	Nanded	Osmanabad	Osmanabad	Osmanabad	Nandurbar
8	Osmanabad	Latur	Gadchiroli	Osmanabad	Hingoli	Osmanabad	Jalna	Jalna	Jalna	Buldhana
9	Dhule	Parbhani	Washim	Jalna	Beed	Parbhani	Parbhani	Parbhani	Beed	Jalna
10	Parbhani	Osmanabad	Beed	Beed	Parbhani	Yavatmal	Dhule	Dhule	Dhule	Beed

Rank	1999–2000	2000–01	2001–02	2002–03	2003–04	2004–05	2005–06	2006–07	2007–08	2008–09
11	Gadchiroli	Dhule	Parbhani	Yavatmal	Yavatmal	Gondia	Beed	Amravati	Amravati	Dhule
12	Beed	Yavatmal	Yavatmal	Dhule	Gondia	Beed	Yavatmal	Beed	Parbhani	Amravati
13	Yavatmal	Beed	Dhule	Parbhani	Dhule	Nandurbar	Amravati	Yavatmal	Nandurbar	Gondia
14	Gondia	Gondia	Gondia	Gondia	Nandurbar	Amravati	Akola	Nandurbar	Yavatmal	Parbhani
15	Bhandara	Akola	Akola	Amravati	Amravati	Dhule	Nandurbar	Gondia	Gondia	Akola
16	Akola	Bhandara	Amravati	Solapur	Akola	Akola	Gondia	Akola	Akola	Yavatmal
17	Solapur	Amravati	Bhandara	Ahmednagar	Ahmednagar	Ahmednagar	Wardha	Wardha	Wardha	Bhandara
18	Ahmednagar	Ahmednagar	Ahmednagar	Akola	Solapur	Bhandara	Bhandara	Bhandara	Bhandara	Wardha
19	Ratnagiri	Ratnagiri	Solapur	Jalgaon	Jalgaon	Wardha	Ahmednagar	Ahmednagar	Ratnagiri	Ahmednagar
20	Amravati	Jalgaon	Ratnagiri	Bhandara	Bhandara	Solapur	Ratnagiri	Ratnagiri	Ahmednagar	Ratnagiri
21	Wardha	Solapur	Wardha	Wardha	Wardha	Jalgaon	Jalgaon	Jalgaon	Jalgaon	Chandrapur
22	Jalgaon	Wardha	Jalgaon	Aurangabad	Aurangabad	Ratnagiri	Solapur	Sindhudurg	Solapur	Solapur
23	Sindhudurg	Chandrapur	Sindhudurg	Satara	Sangli	Sindhudurg	Aurangabad	Aurangabad	Chandrapur	Jalgaon
24	Satara	Aurangabad	Aurangabad	Ratnagiri	Satara	Satara	Sindhudurg	Solapur	Aurangabad	Satara
25	Chandrapur	Satara	Satara	Sangli	Ratnagiri	Sangli	Sangli	Chandrapur	Sangli	Aurangabad
26	Sangli	Sindhudurg	Chandrapur	Chandrapur	Chandrapur	Chandrapur	Chandrapur	Sangli	Satara	Sangli
27	Aurangabad	Sangli	Sangli	Sindhudurg	Sindhudurg	Aurangabad	Satara	Satara	Sindhudurg	Sindhudurg
28	Nashik	Nashik	Nashik	Nashik	Kolhapur	Kolhapur	Kolhapur	Nagpur	Kolhapur	Raigarh
29	Kolhapur	Kolhapur	Nagpur	Kolhapur	Nagpur	Nagpur	Nagpur	Kolhapur	Nashik	Nashik
30	Nagpur	Nagpur	Kolhapur	Nagpur	Nashik	Nashik	Nashik	Nashik	Nagpur	Kolhapur
31	Thane	Thane	Raigarh	Thane	Thane	Thane	Raigarh	Raigarh	Raigarh	Nagpur
32	Raigarh	Pune	Thane	Raigarh	Raigarh	Raigarh	Thane	Thane	Thane	Pune
33	Pune	Raigarh	Pune	Pune	Pune	Pune	Pune	Pune	Pune	Thane
34	Mumbai*	Mumbai*	Mumbai*	Mumbai*	Mumbai*	Mumbai*	Mumbai*	Mumbai*	Mumbai*	Mumbai*

Source: Author's tabulation based on information provided by DES.
Note: Mumbai* refers to Mumbai city and Mumbai Suburban district.

TABLE 3A.5
Sectoral Share in Employment: Maharashtra

Sector	1993–94			1999–2000			2004–05			2009–10		
	All	Rural	Urban	All	Rural	Urban	All	Rural	Urban	All	Rural	Urban
Primary	61.6	82.9	9.8	59.0	82.8	6.1	56.2	80.7	7.5	52.8	79.8	5.0
Secondary	14.5	7.5	31.4	15.0	7.4	32.0	16.9	8.7	33.6	16.8	8.7	31.2
Tertiary	23.9	9.6	58.8	26.0	9.8	61.9	26.9	11.1	58.9	30.5	11.6	63.9
Total	100.00	100.00	100.00	100.00	100.00	100.00	100.00	100.00	100.00	100.00	100.00	100.00

Source: Author's estimates based on the NSS central sample unit record data from the NSS 61st Round (2004–05).

TABLE 3A.6
Unemployment Rate (Percentage) (Daily Status)*: Maharashtra and India

	Maharashtra				All-India			
	Rural		Urban		Rural		Urban	
Survey Period	Male	Female	Male	Female	Male	Female	Male	Female
1993–94	4.60	4.00	6.00	7.80	5.60	5.60	6.70	10.50
1999–2000	6.30	6.90	7.70	10.00	7.20	7.00	7.30	9.40
2004–05	9.0	9.9	8.1	11.2	8.0	8.7	7.5	11.6
2009–10	5.5	8.8	5.0	8.3	6.4	8.0	5.1	9.1

Sources: Government of India (1997a, 2001c, 2006b, 2006c, 2011d).
Note: * Indicates incidence of person-day unemployment, defined as the ratio of unemployed person-days to labour force person-days.

TABLE 3A.7
Distribution of Workers (PS and SS) by Category of Employment: Maharashtra and India

	Rural Maharashtra			Urban Maharashtra			Rural India			Urban India		
	SE	R	CL	SE	R	CL	SE	R	CL	SE	R	CL
1993–94	48.7	7.6	43.7	36.6	49.6	13.8	58.1	6.6	35.3	42.4	39.5	18.1
1999–2000	44.3	7.3	48.4	33.8	51.5	14.7	55.8	6.8	37.4	42.2	40	17.8
2004–05	51.1	7.9	40.9	38.1	46.5	15.5	60.2	7.1	32.8	45.4	39.5	15
2009–10	48.7	6.9	44.4	33.4	54.5	12.1	54.2	7.3	38.6	41.1	41.4	17.5

Sources: Government of India (1997a, 2001c, 2006b, 2006c, 2011d).
Notes: (i) SE denotes self-employed.
(ii) R denotes regular.
(iii) CL denotes casual.

TABLE 3A.8
Decile Group-Wise Estimates of Per Capita Consumption Distribution: Rural Maharashtra

	Share in Private Household Consumption at Current Prices			Per Capita Consumption Per Month at Current Prices			Per Capita Consumption Per Month at 1999–2000 Prices		
Decile Group	1999–2000	2004–05	2009–10	1999–2000	2004–05	2009–10	1999–2000	2004–05	2009–10
0–10	4.4	3.96	4.4	217.9	224.8	445.0	217.9	195.0	240.5
10–20	5.7	5.13	5.6	283.9	291.5	561.6	283.9	252.9	303.5
20–30	6.6	6.04	6.5	325.8	342.7	651.5	325.8	297.3	352.0
30–40	7.5	6.80	7.3	369.5	386.3	734.1	369.5	335.1	396.7
40–50	8.3	7.69	8.0	413.6	436.4	810.0	413.6	378.6	437.7
50–60	9.2	8.62	8.9	457.1	489.6	903.0	457.1	424.8	487.9
60–70	10.3	9.81	10.1	511.5	557.1	1020.9	511.5	483.3	551.7
70–80	11.8	11.41	11.6	587.9	647.6	1168.9	587.9	561.9	631.6
80–90	14.2	14.20	13.9	703.4	806.0	1408.7	703.4	699.3	761.2
90–100	22.1	26.34	23.8	1,097.1	1,495.6	2,404.1	1,097.1	1,297.5	1,299.0
All	100.0	100.0	100.0	496.8	567.8	1,010.9	496.8	492.6	546.3
Lorenz Ratio (At Current Prices) (Percentage)	26.1	31.2	26.8	–	–	–	–	–	–

Source: Author's estimates based on Government of India (2001a, 2006a) and National Sample Survey Office (2011).
Notes: (i) The Lorenz ratio for the year 2009–10 is estimated using the trapezoidal rule from decile group-wise estimates of consumption distribution, while those for the earlier two years are estimated in terms of a fitted Lorenz curve function for expenditure group-wise distribution; hence the ratios are not strictly comparable.
(ii) Per capita consumption at constant 1999–2000 prices for 2004–05 and 2009–10 are worked out using estimates of cost of living indices for agricultural labourers in Maharashtra.

TABLE 3A.9
Decile Group-Wise Estimates of Per Capita Consumption Distribution: Urban Maharashtra

Decile Group	Share in Private Household Consumption at Current Prices			Per Capita Consumption Per Month at Current Prices			Per Capita Consumption Per Month at 1999–2000 Prices		
	1999–2000	2004–05	2009–10	1999–2000	2004–05	2009–10	1999–2000	2004–05	2009–10
0–10	3.2	3.0	2.7	313.9	343.7	598.6	313.9	281.9	–
10–20	4.4	4.2	3.8	428.1	477.2	837.5	428.1	391.4	–
20–30	5.7	5.1	4.7	521.5	580.8	1,036.6	521.5	476.4	–
30–40	6.3	6.1	5.5	609.3	699.5	1,235.8	609.3	573.8	–
40–50	7.4	7.1	6.4	715.6	818.3	1,424.7	715.6	671.3	–
50–60	8.5	8.1	7.5	824.6	930.3	1,674.8	824.6	763.1	–
60–70	10.0	9.8	8.8	975.8	1,126.7	1,971.7	975.8	924.2	–
70–80	12.1	11.7	10.9	1,177.2	1,345.9	2,431.4	1,177.2	1,104.1	–
80–90	15.0	15.1	14.8	1,457.4	1,728.6	3,304.6	1,457.4	1,417.9	–
90–100	27.8	29.9	34.9	2,710.0	3,431.8	7,781.8	2,710.0	2,815.0	–
All	100.0	100.0	100.0	973.3	1,148.3	2,232.0	973.3	941.9	–
Lorenz Ratio (At Current Prices) (Percentage)	35.4	37.8	41.0	–	–	–	–	–	–

Source: Author's estimates based on Government of India (2001a, 2006a) and National Sample Survey Office (2011).
Notes: (i) The Lorenz ratio for the year 2009–10 is estimated using the trapezoidal rule from decile group-wise estimates of consumption distribution, while those for the earlier two years are estimated in terms of a fitted Lorenz curve function for expenditure group-wise distribution; hence the ratios are not strictly comparable.
(ii) Per capita consumption at constant 1999–2000 prices for 2004–05 are worked out using estimates of cost of living indices for industrial workers for urban India.

TABLE 3A.10
Estimates of Average (Mean and Median) Consumption across Social Groups, by Region: Maharashtra (2004–05)

Region	ST		SC		OBC		Others		Total	
	Median	Mean	Median	Mean	Median	Mean	Median	Mean	Median	Mean
Rural Sector										
Coastal	329.5	410.6	460.2	505.6	519.7	676.7	619.4	733.7	481.8	609.0
Inland Western	552.5	610.1	482.4	587.5	558.4	671.5	591.2	721.0	572.0	687.3
Inland Northern	307.3	329.1	337.2	412.4	513.2	602.7	496.5	545.2	413.0	490.9
Inland Central	410.0	572.7	306.2	358.4	369.5	445.0	418.9	579.2	383.9	499.7
Inland Eastern	339.5	413.1	372.6	463.3	464.3	555.2	441.5	600.2	433.3	526.1
Eastern	282.2	379.4	364.5	458.2	415.4	537.8	499.5	572.4	377.0	496.5
Total	331.8	418.6	384.7	457.2	468.7	578.7	539.7	659.4	459.1	567.8
Urban Sector										
Coastal	965.1	1,109.2	937.3	1,096.3	896.9	1,164.1	1,272.0	1,649.8	1,087.9	1,461.4
Inland Western	826.6	877.1	631.9	738.3	737.0	877.9	863.3	1,102.9	797.0	995.0
Inland Northern	552.1	736.4	566.1	806.6	664.6	874.5	741.4	1,030.5	682.8	921.0
Inland Central	927.1	731.8	481.9	598.9	495.5	621.7	500.5	727.1	496.4	667.6
Inland Eastern	629.0	731.7	675.0	799.3	778.3	915.9	652.9	969.0	699.4	909.4
Eastern	496.0	540.7	659.9	763.0	896.8	927.2	770.1	970.2	741.1	882.5
Total	748.7	880.6	730.0	866.6	800.8	967.9	981.1	1,326.8	863.9	1,148.3

Source: Author's estimates based on the NSS central sample unit record data from the NSS 61st Round (2004–05).
Note: In the NSS data, regions in Maharashtra are classified as follows:
1. Coastal region: Greater Mumbai, Suburban Mumbai, Thane, Raigarh, Ratnagiri and Sindhudurg.
2. Inland Western: Ahmednagar, Pune, Satara, Sangli, Solhapur and Kolhapur.
3. Inland Northern: Nandurbar, Nashik, Dhule and Jalgaon.
4. Inland Central: Auragnabad, Parbhani, Beed, Latur, Nanded, Osmanabad, Jalna and Hingoli.
5. Inland Eastern: Buldhana, Akola, Washim, Amravati, Yavatmal, Wardha and Nagpur.
6. Eastern: Bhandara, Gadchiroli, Chandrapur and Gondia.

TABLE 3A.11
Average Consumption, Inequality and Poverty across Districts: Rural Maharashtra

District	1993–94 Average Per Capita Consumption Per Month (Rupees at Current Prices)	Incidence of Poverty (Percentage)	Lorenz Ratio (Percentage)	2004–05 Average Per Capita Consumption Per Month (Rupees at Current Prices)	Incidence of Poverty (Percentage)	Lorenz Ratio (Percentage)
Ahmednagar	269.2	33.4	26.8	622.4	10.8	37.9
Akola	260.3	30.8	23.0	548.4	22.6	37.0
Amravati	282.0	24.2	24.4	475.7	29.4	31.5
Aurangabad	283.2	34.9	30.9	450.4	34.1	33.0
Beed	251.8	34.2	24.3	469.6	36.4	30.5
Bhandara	293.4	23.3	24.4	526.6	30.1	35.4
Buldhana	245.2	37.8	24.1	581.1	21.3	32.5
Chandrapur	284.7	32.0	27.8	623.1	26.3	19.1
Dhule	232.3	45.6	23.6	489.7	27.1	31.9
Gadchiroli	301.4	28.6	30.0	413.4	51.9	37.0
Gondia	–	–	–	484.0	34.6	34.7
Hingoli	–	–	–	613.9	24.8	37.3
Jalgaon	239.8	37.2	23.9	507.9	24.9	26.1
Jalna	280.8	31.3	30.8	638.0	24.3	38.7
Kolhapur	375.0	7.0	25.4	626.7	10.6	36.5
Latur	343.6	24.7	32.5	556.6	36.8	34.1
Nagpur	310.2	24.2	26.9	507.7	30.3	34.5
Nanded	287.3	34.2	31.6	502.1	35.2	31.5
Nandurbar	–	–	–	470.9	44.	34.8
Nashik	270.8	36.0	28.4	468.5	37.5	29.2
Osmanabad	369.9	16.7	34.6	667.3	16.1	36.
Parbhani	301.8	28.6	32.0	478.6	38.7	35.7
Pune	318.7	17.9	25.9	824.9	7.1	39.
Raigarh	398.8	4.9	23.5	651.1	21.1	50.4
Ratnagiri	311.8	24.9	30.0	638.2	16.6	40.1
Sangli	401.6	14.4	33.5	583.9	12.1	33.9
Satara	300.1	22.6	24.9	637.7	9.	33.3
Sindhudurg	286.8	20.5	21.5	565.5	10.7	36.3
Solapur	278.3	31.2	26.9	638.2	10.9	38.1
Thane	430.9	8.3	29.8	627.8	35.2	39.5
Wardha	308.8	27.4	28.1	575.3	11.5	38.5
Washim	–	–	–	516.5	23.2	32.6
Yavatmal	270.4	25.7	22.4	485.9	33.4	30.9
Mumbai	–	–	–	–	–	–
Maharashtra	**302.9**	**26.6**	**28.8**	**570.4**	**24.2**	**34.5**

Sources: Government of Maharashtra (2002, 2009).
Note: Estimates of poverty for 1993–94 and 2004–05 correspond to the official state-level rural poverty lines of ₹194.9 and ₹362.3 per capita per month respectively.

TABLE 3A.12
Average Consumption, Inequality and Poverty across Districts: Urban Maharashtra

	1993–94			2004–05		
District	Average Per Capita Consumption Per Month (Rupees at Current Prices)	Incidence of Poverty (Percentage)	Lorenz Ratio (Percentage)	Average Per Capita Consumption Per Month (Rupees at Current Prices)	Incidence of Poverty (Percentage)	Lorenz Ratio (Percentage)
Ahmednagar	316.4	68.1	30.6	916.6	39.2	36.7
Akola	299.4	71.4	26.8	789.1	55.1	42.4
Amravati	394.5	45.4	27.0	697.6	63.1	35.6
Aurangabad	511.8	46.0	42.9	872.5	53.2	41.5
Beed	344.5	57.8	30.8	464.8	93.4	37.6
Bhandara	397.5	56.5	31.1	986.3	43.4	37.9
Buldhana	283.3	74.1	26.5	804.2	50.2	38.3
Chandrapur	430.1	35.6	25.9	1,199.8	27.4	39.4
Dhule	329.3	62.3	25.7	753.6	48.9	43.
Gadchiroli	622.5	6.1	20.4	836.6	39.5	43.4
Gondia	–	–	–	1,057.1	20.7	36.6
Hingoli	–	–	–	657.2	59.2	36.
Jalgaon	340.0	63.0	29.0	857.2	54.8	37.8
Jalna	349.9	58.5	34.2	1,047.2	20.2	42.4
Kolhapur	470.2	25.1	24.0	873.2	40.1	38.1
Latur	404.2	42.4	27.8	713.8	64.4	36.7
Nagpur	464.3	42.1	34.3	1,040.9	36.8	39.5
Nanded	369.7	57.0	32.0	571.6	75.4	36.
Nandurbar	–	–	–	793.9	58.3	36.1
Nashik	417.5	42.9	28.2	868.5	47.5	37.9
Osmanabad	349.1	58.8	33.5	1,253.3	50.8	48.6
Parbhani	323.6	60.1	27.8	839.5	49.6	39.5
Pune	575.6	27.3	34.1	1,391.8	25.5	47.4
Raigarh	601.6	24.4	32.2	1,332.3	13.7	41.3
Ratnagiri	445.6	29.3	25.1	1,098.8	29.6	39.3
Sangli	386.6	53.3	24.2	685.9	61.7	34.1
Satara	461.8	39.8	33.0	1,566.2	23.4	54.6
Sindhudurg	389.1	53.3	27.2	823.5	48.8	38.8
Solapur	331.4	62.9	26.7	749.6	51.6	34.8
Thane	635.3	15.7	29.1	1,307.1	14.2	42.5
Wardha	412.7	39.1	27	698.0	57.3	39.2
Washim	–	–	–	653.7	60.3	41.8
Yavatmal	355.1	53.0	24.8	764.6	59.4	40.9
Mumbai	721.6	7.8	28.4	1,547.9	8.9	40.0
Maharashtra	**537.2**	**31.2**	**33.8**	**1,200.6**	**28.9**	**41.4**

Sources: Government of Maharashtra (2002, 2009).
Note: Estimates of poverty for 1993–94 and 2004–05 correspond to the official state-level urban poverty lines of ₹328.56 and ₹665.90 per capita per month respectively.

TABLE 3A.13
Estimates of Per Capita Cereal Consumption: Rural and Urban India

Decile Group	Rural India					Urban India				
	1972–73	1983	1993–94	1999–2000	2004–05	1972–73	1983	1993–94	1999–2000	2004–05
0–10	9.1	10.4	10.5	10.5	10.2	8.8	9.2	9.5	9.6	9.7
10–20	12.0	12.5	12.1	11.7	11.1	10.5	10.5	10.6	10.3	10.1
20–30	13.3	13.4	12.7	12.3	11.4	11.2	11.0	10.8	10.8	10.3
30–40	14.6	13.9	13.2	12.6	11.7	11.5	11.3	10.9	10.7	10.2
40–50	15.2	14.8	13.4	12.9	11.9	11.8	11.5	11.0	10.9	10.3
50–60	15.6	15.3	13.8	13.1	12.1	11.9	11.9	11.0	10.8	10.1
60–70	17.1	15.7	14.1	13.4	12.4	12.2	12.1	11.0	10.7	10.1
70–80	17.8	16.3	14.5	13.5	12.5	12.1	12.1	10.8	10.6	10.0
80–90	19.0	17.4	14.7	13.8	12.5	11.8	12.1	10.8	10.6	9.7
90–100	21.3	19.4	15.5	14.2	15.8	11.4	12.1	10.3	10.1	9.4
All	15.5	14.9	13.4	12.8	12.2	11.3	11.4	10.7	10.5	10.0

Sources: Various GOI reports cited in Suryanarayana (2009b).
Note: Estimates of consumption are indicated in kg per 30 days.

TABLE 3A.14
Monthly Per Capita Cereal Consumption by Select Decile Groups: Maharashtra

Year	Population Decile Group (Percentage)					
	0–10	10–20	20–30	30–40	40–50	All
Rural Sector						
1961–62	13.4	11.6	12.6	14.6	14.0	16.1
1972–73	7.7	10.2	11.6	12.1	12.5	12.6
1973–74	9.5	11.2	12.1	12.8	13.5	13.5
1977–78	9.6	11.2	12.1	12.8	13.1	13.6
1983	11.1	12.2	12.8	13.1	13.9	13.8
1986–87	7.9	10.3	10.8	12.0	12.4	11.9
1987–88	10.4	11.6	12.4	12.9	13.4	13.1
1993–94	9.0	10.0	10.6	11.1	11.3	11.4
1999–2000	9.7	10.4	11.0	11.4	11.8	11.5
2004–05	9.7	9.9	11.0	10.5	10.7	10.6
Urban Sector						
1961–62	9.6	10.1	11.2	11.4	11.3	10.8
1972–73	7.7	9.4	9.8	9.5	9.5	9.0
1973–74	8.7	9.9	9.6	9.3	9.4	9.3
1977–78	9.3	10.4	10.3	10.3	10.4	10.0
1983	9.3	9.8	10.2	10.2	10.1	10.0
1986–87	8.3	8.7	9.1	10.2	10.3	9.3
1987–88	10.0	10.6	10.5	10.6	10.0	10.2
1993–94	9.4	9.5	9.8	9.8	9.4	9.4
1999–2000	7.9	9.5	9.5	10.4	9.7	9.5
2004–05	8.6	8.8	8.8	8.8	8.6	8.5

Source: Based on NSS central sample estimates from various NSS reports.
Note: Consumption measured is indicated in kg.

TABLE 3A.15
Per Capita Intake of Calories, Protein and Fat Per Diem by Decile Groups: Rural Maharashtra

Decile Group	1972–73	1983	1993–94	1999–2000	2004–05
Calorie Intake					
0–10	1,063	1,540	1,334	1,466	1,428
10–20	1,420	1,737	1,532	1,627	1,550
20–30	1,588	1,851	1,662	1,786	1,634
30–40	1,695	1,920	1,765	1,862	1,748
40–50	1,819	2,064	1,854	1,982	1,826
50–60	1,959	2,156	1,921	2,090	1,903
60–70	2,056	2,230	2,028	2,146	2,082
70–80	2,152	2,338	2,111	2,168	2,400
80–90	2,371	2,544	2,300	2,366	2,283
90–100	2,826	3,059	2,882	2,627	2,476
All	1,895	2,144	1,939	2,012	1,933
Protein Intake					
0–10	32.1	45.3	40.9	40.3	41.0
10–20	43.1	50.3	44.0	45.6	44.0
20–30	47.4	53.6	47.6	50.6	46.1
30–40	49.7	56.0	50.3	52.7	49.6
40–50	52.4	59.8	52.3	56.2	52.1
50–60	55.5	61.8	54.0	59.3	56.6
60–70	58.5	63.0	56.8	59.3	62.8
70–80	61.4	66.5	58.9	61.1	60.8
80–90	67.9	72.8	64.3	66.8	75.2
90–100	79.0	91.0	79.0	73.1	69.0
All	54.7	62.0	54.8	56.5	55.7
Fat Intake					
0–10	10.3	15.1	16.8	23.8	21.5
10–20	14.3	18.9	21.8	26.5	26.0
20–30	15.4	21.2	24.7	30.0	29.9
30–40	17.7	23.0	27.2	32.1	34.5
40–50	22.5	25.3	30.9	35.8	36.2
50–60	27.9	27.9	33.2	40.3	40.4
60–70	28.6	31.0	35.9	42.4	46.9
70–80	29.2	34.5	38.2	45.3	51.4
80–90	31.9	41.5	44.1	53.2	58.1
90–100	46.3	61.7	62.2	67.7	70.1
All	24.4	30.0	33.5	39.7	41.5

Sources: Government of India (1983, 1986, 1989, 1997b, 2001a, 2001b, 2006a, 2007).
Note: Calories measured are indicated in kcal; protein and fat in grams.

TABLE 3A.16
Estimates of Energy Intake: Rural and Urban India

Decile Group	Rural India					Urban India				
	1972–73	1983	1993–94	1999–2000	2004–05	1972–73	1983	1993–94	1999–2000	2004–05
0–10	1,192.1	1,356.3	1,460.1	1,491.5	1,480.5	1,298.7	1,331.8	1,443.5	1,520.9	1,510.5
10–20	1,591.9	1,681.8	1,731.3	1,730.5	1,681.4	1,575.9	1,588.3	1,702.4	1,731.2	1,687.7
20–30	1,783.4	1,847.9	1,850.0	1,865.3	1,800.0	1,745.9	1,724.0	1,803.5	1,912.6	1,833.0
30–40	1,944.0	1,952.0	1,971.7	1,955.2	1,882.5	1,802.2	1,861.2	1,896.8	1,970.5	1,856.4
40–50	2,115.0	2,111.5	2,056.5	2,049.2	1,959.0	1,980.0	1,912.4	1,992.8	2,092.9	1,944.6
50–60	2,210.0	2,229.6	2,156.3	2,170.6	2,044.3	2,035.5	2,046.0	2,074.6	2,188.1	2,024.0
60–70	2,451.4	2,322.0	2,275.2	2,287.8	2,158.0	2,266.0	2,221.1	2,186.0	2,298.7	2,111.1
70–80	2,581.4	2,506.9	2,410.0	2,403.0	2,290.0	2,382.1	2,294.2	2,296.7	2,467.7	2,209.0
80–90	2,929.0	2,779.5	2,584.7	2,582.5	2,376.9	2,658.8	2,500.7	2,470.5	2,536.0	2,323.0
90–100	3,861.8	3,422.5	3,034.2	2,954.4	2,797.9	3,324.9	3,410.3	2,843.1	2,841.5	2,680.0
All	2,266.0	2,221.0	2,153.0	2,149.0	2,047.0	2,107.0	2,089.0	2,071.0	2,156.0	2,020.0

Sources: Various GoI reports in Suryanarayana (2009b).
Note: Estimates of energy measured are indicated in kcal per capita per diem.

TABLE 3A.17
Average Per Capita Intake of Calorie Per Diem over NSS Rounds, by Major States: Rural Sector

State	27th Round (1972–73)	38th Round (1983)	50th Round (1993–94)	55th Round (1999–00)	61st Round (2004–05)
Andhra Pradesh	2,103	2,204	2,052	2,021	1,995
Assam	2,074	2,056	1,983	1,915	2,067
Bihar	2,225	2,189	2,115	2,121	2,049
Gujarat	2,142	2,113	1,994	1,986	1,923
Haryana	3,215	2,554	2,491	2,455	2,226
Karnataka	2,202	2,260	2,073	2,028	1,845
Kerala	1,559	1,884	1,965	1,982	2,014
Madhya Pradesh	2,423	2,323	2,164	2,062	1,929
Maharashtra	1,895	2,144	1,939	2,012	1,933
Odisha	1,995	2,103	2,199	2,119	2,023
Punjab	3,493	2,677	2,418	2,381	2,240
Rajasthan	2,730	2,433	2,470	2,425	2,180
Tamil Nadu	1,955	1,861	1,884	1,826	1,842
Uttar Pradesh	2,575	2,399	2,307	2,327	2,200
West Bengal	1,921	2,027	2,211	2,095	2,070
All-India	2,266	2,221	2,153	2,149	2,047

Source: Based on Government of India (2007: 54).
Note: Calories measured are indicated in kcal.

TABLE 3A.18
Per Capita Intake of Calories, Protein and Fat Per Diem by Decile Groups: Urban Maharashtra

Decile Group	1972–73	1983	1993–94	1999–2000	2004–05
Calorie Intake					
0–10	1,197	1,400	1,472	1,502	1,430
10–20	1,513	1,593	1,645	1,790	1,588
20–30	1,676	1,720	1,765	1,789	1,663
30–40	1,727	1,789	1,851	1,972	1,747
40–50	1,778	1,886	1,880	1,951	1,781
50–60	1,919	2,000	1,949	1,997	1,833
60–70	1,993	2,049	2,089	2,161	1,935
70–80	2,182	2,218	2,227	2,259	2,008
80–90	2,609	2,696	2,380	2,374	2,096
90–100	3,115	2,930	2,632	2,596	2,389
All	1,971	2,028	1,989	2,039	1,847
Protein Intake					
0–10	32.4	41.3	42.8	43.3	41.5
10–20	59.2	47.4	47.0	48.3	45.9
20–30	51.1	50.0	49.8	49.7	46.8
30–40	51.4	52.0	52.0	55.2	52.0
40–50	51.6	54.0	52.6	54.1	50.9
50–60	52.0	57.5	54.0	55.4	50.5
60–70	54.0	58.5	58.7	58.1	53.0
70–80	58.8	61.5	61.0	60.8	55.0
80–90	69.2	70.2	65.2	64.2	57.8
90–100	73.3	67.6	71.9	69.9	67.0
All	55.3	56.0	55.5	55.9	52.1
Fat Intake					
0–10	14.2	18.0	21.7	25.9	27.5
10–20	22.8	24.1	30.0	40.5	33.9
20–30	28.6	29.0	34.9	41.0	38.2
30–40	30.9	32.1	38.9	42.7	42.8
40–50	33.2	39.0	43.0	48.3	46.2
50–60	39.3	44.2	47.5	51.3	49.6
60–70	43.4	47.1	53.6	57.7	54.8
70–80	53.3	58.0	60.4	62.8	59.0
80–90	66.9	75.0	67.4	70.5	64.8
90–100	86.4	83.4	81.6	85.3	84.2
All	41.9	45.0	47.9	52.6	50.1

Sources: Based on Government of India (1983, 1986, 1989, 1997b, 2001a, 2001b, 2006a, 2007).
Note: Calories measured are indicated in kcal; protein and fat in grams.

TABLE 3A.19
Food and Non-Food Expenditure and Share: Rural Maharashtra (2004–05)

District	Average MPCE (Rupees at Current Prices)			Share of Food in Total Expenditure (Percentage)	Division
	Food	Non-Food	Total		
Mumbai	–	–	–		Konkan
Gadchiroli	241.1	172.3	413.4	58.3	Nagpur
Sindhudurg	328.7	236.8	565.5	58.1	Konkan
Nandurbar	269.3	201.6	470.9	57.2	Nashik
Dhule	277.4	212.3	489.7	56.6	Nashik
Sangli	325.3	258.6	583.9	55.7	Pune
Washim	286.7	229.8	516.5	55.5	Amravati
Jalgaon	281.2	226.7	507.9	55.4	Nashik
Satara	346.5	291.1	637.7	**54.4**	Pune
Aurangabad	244.4	206.0	450.4	54.3	Aurangabad
Kolhapur	338.6	288.1	626.7	54.0	Pune
Solapur	343.5	294.7	638.2	53.8	Pune
Beed	251.0	218.6	469.6	53.5	Aurangabad
Gondia	258.7	225.7	484.0	53.4	Nagpur
Nanded	267.7	234.3	502.1	53.3	Aurangabad
Akola	289.0	259.3	548.4	52.7	Amravati
Nashik	244.5	224.0	468.5	**52.2**	Nashik
Nagpur	264.4	243.3	507.7	52.1	Nagpur
Parbhani	245.2	233.4	478.6	51.2	Aurangabad
Amravati	242.7	232.9	475.7	51.0	Amravati
Ahmednagar	315.9	306.5	622.4	50.8	Nashik
Wardha	288.7	286.6	575.3	50.2	Nagpur
Yavatmal	240.1	245.8	485.9	49.4	Amravati
Buldhana	286.9	294.2	581.1	49.4	Amravati
Raigarh	320.6	330.5	651.1	**49.2**	Konkan
Thane	308.9	318.2	627.8	49.2	Konkan
Chandrapur	305.9	317.3	623.1	49.1	Nagpur
Latur	270.4	286.2	556.6	48.6	Aurangabad
Osmanabad	317.0	350.3	667.3	47.5	Aurangabad
Ratnagiri	302.1	336.1	638.2	47.3	Konkan
Pune	387.9	437.0	824.9	47.0	Pune
Bhandara	246.4	280.3	526.7	46.8	Nagpur
Hingoli	281.8	332.1	613.9	45.9	Aurangabad
Jalna	280.3	357.8	638.0	43.9	Aurangabad
Maharashtra	**293.6**	**276.9**	**570.4**	**51.5**	

Source: Government of Maharashtra (2009).

TABLE 3A.20
Food and Non-Food Expenditure and Share: Urban Maharashtra (2004–05)

District	Average MPCE (Rupees at Current Prices)			Share of Food (Percentage)	Division
	Food	Non-Food	Total		
Beed	265.3	199.5	464.8	57.1	Auranagabad
Sangli	363.5	322.5	685.9	53.0	Pune
Sindhudurg	424.1	399.3	823.5	51.5	Konkan
Nanded	286.9	284.7	571.6	50.2	Auranagabad
Washim	322.6	331.1	653.7	49.4	Amravati
Solapur	369.1	380.5	749.6	49.2	Pune
Wardha	343.1	355.0	698.0	49.2	Nagpur
Hingoli	316.8	340.5	657.2	48.2	Auranagabad
Dhule	360.3	393.3	753.6	47.8	Nashik
Kolhapur	411.7	461.5	873.2	47.2	Pune
Latur	332.4	381.3	713.8	46.6	Auranagabad
Jalgaon	390.8	466.4	857.2	45.6	Nashik
Nandurbar	358.7	435.2	793.9	45.2	Nashik
Amravati	311.9	385.6	697.6	44.7	Amravati
Ratnagiri	483.7	615.1	1,098.8	44.0	Konkan
Ahmednagar	400.1	516.5	916.6	43.7	Nashik
Akola	337.5	451.6	789.1	42.8	Amravati
Parbhani	353.1	486.4	839.5	**42.1**	Auranagabad
Buldhana	336.4	467.9	804.2	41.8	Amravati
Raigarh	555.2	777.2	1,332.3	41.7	Konkan
Jalna	428.6	618.6	1,047.2	40.9	Auranagabad
Yavatmal	309.1	455.5	764.6	40.4	Amravati
Aurangabad	352.1	520.4	872.5	40.4	Auranagabad
Gadchiroli	334.1	502.6	836.6	39.9	Nagpur
Thane	519.5	787.6	1,307.1	39.7	Konkan
Gondia	418.3	638.8	1,057.1	**39.6**	Nagpur
Nashik	342.1	526.4	868.5	39.4	Nashik
Mumbai	604.2	943.7	1,547.9	39.0	Konkan
Nagpur	403.7	637.2	1,040.9	38.8	Nagpur
Bhandara	373.6	612.7	986.3	37.9	Nagpur
Pune	514.4	877.4	1,391.8	37.0	Pune
Satara	574.2	992.0	1,566.2	36.7	Pune
Chandrapur	419.6	780.3	1,199.8	35.0	Nagpur
Osmanabad	413.7	839.6	1,253.3	33.0	Auranagabad
Maharashtra	**479.8**	**720.8**	**1,200.6**	**40.0**	

Source: Government of Maharashtra (2009).

Tables from Chapter 4

TABLE 4A.1
Literacy Rates, by Sex, for State and Districts: 2001 and 2011

Serial Number	State/District Name	Literacy Rate					
		Persons		Males		Females	
		2001	2011	2001	2011	2001	2011
	Maharashtra	**76.9**	**82.9**	**86.0**	**89.8**	**67.0**	**75.5**
1	Nandurbar	55.8	63.0	66.2	72.0	45.2	53.9
2	Dhule	71.7	74.6	81.4	82.6	61.4	66.2
3	Jalgaon	75.4	79.7	85.9	88.0	64.3	70.9
4	Buldhana	75.8	82.1	86.9	90.7	64.1	73.0
5	Akola	81.4	87.6	88.9	92.9	73.4	81.9
6	Washim	73.4	81.7	85.4	90.5	60.6	72.3
7	Amravati	82.5	88.2	88.9	92.7	75.7	83.5
8	Wardha	80.1	87.2	87.2	92.3	72.5	81.9
9	Nagpur	84.0	89.5	90.2	93.7	77.4	85.1
10	Bhandara	78.5	85.1	89.0	93.2	67.8	77.0
11	Gondia	78.5	85.4	89.7	93.5	67.6	77.3
12	Gadchiroli	60.1	70.6	71.9	80.2	48.1	60.7
13	Chandrapur	73.2	81.4	82.9	88.7	62.9	73.7
14	Yavatmal	73.6	80.7	84.1	88.6	62.5	72.4
15	Nanded	67.8	76.9	80.4	86.6	54.4	66.7
16	Hingoli	66.3	76.0	80.7	86.7	51.2	64.7
17	Parbhani	66.1	75.2	79.6	85.7	52.0	64.3
18	Jalna	64.4	73.6	79.2	85.3	49.1	61.3
19	Aurangabad	72.9	80.4	84.9	89.3	60.1	70.8
20	Nashik	74.4	81.0	83.7	88.0	64.4	73.4
21	Thane	80.7	86.2	87.1	90.9	73.1	80.8
22	Mumbai (Suburban)	86.9	90.9	91.6	94.3	81.1	86.9
23	Mumbai	86.4	88.5	90.2	90.5	81.4	86.0
24	Raigarh	77.0	83.9	86.2	90.7	67.8	76.8
25	Pune	80.5	87.2	88.3	92.7	71.9	81.1
26	Ahmednagar	75.3	80.2	85.7	88.8	64.4	71.2
27	Beed	68.0	73.5	80.7	84.0	54.5	62.3
28	Latur	71.5	79.0	82.9	87.4	59.4	70.0
29	Osmanabad	69.0	76.3	80.4	85.3	56.9	66.7
30	Solapur	71.3	77.7	82.0	86.4	59.8	68.6
31	Satara	78.2	84.2	88.2	92.1	68.4	76.3
32	Ratnagiri	75.1	82.4	85.9	91.4	65.8	74.6
33	Sindhudurg	80.3	86.5	90.3	93.7	71.2	79.7
34	Kolhapur	76.9	82.9	87.5	91.3	66.0	74.2
35	Sangli	76.6	82.6	86.3	90.4	66.7	74.7

Source: Government of India (2011a).

TABLE 4A.2
Literacy Rate (7+), by Social Groups, Sex and Sector: 2007–08

	Total	ST	SC	OBC	Others
Total					
Maharashtra	81.0	61.9	77.8	80.9	85.6
Coastal	86.9	66.9	78.4	84.7	91.4
Inland Western	82.4	64.7	77.3	81.5	85.5
Inland Northern	70.1	50.7	72.7	85.6	84.0
Inland Central	71.3	62.4	70.8	67.6	74.2
Inland Eastern	85.1	76.9	83.9	84.4	91.4
Eastern	77.7	63.6	84.5	77.8	89.8
India	71.7	60.5	63.6	70.3	82.1
Male					
Maharashtra	88.2	73.8	86.9	88.4	91.1
Coastal	92.1	83.0	84.5	92.0	94.4
Inland Western	90.1	79.9	88.0	89.6	91.7
Inland Northern	83.6	61.3	84.3	92.8	91.8
Inland Central	80.4	73.3	81.7	77.1	82.4
Inland Eastern	90.6	83.4	90.7	90.2	94.6
Eastern	87.3	76.6	93.8	87.0	95.0
India	80.5	70.9	73.2	80.3	88.4
Female					
Maharashtra	73.4	49.5	68.4	73.0	79.8
Coastal	81.5	50.2	72.3	77.4	88.2
Inland Western	74.2	46.7	66.4	72.8	78.9
Inland Northern	66.0	39.7	58.5	78.3	75.4
Inland Central	61.7	50.2	59.8	57.4	65.5
Inland Eastern	79.2	69.7	77.0	78.2	87.8
Eastern	68.4	53.4	73.6	68.8	85.6
India	62.3	49.7	53.3	59.8	75.4
Rural					
Maharashtra	75.1	58.8	74.4	77.2	78.8
Coastal	76.5	62.4	74.1	78.6	84.7
Inland Western	78.9	58.8	76.9	78.1	81.6
Inland Northern	69.8	50.3	68.5	83.4	76.8
Inland Central	67.3	59.8	68.1	63.1	70.5
Inland Eastern	81.6	73.5	78.2	82.0	89.7
Eastern	75.8	63.1	85.5	76.4	90.4
India	67.0	58.8	60.5	66.7	76.9
Urban					
Maharashtra	89.3	79.4	82.5	90.0	91.2
Coastal	90.5	85.6	79.4	90.5	92.3
Inland Western	88.9	84.2	78.1	88.3	92.1
Inland Northern	87.8	56.3	85.2	90.9	90.6
Inland Central	84.1	86.4	82.3	87.8	83.1
Inland Eastern	91.6	85.9	90.8	92.1	92.6

	Total	ST	SC	OBC	Others
Eastern	85.8	71.4	83.2	88.1	89.0
India	84.3	78.1	75.0	81.8	89.6
Rural—Male					
Maharashtra	84.2	71.3	85.3	85.7	86.9
Coastal	86.7	79.8	82.6	88.6	90.3
Inland Western	87.9	75.9	88.2	86.7	89.4
Inland Northern	80.5	61.4	83.8	92.3	88.6
Inland Central	77.3	71.5	79.7	72.9	79.9
Inland Eastern	88.0	80.1	86.8	88.4	93.3
Eastern	85.3	74.9	94.6	85.9	91.4
India	**77.0**	**69.4**	**70.6**	**77.7**	**84.6**
Rural—Female					
Maharashtra	65.8	45.9	63.0	68.7	70.5
Coastal	66.9	44.5	65.2	69.9	79.0
Inland Western	69.8	40.3	65.9	69.6	73.7
Inland Northern	58.4	38.4	49.3	74.3	63.4
Inland Central	57.0	46.6	56.7	52.7	60.6
Inland Eastern	74.6	65.8	68.2	75.3	85.2
Eastern	66.9	53.9	76.1	67.1	89.7
India	**56.7**	**47.8**	**49.9**	**55.4**	**68.8**
Urban—Male					
Maharashtra	93.6	87.4	89.0	94.9	94.5
Coastal	93.8	95.9	84.9	94.6	94.9
Inland Western	94.0	91.1	87.6	94.8	95.4
Inland Northern	91.3	59.6	85.7	94.0	94.8
Inland Central	90.3	88.6	89.9	95.7	88.5
Inland Eastern	95.7	92.9	95.9	96.1	95.5
Eastern	95.0	100.0	93.0	94.5	99.0
India	**89.9**	**86.1**	**83.1**	**88.3**	**93.8**
Urban—Female					
Maharashtra	84.7	70.6	75.8	84.5	87.7
Coastal	86.9	74.5	73.9	85.7	89.5
Inland Western	82.9	73.2	67.4	80.0	88.3
Inland Northern	84.2	53.1	84.7	87.7	86.1
Inland Central	77.4	83.9	74.2	79.0	77.4
Inland Eastern	87.4	79.3	86.3	87.8	89.5
Eastern	75.5	44.6	70.2	81.1	79.8
India	**78.1**	**69.2**	**66.2**	**74.6**	**85.6**

Source: Author's calculations based on data from National Sample Survey Office (2009b).
Notes: (i) Data presented has been rounded off to one decimal place.
(ii) Regions reported as per NSS specifications.

TABLE 4A.3
Adult Literacy Rate (15+): 2007–08

	Total			Rural			Urban		
	Total	Male	Female	Total	Male	Female	Total	Male	Female
Maharashtra	**77.4**	**86.2**	**68.3**	**70.1**	**81.2**	**58.9**	**87.6**	**92.8**	**81.9**
Coastal	84.9	91.0	78.3	71.6	83.5	60.8	89.2	93.2	84.7
Inland Western	79.3	88.4	69.6	74.9	85.7	64.2	87.1	93.1	80.1
Inland Northern	71.2	81.5	60.6	64.9	77.7	51.9	86.2	90.7	81.6
Inland Central	64.6	76.1	52.5	60.1	72.7	47.1	79.6	87.8	70.9
Inland Eastern	81.9	88.6	74.9	77.5	85.3	69.1	89.9	94.9	89.9
Eastern	72.7	84.7	60.8	70.1	82.3	58.1	83.3	93.9	72.2
India	66.0	76.7	54.9	59.7	71.8	47.5	82.0	88.7	74.6

Source: Author's calculations based on data from National Sample Survey Office (2009b).
Notes: (i) Data presented has been rounded off to one decimal place.
(ii) Regions reported as per NSS specifications.

TABLE 4A.4
Adult Literacy Rate (15+), by Social Groups, Sex and Sector: 2007–08

	Total	ST	SC	OBC	Others
Total					
Maharashtra	77.4	54.8	73.1	77.1	83.1
Coastal	84.9	60.0	73.4	81.8	90.1
Inland Western	79.3	59.9	72.5	78.0	83.1
Inland Northern	71.2	43.6	68.4	82.6	81.6
Inland Central	64.6	54.2	62.4	60.5	68.1
Inland Eastern	81.9	70.3	80.2	81.2	89.5
Eastern	72.7	54.3	81.2	73.1	87.0
India	66.0	51.4	55.6	64.0	78.9
Male					
Maharashtra	86.2	69.3	84.1	86.3	89.7
Coastal	91.0	78.9	82.9	90.4	93.7
Inland Western	88.4	76.3	85.4	87.8	90.5
Inland Northern	81.5	55.8	80.8	91.5	90.8
Inland Central	76.1	67.8	77.1	72.4	
Inland Eastern	88.6	79.2	88.4	88.9	
Eastern	81.7	72.4	92.3	84.4	93.8
India	76.7	63.9	67.5	76.2	86.4
Female					
Maharashtra	68.3	40.2	61.9	67.6	76.1
Coastal	78.3	40.9	67.7	72.8	86.2
Inland Western	69.6	41.4	59.6	67.3	75.3
Inland Northern	60.6	31.8	54.3	73.8	71.3
Inland Central	52.5	40.2	47.4	47.9	57.4
Inland Eastern	74.9	60.4	72.4	74.0	85.3
Eastern	60.8	38.0	69.2	61.6	81.2
India	54.9	38.8	43.3	51.6	71.1

	Total	ST	SC	OBC	Others
Rural					
Maharashtra	70.1	51.0	68.2	72.4	74.8
Coastal	71.6	53.7	67.3	73.5	82.0
Inland Western	74.9	53.3	71.7	73.4	78.5
Inland Northern	64.9	42.7	63.1	80.0	72.8
Inland Central	60.1	51.0	59.4	55.3	64.1
Inland Eastern	77.5	66.9	72.8	78.2	87.2
Eastern	70.1	53.4	82.1	71.3	86.4
India	59.7	49.1	51.3	59.2	72.1
Urban					
Maharashtra	87.6	75.7	79.5	88.4	89.8
Coastal	89.2	83.1	77.1	89.2	91.3
Inland Western	87.1	82.1	74.1	86.5	90.9
Inland Northern	86.2	53.5	82.8	89.1	89.7
Inland Central	79.6	84.4	76.1	84.2	78.5
Inland Eastern	89.9	80.2	89.0	90.8	91.1
Eastern	83.3	66.4	80.2	85.7	87.5
India	82.0	74.0	71.0	79.0	88.4

Source: Author's calculations based on data from National Sample Survey Office (2009b).
Notes: (i) Data presented has been rounded off to one decimal place.
(ii) Regions reported as per NSS specifications.

TABLE 4A.5
Growth of Schools, Teachers and Students: Ratios (1970 to 2010–11)

	1970	1980	1990	2000	2011–12
Schools Imparting Elementary Education					
Total Number of Schools	44,535	51,045	57,744	65,586	100,084
Total Number of School Teachers	177,946	222,070	268,322	313,656	542,070
Total School Enrolment	6,199,325	8,392,356	10,421,602	12,694,398	16,185,891
Secondary Schools (Std VIII to Std X)					
Total Number of Schools	5,313	6,119	9,978	14,767	21,579
Total Number of School Teachers	74,685	114,065	181,842	235,490	174,708
Total School Enrolment	2,077,127	3,309,333	5,794,120	8,274,750	7,038,294
Primary School Ratios					
Total Number of Teachers per Schools	4	4	5	5	5
Total Number of Students per Schools	139	164	180	194	161
Total Number of Students per Teacher	35	38	39	40	30
Secondary School Ratios					
Total Number of Teachers per Schools	14	19	18	16	8
Total Number of Students per Schools	392	541	581	560	326
Total number of Students per Teacher	28	29	32	35	49

Sources: DISE data from Mehta (2004, 2005, 2006, 2007, 2008, 2009) and NUEPA (2011b, 2012b); Ministry of Human Resource Development (2007); School Education Department (2001, 2002, 2003, 2004); SEMIS data from MPSP (2011).

TABLE 4A.6
Upper Primary versus Secondary School Ratios

SN	District	Schools Having Upper Primary Sections	Schools Having Secondary Sections	Ratio of Schools with Upper Primary Sections to Secondary Sections
1	Ahmadnagar	1,496	952	1.6
2	Akola	783	435	1.8
3	Amravati	1,299	677	1.9
4	Aurangabad	1,554	598	2.6
5	Bhandara	584	299	2.0
6	Bid	1,350	637	2.1
7	Buldhana	1,098	495	2.2
8	Chandrapur	1,041	484	2.2
9	Dhule	620	446	1.4
10	Gadchiroli	754	330	2.3
11	Gondiya	744	303	2.5
12	Hingoli	669	179	3.7
13	Jalgaon	1,438	751	1.9
14	Jalna	1,042	323	3.2
15	Kolhapur	1,675	867	1.9
16	Latur	1,342	613	2.2
17	Mumbai & Mumbai (Suburban)	2,264	1,595	1.4
18	Nagpur	1,733	919	1.9
19	Nanded	1,798	634	2.8
20	Nandurbar	599	387	1.5
21	Nashik	1,845	1,023	1.8
22	Osmanabad	926	413	2.2
23	Prabhani	1,052	378	2.8
24	Pune	2,657	1,342	2.0
25	Raigarh	1,288	537	2.4
26	Ratnagiri	1,480	392	3.8
27	Sangli	1,157	602	1.9
28	Satara	1,550	704	2.2
29	Sindhudurg	705	223	3.2
30	Solapur	1,806	894	2.0
31	Thane	3,069	1,586	1.9
32	Wardha	595	282	2.1
33	Washim	634	285	2.2
34	Yavatmal	1,452	615	2.4
	Maharashtra	**44,099**	**21,200**	**2.1**

Sources: MPSP (2011-12); NUEPA (2011b).

TABLE 4A.7
Secondary Schools by School Type

District	Secondary Schools by Categories			
	Secondary Schools (All)	Government	Private Aided	Private Unaided
Ahmednagar	956	32	773	151
Akola	416	18	280	118
Amravati	699	88	531	80
Aurangabad	714	71	334	309
Bhandara	303	39	231	33
Beed	646	70	473	103
Buldhana	525	77	349	99
Chandrapur	512	47	298	167
Dhule	450	17	403	30
Gadchiroli	351	62	213	76
Gondia	309	50	204	55
Hingoli	191	39	104	48
Jalgaon	716	64	614	38
Jalna	360	53	226	81
Kolhapur	847	11	690	146
Latur	610	52	489	69
Nagpur	877	68	645	164
Nanded	664	85	467	112
Nandurbar	374	62	216	96
Nashik	932	112	684	136
Osmanabad	426	55	292	79
Parbhani	417	74	226	117
Pune	1,286	84	883	319
Raigarh	523	20	305	198
Ratnagiri	386	4	311	71
Sangli	615	2	528	85
Satara	697	19	527	151
Sindhudurg	217	1	190	26
Solapur	872	18	698	156
Thane	1,423	63	889	471
Wardha	283	15	221	47
Washim	278	13	219	46
Yavatmal	630	76	471	83
Total	**21,078**	**1,654**	**14,865**	**4,559**

Source: MPSP (2009).

TABLE 4A.8
Female Participation in Education

Year	Percentage of Girls as Primary Students	Percentage of Girls as Secondary Students	Percentage of Women as Primary School Teachers
1960	35.8	26.8	22.1
1965	37.8	28.7	24.8
1970	39.3	30.6	26.4
1975	41.3	34.1	29.1
1980	43	36	31.5
1985	44.7	37.3	35.9
1990	46	40.6	38.4
1995	47.5	43.7	41.1
2008	47.4	48.1	44.9
2010	47	NA	45.2

Source: Based on unpublished data received from the Directorate of Education, GoM.
Note: NA denotes not available.

TABLE 4A.9
Blocks/Municipal Corporations (MNC) with Percentage of Girls Lower than the State Average at Elementary Level

Division Name	District Name	Block/MNC Name	Percentage of Girls Enrolled
Konkan	Mumbai	South	45.0
Konkan	Mumbai	North	45.4
Konkan	Thane	Dahanu	45.4
Konkan	Thane	Talasari	45.5
Konkan	Thane	Navi Mumbai	45.9
Konkan	Mumbai	West	46.1
Konkan	Thane	Mira Bhayandar	46.1
Konkan	Thane	Ulhasnagar	46.3
Konkan	Raigarh	Panvel	46.4
Konkan	Thane	Vasai	46.5
Konkan	Thane	Kalyan	46.5
Konkan	Raigarh	Khalapur	46.6
Konkan	Sindhudurg	Sawantwadi	46.6
Konkan	Thane	Thane Municipal Corporation	46.6
Konkan	Thane	Ambernath	46.8
Nashik	Ahmednagar	Newasa	44.1
Nashik	Jalgaon	Jalgaon Municipal Corporation	44.2
Nashik	Jalgaon	Jamner	44.2
Nashik	Ahmednagar	Kopargaon	44.3
Nashik	Jalgaon	Amalner	44.3
Nashik	Ahmednagar	Rahata	44.6
Nashik	Jalgaon	Chalisgaon	44.6
Nashik	Dhule	Shindkheda	44.6
Nashik	Jalgaon	Bhusawal	44.7
Nashik	Ahmednagar	Rahuri	44.7
Nashik	Ahmednagar	Nagar	45.1

Division Name	District Name	Block/MNC Name	Percentage of Girls Enrolled
Nashik	Ahmednagar	Ahmednagar Municipal Corporation	45.1
Nashik	Ahmednagar	Pathardi	45.2
Nashik	Jalgaon	Bhadgaon	45.2
Nashik	Dhule	Dhule	45.3
Nashik	Jalgaon	Chopada	45.3
Nashik	Jalgaon	Pachora	45.3
Nashik	Nashik	Nashik Municipal Corporation	45.5
Nashik	Ahmednagar	Shrirampoor	45.5
Nashik	Jalgaon	Parola	45.6
Nashik	Dhule	Dhule Municipal Corporation	45.6
Nashik	Ahmednagar	Shevgaon	45.7
Nashik	Ahmednagar	Shrigonda	45.7
Nashik	Ahmednagar	Sangamner	45.7
Nashik	Ahmednagar	Karjat	45.8
Nashik	Nandurbar	Nandurbar	45.9
Nashik	Ahmednagar	Parner	45.9
Nashik	Nashik	Niphad	45.9
Nashik	Jalgaon	Bodwad	46.0
Nashik	Dhule	Shirpur	46.0
Nashik	Jalgaon	Dharangaon	46.1
Nashik	Nashik	Nandgaon	46.2
Nashik	Nashik	Sinnar	46.3
Nashik	Jalgaon	Muktainagar	46.3
Nashik	Jalgaon	Raver	46.3
Nashik	Ahmednagar	Jamkhed	46.3
Nashik	Nashik	Baglan	46.3
Nashik	Nashik	Devla	46.4
Nashik	Nashik	Chandwad	46.7
Nashik	Nashik	Yeola	46.7
Nashik	Nandurbar	Taloda	46.9
Pune	Kolhapur	Panhala	42.7
Pune	Satara	Mahabaleshwar	42.8
Pune	Sangli	Palus	43.9
Pune	Kolhapur	Karveer	44.1
Pune	Sangli	Walwa	44.3
Pune	Satara	Khandala	44.4
Pune	Kolhapur	Hatkalangle	44.5
Pune	Kolhapur	Kolhapur	44.5
Pune	Pune	Haveli	44.6
Pune	Solapur	Barshi	44.7
Pune	Kolhapur	Kagal	44.7
Pune	Pune	Khed	44.8
Pune	Sangli	Tasgaon	45.0
Pune	Satara	Satara	45.1
Pune	Kolhapur	Shirol	45.2

Division Name	District Name	Block/MNC Name	Percentage of Girls Enrolled
Pune	Sangli	Shirala	45.5
Pune	Pune	Daund	45.5
Pune	Pune	Shirur	45.6
Pune	Pune	Indapur	45.6
Pune	Sangli	Miraj	45.7
Pune	Solapur	Mangalwedha	45.7
Pune	Satara	Karad	45.7
Pune	Pune	Pimpari Chinchwad Municipal Corporation	46.0
Pune	Solapur	Madha	46.0
Pune	Pune	Baramati	46.1
Pune	Sangli	Kavathe Mahankal	46.2
Pune	Pune	Purandar	46.2
Pune	Sangli	Sangli Miraj Kupwad Municipal Corporation	46.2
Pune	Satara	Phaltan	46.2
Pune	Kolhapur	Radhanagari	46.3
Pune	Solapur	Sangola	46.4
Pune	Sangli	Khanapur	46.4
Pune	Solapur	Malshiras	46.4
Pune	Satara	Wai	46.4
Pune	Kolhapur	Gadhinglaj	46.5
Pune	Solapur	Karmala	46.6
Pune	Pune	Ambegaon	46.6
Pune	Satara	Man	46.7
Pune	Sangli	Kadegaon	46.7
Pune	Solapur	Pandharpur	46.8
Pune	Solapur	Mohol	46.8
Pune	Sangli	Atapadi	46.9
Pune	Kolhapur	Bhudargad	46.9
Pune	Satara	Koregaon	46.9
Aurangabad	Latur	Ahamadpur	41.8
Aurangabad	Latur	Latur	45.0
Aurangabad	Beed	Ambajogai	45.3
Aurangabad	Beed	Beed	45.5
Aurangabad	Osmanabad	Osmanabad	45.7
Aurangabad	Beed	Kaij	45.8
Aurangabad	Parbhani	Parhbani	45.8
Aurangabad	Aurangabad	Gangapur	45.9
Aurangabad	Latur	Udgir	46.0
Aurangabad	Beed	Parli	46.2
Aurangabad	Beed	Ashti	46.4
Aurangabad	Aurangabad	Khultabad	46.4
Aurangabad	Nanded	Nanded	46.4
Aurangabad	Osmanabad	Bhoom	46.5
Aurangabad	Latur	Jalkot	46.5
Aurangabad	Aurangabad	Kannad	46.6

Division Name	District Name	Block/MNC Name	Percentage of Girls Enrolled
Aurangabad	Jalna	Jalna	46.7
Aurangabad	Parbhani	Sailu	46.8
Aurangabad	Aurangabad	Aurangabad Municipal Corporation	46.8
Aurangabad	Aurangabad	Soyegaon	46.8
Amravati	Buldhana	Buldhana	43.7
Amravati	Buldhana	Deulgaon Raja	43.8
Amravati	Yavatmal	Digras	45.3
Amravati	Buldhana	Mehakar	45.4
Amravati	Buldhana	Lonar	45.9
Amravati	Washim	Washim	46.0
Amravati	Buldhana	Chikhali	46.7
Amravati	Akola	Akola (Municipal Corporation)	46.7
Amravati	Buldhana	Malkapur	46.8
Amravati	Washim	Risod	46.8
Nagpur	Chandrapur	Ballarpur	45.4
Nagpur	Nagpur	Nagpur (Rural)	45.6
Nagpur	Chandrapur	Chandrapur	46.7
Maharashtra			46.9

Sources: Data from DISE in Mehta (2004, 2005, 2006, 2007, 2008, 2009).

TABLE 4A.10
Region-Wise NAR, Primary and Upper Primary Level: 2007–08

	All			Rural			Urban		
	Total	Male	Female	Total	Male	Female	Total	Male	Female
Primary Level (Std I to Std VI)									
India	84.5	85.6	83.1	84.3	85.6	82.8	85	85.6	84.3
Maharashtra	90.8	91.1	90.5	91.5	91.7	91.3	89.7	90.2	89.2
Coastal	86.7	86.5	86.9	88.9	90.2	87.6	85.7	84.7	86.7
Inland Western	94.7	94.3	95.2	94.4	93.4	95.5	95.4	96	94.8
Inland Northern	82.4	83.7	80.9	79.7	81.8	77.1	88.1	87.9	88.3
Inland Central	91.5	92	91.2	91.2	91	91.4	92.4	94	90.4
Inland Eastern	93.8	94.5	93	95.7	95.7	95.6	90.4	92.2	88.2
Eastern	98.2	99.6	97	98.4	100	97.2	97.1	98.1	95.6
Upper Primary Level (Std VI to Std VIII)									
India	58.7	60.7	56.4	56.7	58.9	54.2	65.2	66.7	63.5
Maharashtra	67.1	67.2	62	65.2	64.1	66.5	70.2	72.5	67.7
Coastal	69.5	71.2	67.7	64.4	58.5	72.2	71.6	77.2	66.2
Inland Western	67	68	65.9	65.1	66.6	63.5	72	71.6	72.6
Inland Northern	62.3	63.1	62	56.6	57.8	54.9	79.1	77.7	81
Inland Central	65.3	62.2	68.8	67.8	62.7	73.2	58.6	60.8	56.1
Inland Eastern	66.8	68.9	64.6	66.9	70	63.1	66.7	65.8	67.4
Eastern	72.7	68.9	76.4	71	66.4	74.9	80.9	77	88.9

Source: Author's calculations based on data from National Sample Survey Office (2009b).
Note: NAR is indicated in percentage terms.

TABLE 4A.11
NAR by MPCE Quintiles: Primary and Upper Primary Level: 2007–08

MPCE Groups	India					Maharashtra				
	Total	Rural	Urban	Male	Female	Total	Rural	Urban	Male	Female
Primary Level (Std I to Std VI)										
0–20	79.5	80.1	70	81	77.8	87.8	88.2	84.8	87.1	88.4
20–40	83.6	84.2	77.6	84.5	82.5	90.9	91.9	85	91.7	90
40–60	86.6	87.1	84.1	87.4	85.6	93.6	93.4	93.9	93.3	93.8
60–80	87.7	88.1	86.9	88.8	86.3	90.5	94.3	87.8	91.8	89
80–100	89.3	89	89.5	89.8	88.8	92	93.8	91.5	91.8	92
Upper Primary Level (Std VI to Std VIII)										
0–20	46.7	46.6	48.2	48	45.3	62.8	60.9	83.2	60.1	65.9
20–40	54.2	54.9	49.2	55.8	47.5	64.9	67.8	49.9	62.3	67.4
40–60	60	60.5	57.2	62.9	56.5	62.4	63.8	58.4	65.8	58.2
60–80	65.4	65.4	65.3	67.2	63.2	68.8	72.1	65.3	69.5	67.9
80–100	74.7	72.1	76.3	75.8	73.3	74.8	60	79.3	76.2	73.3

Source: Author's calculations based on data from National Sample Survey Office (2009b).
Note: NAR is indicated in percentage terms.

TABLE 4A.12
NAR, by Social Groups, Primary and Upper Primary Level: 2007–08

	Total				Male				Female			
	ST	SC	OBC	Others	ST	SC	OBC	Others	ST	SC	OBC	Others
Primary Level (Std I to Std VI)												
India	83.0	82.0	84.0	88.0	85.0	83.4	85.0	88.8	80.3	80.4	82.7	87.1
Maharashtra	79.6	92.3	92.1	92.1	79.3	91.8	93.0	92.4	80.0	92.8	91.1	91.9
Coastal	80.1	84.3	86.3	88.4	81.5	79.6	90.0	87.0	80.3	88.3	82.5	89.7
Inland Western	80.0	92.3	96.6	96.0	83.9	94.1	94.5	95.4	72.6	90.1	98.6	96.6
Inland Northern	65.1	88.1	91.6	88.4	67.4	92.3	90.5	93.4	62.2	84.3	93.0	84.4
Inland Central	71.3	96.3	87.5	93.2	68.0	96.3	89.4	93.1	77.0	96.2	85.6	93.4
Inland Eastern	96.8	94.5	94.1	90.8	94.5	91.0	94.9	96.1	99.0	99.1	93.2	83.0
Eastern	100.0	100.0	97.4	98.2	100.0	100.0	100.0	96.0	100.0	100.0	94.9	100.0
Upper Primary Level (Std VI to Std VIII): 2007–08												
India	54.0	55.6	58.2	63.5	55.8	58.0	60.7	64.4	51.9	52.7	55.3	62.5
Maharashtra	55.4	65.0	68.1	69.5	54.7	62.0	66.3	72.6	56.2	69.1	69.9	66.1
Coastal	55.9	67.5	70.9	70.8	52.4	54.7	71.3	76.4	63.5	82.9	70.7	64.7
Inland Western	63.8	58.1	68.1	70.2	100.0	56.8	63.8	72.7	32.1	59.6	72.1	67.4
Inland Northern	36.6	67.2	76.7	64.3	40.2	72.0	75.4	65.9	31.0	47.2	78.0	61.8
Inland Central	66.3	64.4	60.5	68.5	45.5	54.4	53.7	72.1	100.0	77.2	67.6	64.9
Inland Eastern	73.6	66.2	65.9	65.9	61.9	70.0	71.0	65.9	83.2	61.7	60.7	65.8
Eastern	65.9	87.7	68.3	88.7	88.2	84.9	60.1	64.9	54.0	92.7	77.0	100.0

Source: Author's calculations based on data from National Sample Survey Office (2009b).
Note: NAR is indicated in percentage terms.

TABLE 4A.13
NAR, Secondary Levels: Maharashtra: 2007–08

	Secondary Level (Std IX and Std X)		
	Total	Rural	Urban
Male	59.4	57.7	63
Female	51.7	50.7	53.6
ST	33	29.5	54
SC	48.4	46.5	51.8
OBC	61.9	59.5	69.3
Others	57.9	61.1	54.3
		Male	Female
ST		31.1	35.7
SC		47.8	49.1
OBC		67.3	55.8
Others		63.3	52

Source: Author's calculations based on data from National Sample Survey Office (2009b).
Note: NAR is indicated in percentage terms.

TABLE 4A.14
Percentage of Out-Of-School Children: 2007–08

	Never Attended School	Ever Attended But Currently Not Attended	Out-Of-School Children (Column 1 + Column 2)	Males			Females		
				Never Attended	Ever Attended	Out-Of-School (Column 1 + Column 2)	Never Attended	Ever Attended	Out-Of-School (Column 1 + Column 2)
Elementary Level (6–13 Years)									
India	7.9	3.7	11.6	6.7	3.3	10	9.3	4	13.3
Maharashtra	3.4	3.4	6.8	3.3	3.6	6.9	3.6	3.3	6.9
Coastal	3	3.7	6.7	2.1	3.1	5.2	3.8	4.4	8.2
Inland Western	1.8	1.8	3.6	2.1	1.9	4	1.4	1.7	3.1
Inland Northern	11	5.3	16.4	10.5	5.7	16.2	11.7	4.9	16.6
Inland Central	3.7	4.8	8.6	3.8	5.4	9.2	3.7	4.2	7.9
Inland Eastern	1.3	2.7	4	1.3	2.7	4	1.3	2.6	3.9
Eastern	0.4	2.4	2.8	0	4.4	4.4	0.7	0.6	1.3
Secondary Level (14–16 Years)									
India	8.8	24.2	33.0	6.7	22.8	29.5	11.1	25.8	36.9
Maharashtra	2.8	22.4	25.1	1.5	20.7	22.2	4.1	24.3	28.4
Coastal	3.0	24.1	27.1	1.4	18.1	19.5	4.5	29.6	34.1
Inland Western	0.7	17.3	18.0	0.6	17.0	17.6	0.9	17.6	18.5
Inland Northern	7.1	25.1	32.2	2.8	23.9	26.7	12.3	26.5	38.8
Inland Central	5.3	30.3	35.6	3.4	27.9	31.3	7.7	33.2	40.9
Inland Eastern	0.3	18.8	19.1	0.5	19.0	19.5	0.0	18.7	18.7
Eastern	0.0	18.0	18.0	0.0	19.5	19.5	0.0	16.5	16.5

Source: Author's calculations based on data from National Sample Survey Office (2009b).

TABLE 4A.15
Percentage of Out-Of-School Children, by Sector: 2007–08

	Rural			Urban		
	Never Attended	Ever Attended	Out-Of-School	Never Attended	Ever Attended	Out-Of-School
Elementary Level (6–13 Years)						
India	8.6	3.8	12.4	5.4	3.2	8.6
Maharashtra	4.1	3.8	7.9	2.2	3	5.2
Coastal	3.7	2.8	6.5	2.7	4.1	6.8
Inland Western	2.2	2	4.2	0.7	1.3	2
Inland Northern	13.1	7.1	20.2	6.1	1.2	7.3
Inland Central	4.4	5.1	9.5	1.9	4.2	6.1
Inland Eastern	1.4	2.8	4.2	1	2.3	3.3
Eastern	0.4	12.9	13.3	0	0	0
Secondary Level (14–16 Years)						
India	9.8	25.9	35.7	5.5	19.1	24.6
Maharashtra	3.1	23.1	26.1	2.2	21.1	23.3
Coastal	2.7	29.3	32.0	3.2	21.5	24.7
Inland Western	0.7	17.5	18.2	0.9	16.7	17.6
Inland Northern	8.2	24.1	32.3	3.9	27.8	31.7
Inland Central	6.0	29.7	35.7	3.1	32.3	35.4
Inland Eastern	0.4	21.2	21.6	0.0	14.3	14.3
Eastern	0.0	18.2	18.2	0.0	17.3	17.3

Source: Author's calculations based on data from National Sample Survey Office (2009b).

TABLE 4A.16
Percentage of Out-Of-School Children, by Social Groups: 2007–08

	ST			SC			OBC			Others		
	NA	EA	OSC NA+EA	NA	EA	OSC NA+EA	NA	EA	OSC NA+EA	NA	EA	OSC NA+EA
Elementary Level (6–13 Years)												
India	10.7	5	15.7	10	4.4	14.4	8.4	3.3	11.7	4.3	3.1	7.4
Maharashtra	13.5	6.7	20.2	2.7	3.7	6.4	2.5	3.1	5.6	2	2.9	4.9
Coastal	10.4	1.3	11.7	6	5.8	11.8	1.7	4.1	5.8	1.9	3.6	5.5
Inland Western	12	2	14	1.3	4	5.3	1.9	2.3	4.2	1.1	0.9	2
Inland Northern	27.4	12	39.4	7.8	2.6	10.4	3.4	1.9	5.3	4.8	3.7	8.5
Inland Central	5.4	21.4	26.8	0.7	4.7	5.4	6.8	4.9	11.7	2.9	4	6.9
Inland Eastern	1.7	3.4	5.1	3.3	2	5.3	0.7	2.3	3	0.8	3.8	4.6
Eastern	0	1.8	1.8	0	0	0	0.6	3.5	4.1	0	0	0
Secondary Level (14–16 Years)												
India	12.9	32.5	45.4	11.0	28.0	29.0	9.3	23.2	32.5	5.0	20.6	25.6
Maharashtra	9.9	30.6	40.5	3.1	27.0	30.1	1.5	19.7	21.2	2.0	21.1	23.1
Coastal	6.0	30.0	36.0	7.6	27.3	34.9	0.0	24.1	24.1	3.0	22.1	25.1
Inland Western	0.0	32.3	32.3	1.2	35.9	37.1	0.0	12.8	12.8	1.0	13.1	14.1

	ST			SC			OBC			Others		
	NA	EA	OSC NA+EA	NA	EA	OSC NA+EA	NA	EA	OSC NA+EA	NA	EA	OSC NA+EA
Inland Northern	20.9	32.1	53.0	10.7	24.6	35.3	0.6	14.6	15.2	0.6	35.6	36.2
Inland Central	6.9	42.8	49.7	3.9	26.8	30.7	7.3	31.1	38.4	4.1	29.7	33.8
Inland Eastern	0.0	27.2	27.2	0.0	20.8	20.8	0.5	16.8	17.3	0.0	14.7	14.7
Eastern	0.0	13.3	13.3	0.0	8.9	8.9	0.0	20.5	20.5	0.0	12.7	12.7
INDIA	12.9	32.5	45.4	11.0	28.0	29.0	9.3	23.2	32.5	5.0	20.6	25.6

Source: Author's calculations based on data from National Sample Survey Office (2009b).
Notes: (i) NA denotes never attended.
(ii) EA denotes ever attended.
(iii) OSC denotes out-of-school children.

TABLE 4A.17
Dropout Rates: 2007–08

	Total			Male			Female		
	Total	Rural	Urban	Total	Rural	Urban	Total	Rural	Urban
India	6.7	7.5	4.4	6.5	7.1	4.9	6.8	7.9	3.9
Maharashtra	5.3	5.7	4.6	5.4	5.1	5.8	5.2	6.5	3.3
Coastal	7	9	6.3	6.9	5.6	7.4	7.2	12.9	5.3
Inland Western	3.8	4.4	4	4.2	3	6.3	3.7	4.8	1.1
Inland Northern	8.3	3.7	7	7.3	8.4	4	6.7	8.1	3.4
Inland Central	8	3.4	7	6.8	7.2	5.2	7.2	9.1	1
Inland Eastern	4	1.8	3.2	3.8	4.7	2.3	2.6	3.3	1.2
Eastern	1.7	3.5	2	1.3	0	5.3	2.9	3.3	0.6

Source: Author's calculations based on data from National Sample Survey Office (2009b).
Note: Findings are presented in percentage terms.

TABLE 4A.18
Dropout Rates, by Social Groups and Sectors: 2007–08

	Total			
	ST	SC	OBC	Others
India				
Total	11.4	8.6	5.9	5
Rural	12.0	9.3	6.4	6.0
Urban	6.1	6.4	4.4	3.6
Maharashtra				
Total	13.1	6.4	3.7	4.3
Rural	14.8	6.9	3.7	3.9
Urban	3.4	5.8	3.8	4.8
Male	12.0	3.7	3.9	5.5
Female	14.7	9.8	3.5	3.1

	India					Maharashtra				
	Total	Rural	Urban	Male	Female	Total	Rural	Urban	Male	Female
0–20	11.5	11.5	11.8	11.7	11.3	10	9.9	11	9.4	10.6
20–40	8.7	8.3	11.2	8.6	8.7	7.8	6.6	12.7	8.5	7
40–60	6.7	6.8	6.2	6.7	7.3	5.7	5.7	5.3	3.8	7.5
60–80	4.7	4.8	4.5	4.8	4.6	4.1	2.8	5.5	5.1	2.8
80–100	1.5	1.5	1.6	1.6	1.5	1.6	0.5	1.9	2.3	0.7

Source: Author's calculations based on data from National Sample Survey Office (2009b).
Note: Findings are presented in percentage terms.

TABLE 4A.19
Survival of Cohorts by District

Survival until Std VI of Cohort That Started in Std I in 2006		Survival until Std VIII of Cohort That Started in Std III in 2006	
90 per cent and Above	Aurangabad	90 per cent and Above	Aurangabad
	Bhandara		Bhandara
	Gondia		Chandrapur
	Kolhapur		Gondia
	Nagpur		Kolhapur
	Pune		Nagpur
	Ratnagiri		Pune
	Sangli		Raigarh
80 to 89 per cent	Ahmednagar		Sangli
	Akola		Satara
	Amravati		Wardha
	Buldhana	80 to 89 per cent	Ahmednagar
	Chandrapur		Akola
	Jalgaon		Amravati
	Latur		Beed
	Nashik		Buldhana
	Raigarh		Dhule
	Satara		Gadchiroli
	Sindhudurg		Jalgaon
	Solapur		Latur
	Wardha		Nashik
	Washim		Ratnagiri
70 to 79 per cent	Beed		Sindhudurg
	Dhule		Solapur
	Gadchiroli		Washim
	Parbhani	70 to 79 per cent	Jalna
	Jalna		Nandurbar
	Yavatmal		Parbhani
Below 70 per cent	Nanded		Yavatmal
	Nandurbar	Below 70 per cent	Hingoli
	Hingoli		Nanded
	Osmanabad		Osmanabad

Sources: Mehta (2007, 2008, 2009, 2011, 2012).
Note: Mumbai, Suburban Mumbai and Thane were not part of the district-level analysis.

TABLE 4A.20
PS of 6–13-Year-Olds Never Enrolled in School: 2007–08

	India			India Rural			India Urban		
	Total	Male	Female	Total	Male	Female	Total	Male	Female
Worked in Household Enterprise: Own	0.8	1.1	0.5	0.8	1.1	0.5	1	1	0.9
Worked in Household Enterprise: Employee	0	0	0	0	0	0	0	0	0
Worked as Helper in Household Enterprise	6.4	8.3	4.8	6.8	8.6	5.3	4.4	6.9	1.8
Regular Salaried Wage Employee	0.6	0.9	0.3	0.4	0.6	0.2	1.8	2.3	1.2
Casual Wage Labour: Public	0	0	0	0	0	0	0	0	0
Casual Wage Labour: Other	5.7	7.5	4.1	5.7	7.3	4.4	5.5	8.1	2.7
Total	13.5	17.8	9.7	13.7	17.6	10.4	12.7	18.3	6.6

	Maharashtra			Maharashtra Rural			Maharashtra Urban		
	Total	Male	Female	Total	Male	Female	Total	Male	Female
Worked in Household Enterprise: Own	1.6	3.1	1.2	4.1	0		3.4	0	
Worked in Household Enterprise: Employee	0	0	0	0	0		0	0	
Worked as Helper in Household Enterprise	3.7	5.3	0	5.9	2.7		0	0.6	
Regular Salaried Wage Employee	1.2	1.7	0.5	0	0		7.1	1.5	
Casual Wage Labour: Public	0	0	0	0	0		0	0	
Casual Wage Labour: Other	12.3	14.6	9.8	17	13.7		7.3	2.4	
Total	18.8	24.7	11.5	27	16.4		17.8	4.5	

Source: Author's calculations based on data from National Sample Survey Office (2009b).
Note: Findings are presented in percentage terms.

TABLE 4A.21
Proportion of Children (6–13 years) Attending School and Receiving Free Education: 2007–08

	Total			Rural			Urban		
	Total	Male	Female	Total	Male	Female	Total	Male	Female
Maharashtra	76.5	72.8	80.5	91.4	88.6	94.4	53.5	48.4	59.0
Coastal	49.1	44.1	54.3	87.0	84.1	90.4	33.0	25.4	40.2
Inland Western	73.2	68.1	78.9	84.1	79.7	88.9	50.0	44.3	56.8
Inland Northern	82.8	79.3	87.0	89.6	86.0	94.1	68.9	64.5	73.7
Inland Central	93.2	90.0	96.6	96.5	95.2	97.8	84.7	78.0	93.1
Inland Eastern	87.1	85.5	88.8	95.3	93.6	97.3	71.0	68.5	73.6
Eastern	95.7	93.0	98.0	99.5	99.0	100.0	76.4	72.6	83.8

Proportion of Children (6–13 years) Attending School and Receiving Free Education, by Sector and Social Groups: 2007–08

	Total				Rural				Urban			
	ST	SC	OBC	Others	ST	SC	OBC	Others	ST	SC	OBC	Others
Maharashtra	89.7	80.6	82.6	64.5	95.3	93.5	93.3	86.7	67.8	66.0	58.1	47.9
Coastal	93.2	55.6	65.1	35.6	100.0	81.8	89.2	71.9	54.5	47.3	32.1	30.6
Inland Western	70.2	82.4	79.8	67.5	93.6	87.0	88.3	80.3	6.0	71.6	57.4	43.6
Inland Northern	89.0	95.1	78.1	81.5	88.9	93.5	88.7	88.9	75.8	100.0	58.3	75.4
Inland Central	88.9	92.4	93.9	93.2	87.6	99.0	97.8	95.2	100.0	70.0	79.6	89.4
Inland Eastern	94.8	86.2	89.9	76.4	97.4	98.2	94.0	96.1	89.2	72.6	72.9	62.9
Eastern	100.0	88.4	96.6	91.8	100.0	100.0	100.0	94.8	100.0	72.9	75.9	79.5

Source: Author's calculations based on data from National Sample Survey Office (2009b).
Notes: (i) Findings are presented in percentage terms.
(ii) Percentages presented refer to those children who are currently attending schools and receiving free education.

TABLE 4A.22
Results of ASER Tests

	Percentage of Children in Standard 5 Who Are Able to Fluently Read Std II Level Textbooks (All Schools)			
Revenue Divisions	2007	2008	2009	2010
Nagpur	67.3	64.2	69.8	64.6
Amravati	71.4	74.5	72.7	71.0
Aurangabad	71.5	70.8	71.3	71.1
Pune	70.7	77.7	75.2	78.3
Konkan	89.7	88.5	84.0	76.0
Nashik	77.5	71.6	72.0	74.3
Maharashtra	74.1	75.0	73.8	73.1

Percentage of Children in Std V Who Can Accomplish a Division Problem (All Schools)			Everyday Maths: Percentage of Children Who Can Calculate Area (Std V and Std VIII) (All Schools)		
Revenue Divisions	ASER 2007	ASER 2010	Revenue Divisions	Standard 5	Standard 8
Nagpur	31.6	23	Nagpur	17	45.5
Amravati	45	31.2	Amravati	11	41
Aurangabad	33.3	41.4	Aurangabad	21.7	53.5
Pune	51.1	53.1	Pune	33	57
Konkan	71.9	51.3	Konkan	36.5	57.5
Nashik	36.6	40.2	Nashik	28	62.3
Maharashtra	44.3	41.4	Maharashtra	25.1	53.7
All India	42.4	35.9			

Sources: Pratham (2007, 2008, 2009, 2010).

TABLE 4A.23
Percentage of Primary and Upper Primary Schools Who Reported Receiving Grants in Two Recent FYs: Maharashtra and India (2009–10 and 2010–11)

	April 2009–March 2010		April 2010–March 2011	
SSA School Grants	India	Maharashtra	India	Maharashtra
Maintenance Grant	85	92	84	92
Development Grant	81	90	77	76
TLM Grant	88	95	87	93

Percentage of Primary and Upper Primary Schools Who Reported Receiving Grants till November 2009 and November 2011 in Two Recent FYs: Maharashtra and India (2009–10 and 2010–11)

	November 2009		November 2011	
SSA School Grants	India	Maharashtra	India	Maharashtra
Maintenance Grant	59	65	55	66
Development Grant	57	64	51	58
TLM Grant	61	69	52	66

Source: Accountability Initiative (2011b).

Tables from Chapter 5

TABLE 5A.1
Child Sex Ratio

District	2001	2011	Change
Nandurbar	961	932	29
Dhule	907	876	31
Jalgaon	880	829	51
Buldhana	908	842	66
Akola	933	900	33
Washim	918	859	59
Amravati	941	927	14
Wardha	928	916	12
Nagpur	942	926	16
Bhandara	956	939	17
Gondia	958	944	14
Gadchiroli	966	956	10
Chandrapur	939	945	−6
Yavatmal	933	915	18
Nanded	929	897	32
Hingoli	927	868	59
Parbhani	923	866	57
Jalna	903	847	56
Aurangabad	890	848	42
Nashik	920	882	38
Thane	931	918	13
Mumbai (Suburban)	923	910	13
Mumbai	922	874	48
Raigarh	939	924	15
Pune	902	873	29
Ahmednagar	884	839	45
Beed	894	801	93
Latur	918	872	46
Osmanabad	894	853	41
Solapur	895	872	23
Satara	878	881	−3
Ratnagiri	952	940	12
Sindhudurg	944	910	34
Kolhapur	839	845	−6
Sangli	851	862	−11
Maharashtra	913	883	31

Sources: Directorate of Census Operations Maharashtra (2001); Government of India (2011a).

TABLE 5A.2
Per Capita Health Expenditure: Rural

Number	District	2001–02	2002–03	2003–04	2004–05	2005–06	2006–07
1	Thane	162	185	154	167	203	264
2	Raigarh	123	113	121	127	135	145
3	Ratnagiri	131	127	125	132	143	165
4	Pune	214	220	215	205	279	317
5	Satara	97	113	103	110	128	149
6	Solapur	100	102	99	105	120	143
7	Nashik	124	149	132	146	178	195
8	Jalgaon	99	123	108	118	119	144
9	Ahmednagar	74	97	91	102	123	137
10	Dhule	120	131	136	135	171	181
11	Nandurbar	111	151	137	139	224	257
12	Kolhapur	102	117	112	124	139	153
13	Sindhudurg	195	180	178	188	207	250
14	Sangli	102	94	101	104	112	131
15	Aurangabad	108	129	115	117	166	152
16	Jalna	99	108	130	125	143	143
17	Parbhani	132	133	127	127	164	159
18	Hingoli	86	86	118	120	136	136
19	Latur	136	137	120	127	173	169
20	Osmanabad	130	131	144	140	150	158
21	Beed	93	106	114	115	131	141
22	Nanded	123	147	149	153	173	174
23	Akola	169	174	156	171	196	210
24	Amravati	130	137	147	152	169	193
25	Buldhana	102	118	121	116	137	147
26	Yavatmal	112	122	118	123	154	159
27	Washim	102	127	123	127	142	145
28	Nagpur	1227	379	301	351	274	430
29	Wardha	135	131	146	141	150	168
30	Bhandara	148	137	148	165	178	183
31	Gadchiroli	220	270	256	292	317	319
32	Chandrapur	161	157	172	183	220	236
33	Gondia	109	141	160	151	198	218
	Maharashtra	**152**	**142**	**137**	**143**	**167**	**187**

Source: Based on information obtained from the Indian Audit & Accounts Department, Office of the Accountant General (AG), Maharashtra, 2001–07.
Note: Amounts are expressed in Rupees.

TABLE 5A.3
Per Capita Health Expenditure: Urban

Number	District	2001–02	2002–03	2003–04	2004–05	2005–06	2006–07
1	Thane	102	91	101	104	99	100
2	Raigarh	90	89	99	118	109	87
3	Ratnagiri	339	352	429	426	359	361
4	Pune	198	203	221	239	206	217
5	Satara	158	181	173	216	207	187
6	Solapur	217	216	236	238	246	272
7	Nashik	86	83	82	106	95	98
8	Jalgaon	74	76	84	93	89	80
9	Ahmednagar	60	66	65	79	74	68
10	Dhule	311	282	371	346	383	385
11	Nandurbar	38	49	131	159	173	76
12	Kolhapur	149	183	195	196	206	201
13	Sindhudurg	337	364	394	569	562	540
14	Sangli	304	290	309	335	349	355
15	Aurangabad	363	339	365	377	415	430
16	Jalna	145	162	156	161	188	199
17	Parbhani	128	134	150	168	166	155
18	Hingoli	26	30	57	46	157	37
19	Latur	153	171	198	258	367	373
20	Osmanabad	250	275	309	338	382	370
21	Beed	561	617	669	762	797	809
22	Nanded	305	282	300	312	356	335
23	Akola	263	299	286	327	473	591
24	Amravati	146	166	206	198	298	202
25	Buldhana	265	288	286	250	273	251
26	Yavatmal	341	324	425	419	472	418
27	Washim	26	36	88	80	106	40
28	Nagpur	504	426	471	476	501	477
29	Wardha	339	330	344	328	341	413
30	Bhandara	414	474	410	464	478	458
31	Gadchiroli	572	710	1023	941	1110	998
32	Chandrapur	97	97	116	115	130	114
33	Gondia	194	232	283	237	286	425
	Maharashtra	**146**	**143**	**158**	**167**	**175**	**174**

Source: Based on information obtained from the Indian Audit & Accounts Department, Office of The Accountant General (AG), Maharashtra, 2001–07.
Note: Amounts are expressed in Rupees.

TABLE 5A.4
Population Per Public Health Facility in 1991, 2001 and 2011

District	Population Per Sub-Centre		Population per PHC			Population per RH		
	2000	2010–11	1990–91	2001–02	2010–11	1990–91	2001–02	2010–11
Thane	4,743	5,443	25,424	28,953	34,333	142,763	185,781	133,899
Ratnagiri	4,023	4,259	20,985	22,456	24,031	140,600	167,174	134,170
Sindhudurg	3,197	3,244	20,237	20,698	21,169	109,857	87,390	80,441
Raigarh	6,040	6,496	28,230	30,420	35,979	136,016	167,309	124,729
Konkan	**4,531**	**4,953**	**23,927**	**26,133**	**29,631**	**134,807**	**154,839**	**122,164**
Satara	7,802	6,804	30,950	33,956	38,334	177,961	241,087	151,206
Solapur	7,976	6,942	34,872	38,592	38,860	209,234	291,584	157,483
Sangli	7,223	6,963	29,948	33,056	37,767	189,671	216,701	148,549
Kolhapur	6,665	6,722	32,873	34,345	38,560	169,423	190,216	138,814
Pune	6,051	6,257	33,238	35,253	35,129	170,344	202,115	140,514
Western Maharashtra	**7,017**	**6,700**	**32,470**	**35,084**	**37,575**	**181,511**	**223,035**	**146,779**
Ahmednagar	6,674	6,649	32267	36,370	38,438	218,420	248,996	147,603
Nandurbar	NA	4,874	NA	22,633	24,369	NA	110,904	88,336
Dhule	2,928	6,397	24,887	30,782	36,200	167,990	420,687	185,523
Jalgaon	6,624	6,765	30,434	32,874	38,834	154,198	164,369	149,513
Nashik	5,766	6,522	27,278	28,832	36,533	155,142	122,250	129,756
North Maharashtra	**6,128**	**6,365**	**28,722**	**30,943**	**35,576**	**172,331**	**168,570**	**136,131**
Parbhani	2,970	5,570	32,165	33,630	38,452	182,271	130,316	149,002
Nanded	5,848	6,956	31,452	34,175	40,975	165,839	156,228	163,898
Latur	6,795	7,516	30,336	34,566	41,176	166,847	176,669	157,841
Hingoli	NA	7,463	NA	34,714	41,048	NA	166,626	197,030
Jalna	7,632	7,054	34,354	34,345	37,561	188,950	186,445	150,245
Osmanabad	6,144	7,045	26,401	29,841	34,552	154,635	156,666	161,243
Beed	7,013	7,519	33,225	37,749	42,107	186,888	221,773	161,950
Aurangabad	7,298	7,887	34,619	38,508	44,008	212,662	258,552	169,262
Marathwada	**6,428**	**7,144**	**31,744**	**34,795**	**40,210**	**178,559**	**178,718**	**162,244**
Yavatmal	5,350	5,351	29,156	32,275	36,949	132,324	166,755	136,927
Wardha	5,065	5,859	29,031	33,766	39,274	111,977	130,242	106,040
Bhandara	2,249	5,481	28,621	32,014	32,058	166,521	320,139	117,547
Gadchiroli	2,428	3,019	15,965	20,067	25,223	89,806	75,253	94,587
Nagpur	4,846	5,325	27,916	30,289	34,340	157,028	181,736	129,434
Buldhana	6,638	7,378	31,872	33,829	39,726	213,995	251,300	121,515
Washim	NA	6,715	NA	33,671	41,098	NA	140,295	146,779
Chandrapur	4,185	4,573	21,613	24,242	26,730	141,686	108,156	119,256
Gondia	NA	4,967	NA	25,173	30,311	NA	117,475	107,468
Amravati	5,336	5,905	27,462	30,493	35,112	164,770	155,235	140,448
Akola	3,076	6,577	30,383	33,425	39,022	197,493	200,548	195,110
Vidarbha	**4,829**	**5,369**	**26,873**	**29,483**	**34,018**	**151,831**	**150,587**	**125,786**

Sources: Government of Maharashtra (1991–2011, n.d.).
Notes: (i) For the year 2011 we have also taken into account the SDHs that were actually RHs before so that comparability is maintained. Many RHs were upgraded in the last decade into SDHs of 50 as well as 100 beds.
(ii) NA denotes not available.

TABLE 5A.5
Population Per Government Bed

District	2000–01	2007–08	2008–09	2009–10
Thane	1,488.3	NA	1,252.1	1,275.7
Ratnagiri	1,288.4	NA	1,256.7	1,294.9
Sindhudurg	1,667.6	958.9	963.0	1,030.0
Raigarh	2,196.9	NA	1,488.9	1,353.2
Satara	2,499.1	2,519.0	2,431.7	2,463.4
Solapur	2,086.5	2,487.4	2,486.9	877.6
Sangli	1,264.0	1,398.0	2,089.3	2,176.3
Kolhapur	1,930.5	1,613.8	1,557.0	1,865.5
Pune	957.7	NA	1,100.9	1,129.1
Ahmednagar	2,086.0	NA	2,508.3	2,551.2
Nandurbar	1,940.4	NA	1,483.9	1,513.0
Dhule	1,561.2	NA	1,486.6	1,482.5
Jalgaon	1,918.1	NA	2,149.7	2,174.8
Nashik	880.4	NA	1,335.4	1,365.3
Parbhani	1,431.8	3,989.0	4,053.7	1,821.9
Nanded	1,952.7	NA	1,555.2	1,585.9
Latur	NA	NA	NA	NA
Hingoli	2,653.7	2,761.6	2,887.4	2,927.0
Jalna	2,998.1	2,319.7	2,357.2	NA
Osmanabad	1,710.7	1,908.0	1,656.0	NA
Beed	NA	NA	NA	NA
Aurangabad	2,016.0	1,884.9	1,773.3	NA
Yavatmal	1,590.1	NA	1,701.3	1,728.6
Wardha	1,381.8	NA	913.9	1,399.4
Bhandara	766.6	1,145.1	1,157.0	1,168.9
Gadchiroli	NA	NA	NA	NA
Nagpur	804.0	NA	1,569.5	1,417.8
Buldhana	1,719.9	NA	918.3	2,013.3
Washim	2,757.3	NA	2,907.4	2,953.6
Chandrapur	NA	NA	NA	NA
Gondia	810.2	1,872.3	986.8	1,155.9
Amravati	1,550.0	1,435.8	1,459.3	NA
Akola	763.6	NA	1,004.0	717.6

Sources: Government of Maharashtra (1991–2011).
Note: NA denotes not available.

TABLE 5A.6
HR for Health in Maharashtra

Category	Sanctioned	Filled	Vacant	Percentage of Vacancy as against Sanctioned Posts
Maharashtra Medical Health Services Grade A and B	8,558	6,993	15,65	18.3
General State Services Grade A and Grade B	515	217	298	57.7
Health Assistants (Male and Female)	3,842	3,454	388	10.1
Multipurpose Health Workers (Male and Female)	17,903	15,458	2,445	13.7
Additional 2nd ANM at Sub-Centre	6,617	6,617	0	0
Staff Nurse at PHC	1,350	809	541	40.1
LHV at PHC	1,129	923	206	18.3
ANM	787	672	115	14.6

Source: Government of Maharashtra (2012b).

TABLE 5A.7
Select Background Characteristics and Place of Antenatal Care: Maharashtra (2007–08)

Background Characteristics	Full Antenatal Care (Percentage)	Any ANC	Place of ANC*		
			Government Health Facility	Private Health Facility	Community-Based Services
15–19	27.3	91.7	38.6	47.8	2.6
20–24	32.5	92.4	44.8	44.8	2.8
25–29	36.7	91.6	43.9	47	3.5
30–34	38.5	91.2	43.3	47.7	3.4
35+	30.9	87.7	47	43.1	2.7
Number of Living Children					
0	27.7	97.3	57	42.9	0
1	38.8	95.7	38.9	56.6	2.5
2	34.9	92.9	45.8	45.9	2.7
3	30.3	89.5	45.5	37.7	3.9
4 and Above	23.8	81.8	48.5	28.3	4.6
Residence					
Rural	32.6	90	43.7	40.2	3.6
Urban	37.1	96.1	44	59.8	1.8
Education					
Non-Literate	22.2	78.1	47.6	24.7	5.1
Less than Five Years	25	90.1	49.4	32.4	2.7
Five–Nine Years	33.8	95.2	47.7	44.1	2.7
Ten or More Years	45.9	97.9	34.1	66	2.4
Religion					
Hindu	35.1	91.1	42.6	46.5	3.2
Muslim	30.1	94.9	45.4	54.9	1.5
Christian	50.5	100	53.6	36.5	8.2
Sikh	*	*	*	*	*
Buddhist/Neo–Buddhist	33.9	94.2	55.1	31.9	2.2
Jain	58.4	100	10.3	91.8	2.1
Others	51.5	80	50.6	25.6	19

Background Characteristics	Full Antenatal Care (Percentage)	Any ANC	Place of ANC*		
			Government Health Facility	Private Health Facility	Community-Based Services
Social Group					
SC	30.2	93.5	54.4	34.4	2.1
ST	32	81.5	49.8	24.7	6.6
OBC	37.2	94.9	44.2	50.5	2.8
Others	34.2	94.5	36.4	57.8	1.9
Wealth Index					
Lowest	24.1	77.2	48.3	19	7.1
Second	27.1	88.2	51.3	27.6	3.6
Middle	31	91.9	47.4	38.3	3.2
Fourth	34.4	95.4	47.8	48.3	2.1
Highest	46.3	98.3	29.5	74	1.8
Maharashtra (15–49)	33.9	91.8	43.8	46.1	3.1

Source: IIPS (2010).

Notes: (i) * indicates those who received any ANC.
(ii) Totals may not add to 100 per cent due to multiple responses, including 'do not know' and 'missing'.

TABLE 5A.8
Percentage of Women Who Received any ANC and Full Antenatal Care, by Districts: Maharashtra (2007–08)

District	Place of ANC			Any ANC	Full Antenatal Care
	Government Health Facility	Private Health Facility	Community-Based Services		
Nandurbar	40.9	22.1	4.3	60.6	24.3
Dhule	43.2	43.7	4.0	76.2	25.7
Jalgaon	32.0	44.7	1.7	80.3	29.3
Buldhana	38.8	51.1	3.6	93.0	27.7
Akola	40.3	49.7	1.4	91.6	31.0
Washim	23.7	54.5	2.1	95.8	23.0
Amravati	39.7	28.1	7.1	94.8	38.3
Wardha	46.3	49.5	1.5	99.2	36.1
Nagpur	55.8	46.8	4.0	98.2	44.9
Bhandara	67.4	33.4	3.6	97.2	47.4
Gondia	74.8	23.5	4.3	94.3	44.3
Gadchiroli	72.3	8.2	16.5	90.2	43.0
Chandrapur	52.1	45.3	1.0	91.5	38.3
Yavatmal	36.6	51.0	3.4	88.0	28.7
Nanded	35.0	47.9	0.2	97.9	26.2
Hingoli	27.1	41.1	2.2	93.2	21.9
Parbhani	35.6	55.7	2.4	85.4	34.0
Jalna	38.9	48.0	0.7	90.9	28.6
Aurangabad	43.8	45.5	1.3	88.0	14.1
Nashik	39.2	47.8	4.0	89.2	39.3
Thane	51.5	40.3	3.3	95.2	41.5
Mumbai (Suburban)	39.7	59.4	7.5	98.5	33.4

	Place of ANC				
District	Government Health Facility	Private Health Facility	Community-Based Services	Any ANC	Full Antenatal Care
Mumbai	58.2	43.5	1.9	98.9	42.7
Raigarh	47.8	49.5	2.0	95.5	30.8
Pune	43.9	59.8	2.3	97.7	52.7
Ahmednagar	43.1	61.2	2.8	96.6	55.0
Beed	36.9	50.6	1.7	92.4	16.0
Latur	36.3	58.4	1.0	93.7	27.6
Osmanabad	43.1	44.8	0.5	95.5	27.2
Solapur	35.8	61.3	0.0	96.8	32.4
Satara	27.4	74.6	1.3	98.8	55.5
Ratnagiri	57.9	43.1	0.7	96.3	37.2
Sindhudurg	66.7	37.1	3.2	99.5	47.2
Kolhapur	39.0	64.4	0.8	97.4	37.4
Sangli	47.8	55.0	1.4	97.3	49.7
Maharashtra (15–49)	**43.8**	**46.1**	**3.1**	**91.8**	**33.9**

Source: IIPS (2010: Tables 4.2 and 4.5b).

TABLE 5A.9
Institutional Deliveries

	Place of Delivery and Assistance Characteristics by District			
District	Percentage of Women Who Had Institutional Deliveries	Home Deliveries	Home Delivery Assisted by Skilled Persons	Percentage of Safe Deliveries
Thane	71.7	26.1	1.5	73.2
Ratnagiri	73.3	26.5	3.4	76.7
Sindhudurg	92.7	6.8	1.3	94
Raigarh	69.2	30.5	5.9	75.1
Satara	87.4	12.3	3.5	90.9
Solapur	67.1	33.3	6.3	73.4
Sangli	76.1	24.3	2.8	78.9
Kolhapur	89	10.1	3.6	92.6
Pune	83.2	16.7	4.7	87.9
Ahmednagar	80.1	18.7	7.1	87.2
Nandurbar	**25.4**	73	8.6	**34**
Dhule	50.5	48	8.9	59.4
Jalgaon	53.1	46.7	12.1	65.2
Nashik	63.5	35.9	5.3	68.8
Parbhani	64.6	35.4	5.6	70.2
Nanded	55.9	43.4	5.5	61.4
Latur	63.9	35.8	7.5	71.4
Hingoli	**41.5**	57.7	5.8	**47.3**
Jalna	65.5	33.4	6	71.5
Osmanabad	58.9	40.9	10.2	69.1
Beed	68.3	30.6	1.4	69.7

Place of Delivery and Assistance Characteristics by District

District	Percentage of Women Who Had Institutional Deliveries	Home Deliveries	Home Delivery Assisted by Skilled Persons	Percentage of Safe Deliveries
Aurangabad	65.8	33.3	10.2	76
Yavatmal	53.4	45.1	6	59.4
Wardha	81.4	18.6	1.9	83.3
Gadchiroli	**23.5**	76.1	11.1	**34.6**
Nagpur	82.2	18.1	2.2	84.4
Bhandara	56.9	42.8	13.4	70.3
Buldhana	66.6	33.1	3.8	70.4
Washim	65.2	34.7	6.8	72
Chandrapur	54.9	45.5	5	59.9
Gondia	53.6	43.3	9.2	62.8
Amravati	63.6	36.8	2.3	65.9
Akola	74.3	24.8	4.1	78.4
Maharashtra (15–49)	63.5	35.9	5.7	69.2

Source: IIPS (2010).

TABLE 5A.10
Vaccination of Children (12–23 Months), by Background Characteristics: Maharashtra (2007–08)

Background Characteristics	Full Vaccination (Percentage)	No Vaccination (Percentage)
Rural	67.6	1.2
Urban	72.6	0.7
Sex of the Child		
Male	69.9	0.9
Female	68.0	1.2
Birth Order		
1	73.6	0.8
2	69.3	0.4
3	67.2	1.0
4 and More	52.6	3.9
Mother's Education		
Non-Literate	48.9	3.2
Less than Five Years	63.6	1.1
Five–Nine Years	73.2	0.5
Ten or More Years	80.4	0.1
Religion		
Hindu	69.4	1.2
Muslim	63.9	0.9
Christian	(47.1)	(0.0)
Sikh	*	*
Buddhist/Neo-Buddhist	(76.0)	0.0
Jain	64.7	(0.0)
Others	*	*

Background Characteristics	Full Vaccination (Percentage)	No Vaccination (Percentage)
Social Group		
SC	69.9	0.8
ST	52.2	2.7
OBC	74.5	0.5
Others	75.0	0.5
Wealth Index		
Lowest	43.2	4.9
Second	57.5	0.8
Middle	69.4	0.8
Fourth	72.7	0.7
Highest	80.7	0.2
Maharashtra (15–49)	69.0	1.0

Source: IIPS (2010).
Notes: (i) Figures within parentheses indicate that they are based on 10–24 unweighted cases.
(ii) * indicates percentage not shown, based on less than 10 unweighted cases.

TABLE 5A.11
Nutritional Status of Women (15–49 Years) in Maharashtra

Characteristics	BMI < 18.5 kg/m²	Number	Haemoglobin < 12 g/dL	Number	BMI ≥ 25 kg/m²	Number
Maharashtra	36.2	7,914	48.4	8,053	14.5	7,914
Residence						
Rural	45.6	4,018	50.6	4,187	6.9	4,018
Urban	26.6	3,896	46.0	3,866	22.3	3,896
Mumbai (Slum)	23.1	ns	46.0	ns	25.1	ns
Mumbai (Non-Slum)	21.4	ns	47.9	ns	30.4	ns
Social Group						
SC	39.9	1,286	51.9	1,316	12.1	1,286
ST	51.6	800	58.9	824	5.8	800
OBC	35.4	2,352	46.8	2,415	14.2	2,352
Others	31.9	3,470	45.7	3,491	17.5	3,470
Wealth Index						
Lowest	56.7	719	55.3	765	2.1	719
Second	51.0	1,109	54.2	1,140	3.7	1,109
Middle	45.0	1,403	50.7	1,457	7.4	1,403
Fourth	31.9	1,955	47.1	1,997	13.9	1,955
Highest	23.4	2,728	43.7	2,694	26.3	2,728

Source: IIPS and Macro International (2008).
Note: ns indicates not shown in the report.

TABLE 5A.12
Percentage of Children below Five Years Classified as Undernourished and Anaemic in Select States of India: 2005–06

State	Height for Age		Weight for Height		Weight for Age		Anaemia	
	Stunting (SD<–2)	Severe Stunting (SD<–3)	Wasting (SD<–2)	Severe Wasting (SD<–3)	Under–weight (SD<–2)	Severe Under–weight (SD<–3)	Anaemia* (Haemoglobin < 9.99 g/dL)	Severe Anaemia (Haemoglobin < 7 g/dL)
All-India	48.0	23.7	19.8	6.4	42.5	15.8	69.5	2.9
Andhra Pradesh	42.7	18.7	12.2	3.5	32.5	9.9	70.8	3.6
Assam	46.5	20.9	13.7	4.0	36.4	11.4	69.6	2.2
Bihar	55.6	29.1	27.1	8.3	55.9	24.1	78.0	1.6
Chhattisgarh	52.9	24.8	19.5	5.6	47.1	16.4	71.2	2.0
Gujarat	51.7	25.5	18.7	5.8	44.6	16.3	69.7	3.6
Jharkhand	49.8	26.8	32.3	11.8	56.5	26.1	70.3	1.9
Karnataka	43.7	20.5	17.6	5.9	37.6	12.8	70.4	3.2
Kerala	24.5	6.5	15.9	4.1	22.9	4.7	44.5	0.5
Madhya Pradesh	50.0	26.3	35.0	12.6	60.0	27.3	74.1	3.4
Maharashtra	46.3	19.1	16.5	5.2	37.0	11.9	63.4	1.8
Odisha	45.0	19.6	19.5	5.2	40.7	13.4	65.0	1.6
Rajasthan	43.7	22.7	20.4	7.3	39.9	15.3	69.7	6.7
Tamil Nadu	30.9	10.9	22.2	8.9	29.8	6.4	64.2	2.6
Uttar Pradesh	56.8	32.4	14.8	5.1	42.4	16.4	73.9	3.6
West Bengal	44.6	17.8	16.9	4.5	38.7	11.1	61.0	1.5

Source: IIPS and Macro International (2008).
Note: * indicates data on children aged 6–59 months.

TABLE 5A.13
Prevalence of Anaemia among Children below Five Years in Maharashtra

Characteristics	Anaemia* (Percentage)		Number of Children
	Anaemia (Haemoglobin < 10.99 g/dL)	Severe Anaemia (Haemoglobin < 7 g/dL)	
Maharashtra	63.4	1.8	2,269
Residence			
Rural	66.8	2.4	1,308
Urban	58.7	1	962
Mumbai (Slum)	50.2	2.3	ns
Mumbai (Non-Slum)	46.9	0.7	ns
Gender			
Male	66.0	2.6	1,235
Female	60.1	0.9	1,034
Social Group			
SC	64.1	1.2	430
ST	67.6	2.5	285
OBC	62.5	2.8	603
Others	62.3	1.2	951

Characteristics	Anaemia* (Percentage)		Number of Children
	Anaemia (Haemoglobin < 10.99 g/dL)	Severe Anaemia (Haemoglobin < 7 g/dL)	
Wealth Index			
Lowest	71.6	3.1	283
Second	67.5	2.4	361
Middle	60.5	2.6	431
Fourth	67.2	1.2	599
Highest	55.1	0.8	594

Source: IIPS and Macro International (2008).
Notes: (i) * indicates data children aged 6–59 months.
(ii) ns indicates not shown in the report.

TABLE 5A.14
Vitamin A Coverage in Maharashtra

Background Characteristics	Children Who Received at least One Dose of Vitamin A	Children Who Received Three–Five Doses of Vitamin A
Age of the Child		
12–23 months	70.9	20.8
24–35 Months	79.2	37.4
Residence		
Rural	74.3	29.6
Urban	76.3	28.4
Sex of the child		
Male	75.0	29.2
Female	74.7	29.4
Birth order		
1	76.4	30.0
2	77.3	29.4
3	72.5	28.0
4+	65.6	26.8
Mother's Education		
Non–Literate	61.5	29.5
Less than Five Years	70.6	29.9
Five–Nine years	78.5	29.3
10 or more years	82.3	28.9
Religion		
Hindu	75.1	29.4
Muslim	68.7	29.2
Christian	80.6	40.3
Sikh	*	*
Buddhist/Neo-Buddhist	81.5	25.5
Jain	84.1	45.2
Others	(46.2)	(66.7)
Social Group		
SC	76.2	29.4
ST	64.3	29.9
OBC	78.1	29.0
Others	78.4	29.1

Background Characteristics	Children Who Received at least One Dose of Vitamin A	Children Who Received Three–Five Doses of Vitamin A
Wealth Index		
Lowest	60.7	29.6
Second	66.2	29.7
Middle	75.2	28.6
Fourth	77.7	30.0
Highest	81.4	28.8
Maharashtra (15–49)	74.9	29.3
Maharashtra (15–44)	70.5	28.3

Source: IIPS (2010).

Notes: (i) Findings are presented in terms of percentage.
(ii) * Indicates percentage not shown, based on less than 10 unweighted cases.
(iii) Figures within parentheses indicate that they are based on 10–24 unweighted cases.

TABLE 5A.15
Knowledge and Practices Related to Diarrhoea Management

Background Characteristics	Children Suffered from Diarrhoea[1]	Knowledge of Diarrhoea Management	Need to Give ORS	Salt and Sugar Solution	Give ORS	Continue Normal Food	Continue Breastfeeding	Give Plenty of Fluids
Age Group								
15–19	21.7[2]	57.7	31.0	36.8	41.0	3.2	7.2	2.3
20–24	18.1	69.4	39.3	42.7	49.0	4.7	8.4	3.3
25–29	16.6	78.4	41.5	49.8	48.4	4.4	6.1	3.5
30–34	14.0	78.9	35.9	54.8	53.9	4.1	5.2	3.9
35–39	19.3	78.2	32.0	56.5	46.8	3.7	4.3	3.6
40–44		77.3	29.2	55.2		4.3	4.7	3.1
45–49		77.1	30.1	54.6		4.1	5.1	3.8
Residence								
Rural	20.1	72.4	31.9	48.6	42.6	4.3	6.2	3.3
Urban	19.2	81.2	42.1	56.4	48.4	3.7	4.9	3.9
Mother's Education								
Non–Literate	18.7	67.7	23.6	42.6	37.8	4.0	6.1	2.7
< Five years	23.4	74.6	26.5	46.9	40.2	3.6	4.7	3.3
Five–Nine years	20.5	76.1	35.5	53.2	43.0	3.7	5.5	3.1
≥ 10 years	18.8	84.3	53.3	60.5	53.2	5.2	6.4	5.0
Social Groups								
SC	23.1	76.9	36.9	51.7	47.8	4.0	6.0	3.9
ST	19.9	65.2	34.3	46.8	39.7	6.0	8.8	4.6
OBC	20.1	76.3	37.4	55.1	41.8	4.4	6.3	3.8
Others	18.4	78.2	33.2	49.5	46.7	3.3	4.1	2.6
Wealth Index								
Lowest	20.5	62.1	29.2	41.7	41.4	4.7	7.9	3.2
Second	21.4	68.9	26.5	42.1	41.7	4.1	6.5	2.9
Middle	21.1	73.8	28.9	46.3	39.2	4.1	5.9	3.1
Fourth	20.8	77.0	34.9	51.9	44.3	3.9	5.2	3.3
Highest	17.1	83.8	46.5	61.7	51.3	4.3	5.3	4.2
Maharashtra	19.9	75.0	35.2	51.1	44.2	4.2	5.8	3.5

Source: IIPS (2010).

Notes: (i) [1] Indicates last two weeks prior to survey.
(ii) [2] Indicates less than 25 years.

TABLE 5A.16
Coverage of Nutrition-Related ICDS for Children in Maharashtra

Characteristics	Percentage of 0–71-Month-Old Children Residing in an Area Covered by an AWC	Number	Percentage of 0–71-Month-Old Children Who Received Supplementary Food* from an AWC	Number	Percentage of 0-59-Month-Old Children Whose Growth Was Monitored at an AWC**	Number
Maharashtra	74.7	3,782	42.4	3,782	37.4	2,373
Residence						
Rural	97.9	1,750	51.2	1,750	45.4	1,673
Urban	47.8	2,032	21.5	2,032	18.1	700
Mumbai (Slum)	54.5	ns	15.7	ns	11.2	ns
Mumbai (Non-Slum)	22.8	ns	6.3	ns	5.8	ns
Gender						
Male	74.9	2,014	42.0	2,014	36.9	1,275
Female	74.5	1,768	43.0	1,768	37.9	1,098
Social Group						
SC	75.7	609	52.4	609	46.2	390
ST	90.7	473	58.9	473	54.7	350
OBC	82.4	1,012	38.2	1,012	34.3	697
Others	65.1	1,678	35.1	1,678	29.7	931
Wealth Index						
Lowest	96.6	491	54.5	491	43.9	376
Second	90.4	547	63.8	547	57.0	423
Middle	87.8	691	51.5	691	45.8	506
Fourth	73.6	981	32.4	981	30.0	625
Highest	49.3	1,072	15.0	1,072	13.9	442

Source: IIPS and Macro International (2008).
Notes: (i) * Supplementary food includes both food cooked and served at the AWC on a daily basis and food given in the form of take-home rations.
(ii) ** Indicates that weight was taken for growth monitoring.
(iii) ns indicates not shown in the report.

TABLE 5A.17
Breastfeeding Practices in Maharashtra

Characteristics	Percentage of Children below Five Years Who Started Breastfeeding within One Hour of Birth (NFHS-3)	Percentage of Children below Three Years Who Started Breastfeeding within One Hour of birth (DLHS-3)	Percentage of Children below Five Years Who Did Not Receive Pre-lacteal Feeds (NFHS-3)	Percentage of Children below Three Years Who Did Not Receive Pre-lacteal Feeds (DLHS-3)	Percentage of Children below Three Years Who Were Exclusively Breastfed for First Six Months (NFHS-3)	Percentage of Children below Three Years Who Were Exclusively Breastfed for First Six Months (DLHS-3)
Maharashtra	52.0	52.5	67.8	–	53.0	53.9
Residence						
Rural	52.5	52.8	69.3	–	–	53.5
Urban	51.5	51.8	66.2	–	–	55.1
Mumbai (Slum)	50.0	–	60.8	–	–	–
Mumbai (Non-Slum)	71.1	–	78.2	–	–	–
Gender						
Male	53.1	–	67.9	–	–	–
Female	50.8	–	68.0	–	–	–
Social Group						
SC	52.5	56.9	74.6	–	–	49.2
ST	39.7	47.6	69.5	–	–	59.5
OBC	55.1	56.1	71.1	–	–	56.5
Others	53.5	51.1	63.2	–	–	50.7
Wealth Index						
Lowest	43.8	43.3	69.8	–	–	54.3
Second	49.2	51.4	62.4	–	–	54.4
Middle	53.6	55.2	66.6	–	–	52.3
Fourth	53.7	55.6	68.7	–	–	54.2
Highest	54.1	52.5	69.4	–	–	54.6

Sources: IIPS (2010); IIPS and Macro International (2008).

Tables from Chapter 6

TABLE 6A.1
IMR and U5MR in Slums and Non-Slums

	IMR	U5MR		IMR	U5MR
Delhi	40.6	48.5	**Mumbai**	30.3	36.6
Slum	54.1	72.8	Slum	24.9	32.7
Non-Slum	36.1	40.4	Non-Slum	40.1	43.6
Meerut	62.8	77.5	**Nagpur**	42.8	49.9
Slum	71.2	86.1	Slum	48.4	59.5
Non-Slum	55	69.4	Non-Slum	39.2	43.6
Kolkata	41.3	48.8	**Hyderabad**	34.9	40.7
Slum	33.4	44.7	Slum	27.9	33.7
Non-Slum	47	51.6	Non-Slum	36.4	42.3
Indore	42	51.4	**Chennai**	27.6	35.1
Slum	56.4	64.4	Slum	38	46.3
Non-Slum	38.4	48.2	Non-Slum	24.2	31.5

Source: Gupta et al. (2009).

TABLE 6A.2
Nutritional Status of Children (Percentage of Children Stunted, Wasted and Underweight)

	Height for Age	Weight for Height	Weight for Age
Delhi	40.9	15.3	26.5
Slum	50.9	14.5	35.3
Non-Slum	37.9	15.6	23.9
Meerut	43.8	9.5	28.4
Slum	46.2	9.4	26.3
Non-Slum	41.6	9.5	30.3
Kolkata	27.5	15.3	20.8
Slum	32.6	16.8	26.8
Non-Slum	23.1	14	15.6
Indore	32.5	28.9	39.3
Slum	39.6	34	49.6
Non-Slum	30.6	27.6	36.7
Mumbai	45.4	16.2	32.6
Slum	47.4	16.1	36.1
Non-Slum	41.5	16.4	25.8
Nagpur	34.7	16.5	33.6
Slum	47.5	18.1	41.7
Non-Slum	26.5	15.5	28.4
Hyderabad	32.1	9.4	19.8
Slum	32.4	11.1	26
Non-Slum	32	9.1	18.4
Chennai	25.4	18.8	23.1
Slum	27.6	22.8	31.6
Non-Slum	24.8	17.6	20.6

Source: Gupta et al. (2009).
Note: Values shown are those below SD of −2.

TABLE 6A.3
Distribution of Households, by Material of Roof: Maharashtra and India (2001–11)

Material of Roof	2001		2011		Change Percentage	
	Maharashtra	India	Maharashtra	India	Maharashtra	India
Grass, Thatch, Bamboo, Wood or Mud, etc.	10.1	21.9	6.1	15.1	−4.0	−6.8
Tiles	31.0	32.6	21.5	23.8	−9.5	−8.8
GI, Metal or Asbestos Sheets	34.8	11.6	37.3	15.9	2.5	4.3
Concrete	21.1	19.8	30.2	29.1	9.1	9.3
Others	3.0	14.1	4.9	16.2	1.9	2.1

Distribution of Households, by Material of Wall: Maharashtra and India (2001–11)

Material of Wall	2001		2011		Change Percentage	
	Maharashtra	India	Maharashtra	India	Maharashtra	India
Grass, Thatch or Bamboo, etc.	7.3	10.2	5.3	9.0	−2.0	−1.2
Mud or Unburnt Bricks	29.5	32.2	21.7	23.7	−7.8	−8.5
Stone	9.8	9.4	13.4	14.2	3.6	4.8
Burnt Bricks	41.3	43.7	45.9	47.5	4.6	3.8
Others	12.1	4.5	13.7	5.7	1.6	1.2

Distribution of Households, by Material of Floor: Maharashtra and India (2001–11)

Material of Floor	2001		2011		Change Percentage	
	Maharashtra	India	Maharashtra	India	Maharashtra	India
Mud	50.6	57.1	36.1	46.5	−14.5	−10.6
Stone	4.1	5.8	8.3	8.1	4.2	2.3
Cement	13.7	26.5	16.4	31.1	2.7	4.6
Mosaic or Floor Tiles	29.3	7.3	36.8	10.8	7.5	3.5
Others	2.3	3.3	2.4	3.5	0.1	0.2

Source: Government of India (2011c).
Note: Values indicate percentage of households.

TABLE 6A.4
Percentage of Households Having Tap Water as a Source of Drinking Water, by Districts: Maharashtra (2011 and 2001)

State and Districts	Tap Water 2011	2001	Change
Maharashtra	67.9	64	3.9
Mumbai	97.8	96.6	1.2
Mumbai (Suburban)	96.5	98.2	−1.7
Jalgaon	88.7	85.4	3.3
Kolhapur	85.4	76.9	8.5
Dhule	83.9	75.1	8.8
Thane	80.8	76.5	4.3
Pune	80.6	75.2	5.4
Amravati	77.8	70.4	7.4
Nagpur	76.4	70.7	5.7
Raigarh	73.9	56.7	17.2
Satara	73.4	69.2	4.2
Sangli	67.3	65.5	1.8
Wardha	63.5	50.7	12.8
Nashik	63.2	59.3	3.9
Aurangabad	62.4	62.1	0.3
Ratnagiri	60.5	41	19.5
Akola	58.7	60.3	−1.6
Latur	58.4	54	4.4
Solapur	57	54.7	2.3
Nandurbar	56.8	52.4	4.4
Osmanabad	56.6	50.1	6.5
Buldhana	54.1	51	3.1
Ahmednagar	50.4	47.9	2.5
Nanded	47	49.9	−2.9
Yavatmal	43.9	40.7	3.2
Beed	42.4	43.4	−1
Jalna	41.4	43.9	−2.5
Parbhani	41.2	39.1	2.1
Washim	41.1	37	4.1
Chandrapur	40.6	36.3	4.3
Bhandara	38	35.6	2.4
Hingoli	35.9	26.1	9.8
Sindhudurg	30.7	22.3	8.4
Gadchiroli	19.5	17.2	2.3
Gondia	17.5	15.7	1.8

Source: Government of India (2011c).

TABLE 6A.5
Percentage of Households Having Latrines within Their Premises

State and Districts	Latrine within Primises	
	2001	2011
Maharashtra	36.0	53.1
Sindhudurg	32.2	75.9
Nagpur	60.9	75.7
Kolhapur	37.8	74.5
Pune	46.4	73.8
Satara	24.2	71.1
Ratnagiri	28.4	69.4
Mumbai	43.6	67.0
Thane	55.4	67.0
Sangli	32.8	64.9
Raigarh	33.1	62.0
Bhandara	35.5	61.2
Wardha	41.0	56.7
Mumbai (Suburban)	43.5	54.7
Amravati	43.4	53.7
Gondia	26.2	52.4
Aurangabad	38.7	48.9
Nashik	30.8	46.8
Ahmednagar	22.5	46.1
Akola	38.3	46.1
Chandrapur	32.5	43.3
Solapur	21.4	41.3
Latur	24.0	37.6
Jalna	18.9	36.5
Jalgaon	26.7	35.5
Buldhana	22.8	35.3
Washim	19.1	33.8
Nanded	24.4	33.1
Hingoli	15.9	32.4
Dhule	21.3	31.2
Yavatmal	23.1	31.0
Parbhani	25.5	28.8
Nandurbar	20.2	28.7
Osmanabad	22.9	27.7
Gadchiroli	18.8	27.0
Beed	16.8	25.1

Source: Government of India (2011c).

Bibliography

Accountability Initiative. 2011a. 'Analysis of State Budgets: Elementary Education'. Available online at http://www.accountabilityindia.in/sites/default/files/budget-education/apf_-_study_of_state_budgets_brief_mar_7_yamain.pdf (accessed on 31 October 2011).

———. 2011b. 'PAISA 2011: Do Schools Get Their Money?' Available online at http://www.accountabilityindia.in/sites/default/files/state-report-cards/final_paisa_report_2011.pdf (accessed on 8 March 2013).

———. 2013. 'Budget Briefs: Sarva Shiksha Abhiyan, GOI 2012-13'. Available online at http://www.accountabilityindia.in/sites/default/files/ssa_budget_briefs_2013_0.pdf (accessed on 28 February 2012).

Agha, S. 2000. 'The Determinants of Infant Mortality in Pakistan', *Social Science and Medicine*, 51 (2): 199–208.

Black, R., L. H. Allen, Z. A. Bhutta, L. E. Caulfield, M. de Onis, M. Ezzati, C. Mathers and J. Rivera. 2008. Maternal and Child Undernutrition: Global and Regional Exposures and Health Consequences', *The Lancet*, 371 (9608): 243–60.

Central Statistics Office. 2010. *Millennium Development Goals: States of India Report 2010*. New Delhi: Central Statistics Office, Ministry of Statistics & Programme Implementation, Government of India.

Centre for Development Studies. 2006. *Human Development Report 2005*. Thiruvananthapuram, India: State Planning Board, Government of Kerala.

Chandrasekhar, S. and M. R. Montgomery. 2011. 'Broadening Poverty Definitions in India: Basic Needs in Urban Housing', *Human Settlements Working Paper Series, Poverty Reduction in Urban Areas - 27*. London: International Institute for Environment and Development.

Chattopadhyay, A. and V. Durdhawale. 2009. 'Primary Schooling in a Tribal District of Maharashtra: Some Policy Relevance', *International Journal of Educational Administration and Policy Studies*, 1 (5): 070–078.

Chugh, S. 2008. *The Government Primary School Mid-Day Meals Scheme: A Study of Best Practices in the Implementation of Mid-day Meal Programme in Maharashtra*. New Delhi: National University of Educational Planning and Administration.

Development and Planning Department. 2004. *West Bengal Human Development Report 2004*. Kolkata, India: Development and Planning Department, Government of West Bengal.

Directorate of Census Operations Maharashtra. 1951. *Primary Census Abstract, 1951*. Mumbai, India: Ministry of Home Affairs, Government of India.

———. 1961. *Primary Census Abstract, 1961*. Mumbai, India: Ministry of Home Affairs, Government of India.

———. 1971. *Primary Census Abstract, 1971*. Mumbai, India: Ministry of Home Affairs, Government of India.

———. 1981. *Primary Census Abstract, 1981*. Mumbai, India: Ministry of Home Affairs, Government of India.

———. 1991. *Primary Census Abstract, 1991*. Mumbai, India: Ministry of Home Affairs, Government of India.

———. 2001. *Primary Census Abstract, 2001*. Mumbai, India: Ministry of Home Affairs, Government of India.

———. 2011. *Provisional Population Totals, 2011*. Mumbai, India: Ministry of Home Affairs, Government of India.

Duggal, R. and P. Raymus. 2007. 'Understanding Unit Costs: An Exploratory Study of Selected Health Care Facilities in Maharashtra', Unpublished MS. Available with CEHAT, Mumbai.

Government of Bombay. 1949. *Wandrekar Committee Report on Programme of Educational Expansion in the Adiwasi Area of Thane District*.

Government of India. 1983. 'Survey Results: Per Capita Per Diem Intake of Nutrients, NSS 27th Round (October 1972-September 1973)', *Sarvekshana*, 6 (3–4): S1–S88.

———. 1986. 'Results of the Third Quinquennial Survey on Consumer Expenditure, NSS 38th Round (1983)', *Sarvekshana*, 9 (4): S1–S102.

———. 1989. 'Results of Per Capita Consumption of Cereals for Various Sections of Population,

NSS 38th Round (1983)', *Sarvekshana*, 13 (2): S1–S176.

Government of India. 1993. *Report of the Expert Group on Estimation of Proportion and Number of Poor*. New Delhi: Perspective Planning Division, Planning Commission, Government of India.

———. 1997a. *Employment and Unemployment Situation in India, 1993-1994*. NSS 50th Round (July 1993-June 1994), Report No. 409. New Delhi: National Sample Statistical Organisation, Ministry of Statistics & Programme Implementation, Government of India.

———. 1997b. 'Survey Results on Nutritional Intake in India, NSS 50th Round (July 1993-June 1994)', *Sarvekshana*, 21 (2): S1–S214.

———. 2001a. *Level and Pattern of Consumer Expenditure in India 1999-2000*. NSS 55th Round (July 1999-June 2000), Report No. 457(55/1.0/3). New Delhi: National Sample Survey Organisation, Ministry of Statistics & Programme Implementation, Government of India.

———. 2001b. *Nutritional Intake in India 1999-2000*. NSS 55th Round (July 1999-June 2000), Report No. 471(55/1.0/9). New Delhi: National Sample Survey Organisation, Ministry of Statistics & Programme Implementation, Government of India.

———. 2001c. *Employment and Unemployment Situation in India, 1999-2000*. NSS 55th Round, (July 1999-June 2000), Report No. 458. New Delhi: National Sample Statistical Organisation, Ministry of Statistics & Programme Implementation, Government of India.

———. 2001d. *Census of India 2001: Houselisting and Housing Census Data Tables, Maharashtra*. New Delhi: Office of the Registrar General & Census Commissioner, Ministry of Home Affairs, Government of India.

———. 2004. *School Water Supply, Sanitation and Hygiene Education: India*. Technical Note Series. Department of Drinking Water Supply, Ministry of Rural Development, Government of India.

———. 2006a. *Level and Pattern of Consumer Expenditure, 2004-2005*. NSS 61st Round (July 2004-June 2005), Report No. 508(61/1.0/1). New Delhi: National Sample Survey Organisation, Ministry of Statistics & Programme Implementation, Government of India.

———. 2006b. *Employment and Unemployment Situation in India, 2004*. NSS 61st Round (January–June 2004), Report No. 515, Part I. New Delhi: National Sample Statistical Organisation, Ministry of Statistics & Programme Implementation, Government of India.

———. 2006c. *Employment and Unemployment Situation in India, 2004*. NSS 61st Round (January–June 2004), Report No. 515, Part II. New Delhi: National Sample Statistical Organisation, Ministry of Statistics & Programme Implementation, Government of India.

———. 2007. *Nutritional Intake in India 2004-2005*. NSS 61st Round (July 2004-June 2005), Report No. 513(61/1.0/6). New Delhi: National Sample Survey Organisation, Ministry of Statistics & Programme Implementation, Government of India.

———. 2009. *Report of the Expert Group to Review the Methodology for Estimation of Poverty*. New Delhi: Planning Commission, Government of India.

———. 2010. *Report of the Committee on Slum Statistics/Census*. New Delhi: Ministry of Housing and Urban Poverty Alleviation, National Buildings Organisation, Government of India.

———. 2011a. *Census of India 2011: Provisional Population Totals: Maharashtra*. New Delhi: Office of the Registrar General & Census Commissioner, Ministry of Home Affairs, Government of India.

———. 2011b. 'Census of India 2011: Release of Provisional Population Totals of Maharashtra State: Maharashtra at a Glance'. Available online at http://censusindia.gov.in/2011-prov-results/data_files/maharastra/maha_at_aglance.pdf (accessed on 4 July 2011).

———. 2011c. *Census of India 2011: H–Series: Houses, Household Amenities and Assets, Houselisting and Housing Census Data Tables, Maharashtra*. New Delhi: Office of the Registrar General & Census Commissioner, Ministry of Home Affairs, Government of India.

———. 2011d. *Key Indicators of Employment and Unemployment in India 2009-10*. NSS 66th Round (July 2009-June 2010), Report No. NSS KI (66/10). New Delhi: National Statistical Organisation, Ministry of Statistics & Programme Implementation, Government of India.

———. 2012a. 'Nirmal Bharat Abhiyan', *Ministry of Drinking Water and Sanitation, Government of India*. Available online at http://tsc.gov.in/tsc/NBA/NBAHome.aspx (accessed on 23 October 2011).

———. 2012b. 'Nirmal Gram Puraskar', *Nirmal Bharat Abhiyan, Ministry of Drinking Water and Sanitation, Government of India*. Available online at http://nirmalgrampuraskar.nic.in (accessed on 23 October 2011).

———. 2005–12. *India Health Profile*. New Delhi: Central Bureau Of Health Intelligence.

Government of Maharashtra. 1970–2009. Unpublished reports available with the Directorate of Education, DES.

———. 1993. *Report of the Expert Committee on Inclusion of Communities in the List of Scheduled Castes, Vimukta Jati, Nomadic Tribes and Other Backward Classes, in the State of Maharashtra*. Pune, India: Department of Social Welfare.

———. 2000. *Socio-Economic Information of Tribals in Tribal Area of Maharashtra State*. Pune, India: Tribal Research & Training Institute, Government of Maharashtra.

Government of Maharashtra. 2002. *Human Development Report Maharashtra 2002*. Mumbai, India: Government of Maharashtra.

———. 2009. *A Report on 'Household Consumer Expenditure' Based on Data Collected in Central, State and Pooled Samples of 61st Round of National Sample Survey (July, 2004–June, 2005)*, Mumbai, India: Directorate of Economics and Statistics, Planning Department.

———. 2010. *Economic Survey of Maharashtra 2009-10*. Mumbai, India: Directorate of Economics and Statistics, Planning Department, Government of Maharashtra.

———. 2011. *Economic Survey of Maharashtra 2010-11*. Mumbai, India: Directorate of Economics and Statistics, Planning Department, Government of Maharashtra.

———. 2012a. *Economic Survey of Maharashtra 2011-12*. Mumbai, India: Directorate of Economics and Statistics, Planning Department, Government of Maharashtra.

———. 2012b. *Public Health Department: Annual Report 2012*. Mumbai, India: Public Health Department, Government of Maharashtra.

———. 2012c, Report of Public Health Department (Unpublished), Pune, Family Health and Welfare, Government of Maharashtra

———. 1991–2011. Various District Socio-Economic Reviews. Mumbai, India: Department of Economics and Statistics, Planning Department, Government of Maharashtra. Available online at http://mahades.maharashtra.gov.in/ (accessed on 4 July 2011).

———. 2001–07. *Civil Budget Estimate*. Mumbai, India: Public Health Department Finance Accounts.

———. n.d. 'Directorate of Health Services: Public Health Department'. Available online at www.maha-arogya.gov.in/ (accessed on 4 July 2011).

Government of Orissa. 2004. *Human Development Report 2004: Orissa*. Bhubaneswar, India: Planning and Coordination Department, Government of Orissa.

Government of Uttar Pradesh. 2003. *Human Development Report 2003: Uttar Pradesh*. Lucknow, India: Planning Department, Government of Uttar Pradesh.

Govinda Rao, M. and Mita Choudhury. March 2012. 'Health Care Financing Reforms in India', Working Paper No: 2012–100. National Institute of Public Finance and Policy.

Gupta, K. F. Arnold and H. Lhungdim. 2009. *Health and Living Conditions in Eight Indian Cities: National Family Health Survey (NFHS-3), India, 2005-06*. Mumbai, India: International Institute for Population Sciences and Calverton, MD: ICF Macro.

Health Education to Villages. n.d. 'Rajmata Jijau Mother-Child Health and Nutrition Mission: About the Nutrition Mission'. Available online at http://hetv.org/nutritionmission/about/index.html (accessed on 7 March 2012).

IIPS. 1995. *National Family Health Survey (MCH and Family Planning) (NFHS-1), India, 1992–93: Maharashtra*. Bombay, India: International Institute for Population Sciences.

———. 2001. *Reproductive and Child Health Project, Rapid Household Survey (Phase I & II): District Level Household and Facility Survey (DLHS-1), India, 1998–99: Maharashtra*. Mumbai, India: International Institute for Population Sciences.

———. 2006. *Reproductive and Child Health: District Level Household Survey (DLHS-2), India, 2002–04: Maharashtra*. Mumbai, India: International Institute for Population Sciences.

———. 2010. *District Level Household and Facility Survey (DLHS-3), India, 2007–08: Maharashtra*. Mumbai, India: International Institute for Population Sciences.

———. 2012. *Comprehensive Nutrition Survey in Maharashtra (CNSM), 2012: Fact Sheet, Provisional Data*. Mumbai, India: International Institute of Population Sciences.

———. n.d. *Key Indicators for Maharashtra from NFHS-3*. Mumbai: International Institute for Population Sciences.

IIPS and Macro International. 2008. *National Family Health Survey (NFHS-3), India, 2005–06: Maharashtra*. Mumbai, India: International Institute for Population Sciences.

IIPS and ORC Macro. 2001. *National Family Health Survey (NFHS-2), India, 1998–99: Maharashtra*. Mumbai, India: International Institute for Population Sciences.

Indian Institute of Education. 2004. *Developing a Quality Improvement Plan For Rural Education in Maharashtra*. Pune, India: Indian Institute of Education.

Institute of Applied Manpower Research. 2011. *India Human Development Report 2011: Towards Social Inclusion*. New Delhi: Oxford University Press.

Isalkar, U. 2011. 'Health Dept to Implement Scheme for the Poor', *The Times of India*, 24 May. Available online at http://articles.timesofindia.indiatimes.com/2011-05-24/pune/29577397_1_bpl-families-rsby-rashtriya-swasthya-bima-yojana (accessed on 14 July 2011).

Jayachandran, U. 2002. *Socio-Economic Determinants of School Attendance in India*. Working Paper No. 103. New Delhi: Centre for Development Economics, Delhi School of Economics, University of Delhi.

———. 2007. 'How High Are Drop Out Rates in India?', *Economic & Political Weekly*, 42 (11): 982–83.

———. 2010. *Socio-Economic Analysis of Elementary Education in India*, Ph.D. Thesis submitted to the Department of Economics, Delhi School of Economics, New Delhi.

Kishor, S. and Gupta, K. 2009. *Gender Equality and Women's Empowerment in India*. National

Family Health Survey (NFHS-3), India, 2005-06. Mumbai, India: International Institute for Population Sciences and Calverton, MD: ICF Macro.

Kumar, A. K. S. 2007. 'Why are Levels of Child Malnutrition Not Improving?', *Economic & Political Weekly*, 42 (15): 1337–45.

Kurian, O. C., S. Wagle and P. Raymus. 2011. *Mapping the Flow of User Fees in a Public Hospital*. Mumbai, India: Centre for Enquiry into Health and Allied Themes.

MHADA. 2008. 'Jawaharlal Nehru National Urban Renewal Mission', *Maharashtra Housing and Area Development Authority*. Available online at http://mhada.maharashtra.gov.in/?q=jnnurm (accessed on 10 November 2011).

Mehta, A. C. 2004. *Elementary Education in India: Where Do We Stand? Analytical Report 2003*. New Delhi: National Institute of Educational Planning and Administration.

———. 2005. *Elementary Education in India: Where Do We Stand? State Report Cards 2004*. New Delhi: National Institute of Educational Planning and Administration.

———. 2006. *Elementary Education in India: Where Do We Stand? State Report Cards 2005*. New Delhi: National Institute of Educational Planning and Administration.

———. 2007. *Elementary Education in India: Where Do We Stand? State Report Cards 2005-06*. New Delhi: National University of Educational Planning and Administration.

———. 2008. *Elementary Education in India: Where Do We Stand? State Report Cards 2006-07*. New Delhi: National University of Educational Planning and Administration.

———. 2009. *Elementary Education in India: Where Do We Stand? State Report Cards 2007-08*. New Delhi: National University of Educational Planning and Administration.

———. 2011. *Elementary Education in India: Where Do We Stand? State Report Cards 2008-09*. New Delhi: National University of Educational Planning and Administration.

———. 2012. *Elementary Education in India: Where Do We Stand? State Report Cards 2009-10*. New Delhi: National University of Educational Planning and Administration.

Ministry of Drinking Water and Sanitation. 2011. 'National Rural Drinking Water Programme (Rajiv Gandhi National Drinking Water Mission)', *Ministry of Drinking Water and Sanitation, Government of India*. Available online at http://indiawater.gov.in/imisreports/nrdwpmain.aspx (accessed on 10 November 2011).

Ministry of Human Resource Development. 2007. *Selected Educational Statistics 2004-05*. New Delhi: Department of Higher Education—Statistics Division, Ministry of Human Resource Development, Government of India.

Ministry of Rural Development. 2009. *Movement Towards Ensuring People's Drinking Water Security In Rural India: Framework for Implementation 2009-2012*. New Delhi: Department of Drinking Water Supply, Ministry of Rural Development, Government of India.

Mishra, S., R. Duggal, L. Lingam and A. Pitre. 2008. *A Report on Health Inequities in Maharashtra*. Pune, India: SATHI (Support for Advocacy and Training into Health Initiatives).

Mishra, S., R. Duggal and P. Raymus. 2004. 'Health and Healthcare Situation in Jalna, Yavatmal and Nandurbar'. *Report submitted to UNDP, Planning Commission, Government of India and State Planning Board, Government of Maharashtra*.

MPCB. 2007. *State of Environment Report for Maharashtra*. Mumbai, India: Maharashtra Pollution Control Board and Indira Gandhi Institute of Development Research and New Delhi: Ministry of Environment and Forests, Government of India.

MPSP. 2009. 'Data from Secondary Education Management Information System (SEMIS), 2008-2009', Unpublished MS. Available with Maharashtra Prathamik Shikshan Parishad, Mumbai.

———. 2010. 'Data from Secondary Education Management Information System (SEMIS), 2009-2010', Unpublished MS. Available with Maharashtra Prathamik Shikshan Parishad, Mumbai.

———. 2011. 'Data from Secondary Education Management Information System (SEMIS), 2010-2011', Unpublished MS. Available with Maharashtra Prathamik Shikshan Parishad, Mumbai.

———. 2012. 'Data from Secondary Education Management Information System (SEMIS), 2011-2012', Unpublished MS. Available with Maharashtra Prathamik Shikshan Parishad, Mumbai.

———. n.d. 'Annual Working Plan and Budget, 2011–12', Unpublished MS. Available with Maharashtra Prathamik Shikshan Parishad, Mumbai.

Municipal Corporation of Greater Mumbai. 2010. *Mumbai Human Development Report 2009*. New Delhi: Oxford University Press.

Mutatkar, R. 2007. *Social Group Disparities, Ethnicity and Poverty in India*, Unpublished Ph.D. Thesis submitted to the Indira Gandhi Institute of Development Research, Mumbai.

Mutatkar, R. K. 2004. *Action Strategies for Health and Education in Tribal Nandurbar: Maharashtra Human Development Action Research Study*. Mumbai, India: Indira Gandhi Institute of Development Research.

NACO. 2008. *HIV Sentinel Surveillance and HIV Estimation in India 2007: A Technical Brief*. National AIDS Control Organisation, Ministry of Health & Family Welfare, Government of India.

National Sample Survey Office. 2009a. *Instructions to Field Staff, Volume I, Design, Concepts, Definitions and Procedures*. Socio-Economic Survey, NSS 64th Round (July 2007-June 2008). New Delhi: National Statistics Organisation, Ministry of Statistics & Programme Implementation, Government of India.

———. 2009b. *Schedule 25.2: Participation and Expenditure in Education*. Socio-Economic Survey, NSS 64th Round (July 2007-June 2008). New Delhi: National Statistics Organisation, Ministry of Statistics & Programme Implementation, Government of India.

———. 2010a. *Some Characteristics of Urban Slums: 2008-09*. NSS 65th Round (July 2008-June 2009), Report No. 534(65/0.21/1). New Delhi: National Statistics Organisation, Ministry of Statistics & Programme Implementation, Government of India.

———. 2010b. *Housing Condition and Amenities in India 2008-09*. NSS 65th Round (July 2008-June 2009), Report No. 535(65/1.2/1). New Delhi: National Statistics Organisation, Ministry of Statistics & Programme Implementation, Government of India.

———. 2010c. *Migration in India, 2007-2008*. NSS 64th Round (July 2007-June 2008), Report No. 533(64/10.2/2). New Delhi: National Statistics Organisation, Ministry of Statistics & Programme Implementation, Government of India.

———. 2011. *Key Indicators of Household Consumer Expenditure in India, 2009-10*. NSS 66th Round (July 2009-June 2010), Report No. NSS KI (66/1.0). New Delhi: National Statistical Organisation, Ministry of Statistics & Programme Implementation, Government of India.

National Sample Survey Organisation. 1997. *Housing Conditions in India*. Report No. 429. New Delhi: National Sample Survey Organisation, Ministry of Statistics & Programme Implementation, Government of India.

———. 1998. *The Aged in India: A Socio-Economic Profile*. NSS 52nd Round (July 1995-June 1996). Report No. 446 (52/25.0/3). New Delhi: National Sample Survey Organisation, Ministry of Statistics & Programme Implementation, Government of India.

———. 2003. *Condition of Urban Slums 2002: Salient Features*. Report No. 486(58/0.21/1). New Delhi: National Sample Survey Organisation, Ministry of Statistics & Programme Implementation, Government of India.

———. 2004. *Housing Condition in India: Housing Stock and Constructions*. NSS 58th Round (July 2002-December 2002), Report No. 488(58/1.2/1). New Delhi: National Sample Survey Organisation, Ministry of Statistics & Programme Implementation, Government of India.

———. 2005. *Housing Condition in India: Household Amenities and Other Characteristics*. NSS 58th Round (July 2002-December 2002), Report No. 489(58/1.2/2). New Delhi: National Sample Survey Organisation, Ministry of Statistics & Programme Implementation, Government of India.

———. 2006. *Morbidity, Health Care and the Condition of the Aged*. NSS 60th Round (January–June 2004), Report No. 507(60/25.0/1). New Delhi: National Sample Survey Organisation, Ministry of Statistics & Programme Implementation, Government of India.

———. 2012. *Utilisation of Medical Services*. NSS 42nd Round Schedule 25.7 (1986-87). New Delhi: National Sample Survey Organisation, Ministry of Statistics & Programme Implementation, Government of India.

Nayar, K. R. 1997. 'Housing Amenities and Health Improvement: Some Findings', *Economic & Political Weekly*, 32 (22): 1275–79.

NHRM. 2009. 'Maharashtra State Report'. Available online at http://www.mohfw.nic.in/NRHM/Documents/Non_High_Focus_Reports/Maharashtra_Report.pdf (accessed on 13 July 2011).

———. 2010. *Rural Health Statistics in India 2010*. New Delhi: National Rural Health Mission, Ministry of Health & Family Welfare, Government of India.

———. 2011a. *Fourth Common Review Mission: Maharashtra 2010*. New Delhi: National Rural Health Mission, Ministry of Health & Family Welfare, Government of India. Available online at http://www.mohfw.nic.in/NRHM/CRM/CRM_files/4th_CRM/Statewise/Maharashtra%204th%20CRM%20Report.pdf

———. 2011b. *Fourth Common Review Mission Report 2010*. New Delhi: National Rural Health Mission, Ministry of Health & Family Welfare, Government of India.

———. 2011c. *Programme Implementation Plan, PIP 2011-12, NHRM, Maharashtra*. New Delhi: National Rural Health Mission, Ministry of Health & Family Welfare, Government of India.

NUEPA. 2011a. *Elementary Education in India: Progress towards UEE, DISE Flash Statistics 2009-10*. New Delhi: National University of Educational Planning and Administration. Available online at http://www.dise.in/Downloads/Publications/Publications%202009-10/Flash%20Statistics%202009-10.pdf (accessed on 31 October 2011).

———. 2011b. *Elementary Education in India: Where Do We Stand? State Elementary Education Report Card: 2010-11 (Provisional)*. New Delhi: National University of Educational Planning and Administration.

———. 2012a. *Elementary Education in India: Progress Towards UEE, DISE Flash Statistics 2010-11*. New Delhi: National University of

Educational Planning and Administration. Available online at http://www.dise.in/Downloads/Publications/Publications%202010-11/Flash%20Statistics-2010-11.pdf (accessed on 10 November 2012).

NUEPA. 2012b. *Elementary Education in India: Where Do We Stand? State Elementary Education Report Card: 2011-12 (Provisional)*. New Delhi: National University of Educational Planning and Administration.

Office of the Registrar General. 2000. *Sample Registration System: Statistical Report 1998*. New Delhi: Office of the Registrar General, India, Ministry of Home Affairs, Government of India.

———. 2003. *Sample Registration System: Statistical Report 2001*. New Delhi: Office of the Registrar General, India, Ministry of Home Affairs, Government of India.

———. 2004. *Sample Registration System: Statistical Report 2002*. New Delhi: Office of the Registrar General, India, Ministry of Home Affairs, Government of India.

———. 2005. *Sample Registration System: Statistical Report 2003*. New Delhi: Office of the Registrar General, India, Ministry of Home Affairs, Government of India.

———. 2006. *Sample Registration System: Statistical Report 2004*. New Delhi: Office of the Registrar General, India, Ministry of Home Affairs, Government of India.

———. 2007. *Sample Registration System: Statistical Report 2005*. New Delhi: Office of the Registrar General, India, Ministry of Home Affairs, Government of India.

———. 2008. *Sample Registration System: Statistical Report 2006*. New Delhi: Office of the Registrar General, India, Ministry of Home Affairs, Government of India.

———. 2009. *Sample Registration System: Statistical Report 2007*. New Delhi: Office of the Registrar General, India, Ministry of Home Affairs, Government of India.

———. 2010. *Sample Registration System: Statistical Report 2008*. New Delhi: Office of the Registrar General, India, Ministry of Home Affairs, Government of India.

———. 2011. *Sample Registration System: Statistical Report 2009*. New Delhi: Office of the Registrar General, India, Ministry of Home Affairs, Government of India.

———. 2012. *Sample Registration System: Statistical Report 2010*. New Delhi: Office of the Registrar General, India, Ministry of Home Affairs, Government of India.

Office of the Registrar General & Census Commissioner. 2006. *Population Projections For India and States 2001-2026: Report of the Technical Group on Population Projections Constituted by the National Commission on Population*. New Delhi: Office of the Registrar General & Census Commissioner, Ministry of Home Affairs, Government of India.

PIB. 2011. 'Rashtriya Swasthya Bima Yojana (RSBY): Some Initial Trends', *Republic Day 2011 Feature, Labour*, 21 January. New Delhi: Press Information Bureau, Government of India. Available online at http://www.pib.nic.in/archieve/others/2011/jan/d20 1012101.pdf (accessed on 14 July 20

Planning Commission. 200 *Towards Faster and More Inclusive Growth. Approach to the 11th Five Year Plan (2007–2012)*. New Delhi: Planning Commission, Government of India.

———. 2007. 'Strengthening State Plan for Human Development (SSPHD): Sectorwise Gross District Domestic Product (GDDP) for the Year: 2006-07'. Available online at http://planningcommission.nic.in/plans/stateplan/ssphd/ddpdata/Maharashtra/maharastra%20DDP%202006-07.pdf (accessed on 13 July 2011).

———. 2008. *Eleventh Five Year Plan (2007–2012): Social Sector, Volume II*. New Delhi: Oxford University Press.

———. 2011. *Faster, Sustainable and More Inclusive Growth: An Approach to the Twelfth Five Year Plan (2012-17)*. New Delhi: Planning Commission, Government of India.

Pratham. 2005. *Annual Status of Education Report (Rural) 2005*. Mumbai, India: Pratham Resource Centre.

———. 2006. *Annual Status of Education Report (Rural) 2006*. Mumbai, India: Pratham Resource Centre.

———. 2007. *Annual Status of Education Report (Rural) 2007*. Mumbai, India: Pratham Resource Centre.

———. 2008. *Annual Status of Education Report (Rural) 2008*. Mumbai, India: Pratham Resource Centre.

———. 2009. *Annual Status of Education Report (Rural) 2009*. Mumbai, India: Pratham Resource Centre.

———. 2010. *Annual Status of Education Report (Rural) 2010*. Mumbai, India: Pratham Resource Centre.

———. 2011. *Annual Status of Education Report (Rural) 2011*. Mumbai, India: Pratham Resource Centre.

———. 2012. *Annual Status of Education Report (Rural) (Provisional) 2011*. Mumbai, India: Pratham Resource Centre.

Rao, M. Govinda and Mita Choudhury. March 2012. Health Care Financing Reforms in India, Working Paper No: 2012-100. National Institute of Public Finance and Policy.

RGJAYS. 2013. 'Rajiv Gandhi Jeevandayee Arogya Yojana', *Rajiv Gandhi Jeevandayee Arogya Yojana Society*. Available online at http://www.jeevandayee.gov.in/RGJAY/Society (accessed on 25 March 2013).

Rathi, P. 2011. 'Evaluation of 'Rashtriya Swasthya Bima Yojana', a Health Insurance Scheme for below Poverty Line People in Amravati'.

Available online at http://www.scribd.com/doc/58131645/Handout-Evaluation-of-Rashtriya-Swasthya-Bima-Yojana-GHC (accessed on 14 July 2011).

Registrar General, India. 2009. *Compendium of India's Fertility and Mortality Indicators, 1971-2007: Based on the Sample Registration System (SRS)*. New Delhi: Office of the Registrar General & Census Commissioner, Ministry of Home Affairs, Government of India.

———. 1999–2011. *SRS Bulletins: Sample Registration System*. New Delhi: Registrar General, India, Vital Statistics Division, Ministry of Home Affairs, Government of India.

School Education Department. 2001. *Selected Educational Statistics, 2000-2001*. Mumbai, India: Mantralay, Government of Maharashtra.

———. 2002. *Selected Educational Statistics, 2001-2002*. Mumbai, India: Mantralay, Government of Maharashtra.

———. 2003. *Selected Educational Statistics, 2002-2003*. Mumbai, India: Mantralay, Government of Maharashtra.

———. 2004. *Selected Educational Statistics, 2003-2004*. Mumbai, India: Mantralay, Government of Maharashtra.

Sen, T. K., H. K. A. Nath, M. Choudhury and S. Das. 2010. *Matching Human Development Across Maharashtra with Its Economic Development*. New Delhi: National Institute of Public Finance and Policy.

SHSRC. 2009. *Health Status Maharashtra: 2009*. Mumbai, India: Public Health Department, Government of Maharashtra.

———. 2010. *Health Status Maharashtra: 2010*. Mumbai, India: Public Health Department, Government of Maharashtra.

———. 2011. *Proposal for Strengthening Karnataka State Drug Logistics and Warehousing Society based on the TNMSC Model, Bangalore*. Pune, India: State Health Systems Resource Centre.

———. 2012, Health Status Maharashtra, 2012, Mumbai, India, Public Health Department, Government of Maharashtra.

Social and Rural Research Institute. 2009. *All India Survey of Out-of-School Children of Age 5 and in 6-13 Years Age Group*. New Delhi: Department of Elementary Education and Literacy, Ministry of Human Resource Development, Government of India. Available online at http://www.educationforallinindia.com/Survey-Report-of-%20out-of-school-children-IMRB-MHRD-EDCil-2009.pdf

Sonowal, C. J. 2010. 'Factors Affecting the Nutritional Health of Tribal Children in Maharashtra'. Available online at http://www.krepublishers.com/02-Journals/S-EM/EM-04-0-000-10-Web/EM-04-1-000-2010-Abst-PDF/EM-04-1-021-10-081-Sonowal-C-J/EM-04-1-021-10-081-Sonowal-C-J-Tt.pdf (accessed on 25 August 2012).

Sood, N. 2010. *Malnourishment among Children in India: Linkages with Cognitive Development and School Participation*. New Delhi: National University of Educational Planning and Administration.

State Bureau of Health Intelligence and Vital Statistics. 2009. *Survey of Causes of Deaths Scheme (Rural)*. Pune, India: Directorate of Health Services, Department of Public Health, Government of Maharashtra.

———. 2010. *Survey of Causes of Deaths Scheme (Rural)*. Pune, India: State Bureau of Health Intelligence and Vital Statistics, Directorate of Health Services, Department of Public Health, Government of Maharashtra.

State TB Office. 2009. *RNTCP Performance Report: Maharashtra 2009*. Pune, India: Government of Maharashtra.

Suryanarayana, M. H. 2008. 'What Is Exclusive about 'Inclusive Growth'?', *Economic & Political Weekly*, 43 (43): 91–101.

———. 2009a. 'Intra-State Economics Disparities: Karnataka and Maharashtra', *Economic & Political Weekly*, 44 (26–27): 215–23.

———. 2009b. 'Nutritional Norms for Poverty: Issues and Implications', Concept paper prepared for the Expert Group to Review the Methodology for Estimation of Poverty. Available online at http://planningcommission.nic.in/reports/genrep/surya.pdf (accessed on 2 March 2013).

———. 2011. 'Expert Group on Poverty: Confusion Worse Confounded', *Economic & Political Weekly*, 46 (46): 36–39.

Suryanarayana, M. H., A. Agrawal and K. S. Prabhu. 2011. *Inequality-adjusted Human Development Index for India's States*. New Delhi: UNDP.

Symington, D. 1938. *Report on the Aboriginal and Hill Tribes of the Partially Excluded Areas in the Bombay Presidency (Symington Report)*. Bombay, India: Government of Bombay.

TBC India. 2013. 'About RNTCP'. Available online at http://www.tbcindia.nic.in/RNTCP.html (accessed on 13 March 2013).

The Right of Children to Free and Compulsory Education Act, 2009. Gazette of India. 27 August 2009.

UNDP. 1999. *Public Report on Basic Education in India*. New Delhi: Oxford University Press.

———. 2005. *Human Development Report 2005: International Cooperation at a Crossroads: Air, Trade and Security in an Unequal World*. New York, NY: United Nations Development Programme.

———. 2010. *Human Development Report 2010: The Real Wealth of Nations: Pathways to Human Development*. New York, NY: Palgrave Macmillan.

UNICEF. 2011a. *Children in Maharashtra: An Atlas of Social Indicators*. Mumbai, India: Planning Department, Government of Maharashtra and United Nations Children's Fund.

UNICEF. 2011b. 'Programming Guide for Infant and Young Child Feeding', *UNICEF Programming Guide*, May 2011. Available online at http://www.unicef.org/nutrition/files/Final_IYCF_programming_guide_2011.pdf (accessed on 12 November 2011).

———. 2012. *WASH Atlas: Unpacking the Census 2011 Data on Water and Sanitation, Maharashtra*. Mumbai, India: United Nations Children's Fund.

UNFPA. 2007. *State of World Population 2007: Unleashing the Potential of Urban Growth*. New York, NY: United Nations Population Fund.

Index

Bombay Nursing Home Registration Act, 1949, 130
box plot, 14n6

calorie intake, 41–43
cereal consumption, 41–43

data collection management, 131
demographic profile of Maharashtra, 46
district-wise HDI, 2001 to 2011, 11–17

economic development, defined, 1
economic growth, 5, 9
    agricultural sector, 28
    child poverty, 40
    consumption distribution, 35–37
    disaggregate profile, 39–41
    distribution of employment and workforce, 33–35
    district-level profile, 30–33
    incidence of poverty, 36, 38–41
    inter-district disparities in per capita income, 30–31
    levels of living, 37–38
    macro profile, 28–30
    tertiary sector, 30
    1999–2000 to 2008–09, 29
education, 5–6. *See also* literacy rate
    access to, 51–52
    analysis of infrastructure, 64
    attendance rates, 54–56
    budget, allocations and achievements, 66–67
    children's proficiency in mathematics, 62–63
    completed at least 10 years, percentage, 47
    enrolments, 51–52
    female enrolments, 52–54
    female literacy, 47–48
    of Katkari tribe, 64–65
    literacy rate, 48–51
    NFHS and DLHS data for, 47–48
    out-of-school children and dropouts, 56–60
    PAISA survey, 68
    planning for improvements in, 66
    primary schooling for tribals, 66
    quality of, 61–63
    reading and arithmetic abilities of children, 61–62
    schooling incentives, 60–61
    school resources, 63–64
    teachers, 63–64
Eleventh and Twelfth Five Year Plans, 7–8

female education and effect on child health and nutrition, 47–48
female enrolments in education, 52–54

global HDR 2010, 1–2
    conclusions, 3
    education and health, 2
    HDI achievements, 2
    human development perspective, 2
    interstate disparities, 2
Gross Enrolment Ratios (GERs) for schooling, 11
    2001 and 2011–12, 18

health, 6
    accessibility of health care, 91
    anaemia, prevalence of, 97–98
    antenatal care, 86–88
    childcare and feeding practices, 99–100
    childhood diarrhoea, 99
    child immunization and postnatal care, 89–90
    child sex ratio, 72–73
    child survival indicators, 75–76
    community-based monitoring (CBM) initiative, 93
    cost of healthcare, 90–91
    crude birth rate, 72
    crude death rate, 72
    demand-side financing in, 92–93
    financial allocation for medicines, 91
    government initiatives, 91–94
    HIV prevalence, 91
    implications for, 71
    infant mortality rate (IMR), 6, 11, 73–75
    infrastructure and facilities, 79–82
    input indicators, 77–84
    institutional births and safe deliveries, 88–89
    life expectancy, 73
    maternal deaths, 76–77
    obesity, 97–98
    outcome indicators, 72–77
    overweight, 97–98

per capita health expenditure, 79
personnel, 82–83
PHCs, 81
pricing of essential drugs, 91
process indicators, 84–90
public provisioning of health care, 77–79
specialists, 83
total fertility rate (TFR), 72
U5MR measures, 75–76
utilization of health care, 85–86
vitamin A coverage, 98–99
housing amenities, 110–13
    access to water, 113–17
    condition of dwellings, 111–12
    sanitary conditions, 117–21
housing programmes, 113
human capabilities, enhancement of, 45
human development
    defined, 1
    global overview, 1–3
    pathways to, 1
Human Development Commissionerate, 7
human development index
    across States and India, 2010–11, 23
    design, 25
human development indicators, 22
human development in Maharashtra
    district-wise, radar profile, 21
    district-wise, 2001 to 2011, 11–17
human development policy, imperatives for, 126–31

immunization coverage, 102
inclusive human development, 7–8
income distribution, 19–20
India Human Development Report (IHDR) 2011, 3–4
    Maharashtra, scenario in, 3–4
    proportion of population below poverty line, 4
    public expenditure on health and education, 4
    ranking of Indian states, 4
    set of indicators used, 3n1
    state-wise analysis, 3
    U5MR and underweight children, 4
inequality-adjusted human development index (IHDI), 21–24
    2010–11, 23
    loss due to inequality, 2010–11, 23
infant mortality rate (IMR), 6, 11, 18–20, 73–75
    for 2001 and 2011, 12
infant survival rate (ISR), 11
Integrated Child Development Services (ICDS), 99
inter-regional variations
    availability of HR, 83–84
    growth performance, 5
    immunization coverage, 102
    literacy rate, 49–51
    nutrition status, 103
    primary-level NARs, 69
    provisioning of subcentres, PHCs and RHs, 101
    trends in IMR, 75

Katkari tribe, 9, 93–94
    education of, 64–65

literacy rate, 48–51. *See also* education
    adult (age 15+), 51
    2001 and 2011, 17–18
    at disaggregated level of social groups, 49
    district profile, 49
    gender parity index (GPI), 49
    inter-regional variations, 49–51
    Maharashtra Human Development Report, 2002, 6
    for social groups, 49–50
Lorenz ratio, 36

Maharashtra Human Development Report, 2002, 5–7
    access to basic education, 6
    density of population, 5
    distribution of economic growth, 5
    economic growth, 5, 9
    education and health indicators, 5–6
    highlights of, 27
    income distribution, 9
    income level, 5
    life expectancy, 6
    literacy rates, 6
    migration rate, 5
    nutritional and health status, 6
    population, 5
    preventive health care, 6
    primary school participation, 6
    primary sector, 5
    proportion of population below poverty line, 9
    secondary school participation, 6
    sex ratio, 5
    unemployment and regional disparities, 5
Maharashtra Human Development Report, 2012
    concept of 'inclusion', 9
    content highlights, 8–10
Mahbub-ul-Haq, 1
malnutrition, 71, 94–97, 100
Medical Termination of Pregnancy Act, 1971, 130
Mid Day Meals (MDM), 61
migration, 107–109

National Institute of Public Finance and Policy (NIPFP), 78–79
National Rural Health Mission (NRHM), 91–92
neonatal mortality, 47
Net District Domestic Product (NDDP), 2008–09, 32
Net State Domestic Product (NSDP)
    per capita, 1999–2000, 31
    sectoral distribution, 1999–2000, 30
nutritional and health status, 6, 94
    district-wise food security profile, 42–43
    rural–urban profile, 41–42

out-of-school children and dropouts, 56–60, 69–70

PCPNDT Act, 130
Per Capita Net District Domestic Product (PCNDDP), 11
principal activity status, 35n4
protein intake, 41–43
pucca structures, 109

radar chart, 21n8
Rajiv Gandhi Jeevandayee Arogya Yojana (RGJAY), 92–93
RJMCHNM, 95

schooling incentives, 60–61
Sen, Amartya, 1
slums, 106–107
standard of living, 1

State Health Systems Resource Centre (SHSRC), 80
state human development reports (SHDRs), 25
subsidiary economic activity status, 35n4

urbanization, 106–07
    migration and, 107–09
    poverty and, 106–07

water, access to, 113–17
well-being
    defined, 1
    link with health and, 105–06
whiskers, 14n6
Workforce Participation Rate (WPR), 34–35